Mercantilism in a Japanese domain

The merchant origins of economic nationalism in 18th-century Tosa

This book explores the historical roots of economic nationalism within Japan. By examining how mercantilist thought developed in the eighteenth-century domain of Tosa, Luke Roberts shows how economic ideas were generated at the regional level.

During the Edo period (1600–1867), Japan was divided into over 230 competitive states, many of which wished to reduce the dominance of the shogun's economy. The seventeenth-century Japanese economy was based on samurai notions of service – especially the duty performed by the domainal lord to the shogun – and a rhetoric of political economy that centered on the lord and the samurai class. This "economy of service," however, led to crises in deforestation and land degradation, government fiscal insolvency and increasingly corrupt tax levies, and finally a loss of faith in government.

Commoners led the response with a mercantilist strategy of protection and development of the commercial economy. They resisted the economy of service by creating a new economic rhetoric that decentered the lord, imagined the domain as an economic country, and gave merchants a public worth and identity unknown in Confucian economic thought. This thought and activity changed domainal government, and played an important role in the decline of shogunal authority, producing proto-nationalist practices and rhetoric that influenced Meiji era national development.

Luke S. Roberts is Assistant Professor of Japanese History in the History Department at the University of California at Santa Barbara

Mercantilism in a Japanese domain

The merchant origins of economic nationalism in 18th-century Tosa

Luke S. Roberts

CAMBRIDGE
UNIVERSITY PRESS

PUBLISHED BY THE PRESS SYNDICATE OF THE UNIVERSITY OF CAMBRIDGE
The Pitt Building, Trumpington Street, Cambridge, United Kingdom

CAMBRIDGE UNIVERSITY PRESS
The Edinburgh Building, Cambridge CB2 2RU, UK
40 West 20th Street, New York NY 10011–4211, USA
477 Williamstown Road, Port Melbourne, VIC 3207, Australia
Ruiz de Alarcón 13, 28014 Madrid, Spain
Dock House, The Waterfront, Cape Town 8001, South Africa

http://www.cambridge.org

First published 1998
First paperback edition 2002

Typeface Caledonia 10/13 pt, in Quark XPress™

A catalogue record for this book is available from the British Library

Library of Congress Cataloguing in Publication data
Roberts, Luke Shepherd.
Mercantilism in a Japanese domain: The merchant origins of economic nationalism in 18th-century Tosa / Luke S. Roberts.
     p.   cm.
Includes bibliographical references
ISBN 0 521 62131 3
1. Tosa-han (Japan) – Economic conditions.   2. Mercantile system – Japan – Tosa-han –
History – 18th century.   3. Japan – Commercial policy – History – 18th century.   I. Title.
HC463.T593R63 1998   97-18070
380.1′0952′33–dc21   CIP

ISBN 0 521 62131 3 hardback
ISBN 0 521 89335 6 paperback

To Yachiyo

Contents

Maps, tables, and figures

Maps

Tables

Figures

Acknowledgments

This book has taken many years to research and write, and during that time I have incurred a tremendous debt of gratitude to many people and institutions.

The following institutions and people provided me with generous financial support: The Japan Foundation for a doctoral dissertation research fellowship in 1987–8, which enabled me to travel to and live in Tosa to do my research, and a faculty research fellowship in 1994–5, which enabled me to tie up loose ends on this project while working on a new project; Princeton University, which provided me with generous fellowship support, including a Harold W. Dodds Fellowship while I was a graduate student. My thanks go to the UCSB Academic Senate for granting research funds. I thank Yamauchi Toyoaki, Yamauchi Toyoharu, Yamauchi Shizumoto, and the Yamauchi Shrine Treasury and Archives, who generously replaced my copy of the published seventeenth-century portions of the *Yamauchi-ke shiryō*, when they learned that my own copy had been lost to flood. After my first two-year residence in Kōchi, Dr. Okamune Shigehisa and Okamune Tomoko kindly provided me with hospitality and lodging during my numerous follow-up research trips.

I owe a great debt to the following people for their help with the writing and rewriting of this manuscript. Foremost, Marius B. Jansen for his continual guidance and thoughtful criticism; secondly, to my sister Sally Roberts for a detailed editorial reading of an early version of this manuscript. I am also grateful for many detailed comments on drafts at various stages from Martin Collcutt, Fujita Teiichirō, Sheldon Garon, David Howell, Joan Judge, Tetsuo Najita, Conrad Totman, Constantine Vaporis, Anne Walthall, Kären Wigen, my editor Herbert Gilbert at Cambridge University Press, and the two anonymous readers. This book has grown and improved immeasurably because of their advice. What shortcomings remain are my responsibility.

I owe a special debt of scholarly inspiration to two people. The former president of Kōchi University, Sekita Hidesato, wrote a fascinating article on Tosa domain paper policy in early modern Tosa, which led me to begin research on this topic. The research of Fujita Teiichirō of Dōshisha University provided me with my initial theoretical framework, and his helpful criticisms and assistance at later stages are greatly appreciated.

I owe a different debt of a very high order to the extremely friendly assistance I received from individuals too numerous to name at the following archives and institutions in Tosa. The Kōchi Prefecture Library and the Tosa Shidankai provided me with a desk I could call my own. Ishizu Kazuko of the Tosa Shidankai provided me with publishing assistance and daily afternoon tea. The Kōchi City Library always kept a desk open for me in the local documents section, where Sumida Michiko and Yasuoka Norihiko generously aided me with locating and interpreting documents. At the Yamauchi Shrine Treasury and Archives, Mr. Matsuyama and Okamura Masaki provided helpful assistance and made me feel at home. The people of Aki City Library and the Aki City Board of Education, especially Inoue Hideo and Komatsu Eiji, gave me much helpful assistance with the Gotō Family Documents. I would like to thank the people of the above four archives for most generously giving me the freest access possible to the documents in their care. I would also like to thank Kōchi University for providing me with the many advantages of research-student status and access to the many fine professors there. The Kōchi Prefecture Pulp and Paper Institute provided me with an invaluable two weeks of experience in making paper in the manner of the early modern period. Finally, thanks to the Kainan Shigakkai and the Tosa Shidankai for providing me with a chance to present some of my research and receive helpful criticism during early stages of this project.

The pre-modern Chinese had their four great books to guide them through life and scholarship. While in Tosa I had my four great friends. I owe them debts both scholarly and personal that I cannot adequately express. These are Professor Akizawa Shigeru of Kōchi University and Moriguchi Kōji, Yorimitsu Kanji, and Takahashi Shirō of Kōchi Prefecture Library. Tosa is a very special place. Being able to easily interact with the people of Tosa has been one of the great fortunes of my life. I return their friendship and give my special thanks to all of the people of Tosa I have met.

My deepest thanks and appreciation go to my wife Yachiyo, whose love and care have kept me going for many years, and to my children May and Ken, who make me proud that I am their father.

Dates and units of measurement used in the text

The early modern Japanese used a different calendar from the modern one. Each year included twelve months of thirty days, and sometimes an inserted intercalary month as well, to make up for slippage in the lunar and solar cycles. An intercalary seventh month, for example, followed the normal seventh month. Each month of the early modern year usually began about one month later than the corresponding month of the modern Western calendar. For example, the second day of the twelfth month of the fifth year of Meiji was the same day as December 31, 1872. The next day, January 1, 1873, the Japanese began using the modern Western calendar.

Years were counted by a succession of eras. The eras were not decided according to reigns, but by astrological considerations. The shortest era in the early modern period lasted only one year, and the longest lasted twenty years. The Tenmei era, for example lasted from the fourth month of 1781 to the first month of 1788, when it was succeeded by the Kansei era, which lasted until the second month of 1801.

I have given the Japanese days and months and the most approximate Western calendric year in the following manner. I write the fourteenth day of the fifth month of the first year of Tenmei as 5/14/1781. If the month were an intercalary month, I would write "intercalary 5/14/1781." I identify in the footnotes many manuscript documents by the date of composition, and many quotations from manuscript diaries by the date of entry. When a day is unknown but the month and year are known, I write, for example, 12/?/1781.

I have used in the text the following early modern units of measurement. Their approximate Western equivalents are as follows:

silver weight: 1 *kan* = 1,000 *monme* = 3.75 kg = 8.25 lb
rice volume: 1 *koku* = 180 l = 5.1 bushels
land area: 1 *tan* = 991.7 m^2 = 1/4 acre

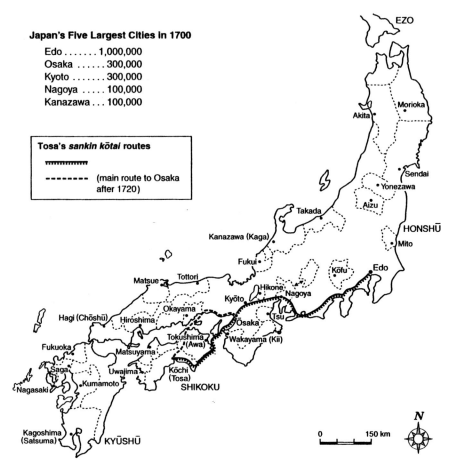

Japan's Five Largest Cities in 1700

Edo 1,000,000
Osaka 300,000
Kyoto 300,000
Nagoya 100,000
Kanazawa . . . 100,000

Tosa's *sankin kōtai* routes

ʳʳʳʳʳʳʳʳʳʳ

- - - - - - - (main route to Osaka
after 1720)

EZO

Morioka

Akita

Sendai

Yonezawa

Aizu

Takada

HONSHŪ

Kanazawa (Kaga)

Mito

Fukui

Kōfu

Edo

Matsue

Tottori

Hikone

Nagoya

Kyōto

Okayama

Tsu

Hagi (Chōshū)

Hiroshima

Ōsaka

Tokushima
(Awa)

Wakayama (Kii)

Fukuoka

Matsuyama

Saga

Uwajima

Kōchi
(Tosa)

Nagasaki

Kumamoto

SHIKOKU

Kagoshima
(Satsuma)

KYŪSHŪ

0   150 km

N

Japan, with the largest domains and major cities

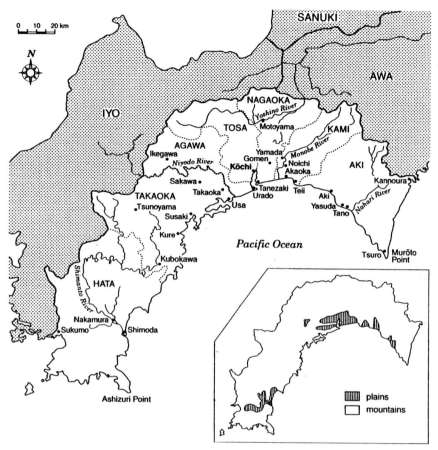

Tosa
(Source: adapted from map in Hirao Michio, *Tosa-han*, Yoshikawa Kōbunkan, 1965)

1

Introduction

The development of the modern nation-state of Japan is based, in part, upon common belief in and support of a nationally organized political economy. *Kokueki* thought as developed in Japanese domains in the eighteenth century was the origin of such belief. The word kokueki, meaning "prosperity of the country," was a neologism in eighteenth-century Japanese – the key term in a newly developing mercantilist economic thought and ideology (*kokueki shisō*) of many domainal states in Japan of the late Edo period. Because it was a proto-national vision of economic organization, kokueki played a highly influential role in the creation and development of the Meiji period (1868–1911) nation-state of Japan, and continues to resonate in modern times.

As this book will demonstrate, kokueki thought played importantly in the latter half of the Edo period, justifying a great proliferation of domainal economic initiatives. Tokushima domain became a famous producer of indigo, Aizu domain of lacquerware, and Matsue domain of ginseng during the eighteenth century, all revealing a high degree of domain government involvement in the development of these industries under the bannerhead "Prosperity of the Country." A key issue is that the "country" in each case referred to the domainal country (*ryōgoku, okuni*) and not to the whole of the Japanese archipelago. Japan was undergoing a process of linguistic and cultural unification in the Edo period, but the space of the archipelago included a collection of many states that were individually strengthening their nature as countries in the realm of economic policy. The situation in Japan is perhaps best imagined as roughly comparable to "Germany" or "Italy" at the beginning of the nineteenth century, culturally and to a degree politically unified, but not unified upon nationalist lines. More than 230 states existed within the larger polity of shogunal Japan. Kokueki thought developed out of the internal dynamic of the miniature "international" economic order within the Japanese islands. It represented a shift away from an economy of service structured primarily on a hierarchy of samurai households, toward a state legitimating itself through the protection and development of the commercial economy of the territory enmeshed in intercountry trade.

This book will focus on the domain of Tosa, a large realm encompassing the southern half of the island of Shikoku, in order to explore the origins and development of kokueki thought and its political, social, and economic meanings. Scholars of kokueki thought to date have placed its origins in the 1760s and have argued that it was the invention of domain bureaucrats who were desperately trying to alleviate troubled finances by legitimating government intrusion into commercial activity. Domainal subjects are seen variously as beneficiaries or victims of this new thought and policy, but uniformly as recipients. Yet, this study of Tosa will show that kokueki thought originated much earlier than believed, in the 1730s, and that its primary exponents and developers in the mid-eighteenth century were merchants, not samurai bureaucrats. Merchants made frequent appeals to "the prosperity of the country" to justify the public value of their activity and thereby gain governmental support. The samurai bureaucrats learned and adopted kokueki thought in the late eighteenth century through dialogue with the merchants and adapted it to legitimize their changing role in the domainal commercial economy and to collect taxes therefrom. Samurai appropriation did not stop the dialogue. Thereafter, merchants, consumers, and to a lesser degree peasants continued to use kokueki ideologically to justify the public worth of their economic activity.

Kokueki *and nationalism*

The creation of kokueki mercantilist thought and its development into an ideology used by many domains in the latter half of the Edo period can be situated as an important topic of research for the understanding of the historic development of nationalism. When the islands of Japan were drawn into the world of nations at Western insistence, in 1853, when Commodore Perry appeared in Edo bay, the Japanese islands were nearly isolated from the world economic order. Overseas trade had flourished in Japan in the late sixteenth century and, despite the political effects of the so-called *sakoku* edicts of the 1630s, trade with China, Korea, the Dutch, and Southeast Asia continued to grow throughout the seventeenth century. A period of decline, however, can be traced to the early eighteenth century when mines in Japan began to produce less precious metal. Rather than developing new export items, the shogun of the time instead encouraged the production of import substitutes, such as fine silk and ginseng, thus bringing a steady decline in legal overseas trade from the beginning of the eighteenth century. After the early eighteenth century, trade was maintained primarily as a means of sustaining information networks and/or political relations with the traditional trading partners.[1] This situation ended when Perry arrived, bearing miniature trains and telegraphs and a mission to force Japan to become part of a Western-led international economic order.[2]

Eagerly anticipating the departing wake of Perry's ships, representatives of numerous Western countries steamed into Japanese waters demanding inclusion in Japan's international trade and commerce. This series of events provoked a crisis in the legitimacy of the shogunate, which had based its legitimacy not on the control of international trade, but rather on its dominance of the protocol of international relations.[3] The Western nations forced their own protocol and vision of foreign relations upon the shogunate; a vision that, as symbolized by the signing of the Treaty of Amity and Commerce with the United States in 1858, demanded that the management of commerce be the primary object of foreign relations. Because many domains had much experience in "internationally" organized commercial development, their leaders and merchants were better situated than the shogunate to appreciate and enact this new pattern of foreign relations.

The strongly mercantilist concepts that were part of kokueki thought possessed numerous similarities to the economic nationalisms of the nineteenth-century West. In 1868, when the shogunate was overthrown by a coalition of domains, leaders emerged from these realms to direct the creation of the new nation-state of Japan. Kokueki thought came to play a central role in conceptually organizing the development of this new nation as they strove to increase Japan's industrial and commercial potential.[4] Certainly, a key problem for understanding this transition is how the idea of kokueki, which was developed for a domainal state, came to be appropriated by the Meiji Japanese nation-state and, similarly, how a "domain" can create a "national" economic ideology. This issue seems more complicated than it really is because it involves certain historiographical silences created by the use of anachronistic terminology.

---

[1] My focus here is economic. Intellectually, study of Chinese culture and Western culture continued to grow in importance throughout the Edo period: Marius Jansen, *China in the Tokugawa World*; Donald Keene, *The Japanese Discovery of Europe, 1720–1830*.

[2] Ronald Toby, *State and Diplomacy*, which focuses upon earlier indigenous views of foreign policy rather than the late eighteenth-century view of "closed country" (itself inspired by Western conceptions), provides the best English language interpretation of foreign relations in the seventeenth and eighteenth centuries.

[3] Toby, *State and Diplomacy*.

[4] Thomas Smith, *Political Change and Industrial Development in Japan: Government Enterprise, 1868–1880*, provides the basic general survey of government economic policy during this period. Fujita Teiichirō has explored how *kokueki* thought was used extensively by a wide range of people in the early Meiji period in three articles beginning with the title "Meiji zenki no 'kokueki' shisō," and in "'Kyōkyūsha engi sōkō' no shōkai." Other commentators on early Meiji kokueki thought include Morikawa Hidemasa, *Nihongata keiei no genryū*.

Close scrutiny reveals that the basic terminology of the modern nation-state was created by domainal countries in the Edo period.

Various scholars have followed diverse threads into the tangled historical weave of modern nationalism. Research on the development of language, ethnicity, political organization, and culture emphasizes the fact that, nationalist claims to the contrary, these have only been woven together into a clearly national fabric over the past few centuries in even the oldest of modern nations.[5] Modern nations project their identities into the distant past, erasing previous forms of collective identity and consciousness from their memories. There exists also an extensive collection of pressures acting on historians of our own national era to write history that makes the modern nation the significant frame of reference.[6] Contemporary patterns of rhetoric arising from our national consciousness make it easy to subsume other forms of group identification into a modern national framework and thereby make it difficult for us to appreciate the centrality of other forms of consciousness to people of the past. Creating a common national heritage and forgetting an uncommon past are part of the continuous nationalist project of creating identification with the imagined community of the contemporary nation.

Currently, historians of Japan using Japanese terms enlist a wide range of anachronisms to describe the Edo period. Many of these reflect nationalist aspirations. Today Japan is the sole *kuni*, or "country," upon the archipelago. However, most uses of the term "kuni" (read "*koku*" in compound words) as applied to Japan are typically creations of the very late Edo period, words of uncommon usage in that era, or even Meiji period neologisms. Sakoku (meaning isolated country), *Nihon kokka* (state of Japan), *bakuhansei kokka* (*bakufu* domain state), *kokugaku* (national studies), *kokusei* (national governance), etc., are all terms used commonly by modern historians to inject the image of a multidimensional nation of Japan into our understanding of the Edo period.[7] Similarly, Meiji period terms such as *han* function to erase awareness that in the Edo period there were many kokka and kuni within the modern territory of Japan. Scholars of Japan writing in the English language have followed the Japanese lead and use the feudal term "domain" to describe the realms of the lords, and they use the terms "country," "state," and "nation" to describe the polity of the whole archipelago; these terms do not conflict with projecting the modern unity of Japan as a nation-state into the past.

[5] E. J. Hobsbawm, *Nations and Nationalism*, pp. 15–45.
[6] Prasenjit Duara, *Rescuing History from the Nation*, pp. 27–33, 51–68. Indeed, for such reasons I could not escape having to put "Japan" into the title of this book.
[7] For the history of the word "*sakoku*," see Toby, *State and Diplomacy*, pp. 11–22; for "*kokugaku*," see Peter Nosco, *Remembering Paradise*, p. 94.

It is worth reviewing the political language of the Edo period to see from where the political terms of the Japanese nation-state emerged. In the Edo period, Japan was primarily known as the *tenka*, "all under heaven." This symbolized its unity under the imperial descendants of the heavenly sun.[8] The shogun based his authority on the pacification of the tenka by his conversion of all samurai into vassals or subvassals of his household.[9] The lordly vassals of the shogun each ruled their own domains (*ryōbun*) formally granted in fief from the shogun. The term kokka emerged primarily from rhetoric used within domains. Although the term sometimes conflated the person of the ruler and realm he ruled – typical for this era – the term kokka increasingly was used to refer to the domain and its ruling institutions.[10] A survey of mid-eighteenth-century writings of samurai in Tosa reveals to us that the domain was not only a kokka, it was ruled by a "lord of the country" (*kokushu*) whose holy mediation (*intoku*) directly brought the benefits of a Confucian heaven (*ten*) and the gods of the land and sky (*jingi*) to the people of the country (*kunitami, kokumin*). Tosa possessed a capital of the country (*kunimiyako*) and had its own distinctive country polity (*kokutai*).[11] It is of great significance that the new leaders of the Meiji Restoration forewent calling their government a tenka, and called it instead a kokka, and used such terms as kokumin, kokutai, and kokueki to describe the Japanese people, their distinctive national polity, and a major objective of their government. They were clearly adopting the political rhetoric of the domains as a model for creating a nation-state rather than the rhetoric of the shogunate.[12]

The word kuni, which in modern usage is limited to meaning "country," was used with a great variety of meanings in the Edo period. Historically, it was used to refer to Japan (*Wakoku, Nihonkoku*) from at least the sixth century when the rulers of Japan carried on political correspondence with the Tang and Sui of China and the Silla of Korea. Yet, at this time, "kuni" was not the monopoly of "Japan." Kuni was also used to refer to each of the sixty-six administrative districts (what are now called provinces) within Japan, each under the authority of an imperially appointed governor.[13] Much later, in the Edo period, people

---

[8] This point made by Fujita in *Kinsei keizai*, pp. 203–16, and artfully summarized by Miyamoto Mataji in Miyamoto Mataji, ed., *Kokka kanjōroku*, pp. 197–9.
[9] Eiko Ikegami, *The Taming of the Samurai*, pp. 151–63.
[10] It should be noted also that for many domains of preunification lineage, the notion of *kokka* historically preceded the creation of the Tokugawa shogunate. Katsumata Shizuo with Martin Collcutt, "The Development of Sengoku Law."
[11] I explore this issue in detail in "Tosa to ishin – 'kokka' no sōshitsu to 'chihō' no tanjō."
[12] This strain of my argument develops and expands on Albert Craig's description of the development of domain nationalism and its subsequent contribution to Japanese nationalism. *Chōshū in the Meiji Restoration*, pp. 17–25, 143–64, 299–300, 358–9.
[13] The many uses of the term suggest that *kuni* meant a large territory under the control of a powerful but not neccessarily sovereign authority. The various kuni described in Japanese

referred to Japan as a kuni in contradistinction to culturally foreign countries and in reference to the religious territory of *shinkoku*, "the country of the gods," a mythicoreligious definition originating in the eighth-century text, the *Kojiki*. The former imperial provinces no longer had any administrations in the Edo period, but remained on the cultural map as commonly used definers of territorial regions called kuni (or synonymously *shū*). They nevertheless retained a minimal administrative validity, because when the shogun ordered population registers and maps to be made, he had them organized along the borders of the provincial kuni. This has been interpreted as important evidence of the shogun's styled role as a servant of the emperor, one important means by which he legitimated his authority. Kuni was also the most common term used for large domains such as Tosa. The domain of Tosa happens to be contiguous with the imperial province of Tosa, and one might argue that the prevalent use of the word kuni in Tosa rhetoric is little more than recognition of its boundary with the former imperial province. However, people within domains much smaller and much larger than former provinces also used the term kuni to refer to their domains.[14] In Edo period parlance, *takoku* meant a different domain or province, and *takoku no hito* meant a person from such a place. Today these words mean non-Japanese countries and people. In the Edo period, China, Korea, Holland, and the Ryūkyū kingdom (now part of Japan) were *ikoku*, which meant "different countries" or "strange countries." This denoted a conception of cultural difference, but takoku and ikoku were both variations of koku. In short, in the early modern period, the word kuni had many levels of meaning that varied according to the situation. (It is worth noting that this is roughly comparable to the multivariant use of the word "country" in premodern and early modern English.) Each kuni was construed by different characteristics, but no one kuni was more authentic than another.

This befit a time when "household" (*ie*) was a political unit of primary importance and "country" was not as politically potent a concept as it is today. However, under the cultural, economic, and military pressure of the West, the leaders of the Meiji Restoration unified the religious entity, the cultural entity, and the idea of a geopolitical country into a single nation-state. The significance of the new leaders' appropriation of the rhetoric of the domainal country is brought into higher relief when we consider the concerted erasure of real and

---

documents as existing on the Korean peninsula and in Japan changed with the changing configuration of the authority of elites.

[14] Examples of such usage in Uwajima domain and Yanagawa domain (both much smaller than provinces) can be found in Fujita Teiichiro, *Kinsei keizai shisō no kenkyū*, pp. 61–77, 123–5. The case of Morioka domain and other large domains having boundaries not contiguous with provinces is extensively and provocatively discussed in this light in Yokoyama Toshio, "'Han' kokka e no michi – shokoku fūkyō fure to tabinin."

rhetorical domainal nationalism that followed. One of the first actions of the new Meiji government was to rename all of the domains han, thus emphasizing their ultimate subordination to a national form of imperial rule. After the restoration the only publicly recognized kuni in Japan was to be Japan itself. This act of naming was one of the many steps the Meiji government made to promote a new national unity in its early unsettled years of development. In the face of persistent divisiveness along domainal and household boundaries the han were abolished in 1871, recreated into *ken*, and the ruling samurai households were disenfranchised. Following this, the geographical borders of most of these domains-cum-ken were redrawn and redrawn yet again, and their administrators (mostly former samurai) transferred throughout Japan in order to erase old loyalites to household and kuni.[15] The tradition, created out of the needs of the early Meiji state, still lives with us. It has affected not only our historical terminology, but also our historical perspective. Today Edo period domains are uniformly referred to in the historical literature as han. Han was a Chinese word never used officially in the early modern period to describe domains. Even its private use was rare until the arrival of Commodore Perry forced a new political agenda upon many samurai within Japan.

The interests involved in this linguistic change are evident even in the eighteenth century. Arai Hakuseki was the first person to apply the term han to the Japanese context, when he used it to mean domainal lords, thereby indicating that their function was to protect the shogun. Hakuseki was a famous eighteenth-century advocate of centralizing all ruling authority and ceremonial activity into the hands of the shogun.[16] Neither the imperial court nor independent domains were a vital part of his vision of shogunal rule. His thought and activity were thus threatening not only to the kuni of the domains, but also to the tenka of the imperial tradition. His choice of the word han fit with this approach, and in a sense, his vision was prophetic of what would happen to domains in the Meiji Restoration.

The transition to creating the new nation-state was modeled partially on domain experience, but ultimately destroyed the domains themselves. The fledgling Meiji administration immediately began legitimating itself with the same domain-produced combination of ideology centered on the lord and on the economic country, only the lord was the emperor and the country was Japan. This link had not previously been important for Japan as a whole. Japan ceased being the tenka, "all under heaven," and became the kokka, a nation among nations. The object of service became the country of Japan and the

---

[15] Matsuo Masahito, *Haihan chiken.*
[16] Kate Nakai, *Shogunal Politics: Arai Hakuseki and the Premises of Tokugawa Rule*, pp. 135, 141–7, 235–6.

emperor, whom the leaders came in time to associate with the essence of national structure and identity, the kokutai.[17] The former kokka within Japan disappeared not only in reality but, to a large degree, from historical memory, an excellent illustration of Ernest Renan's oft-cited statement, "Well, the essence of a nation is that all of its individuals have much in common, and also that they have forgotten many things. . . . Forgetting and – I'll even add – historical error is a factor in the formation of a nation."[18]

The points with regard to language that I have made thus far are significant not only for our understanding of the lineage of some threads of Meiji nationalist rhetoric, but also for our understanding of the nature of Edo period politics. I feel that the word kuni when referring to domains is sometimes, if not always, best translated as "country" because of the protonational significance of domainal political identities.[19] I will use "domain" as a translation for ryōbun, and "household" as a translation of ie and *kachū*. I will follow received practice in calling Tosa a domain when I do not wish to emphasise the protonational characteristics, and use the term domainal country when I wish to highlight the protonational characteristics of what I am talking about. This may be inconsistent, but faithfully reflects the fact that the people of the day were inconsistent as well, and I hope by my usage to highlight the developing nature of domainal politics within the Edo period. I have two objections to the use of the word han: The first, as described above, is that it makes us that much less sensitive to the emerging "countryness" of many of the large domains. One might argue that the scholars who use the term *han kokka* have overcome this limitation, which is somewhat true. However, I still do not like the term, not only because of its anachronism, but because – and this is my second objection to the use of the term han – the term unifies the rule of the lord's household and the rule of the domain, where they were not neatly unified in their day. A distinguishable dynamic of Edo period domainal politics emerges from the complex interplay between notions of household and country.

---

[17] Carol Gluck analyzes the complicated process leading to the eventual unification of the emperor with the *kokutai*, *Japan's Modern Myths*, pp. 36–7, 120–7.

[18] Ernest Renan, *Oeuvres Complètes de Ernest Renan*, tome 1, pp. 891–2. "L'oublie et je dirai même l'erreur historique, sont un facteur de la formation d'une nation. . . . Or l'essence d'une nation est ce que tous les individus aient beaucoup de choses en commun, et aussi que tous aient oublié bien des choses" [My translation]. I have inverted the order of the two phrases in the original for rhetorical effect.

[19] I shy away from translating the term kuni into "nation" or "national," which I prefer to regard as a distinctly modern weave of ethnic, linguistic, and political-economic beliefs. Notions of ethnic and linguistic difference were not of great political importance to domainal countries. Rather, these elements took on growing importance in the eighteenth century to the notion of Japan. Harry Harootunian, *Things Seen and Unseen*. It is unfortunate, and a source of great consternation to me, that the English word "country" has no adjectival form. This has led me to use reluctantly the term "international economy" and "economic nationalism" with the understanding that the meanings are strictly limited to political economic relations and thought.

Han kokka is sufficient to describe a conflict of interest between domain and shogun, but it encourages us to ignore the very real occasions of conflict of interest hidden behind usage of the rhetoric of service to the lord's household or service to the domainal country, two fundamentally different notions of political economy. This conflict is what structures the present book's narrative about the development of kokueki thought.

Benedict Anderson has argued in *Imagined Communities* that an important element of modern nationalism is the widespread imagining of a common national community enabled and encouraged by the spread of print culture.[20] The growing influence from the early seventeenth century of a printing industry centered in Osaka, Kyoto, and Edo can indeed be related to the development of a strong Japanese cultural identity in the Edo period.[21] The great elaboration of the rhetoric of cultural difference defining Japaneseness that we find in the Edo period undoubtedly owes itself to the spread of print culture and played an important role in later Meiji nationalism.[22] However, I will argue in this book that the economic imagination, the imagining of a nationally organized political economy, is also a key element of modern nationalism. The creation of kokueki thought in domains in the eighteenth century and its emergence into public rhetoric represented the beginning of a key shift away from an economic vision based upon service between heads of households, where relationships between the ruling samurai lords functioned as the primary legitimating structure of economic activity. Kokueki thought imagined that the commercial economy of a political territory was indeed worth sacrificing self-interest for, a symbol of the public good more immediately relevant to merchant interests than samurai interests.[23] In so arguing, I am adapting Anderson's emphasis on the creation of (following Duara's criticisms I feel "expansion of" is the better way to interpret the change) a form of collective consciousness originating in the development of an "international" capitalist economy.[24] By emphasizing the economic imagination, I hope to add a new dimension to the discussion of the development of nationalism. This book will pose a critique of modern nationalism by focusing

[20] Benedict Anderson, *Imagined Communities: Reflections on the Origins and Spread of Nationalism.*
[21] Henry D. Smith, II, "The History of the Book in Edo and Paris."
[22] Mitani Hiroshi, *Meiji ishin to nashonarizumu*, pp. 5–34; David Howell, "Ainu Ethnicity and the Boundaries of the Early Modern Japanese State"; Ronald Toby, "The Carnival of the Aliens: Korean Embassies in Edo Period Art and Popular Culture."
[23] It is in their bureaucratic identity as officials of the state that samurai come to appropriate kokueki thought. Their appropriation of kokueki thought is a key stage in making it a successful ideology.
[24] I find Anderson's book (as extraordinarily insightful as it is and as deeply instructive to me as it has been) curiously silent on economic relations and thought. This is all the more perplexing because Anderson highlights Marxist historiography and relies upon the notion of print capitalism. Prasenjit Duara's criticisms can be found in *Rescuing History From the Nation*, pp. 52–6.

on kokueki as a historically contingent rhetorical strategy for asserting the public worth of private trade.

I have thus far used the modern Japanese state and nationalism as a frame of reference for viewing kokueki thought. This is legitimate because kokueki thought was appropriated by creators of the early Meiji state. They saw the relevance of domainal kokueki to their predicament, while transforming the scale of its rhetoric to the young nation-state of Japan in its international context. However, the origins of kokueki thought can only be understood in its eighteenth-century context. We can understand the needs and responses that are the origins of kokueki thought only with a "thick description" of the politics, economics, and various ideologies of the eighteenth-century domain as a frame of reference. Therefore, this study will primarily emphasize the rapidly changing contexts of the eighteenth-century domain, while occasionally making reference to the issues of the growth of nationalism, which is the larger narrative into which this study fits.

The appearance of kokueki thought marked an important ideological shift in eighteenth-century Japanese domains. The increasing use of kokueki thought within domain state governments carried important political implications, because it facilitated a shift from a lord-centered toward a country-centered political imagination. Expounders of working for the "prosperity of the (domainal) country" through the support of export industry and commerce were subtly redefining what was considered the public good and what the purpose of government should be. Before the invention of the rhetoric of kokueki in the early eighteenth century, the dominant samurai discourse defined an activity, including economic activity, as public by linking it to the lord of the domain. Traditionally defined, service (*goyō*) and faithful duty (*hōkō*) to one's lord were public (*kō*) actions, and actions not for the benefit of one's lord were private (*shi*), and all private actions were tinged with selfishness (*shii*).[25] A daimyo served the shogunal house, defined as kō, and daimyo retainers served the daimyo house, defining it as kō, and members of a retainer's house served

---

[25] This can be seen in the fact that the term *kō* or *oyake* can mean both "public authority" and "the lord." My thinking owes much to Aruga Kizaemon's exploration of the concept of kō in *Aruga Kizaemon chosaku shū*, vol. 4, pp. 179–283. In the English literature, I have found Mary Elizabeth Berry's "Public Peace and Private Attachment: The Goals and Conduct of Early Modern Power in Early Modern Japan" and most especially Mark Ravina's "State Building and Political Economy in Early Modern Japan" to be superb discussions of the complex net of coexisting notions of public authority. Ravina's forthcoming book, *Land and Lordship in Early Modern Japan* should further develop this discussion. Because we continue to depend upon the concept of "state," we have yet to develop a satisfactory appreciation of the nonterritorial nature of public authority embodied in the concept of household. Eiko Ikegami's *The Taming of the Samurai*, pp. 164–71 presents a nonterritorial approach to public authority that deserves further exploration. I also find Mary Berry's close analysis of changing notions of political space in *The Culture of Civil War in Kyoto* to be promising.

him, defining him as kō. Commoners were subject to numerous exactions in the name of this service, and those commoners able to organize others to perform these duties were accorded public status and privileges. Public activity, including economic, was generally organized along lines of service, and the polity was imagined as a hierarchy of obligations of service between or within households.

The lives of samurai were most fully incorporated into this structure, and thus were the most "public" of the four classes. Members of the lesser classes might find opportunities to be incorporated into public activity through service. With regard to commerce, only merchants in the service of the lord, *goyō shōnin*, possessed a public worth, symbolized by their possession of certain samurai privileges.[26] Yet in general, merchants were the least "public" of the classes. NeoConfucian orthodoxy, for example, held a low view of merchants. This was rationalized with physiocratic economic logic: Peasants created new wealth from the earth, craftsmen transformed materials into more useful things, but merchants did not produce any real wealth at all, contributing least to society, and furthermore their role exchanging goods naturally encouraged them to seek "selfish" profit. They were often regarded as parasites, or at best understood as having their proper place, but hardly seen as heroes of public duty. Within the newly developed rhetoric of kokueki thought, however, the trading activities of any merchant, not merely those serving the lord, became crucial to the "prosperity of the country" and, by extension, of the people and government. Furthermore, kokueki thought established the public value of merchant activity with no reference to serving the lord (*otome*), but rather with reference to increasing the prosperity of the kuni, or country. The hierarchical arrangement of households, which was at the heart of samurai politics and of which the lord may be seen as merely the pinnacle, became superfluous within this new rhetoric of kokueki. This imagined entity, the economic country, came to signify the public interest, and within the discourse of kokueki thought, individuals had to link themselves to this definition of the public interest in order to perceive their public identity. The country became something worth sacrificing self-interest for, such that a sugar merchant of Tosa could declare in a petition in 1816, "Ever since the production of sugar was initiated in this country of Tosa, I have given it my all, thinking of nothing but the prosperity of the country."[27] The development of kokueki thought was, in short, creating an important element of modern nationalism.

[26] These privileges, reserved to samurai in principle, might include any or all of the following: the right of audience with the lord, the right to use a family name in public documents, and the right to bear a sword.

[27] Watanabe Mitsushige, "Tosa-han tōgyō shikō," p. 66.

Tosa is an example of the larger, peripheral domains in which kokueki thought was developed earliest and realized most fully in policy. These domains increasingly carried out policies that can be described as mercantilist or economic-nationalist, which they justified by appeals to the concept of kokueki. Just as nation-states were created not in isolation, but through their interaction, the domains influenced each other's development greatly. Matsuyama domain, for example, launched a program to increase paper production in its domain in 1768 with the proclamation, "We hear that this is being done in many other domains, most especially successful in Tosa, Uwajima, and Ōzu, and brings prosperity to their countries."[28] In this way, domains influenced each other not only in actual policy, but also in the rhetoric with which they justified it, facilitating the spread of kokueki thought into many of the. islands' regions. These domains were territorial states whose beginnings predated the origins of kokueki thought. Furthermore, when they were unified into a compound polity at the beginning of the seventeenth century, they were integrated by ties of service between lord and servant, most importantly enacted in the alternate attendance system. This system of service created the export-oriented "international" economy that was the context in which kokueki could first emerge as a meaningful imagining. What were these domains, and what was the nature of the shogunal government that ruled over this collection of states? A brief review of their origins will help clarify the structures out of which kokueki thought grew.

The creation of the Tokugawa polity

The historical literature credits the development of territorial states to warlords in many regions of the Japanese islands. These warriors created "domainal countries" (ryōgoku) during the Sengoku (Warring States) period (1467–1568). There were hundreds of these domains – small ones encompassing only a few villages and large ones the size of present-day New York State. Nearly all were in competition with their neighbors, and the needs of continuous warfare led lords to create military governments that were nearly, or in some cases wholly, independent of the dying estate system controlled by Kyoto aristocrats and religious institutions. Although the vicissitudes of warfare made many of these individual realms short lived, patterns of domainal organization became the foundation of the early modern political order.

Two major organizing concepts for these domains were the "household" and the "country," and as even the modern term for nation-state in Japanese sug-

---

[28] Matsuyama-shi Shiryōshū Henshū Iinkai, *Matsuyama-shi shiryō shū*, vol. 6, p. 502.

gests (kokka: etymologically "country-household"), the greater part of succeeding political history on the Japanese islands can be understood in terms of the tensions between, or fusions of, these two ideals.[29] Of the two, the idea of the household, the ie, functioned as the major organizing principle for the ruling samurai class. All of the warriors who lived within the domainal territory had their own households, made up of the estate, family, and servant/retainers. The daimyo recognized and guaranteed the continuity of these warrior households, at the same time subsuming them into his own large "household" (kachū) of which he was ritually known as the head and fictive father. All of the retainers were members of the lord's household, and the domain with its people was his estate to share with them in grants of fief. From the perspective of this "household" of samurai, the domain and its people were primarily so much "territory" or "possession" (ryō) and did not bear a public valence. As lesser samurai became retainers of larger samurai (who were becoming the lords), they received from their new overlord confirmation of the possession of their ryō in letters of enfeoffment. Fief holders provided for their households and financed their military and other service to the lord with fief income and conscripted labor from their fief villagers. A ryō was a means to sustain the household for war and could be enlarged or lessened or even transferred to a different location, without affecting the essential integrity of the household. The only way to truly destroy a household was to kill all inheriting family members.

If "household" was the primary concept ordering relations among retainers, the creation of a state (kokka) identity for the daimyo possessions emerged out of the relations between peasants and the lord. Peasants were responsible to pay crop taxes (nengu), incidental produce taxes (komononari), and corvée labor services (yaku) to whichever samurai held the territory on which they lived. Retainers held administrative and judicial authority over their fiefs as well. Some retainers taxed and ruled more harshly than others. Because the daimyo was overlord to the retainer and had an interest in asserting his authority, peasants could appeal to the lord for "fair treatment" if a retainer were too harsh. When peasants resisted the exactions of fief holders through appeals to the lord, the usual result was greater domainwide standardization of tax rates and laws. Such protest often invited an extension of the lord's administrative control and urged the growth of an extensive and independent domainal administration that could allow the lord to pose as a fair government authority, *kōgi*,

---

[29] Mark Ravina has best reviewed the literature and adds his interpretations in "State Building and Political Economy in Early Modern Japan." See also Katsumata Shizuo with Martin Collcutt, "The Development of Sengoku Law."

of the state. In this guise, such Sengoku lords as the Imagawa of Mikawa and the Takeda of Kai issued law codes for their domains.[30]

This encouraged the gradual reduction of samurai fief rights, which were absorbed into the rights of the domain-state possessed by the lord. Some daimyo households maintained a fief system, but greatly attenuated the judicial and administrative rights of retainers. Other daimyo households abolished fief administrative rights altogether and developed unified domain administrations, providing annual payments to the retainers from the domain warehouses (although for reasons of maintaining household status this was often fictionalized as tax coming from fiefs). In almost all domains, most of the samurai retainers were forced to live in the lord's castle town and become servants in his administration and army. They were divorced from independent sources of economic and political power and became completely dependent upon the survival of the lords' household.

The importance of the samurai household as such did not decline with the development of a state identity and administration. The kachū organization continued to be the foundation of the military and provided the basic structure upon which civil government itself was created. The lord remained at the center of the "house" through an immense number of ritual observances forced on all retainers and through the organization of political power. As the lord's domainal government grew, retainers came to serve in posts in this administration. The status of a samurai within the "household" determined the civil and military posts in which he was eligible to serve: House elders (karō) were the elite who possessed the largest fiefs and served in chief administrative posts and as generals. Their nearness to the lord and consequent high public value were often symbolized by granting use of the lord's family name. Samurai lower in the household hierarchy had smaller fiefs and filled more menial posts in the military and government. Because the lord's government was staffed and run by his samurai, they were able to continue to collectively protect the interests of their own households within the context of a domain with a unified code of laws and behavior and privately pursue their own ambitions within the framework of the lord's household.[31] Yet, the whole domain came to be subject to service to the hegemon of Japan.

The islands of Japan were unified into a tightly controlled coalition of domain states between 1568 and 1615. Oda Nobunaga, Toyotomi Hideyoshi, and Tokugawa Ieyasu were a succession of three daimyo lords who developed into overlords of the other daimyo through conquest and negotiation. Oda

[30] Michael Birt, "Samurai in Passage"; Sasaki Junnosuke with Ronald Toby, "The Changing Rationale of Daimyo Control in the Emergence of the Bakuhan State."
[31] Kasaya Kazuhiko, *Kinsei bukeshakai no seiji kōzō*, pp. 88–102.

Nobunaga lorded a small domain in central Honshū, from which he led an army into Kyoto in 1568. Adeptly using the newly imported technology of guns, he conquered most of central Japan in the following decade. Nobunaga enlarged his own realm thereby, but also partitioned much of this territory to his vassals, allowing them to create their own domains. One such vassal was Toyotomi Hideyoshi. Hideyoshi had begun life as a commoner servant of Nobunaga but developed into an extraordinarily adept politician and general. At the time of Nobunaga's assassination by a dissatisfied vassal in 1582, Hideyoshi was daimyo of Himeji domain and was serving as general of Nobunaga's western army. Hideyoshi led this army to defeat the assassin and take the banner of leadership himself. Hideyoshi's armies spread throughout Japan, and he defeated the last major lord in 1590, achieving hegemony over the islands. As Mary Berry argues, Hideyoshi is notable not merely for transforming his vassals into lords of domains, but also for frequently allowing defeated enemy lords to retain rule of their realms (or a depleted portion thereof) in return for their recognition of his suzerainty. Hideyoshi attempted to create a federation of lords under his authority.[32] Hideyoshi assumed some of the trappings of the traditional imperial state, such as the title of regent to the emperor, and he began the practice of collecting maps, and cadastral and population surveys based on the imperial province system. But Hideyoshi remained head of a coalition of the households of daimyo lords that was his essential power base. His control of lords through the household rhetoric of service was far more thorough than his control of cultivators through cadastral and population surveys. As Philip Brown has argued, these surveys were of dubious quality, often unable to be of practical use.[33] Peasants were controlled rather more effectively through corporate village agreements with samurai rulers, and it was the duty samurai households owed their overlord that was the primary justification for exactions. When Hideyoshi died in 1598, he left behind an infant heir and an unstable association of daimyo. The lords split into eastern and western coalitions, and in 1600 the eastern armies, under the leadership of Tokugawa Ieyasu, emerged from the battlefield victorious. Following the pattern set by Hideyoshi, Ieyasu granted many lands as domains to allies and vassals, confiscated a large portion of the lands of his enemies, but also allowed some of them to retain possession of realms in return for promises of fealty. All of the lords of Japan came to recognize his leadership in the settlement following the battle. Ieyasu had the emperor name him shogun in 1603, and his descendants reigned as shoguns in Japan until 1867.

---

[32] Mary Elizabeth Berry, *Hideyoshi*, pp. 66–98.
[33] Philip Brown, *Central Authority and Local Autonomy in the Formation of Early Modern Japan*.

A political order based upon hierarchies of samurai households in charge of their domainal territories (ryōbun) was implemented throughout the islands. A quarter of the archipelago was ruled directly by the Tokugawa household, and the remaining three quarters was divided into more than 250 domains, each ruled by its own daimyo lord. During the Tokugawa period, a daimyo was defined as a samurai who was granted directly from the shogun a realm assessed to produce the equivalent of over ten thousand *koku* of rice. These lords were vassals (*kerai*) of the Tokugawa shogun, fictively members of his extended household. They served the shogun as their vassals served them, and the shogun required them to perform many costly services that forced them to mobilize the resources of their domains to that end. Many of the lords (those who had already been counted as vassals by the time of the battle of Sekigahara) were eligible to serve in the senior positions of the shogun's government, which was called the *bakufu*. The fact that lords filled the policy-making positions of the bakufu led it to mediate between protecting the interests of the lords and their domains and the centralizing influence of the shogun, much in the same way that the household structure of the domains functioned.[34]

With regard to the management of their own realms, the lords were required to enforce the broad outlines of bakufu law and obey occasional arbitrary directives from the shogun, but they were expected to be rulers – not bureaucrats from Edo. When the daimyo Hosokawa Tadatoshi was granted the large realm of Higo (Kumamoto) in 1632, he made three separate drafts of basic law for his new realm and sent them to his friend, the senior councilor Inaba Masakatsu, in order to have the shogun Iemitsu recommend the most appropriate one. Masakatsu answered abruptly in a letter, "Higo has been entrusted to you. You have been charged with governing it. At a busy time like this I don't think it would be wise to bother the shogun with such questions. . . . I think it is fine if you use whichever of the three versions you like. . . . I mentioned this to [our friend] Sakakibara who joked, 'The bigger the realm the shogun gives Tadatoshi the bigger the fool he becomes!'".[35] The realms, such as Higo, were territories that lords were expected to rule as they saw fit. This, and very diverse regional geography and histories, led to a fair variety in governments throughout Japan.

The some 250 realms of these lords were physically diverse in character, ranging from large domains of more than a million people to small domains of fewer than ten thousand. Many of the smaller domains in the Kinai and Kanto

---

[34]   Harold Bolitho, *Treasures Among Men*. This can also be seen as reflecting the tendencies that Mary Berry characterizes as the development of a "federal" polity under Hideyoshi, *Hideyoshi*, pp. 147–67.
[35]   Yamamoto Hirofumi, *Edojō no kyūtei seiji*, pp. 176–9.

plains consisted of dispersed parcels on a politically very complicated landscape. Their rulers had comparatively little authority over their people. They had the right to collect basic taxes and the right to adjudicate the few disputes that did not cross out of their tiny realm boundaries. By contrast, large peripheral domains functioned in many respects as small countries. Most of the larger domains were contiguous realms. Their populaces generally had no direct contact with any government other than that of the domain.[36] As a rule, the bakufu sent in no officials to advise, oversee, or interfere with domain government. The administrations of larger domains had full rule over the people, economies, and wealth of their realms and could control such factors as immigration and emigration, and imports and exports through many means such as tariffs, quotas, bans, and the issuance of paper currency.[37]

The alternate attendance system and domainal export economies

Despite the greater independence of the larger peripheral domains versus the smaller, centrally located domains, the alternate attendance system instituted by the bakufu exerted a tremendous influence upon all domains alike. The alternate attendance system required the lords of domains to live in Edo every other year with a large retinue of retainers prepared to do service to the bakufu in the form of guard duty, fire prevention, or participation in ceremony. The lords also maintained their families in palaces in Edo as hostages to the bakufu. The alternate attendance system was designed to the political end of deterring the lords from carrying out rebellions against the Tokugawa house. It met this end very well, but was far greater in significance. It actively bound together the whole economy and society of Japan. The constant traffic of lords, retainers, and bearers to and from Edo circulated their culture into Edo and from there back out again, contributing to the cross-fertilization of the regional cultures of the islands.[38]

Most germane to the issues related to this book, the alternate attendance system quickly transformed domainal economies into export-dominated economies. The lords were themselves required to pay for the enormous expense of constructing and maintaining their numerous Edo residences, as well as the

---

[36] Harold Bolitho, "The Han," pp. 183–234, in John Hall, ed., *Early Modern Japan*.
[37] John Hall, "Foundations of the Japanese Daimyo," in Hall and Jansen, eds., *Studies in the Institutional History of Early Modern Japan*; Bolitho, "The Han." It should be noted that even large domains lacked the same degree of independence with regard to economic policy when they were situated on the five shogunal highways that covered the southeastern region of Japan between Kyoto and Edo. The shogun had jurisdiction over the highways even if they passed through a domain; Constantine Vaporis, *Breaking Barriers*, pp. 28–31.
[38] Constantine Vaporis, "To Edo and Back."

general costs of living and traveling outside their domains. An example from Tosa in the 1690s can illuminate the scale. Tosa annually moved from 1.5 to 3 thousand people and their baggage the 500-mile trek over mountain, sea, and coastal highway between home and the great metropolis of Edo. In 1697, 2,813 Tosa people in Edo had come with the lord.[39] On that journey, additional porters, innkeepers, shippers, and food suppliers had to be paid. In the spring of 1694, a time of Edo residence, the domain population statistics recorded 4,556 Tosa people in Edo.[40] Suppliers of food and other goods to these people in Edo, as well as carpenters and artisans for the mansions, had to be paid. The samurai who traveled needed extra stipends. In the domain budget for 1688, 300 kan out of 3,953 kan of total expenses were devoted to the journey itself, and 1,422 kan were devoted directly to Edo residence expenses. Of the remainder, 1,042 kan went to pay off loans incurred in Edo and Osaka, leaving only 1,189 kan for other expenses.[41] It can be said without exaggeration that well over half of Tosa's expenses were related to the costs of the alternate attendance system, and as Toshio Tsukahira's research has shown, this is true for nearly all domains for which we have data. Altogether, costs that can be traced to the alternate attendance system regularly consumed from 40 percent to 70 percent of the budget of any domain administration.[42] This enormous expense outside of the domain required a concomitant amount of exported tax goods in payment, influencing the structure and development of the Edo period's political economy.[43] The alternate attendance system itself and its economic influences lasted throughout the early modern period, certainly the single most important institution affecting economic life.

The Kinai region, which centered on the manufacturing city of Kyoto and the great port of Osaka, emerged as the hub of this great economic activity. This was because it possessed a large urban population of consumers and the finest agriculture and artisan production in the archipelago. High-quality goods from the Kinai were exported throughout the islands, most especially to Edo. Daimyo and their retinues in domains and Edo were important consumers of many Kinai goods, such as the high-quality silks of Kyoto, cotton cloth of Osaka, weapons of Sakai, and sake of Nada. The area was directly controlled by the bakufu or by lords of fiefs too small to effectively interfere in the commercial economy, and Osaka's position was further enhanced by legal protections granted the market by the shogun, who declared ownership of the city in 1619.

---

[39] 1697 According to a *shūmon aratame* report in *TMK*, vol. 86, ff. 55–7; other numbers cited in Vaporis, "To Edo and Back," p. 30.

[40] From shūmon aratame statistics in *TMK*, vol. 83, f. 39.

[41] Hirao Michio, *Kōchi-han zaisei shi*, pp. 36–9.

[42] Toshio Tsukahira, *Feudal Control in Tokugawa Japan*, pp. 88–102.

[43] Furushima Toshio, "Shōhin ryūtsū no hatten to ryōshū keizai."

Osaka developed in the early seventeenth century into the central market for the goods collected as taxes by lords.

Most domains in western and northwestern Japan exported tax goods primarily to Osaka, whereas a far smaller number of northeastern domains exported primarily to Edo. Osaka harbors were filled with thousands of cargo boats daily. Lords periodically sent boats filled with rice, lumber, paper, and other goods to be sold. Because sales income was sporadic and expenses were constant for any daimyo, they borrowed large sums of money from designated financing merchants in Osaka in return for promises to sell these merchants the tax goods against the debt (or hand over the proceeds if sold elsewhere) when they came in. When these goods did not suffice to cover expenses, the lords exported other products they were able to collect through the implementation of export monopolies.[44]

The merchants in control of the tax goods trade not only gained profits from their role in marketing, but had possession of large amounts of lending capital. Lords received bills of credit from the Osaka merchants who marketed their tax goods. With these bills of credit, they paid many of their expenses to retailers in Edo, who then used the bills toward the purchase of new wares from Osaka. The mechanism of credit between Osaka and Edo left large sums of interest-free tax money in the hands of Osaka exchange merchants for weeks or months at a time, which they used in their role as moneylenders.[45] Merchants who sold goods for the lords developed into powerful creditors who invested in private enterprises and goods throughout Japan. The Japanese islands became economically integrated around Osaka, which became known as the "Kitchen of the Realm," into which raw materials flowed and out of which finished products and orders for more goods were sent.

Yasuoka Shigeaki has shown that although Osaka had many of Japan's leading industries and was a major exporter, it was still a net importer of goods. At the end of the seventeenth century, port records reveal that it imported three times as much as it exported. In short, Osaka, like Edo, was an important consumption center. Although trade in goods would have depleted Osaka of its capital resources quickly, Yasuoka astutely notes that interest payments flowing into Osaka probably far exceeded this deficit in the value of actual goods.[46] In the eighteenth and early nineteenth centuries, Osaka and Kyoto's industry dominance declined because of the diffusion of production to the regions. Even so, Osaka remained at the head of a large credit pyramid extending throughout Japan. It did not lose its dominance of the financial market until the Meiji

[44] Miyamoto Mataji, *Ōsaka*, especially ch. 3. Yoshinaga Akira, *Kinsei no senbai seido*.
[45] This is described well in Yamaguchi Tetsu, "Bakuhansei shijō no saihen to shōhin seisan."
[46] Yasuoka Shigeaki, "Bakuhansei no shijō kōzō."

government abolished the domains and the lords no longer sent their goods to the Osaka market. The alternate attendance system created in this way a pyramid of wealth and credit in the Japanese economy. The chief Osaka merchants became rich because the alternate attendance system funneled wealth into the cities and into the hands of the large exchange merchants. Conversely, the constant drain on the domain economy to finance the lord's Edo-related expenses constricted and disrupted local lending markets.

The importance of the credit ties to Osaka can hardly be overestimated. As can be seen from the example of Tosa, the domain often sold in Osaka to satisfy creditors even when the local Tosa market would have been much more profitable. From the eighteenth century on, even though it was often more profitable to sell rice in Tosa, the domain still exported to Osaka.[47] The same was true with paper. In 1791, a samurai wrote a memorial to the junior administrator Mori Yoshiki suggesting that the domain should not sell its paper in Osaka, but Mori had to respond, "It is a very good suggestion, but if we do not ship it to Osaka then our borrowing position would become worse. Although the opinion is reasonable, it is impossible to stop shipping paper to Osaka."[48]

Not only lords, but independent domain merchants as well, frequently exported to "The Three Cities" of Osaka, Kyoto, and Edo (primarily to Osaka, which had numerous merchants who specialized in reexporting goods to the other two cities). They chose to do so for two major reasons. First, the three cities were enormous centers of consumption, and until the eighteenth century at least, their prices and marketing facilities were generally better than in the countryside. Second, the merchants of the big cities were major sources of commercial credit. They often lent money to provincial merchants to ensure a steady inflow of goods. Even when prices were favorable in the domain, many merchants exported to Osaka to pay off their commercial loans. Like the lords who ruled them, they developed long-term trading relationships with Osaka merchants through bonds of debt.[49]

The domainal merchants who dealt with the Osaka merchants were of two types. The ones who were dominant in the seventeenth century dealt in the lord's tax goods or filled his needs. They were called goyō shōnin. They often helped the lord ship his goods to Osaka and imported luxury products for him.

[47] Yamazaki Ryūzō, *Kinsei bukkashi kenkyū*, pp. 69, 110–1, 200–5 gives comparative prices, which were generally 85 percent to 125 percent of the Osaka market price except for during the mid-eighteenth century. When one considers transportation costs and marketing fees, even a lower price in Tosa could be more profitable.

[48] In his office diary ms. *Sansei nichiroku*, vol. 1, entry for 9/4/1798, in the Kōchi Prefecture Library.

[49] Yasuoka Shigeaki, "Bakuhansei no shijō kōzō," pp. 245–98. Ōno Mizuo, "Bakuhanseiteki shijō kōzō ron."

They played importantly in the rapid expansion of the Osaka marketing structure in the first few decades of the seventeenth century. The domainal and even the Osaka merchants who thrived in the mid-seventeenth century generally did so through their role in the export of tax goods or as purveyors to the lord.[50]

Trade in products that remained in commoners' possession after taxes was carried on by merchants of lesser stature. Such merchants and trade existed from the beginning of the Edo period, but they had grown vastly in collective importance by the end of the seventeenth century. Many local merchants exported to wholesale merchants in Osaka, called *toiya* or *tonya*, who also became quite wealthy and economically powerful. From the mid- to late seventeenth century these Osaka merchants increasingly organized themselves into associations or guilds, called *nakama*.[51] These associations functioned to preserve each merchant a market share, protect prices, and strengthen their hand vis-à-vis the people who shipped goods to Osaka, both domain lords and domainal commoners. The merchants who shipped goods from the domains had to deal with these associations largely on the associations' terms. This, of course, provided potential for conflict; domainal merchants sometimes sold goods illegally to Osaka merchants who were not members of the pertinent association or tried to get associations to change their fees and terms of trade.

The bakufu and the domain governments sometimes entered into these conflicts. Domains would often support their merchants' claims against the associations in the court of the Osaka magistrate. Or sometimes they would allow domain merchants to obviate conflict by permitting their use of the domain government's marketing compound and warehouse, the *kurayashiki*, in Osaka. The bakufu frequently supported its own Osaka merchants and tried to suppress some domainal policies.[52] Conflicts of interest with the bakufu increased from the late eighteenth century as domains became less devoted to the economy of service and increasingly committed to the interests of their own trade economies. Kokueki thought encouraged such centripetal tendencies in the relationship between domains and the shogun.

Research on domainal economic policy and **kokueki** thought

Tosa was one of the earliest sites of the creation of kokueki thought, possibly the earliest, although the currently undeveloped state of this field of research precludes more than speculation on the matter of primacy. At any rate, the

---

[50] Wakita Osamu, "Kinsei toshi no kensetsu to gōshō."
[51] The classic source on this topic is Miyamoto Mataji, *Kabunakama no kenkyū* (1938).
[52] Although because of the bakufu's nature as a mediator of shogunal and domainal interests, its policies were not always consistent.

crucial issue is the type of domain for which kokueki made most sense. Tosa was generally similar in type to other domains, such as Sendai and Kumamoto, which also made extensive early use of kokueki thought, in the last half of the eighteenth century. Like these other domains Tosa was a large, geographically contiguous realm relatively distant from the economically advanced Kinai region of Japan. It was not well suited for specialization in rice production, and thus the people sought the development of numerous other products for export. It was also politically stable and powerful, both internally and vis-à-vis the central government. As will be argued below, merchants of Tosa and other domains with similar conditions developed the concept of kokueki in the early eighteenth century. By arguing that their activities were for the benefit of the "prosperity of the country," they could justify their requests for assistance from their governments, which were sufficiently powerful to be of use to the merchants. By the latter half of that century, the samurai leadership of many of these domains had adopted the mercantilist premises of this thought, and working for the prosperity of the country developed into an important ideological tool of government, adding a political dimension to the decline of the Osaka-centered economic order of the archipelago. Because a number of large domains followed similar trajectories, I will set Tosa in the context of other domains and the research on "domain nationalism."

Prewar historical writing on the early modern period generally imagined a monolithic Japan under the rule of the shogun. History of the Japanese islands during the early modern period focused on the shoguns and their chief advisors. Domains were interpreted as small imitations of bakufu rule or as passive objects of shogunal control. Their lords became significant only when they participated in bakufu affairs. Only in the story of the final years of the collapsing shogunate did they suddenly come to appear as actors, on two sides of a battle over the continued existence of the bakufu. This history reflected both the elitist tendencies of the prewar period and the tendency of a period of nation building in Japan to project the image of a monolithic nation into the past. As elitism in society has lessened and as the Japanese nation has become more of an accepted belief rather than a project, the highly centralized interpretation of the early modern period has been in slow decline.

The research of Itō Tasaburō, begun in the 1930s, inaugurated domainal studies as a field of Japanese historical interest rather than local interest. Interest in domains themselves as opposed to the Tokugawa shogunate has risen steadily since the postwar period. Since that time, recognition of the potentially independent roles of domains within the early modern polity inspired much work on domain–bakufu relations and led most historians to adopt the term *bakuhan taisei*, or "bakufu-domain political structure," that was coined by Itō.[53] From the 1950s many scholars began showing that domains pursued policies different from the bakufu, stressing their special character in contrast to previous descriptions of the domains as imitative of the bakufu.

Tōyama Shigeki saw a growing divergence between the interests of domainal and shogunal rule as a factor in the collapse of bakufu authority in the nineteenth century. He created the term han kokka, domain-state, to describe the growing independence of domains and their increasingly centralized bureaucracies.[54] His description of the domains as becoming increasingly absolutist – in the Marxist sense of being centralized, bureaucratic, and based on the interests of rural capital – sparked more than a decade of debate within circles of Marxist historiography over the meaning of domain reforms. Some scholars argued that domain reforms were mainly feudal-reactionary, and some that domain reforms were becoming more oriented to the rising bourgeoisie represented by the landlord-entrepreneur farmers called the *gōnō*. Among those who accepted the idea that the domain reforms became progressive – meaning absolutist – there was debate concerning the timing of the transition, whether the Kansei reforms of the 1790s or the Tenpō reforms of the 1830s were more important in representing a shift of domain policy support away from the small, independent peasant household toward the landlord-entrepreneur farmer. Shift to the latter was considered to be a sign that regional commerce had spread enough that the domains tried to make a power base upon the interests of rural capital.[55] Another trajectory of the debate compared the success of domainal and bakufu reforms. The research generally affirmed that the bakufu largely failed in its attempts, whereas some domains succeeded.[56] The domainal research of Marxist historians focused largely on state policy toward agriculture and the villages.

At the same time, scholars raised in the classes of Honjō Eijirō at Kyoto University carried out research focusing upon the many aspects of urban commerce in Japan, especially Osaka. They were non-Marxist, liberal economists and saw themselves as nonideological. Among this group, Horie Yasuzō wrote *Wagakuni kinsei no senbai seido* (1933), which is the earliest monograph with extensive discussion of domain commercial monopsonies and monopolies.

---

[53] Fujino Tamotsu, *Bakuhan taisei shi no kenkyū*, is the classic of bakufu-domain research. Itō Tasaburō's works are collected in *Kinseishi no kenkyū* (4 vols.).

[54] Tōyama Shigeki, *Meiji ishin*, pp. 25–44. An excellent example of English language research with an interest in domain nationalism is Albert Craig, *Chōshū in the Meiji Restoration*.

[55] Ikeda Norimasa, "Tenpō kaikaku ron no saikentō – Tosa-han o chūshin ni shite"; Hayashi Motoi, "Hōreki Tenmei ki no shakai josei"; Hatanaka Seiji "Hōreki Tenmei ki Setonaikai shohan ni okeru keizai seisaku to sono kiban."

[56] Gotō Yasushi, "Bakusei kaikaku – toku ni Tenpō kaikaku ni tsuite." For a dissenting view see Okamoto Ryōichi, "Tenpō kaikaku," pp. 242–50.

Yoshinaga Akira summarized the subsequently extensive research on domain commercial monopsonies and monopolies in 1973 in *Kinsei no senbai seido*. As Yoshinaga notes, the research has focused largely on the institutional aspects of these commercial schemes. Scholars have uniformly interpreted the development of domain government commercial projects as being originated by domainal administrators, who were attempting to locate income for impoverished domain finances by tapping the growing commercial life of their domains. There has been relatively little research on the class interests involved and almost no research on the ideological aspects of these ventures.

Fujita Teiichirō was the first scholar to identify and research the ideology and thought that justified this activity. He saw in the appearance of kokueki thought an important departure from the dominant view of the economy that centered upon the paternalistic benevolence of the lord (*osukui*) and the obedient dutifulness of the common people. Kokueki, he argued, did not incorporate issues of morality, but rather created the basis for the development of economic theory by envisioning the domainal economic unit and placing an emphasis on issues such as economic growth, balance of trade, the importance of finance and marketing.[57] He argued more recently, in an article on kokueki in an encyclopedia of Japanese history, that Japan formed of itself a miniature international economic order, with domain states being the countries. He writes, "It can be said that kokueki became a profitable [form of economic] understanding only when many states coexisted within an international order which considered commercial exchange and monetary exchange as natural."[58] This perspective opens the way to exploration of the social origins of kokueki thought and to the meaning of the concept of economic country itself. Fujita has indeed suggested and explored many of the links between Edo period kokueki thought and Meiji period kokueki thought in research on economic proposals in petitions of the early Meiji period.[59] Yet his analysis of the class interests parallels that of previous research on domain monopsonies and monopolies. Fujita has argued that "domain economists," bureaucrats in charge of domain finances, were the creators of the concept of kokueki and its associated policies. In this scheme of things, merchants and peasants are the object of new economic policies engineered by these bureaucrats and recipients of this new rational system of economic thought. Kokueki appears as a Japanese-bred form of cameralism. Fujita's extensive exploration of this topic initially inspired little research by

---

[57] Fujita Teiichirō, *Kinsei keizai shisō no kenkyū – kokueki shisō to bakuhan taisei*. A more recent general summary of his thesis is in "Tokugawa keizai shisō no tassei to genkai – 'kokueki' shisō o chūshin ni."
[58] *Kokushi daijiten*.
[59] Three articles beginning with the title, "Meiji zenki no 'kokueki' shisō."

others. Coming from the non-Marxist approach of his mentor, Miyamoto Mataji, he was in a milieu that paid much attention to economic institutions but had little interest in ideology.

Yet Fujita's lack of emphasis on class interest and struggle made his work seem ahistorical to the Marxist scholars of the day.[60] Fujita saw the new relationships associated with kokueki thought as generally beneficial to all concerned, including the merchants and peasants, because the new policies often led to economic growth that benefited the domainal economies. In the early seventies, Sugi Hitoshi and Fukaya Katsumi were the first scholars to respond creatively to Fujita's thesis of the importance of kokueki thought. Fukaya responded in his article on the ideology of peasant protests by emphasizing the conflict of interest between domain and peasant, and he identified kokueki as a scheme to increase taxation. This article is an excellent description of the ideological sources of resistance to government taxation by peasants, based on their assertion of a "right to subsistence," but Fukaya considered kokueki and *kokusan senbai* (domain products monopolies) to be effectively the same thing, and kokueki as nothing but an ideology masking state interests.[61] Sugi Hitoshi identified kokueki in the same way and looked at the development in the early nineteenth century of a competing *minpu*, "enrich the people," ideology among peasants involved in sericulture.[62] He regarded this minpu ideology as coming naturally out of rationalization of production by peasants – along the lines of the physiocrats identified by Thomas Smith – and also as an ideology of resistance to domainal kokueki thought.[63] The tendency to identify kokueki simply with the rulers is also visible in the more recent interpretation of Aoki Michio, who describes kokueki as domain products monopolies aiming to:

increase domain government income by encouraging the production of products other than rice. . . . In order to successfully make people understand the profits of this production as domainal prosperity (kokueki), and increase their desire to produce, the domain had to imbed a clear consciousness in the retainers and common people of the domain as a 'country' vis-à-vis the bakufu and other domains.[64]

Aoki's point that the use of kokueki is related to the development of a national consciousness is important, but his paradigm is also top down, and kokueki is but an ideological tool used to support state commercial monopolies. These scholars have generally emphasized a conflictual rather than a dialogic model

---

[60] This is expressed in the 1966 review of his work in *Shigaku zasshi*, reprinted in *Nihon rekishi gakkai no kaikan to tenbō*, vol. 8, p. 407. Also see the review in *Nihon rekishi*, no. 222 (November 1966), pp. 109–11.
[61] Fukaya Katsumi, "Hyakushō ikki no shisō" (1973).
[62] Sugi Hitoshi, "Kasei ki nōson ni okeru minpuron no keisei" (1972).
[63] Thomas Smith, "Okura Nagatsune and the Technologists."
[64] *Kindai no yochō*, pp. 91–115, quotation from p. 94. See also his "Murakata sōdō," pp. 272–9.

for understanding the development of kokueki thought and have ignored merchants as actors.

The link between kokueki thought and domain export policies has also been increasingly treated by scholars other than Fujita in a neoliberal vein. In the past two decades more scholars of economic history in Japan have become less interested in issues of class conflict and tend more toward essentially modernizationist paradigms (belatedly from an American perspective but right in tune with national economic preeminence) and capitalist modes of economic analysis.[65] Also, from the quite different perspective of cultural studies, interest in issues of nationalism and regional identity has risen in Japan recently as well, increasing the relevance of Fujita's research.[66] A sign of this is that recent researchers have begun to interpret domain export policies in terms of the significance of kokueki thought, but the field is still small.[67]

The interpretation of kokueki thought presented to date is one largely devoid of commoner roots. Fujita has mainly used samurai-generated materials and has come to the conclusion that kokueki thought was a conceptual and ideological tool created by domain economic bureaucrats who wanted to alleviate domain financial difficulties.[68] This parallels the general interpretation of domain export policies, which tends to describe these policies as administrative creations, rather than as an administrative response to the demands, needs, and ideas of various commoners. A further implication of the dependence on the documents of domain administrators for the analysis of kokueki thought is that it becomes difficult to separate the range of kokueki thought from administrative policies. This has been one source of the above-described tendency among scholars to approach kokueki and kokusan senbai as identical.

There are two pieces of research that do not fit into the interpretation I have given thus far. Taniyama Masamichi deals with the active use of kokueki thought and rhetoric by peasants of the Kinai region in the Kasei period (1804–29).[69] He sees these highly commercialized peasants of the Kinai region using the rhetoric of kokueki to organize broadly across their region in order to protest and defend

---

[65] The *Nihon keizaishi* series published by Iwanami shoten (1987–90, 5 vols., Hayami Akira et al., eds.) includes and summarizes much of the best work of these scholars. Their approaches are diverse, but the collection mainly stands out for its use of contemporary liberal economic theory.

[66] This trend is typified by Tsukamoto Manabu's *Kinsei saikō – chihō no shiten kara*. Tamura Sadao introduces much of the recent literature in this vein in his volume of essays, *Nihon shi o minaosu*.

[67] Nishikawa Shunsaku and Amano Masatoshi, "Shohan to sangyō to keizai seisakushi," pp. 206–10, in Shinbo Hiroshi and Saitō Osamu, eds., *Kindai seicho no taidō*; Aoki Michio, *Kindai no yochō*, pp. 91–115, and his "Murakata sōdō to minshūteki shakai ishiki," pp. 272–9; Doi Sakuji, *Bakuhansei kokka no tenkai – Hiroshima-han o chūshin ni shite*, pp. 500–54.

[68] One of his articles, however, does deal with the thought of a merchant in the 1790s, Fujita Teiichirō, "Kansei ki jōka machi shōnin no shisō – Ōkōchi Tadashi cho *Tatoeba* ni tsuite."

[69] Taniyama Masamichi, *Kinsei minshū undō no tenkai* (1994), pp. 348–9.

their commercial activity. Insofar as the region of these peasants was not domainal, Taniyama notes that the interests reflected could not be those of a political administration; rather they were using kokueki to describe their sense of a common economic fate bound by commercial relationships. Taniyama regards the peasants as having appropriated and significantly transformed a rhetoric previously monopolized by domain governments, and reveals them as using kokueki for their own ends as a rhetoric aimed at bakufu officials.

Taniyama's focus on what may be called the contested meanings of kokueki and his emphasis on its ideological uses by people outside of government parallel my own project in this book. The other work that does not fit the top-down mode of understanding kokueki is that of Hirakawa Arata, who has studied the petitions of commoners to domain government leaders and has noted their importance in suggesting domainal involvement in commercial activities. Although Hirakawa does not explore the ideological aspects of kokueki thought, he posits an increase in dialogue between domain and merchant that arose out of the greater commercialization of domainal economies, and he focuses on the issue of increasing domainal sensitivity to "public opinion" (*seron*).[70]

This book emerges out of this historiographical context. It focuses on the dialogic, arguing that domain merchants created the essential features of kokueki in the early eighteenth century, and domain officials gradually adopted and adapted it in their relations with these merchants. At the same time, whereas the above-mentioned research situates the earliest beginnings of kokueki thought among domainal samurai in the 1760s and its prominent use from the first decades of the nineteenth century, this book will point to its earlier origins and centers on an analysis of a large body of petitions from the 1750s and 1760s in Tosa, which shows that a rich and well-developed kokueki thought was already used by the townsmen and port merchants of Tosa. They envisioned a system of domainal countries involved in exporting and importing products. They possessed a clear vision of Tosa as a country whose economic well-being depended heavily upon its management of trade across the border. They considered it the proper role of government to assist the development of the Tosa economy defined in this way. They possessed a great diversity of opinions on the best means to achieve this goal. Many argued for government intervention in trade, and yet others for free trade, both making equal appeals to the concept of kokueki. These various approaches to economic management are all part of the central innovation, which is the imagining of such an economy in the first place, setting up, in effect, a debate over free and managed trade that continues to this day – a debate appropriate for national economies.

[70] Hirakawa Arata, "Chiiki keizai no tenkai" (1995).

In a sense the domainal-country economy they envisioned was already coming into being, as a result of the development made under the influence of the alternate attendance system, yet the creation of kokueki allowed them to better conceptualize and attach a public meaning to this economy. The experience of individual merchants was one of shipping goods to distant places or of competing with goods brought from distant areas of production. It was paying taxes each time one crossed the border of the lord's domain with goods, or being forbidden to send certain products across the border. It was finding it difficult to sell products nearby, while finding it easy to sell in Osaka. It was finding that borrowing capital from Osaka merchants meant having to ship goods to those merchants even when they offered low prices. Conceptualizing a "national economy" out of this experience was an act of will that enabled commoners to respond to and influence economic change, because it was used to influence their own behavior and government policy. The expanding acceptance of the system of thought associated with the term kokueki created a consensus of understanding that empowered people and governments to respond to changes that could not be well controlled with orthodox neo-Confucian views or more fundamental samurai views of the political economy tied into household organization.

Since kokueki was an ideological justification for new forms of government involvement in commerce, interaction between samurai government officials and merchants was essential to the spread of kokueki thought. Samurai, indeed the finance officials identified by Fujita, adopted and adapted kokueki thought and incorporated the needs of the domainal state for income and legitimation. However, the issue of origins is important. The interactive framework allows us to see the continuing relations between commoners and the samurai in the formation of a new vision of the role of the state in the economy and to correctly identify the interests and the worldview that produced it. Because it was a vision of the economy that was not lord-dependent but rather centered on the country, the creation and then the gradual inclusion of this ideology into domain-states represent a key event in the lineage of the modern nation-state. The key importance of kokueki is that it "de-centered" the lord and "centered" the country in political economic thought and thereby began changing the relationship between government and its people. This exploration of kokueki thought in Tosa will be, at the same time, a story of how commoners significantly affected government policies and the ideology of rule. Behind the facade of an autonomous elite, the "ruled" were politically active and engaged at many levels.[71]

---

[71] This argument owes much to Tetsuo Najita's *Visions of Virtue: The Kaitokudō Merchant Academy in Tokugawa Japan*. Note especially pp. 8–9, where he discusses the need to avoid a hard dichotomy of ruled and ruler.

Tosa officials were among the first of any domains in Japan to begin using kokueki thought as justification for policy. The documents of Tosa show that kokueki thought existed at least as early as the 1720s (instead of the period from 1750 to 1790 as has been previously argued). The rulers increasingly found kokueki thought attractive and useful in responding to some increasing ecological, economic, and financial problems of rule. One of the central duties and justifications of domain government was the disbursement of famine relief (osukui) to prevent death and maintain people in their occupations. The provision of relief was an important symbol of the personal benevolence of the lord. Failure implied his lack of benevolence and by extension a lack of worthiness of his government. From the late seventeenth century, however, famines increased in severity and frequency, and most domain governments were patently unsuccessful at relief. In addition, in most domains debt problems became more serious in the eighteenth century than in the seventeenth century. This led to increasing taxation of agriculture in some domains, to increasing control of commerce through monopolization and privileging, and to extensive use of special levies on the populace. These appropriations harmed livelihoods, and many people came to feel that they directly contravened the duty of government to maintain people in their professions. Furthermore it was known to all that one of the main reasons for extensive domain debt was service to the bakufu and the expense of life in Edo. Kokueki thought suggested answers to some of these problems because its logic justified the following: the creation of new industries to provide a more stable economy and employment; an increase in export production to counteract the debilitating effects of the drain on the economy of the alternate attendance system; altering the relationship to Osaka marketers and creditors to strengthen the hand of the domain government and merchants; and reduction in service to the bakufu and participation in Edo life by the lord. Because of its legitimating potential, the rulers of domains often used the argument that they were working for the "prosperity of the country" in many of their commercial policies from the late eighteenth century.

When the rulers argued they were working for the prosperity of the country they were, like the merchants, legitimating their behavior in terms not centered on the lord himself. Thorough use of kokueki thought as an ideology of rule would have erased the role of the lord and the household structure of government itself. Because kokueki thought was used extensively only in the restricted situation of commercial policy, however, it was not threatening. Its influence in other areas of policy was diffuse. Furthermore, the increasing focus on the regional economy expressed in kokueki thought occurred simultaneously with other methods of increasing focus on the personal rule of the lord in the domain. In Tosa from the mid-eighteenth century, the administrators styled their lords as enlightened and benevolent rulers and emphasized the lords' association with the "country" of Tosa. The lords' realm and the "country" were identical. Tosa's rulers were successful in using an ideological mix that was simultaneously lord-centered and country-centered by associating the identity of the lord with that of the country.

This book presents a picture of the origins of kokueki thought highly contextualized in the economic and political history of Tosa domain. Without this contextualization it is impossible to adequately answer questions such as "Why the early eighteenth century?" or "Why did samurai bother to adopt an outside ideology?" Chapters 2, 3, 4 and 5 are structured to set up the main argument of the book, which is summarized above and developed in the last four chapters. Chapter 2 describes the seventeenth-century formation of the Yamauchi household and its domain within the general political context of early modern Japan. It describes the factors of size and location of the domain that had important implications for the development of kokueki thought and for its successful application as ideology. Particular emphasis is placed on domainal economic organization and its relation to the ideology of the ruling samurai class. Chapter 3 describes the processes creating a crisis that came to face Tosa people and their government in the mid-eighteenth century. I interpret the economic crisis as resulting from development according to the seventeenth-century settlement and thus leading to a need for policy change and the rhetoric to support it. Chapter 4 describes the eighteenth-century crisis in domain finances and its subsequent recovery after the 1780s, raising the question of how the domain was able to enact a very real turnaround. Chapter 5 describes the nature of mid-eighteenth-century popular disillusionment with government and discusses the petitions and memorials the people of Tosa submitted to the lord via a newly created petition box. This chapter also discusses how the paternalistic language that the rulers used and in which so much contemporary history was recorded hides the interactive aspects of domain government. The remainder of the book presents the development of kokueki thought and its adoption and adaptation by the samurai rulers in light of the mid-eighteenth-century crisis described above. Chapter 6 explores the ideological origins and development of kokueki thought, primarily based on an analysis of petitions, showing its intimate relationship to the commercial and urban class, and its gradual adoption by the retainer class. Chapter 7 explores the pivotal Tenmei reforms begun in 1787 and the growing resistance to the performance of bakufu duty. Chapter 8 examines domain commercial economic policy from the 1780s to the 1870s mainly to assess the role that kokueki thought played as an ideology of government–commerce interaction and to assess the role it may have played in altering the relationship between the domain and the bakufu. The Conclusion summarizes and includes speculation on the relationship between kokueki and nationalism in early Meiji history on the archipelago.

2

The geography and politics of seventeenth-century Tosa

When all of the lords [of Ieyasu's camp] were gathered Katsutoyo announced, 'We should set our horses toward Kamigata. . . . The reason Ieyasu is pausing is because he worries about the dangers of the road there. If that is the case, I will open my castle of Kakegawa to him and hand it over to one of his trusted retainers, and I will give him a hostage as dear to me as myself. . . .' Then twelve or thirteen of the lords signed together [a document that they would do likewise]. . . . On the way out, Ieyasu grabbed Katsutoyo's sleeve and said, with tears in his eyes, 'I owe everything to you this time'.
Recollections of Yamauchi Katsutoyo's page, Tanikawa Shichizaemon[1]

Samurai were at the heart of the early modern political order, and their vision of human relations dominated the political structure and the economy. They were warriors whose success depended on faithful service to the right lord. Yamauchi Katsutoyo received the domain of Tosa in 1600 for his service to Ieyasu at the battle of Sekigahara. This realm made Katsutoyo wealthy, yet it was a domain and a wealth that he had to be ready at any moment to devote to his overlord's command. Katsutoyo demanded no less from his retainers, whom he enfeoffed, and not much less from leading merchants and peasants, who were required to help Katsutoyo and his descendants serve.

The hierarchy of service became the engine of tremendous economic and social change in Tosa, converting its landscape forever. The key link and the symbol used to legitimate the economic activity and change was the relationship between the lord of Tosa and the shogun. This relationship was metaphorically spread out and repeated in bonds of duty and benevolent reward over the social terrain of Tosa, defining the public value of the economic activity of the domain by linking it to this economy of service. This was the structure that transformed domainal territories throughout the islands of Japan into export economies in the seventeenth century. The surveys of agricultural productivity, shipping capacity, and so forth, were made to enable this economy to function. They also provided standards by which to limit the extent of service demanded under

[1] *KTK*, pp. 320–1.

normal circumstances. Yet, the ideology of the economy of service always permitted demanding the ultimate sacrifice from anyone who claimed to benefit from it – most typically the samurai. Service to the shogun left domains particularly vulnerable ideologically, because it did not provide them with an effective rhetoric of resistance. In the eighteenth century, *kokukeki* thought emerged into public discourse to fill this gap. It emerged out of the seventeenth-century context, which will be explored in this chapter.

Yamauchi Katsutoyo receives Tosa from the Tokugawa

After the battle of Sekigahara, Ieyasu confiscated Tosa from its lord, Chōsogabe Morichika, who had sided with the losing Western armies. Yamauchi Katsutoyo was then a fifty-five-year-old warrior and lord of the small domain of Kakegawa in Honshū. The transfer of power in Tosa to Katsutoyo reflects the shift from the Sengoku warrior's lingering devotion to his fief to the early modern warrior's devotion to his lord and his household. Katsutoyo is the archetype of all his warriors: rootless people whose success depended upon able performance as vassals. Katsutoyo lost his father to battle at age fourteen in 1559 and became a *rōnin*, a wandering samurai looking for a lord. He finally found a lord in Oda Nobunaga in 1573 and was fortunately placed in the unit of Kinoshita Tōkichirō, later known as Toyotomi Hideyoshi. When Nobunaga was assassinated in 1582, Hideyoshi stepped in to take over leadership. Over the next eight years, Hideyoshi led the armies that conquered all of Japan, and in 1590 he became its first undisputed ruler in well over a century.

As Hideyoshi expanded his dominion, he rewarded Katsutoyo with larger fiefs, but this meant frequent transfers from one realm to another. Under Hideyoshi, Katsutoyo's fief amounts advanced in eight stages from a small holding of 400 *koku* in Karakuni to, in 1590, a 50,000 koku (later raised to 60,000 koku) domain at Kakegawa, a castle town on the coast of Honshū near Shizuoka. By this point, he had achieved status as a minor lord in his own right. His band of retainers grew proportionately, from his single faithful lackey, Gotō Tameshige, to nearly two hundred mounted samurai, and many hundred retainers of lesser status.[2] These samurai included family, such as his younger brother Yasutoyo, and brother-in-law Andō Yoshiuji.[3] They also included friends such as Hayashi Kazukichi, who had made a pact with Katsutoyo when they were both

---

[2] I will maintain the distinction between *samurai* (retainers with the right of audience, the right to bear two swords and the right of entry in the domainal register of retainers [*bugen'iri*]), and lower status retainers such as *ashigaru* (musketeers and archers), *kachi* (footsoldiers), and others not possessing these rights. All were *bushi* (warriors) or *hōkōnin* (military servants), but samurai made up only the top 10 percent of retainer households.

[3] *KTK*, pp. 75–83, 109.

rōnin to hire the other if one of them found the elusive charm of success.[4] A few were local samurai of Katsutoyo's fief land who joined his band and then were enticed with larger fiefs to move on with Katsutoyo as his own star rose.[5] Although Katsutoyo granted his retainers fiefs, his own repeated transfers effectively cut the retainers from any land-based roots they might have traditionally possessed or developed. Their fortunes were as dependent upon service to Katsutoyo as his fortunes were upon serving the hegemon.

The actual military contribution of Katsutoyo's small army in the battle of Sekigahara was not great, but Tokugawa Ieyasu richly rewarded Katsutoyo because he was one of the first Toyotomi daimyo to give 100 percent to Ieyasu, and the example brought Ieyasu many more strong allies. Recognizing Yamauchi weakness, Ieyasu delegated his own representatives in the final month of 1600 to send forces to Tosa, along with a contingent of Katsutoyo's warriors under his brother Yasutoyo, to demand the transfer of the castle and realm to the Yamauchi clan. However, a large number of the Tosa samurai, especially the self-made rural samurai (*ichiryō gusoku*), hoped to renegotiate the terms of defeat. They knew that some of the lords on the losing side, such as the Mōri of Chōshū domain, had been allowed to keep portions of their domains. The rural samurai did not want to lose the Chōsogabe, who had protected their interests, nor did they want rule by a foreigner from the mainland, certain to bring his own more urbanized samurai in train.[6] They gathered in the lord's city of Urado and occupied the castle, firing on the boats of the Tokugawa emissary and refusing to hand it over unless Morichika were granted half of Tosa to rule. A standoff continued for weeks, but the incoming forces finally found a few Chōsogabe allies, senior urban retainers – professionally mobile and concerned for Morichika's welfare – who secretly opened up the gates to the castle. The castle was then stormed, and the victors sent a shipload of 273 heads back to Osaka as grisly proof of their labors.[7]

The central role of Tokugawa Ieyasu's forces in the transfer spells out Katsutoyo's full dependence upon Ieyasu for his possession of Tosa. Because Katsutoyo's right of possession was based only on the word and force of Ieyasu, Yamauchi allegiance was naturally to the Tokugawa and not to the people of his new domain. Indeed, the violent transfer of lordship made relations between the rural warriors and the Yamauchi especially tense and adversarial at the

---

[4] Kubokawa-chō Shi Henshū Iinkai, *Kubokawa-chō shi*, p. 79.
[5] An example of this kind would be the retainer Higashino Yukinari. *KTK*, p. 117; Kōchi-ken Jinmei Jiten Henshū Iinkai, *Kōchi-ken jinmei jiten*, p. 297.
[6] Yamamoto Takeshi, "Chōsogabe seiken no henshitsu to ichiryō gusoku."
[7] Marius B. Jansen provides an excellent account of the transfer in "Tosa in the Seventeenth Century," pp. 89–129, in Hall and Jansen, eds., *Studies in the Institutional History of Early Modern Japan. KTK*, pp. 392–427.

beginning of rule. Katsutoyo himself arrived with the remainder of his army on the second day of 1601. He met with the initial contingent of his forces led by his brother on the eighth, and Ieyasu's deputy forces soon returned to Osaka.

The Yamauchi army remained outnumbered by the Tosa warriors, and the Yamauchi were still fearful of rebellion, which explains a treacherous stratagem Katsutoyo used to assert his military authority. In the third month of 1601, he sponsored a sumo tournament on the beach below his newly acquired castle at Urado to celebrate his entry. However, he turned the celebration to horror when he used the occasion to grab over seventy of the more fractious Chōsogabe rural retainers and had them crucified before the waves. Soon, other local samurai who had initially resisted Yamauchi possession were hunted down in the countryside. Only a very few, including some of those previously disaffected with Chōsogabe rule, were hired as samurai to become members of Katsutoyo's own retainer corps, now rapidly expanding.[8] Katsutoyo chose rather to locate most of his new samurai in distant Kyoto and Osaka.[9] The senior retainers of the Chōsogabe were banished from the domain, becoming rōnin forced to look for positions with other lords. The remaining rural retainers of Tosa, who were still many in number, were permitted to continue farming, but as peasants deprived of samurai status.

Over the decade, relations with the populace gradually improved. From early on, local elites such as the former rural samurai were incorporated into domain administration as village headmen and elders. A very few were even guaranteed their status as rural samurai (newly termed gōshi). Overt hostility became a thing of the past after a last minuscule attempt at rebellion in 1615 (in conjunction with the siege of the Toyotomi castle in Osaka by Ieyasu), and increasingly the two "camps" became cooperative and integrated. Beginning in 1644, a far greater number of former rural samurai were allowed to gain gōshi status on the condition that they sponsor land reclamation. However, the original conflict set up a paradigmatic relationship and allowed the Chōsogabe identity (increasingly including many members with fictional ties), mixed up with gōshi identity, to be one of resistance to domain authority. As Marius Jansen has shown, this played an important role in Tosa politics as late as the collapsing years of the

---

[8] One major source of disaffection for many in Tosa was the succession dispute between the two sons of Chōsogabe Motochika: Morichika and Chikatada.

[9] One document lists 23 former Chōsogabe retainers employed by the Yamauchi, but only 7 were taken on in the first five years of Yamauchi rule (most as sub-retainers at that). This is from among at least 116 enfeoffed retainers hired between 1600 and 1605. Kurokawa Masamichi, ed., *Tosa monogatari*, vol. 2, pp. 156–62, provides a list made in the mid-seventeenth century of where Chōsogabe samurai found employment after the demise of the household. Mutō Yoshimichi, comp., *Nanroshi*, vol. 5. pp. 178–9, 196–201, 222–3, provides dates of first employment supplementable by ms. "Kanbun hachinen bugenchō" in the Kōchi Prefecture Library which provides summary lineage histories.

bakufu, two and one half centuries later.[10] The resentment has had tremendous staying power. It is surprising to see that even today some Tosa people get hot under white collars over the subject of the "Yamauchi invaders." The conquest is the event most symbolic of the threat to local identity posed by relationships with the outside ever since, as Tosa increasingly loses its form into that of a more homogenized "Japan"; it is a symbol of the anxiety over the decline of local autonomy.

The Yamauchi brought about rapid changes in the economy of Tosa to enable them to perform service for the Tokugawa. Ieyasu had granted out Tosa to Katsutoyo, but this was not merely as a gesture of thanks for support. Katsutoyo became Ieyasu's vassal and owed him nearly any service he might request. This relationship bound the Yamauchi clan to the Tokugawa clan for generations. Their primary duty was to supply an army should Ieyasu and his descendants need it, such as demanded at the siege of Osaka castle in 1614–15. Shogunal military emergencies became a thing of the past after the Shimabara peasant rebellion of 1637, but by the 1630s the alternate attendance system had become firmly established, and this was considered a primary form of military duty – in the form of providing guards for the city of Edo. Another duty, extremely important to both the shogun and the domains, was to assist the shogun in the construction of cities and castles. The large armies and construction teams had to be supported by the economies of the lords' domains.

The basis of the amount of earliest service to the Tokugawa is unclear for many domains, but soon the standard for calculating the amount of service to the shogun came to be the *omotedaka*, or "official *kokudaka*." It is important to consider briefly how these numbers were assigned, to gain a greater appreciation of the great diversity of domainal economies and the true nature of the kokudaka system. Because local geography made rice cultivation impossible in many regions of the Japanese islands, local land surveys mathematically converted the production of nonrice products, such as wheat or beans, into a rough value equivalent of rice. At the village level of assessment, the evaluators also fudged the numbers to take into account economic factors such as distance from market and special costs of production. This was to make sure that the number would be a reasonable basis for making tax demands on the village.[11] Ostensibly, these totals were then added up within the domain, and domain lords then submitted the totals to Hideyoshi (or later to the Tokugawa shoguns). These estimates of economic power based on land surveys became the

[10] *Sakamoto Ryōma*, pp. 27–30, 49–50.
[11] Philip Brown provides a detailed and stimulating discussion of many problems associated with the actual land surveys as carried out in Kaga domain in *Central Authority and Local Autonomy in the Formation of Early Modern Japan*, pp. 58–88.

kokudaka of the domain. This indeed was the case for several lords, but there were very many exceptions to this ideal. The Matsumae in the far north had a domain based on herring fishing and trade with the Ainu, and their retainers were enfeoffed with the product of fishing villages. Their kokudaka status was a pure fiction in that it was based on no survey, but on a rough estimate of what service to the Tokugawa they were able and willing to bear.[12] Lest this be thought an extreme exception, even the Mōri of Chōshū domain, lords of a rice-producing realm that had been surveyed, had an internal debate over the amount of the kokudaka to submit to the shogun in 1605. They provided their domain representative in Edo with various appropriate-seeming calculations with numbers ranging from 296,000 koku to 428,000 koku, and gave him a carte blanche to choose the number he thought most appropriate in the political context. Political questions determined the final result.[13] Thus, the kokudaka of a domain recognized by the bakufu, also called the omotedaka, was not a measure of rice production, nor even, with some domains, simply a measure of agricultural productivity. Nevertheless, these numbers were of prime economic importance, because the kokudaka became the standard by which the shogun determined the amount of service he would demand from each lord.

The Chōsogabe of Tosa had their own internal land survey, which had been carried out in the 1590s and attempted to measure the amount of cultivated land area in Tosa. It is not clear whether this amount was actually reported to Hideyoshi or not. Their land survey disclosed 248,300 *tan* (one tan equals one fourth of an acre) of land, easily able to produce far more than the omotedaka of 98,000 koku that was the basis for their service to Hideyoshi.[14] Although the land had not changed and no new surveys were carried out, the omotedaka of Tosa changed in 1604, when Tokugawa Ieyasu ordered all of the lords of western Japan to submit to him a domain production assessment along with the totals of tax collected in 1604.[15] Yamauchi Katsutoyo had his retainers carry out a desktop calculation based upon the Chōsogabe cadastral registers and worked out a kokudaka of 202,626 koku.[16] This amount came to be the standard for the calculation of service to the bakufu for most duties, and these costs can be linked roughly to the domain kokudaka.

[12] David Howell, *Capitalism from Within*, pp. 28–9, 34–5.
[13] Akizawa Shigeru, "Keichō jūnen Tokugawa gozenchō ni tsuite," pt. 1, p. 36.
[14] Akizawa Shigeru, "Toyotomi seikenka no daimyō kokudaka ni tsuite – Chōsogabe shi kokudaka kō."
[15] Akizawa Shigeru, "Keichō jūnen Tokugawa gozenchō ni tsuite."
[16] Thirty-six percent of the total was a calculated conversion into rice equivalents from crops such as wheat, millet, and beans produced in fields on terrain unsuitable for rice production. Yokogawa Suekichi, "Tosa no kokudaka," *Kōchi-ken shi, kinsei hen*, p. 50.

Rice was the ideal export item for lords in the seventeenth century, but it was not an important export of Tosa. Maps reveal Tosa to be a very large domain, but this physical size was not matched by extensive agricultural production. Even though the long southern summers permitted the double cropping of rice in Tosa, the productivity of the land was minuscule in comparison with the teeming central plains of Japan. This was because Tosa has an extremely mountainous terrain, which allowed room for only small and scattered plains suitable for rice agriculture. A contrast with the domain of Hikone in the developed heart of Honshū highlights Tosa's low agricultural productivity. Hikone was one-eighth the land area of Tosa, but its assessed agricultural yield in the early Edo period was 300,000 koku, a full 100,000 koku more than Tosa at that time. A rough calculation from these numbers makes Hikone twelve times as productive. By this comparison Tosa appears to have been a very poor region. However, other factors, not well recorded in the surveys of agricultural yield, made Tosa far richer than the kokudaka suggests. Compared with Hikone, Tosa had special advantages; hundreds of miles of ocean front and extensive green blankets of ancient forest covering the mountains. In lieu of rice, lumber, fish, tea, and paper all came to play important roles in the economy of Tosa as export products.

Initially, these products were largely controlled by the economy of service. Based on the Chōsogabe registers, Katsutoyo quickly granted out the lion's share of the agricultural land as fief to his retainers. He granted his brother Yasutoyo 20,000 koku and the western castle of Nakamura. Five senior retainers received small castles located strategically within the large domain and fiefs ranging from 1,100 to 10,000 koku.[17] Over a hundred remaining samurai were granted fiefs ranging from 20 to 7,000 koku and residences in the castle town. Katsutoyo's own demesne was a mere 45,000 koku. Out of this, he disbursed stipends to hundreds more retainers of lesser status than samurai. Yet Katsutoyo was able to carry out his duties to Ieyasu because his retainers owed him most any service he might request. Indeed, this economy of service was applied to the whole domain of Tosa, and common people who aspired to wealth and/or public identity were bound in much the same way as samurai to frame their identity within the bounds of service to the lord.

The four administrative regions of Tosa: Castle town, port, mountain, and village

The Yamauchi divided Tosa into the four administrative regions of castle town, ports, mountains (forest), and villages, corresponding to the functions of com-

---

[17] Hirao Michio, *Tosa-han*, pp. 10–11. These amounts are all *jidaka*.

merce, shipping and fishing, lumber production, and grain production. Each was assigned a special magistrate who reported directly to the senior administrators of the domain. Although the four divisions were based on a mixture of natural and historic divisions in the local economy of production and trade, the different social and political qualities of each region were greatly affected by the administrative control set up by the Yamauchi, assigning them a place in the hierarchy of service to the bakufu.[18]

The creation of a large castle town was crucial to the Yamauchi. Its importance can be surmised from the fact that Katsutoyo decided to move the castle even before he arrived in Tosa. The Chōsogabe castle had been at Urado point, on a narrow strip of land jutting into the mouth of Urado bay (now known as Kōchi bay). The location was defensible but permitted little room for the development of a town around the citadel. Even Katsutoyo's small retainer band could not all find residences in this tiny town, and some remained in Osaka and Kyoto waiting for the new city to be completed.[19] Katsutoyo needed a new city that could give him far more control of retainers and merchants in Tosa than had been achieved by the Chōsogabe, and he chose a small hill between two rivers in a plain at the head of the bay, about five miles to the north of Urado. Parts of Urado castle were moved to the new location, and laborers collected stone and lumber from the surrounding land to enlarge the new edifice. Samurai hoisted their kimonos and worked in the muck alongside commoners conscripted to the job. Even children were conscripted to carry earth, being paid one copper coin for each bucketful. At night, barrels of sake were brought out, musicians played, and all danced upon the new earth to pack it down tightly behind the rising stone ramparts. The people of Tosa labored for years hauling rocks and earth and constructing the buildings of the castle, palace, and surrounding city, according to the plan laid out by the chief building magistrate, Dodo Echizen. The location of the new city at the head of Tosa bay was much better suited for the development of a large town from which to control trade. Katsutoyo further pursued policies that made Kōchi quickly come to function as the hub of Tosa.

First of all, he was successful at having most of his middle-level samurai retainers live in the castle town or suburban villages. Unlike the Chōsogabe rural warriors, Katsutoyo's retainers had no traditional fiefs to be removed from, and this made it easy for Katsutoyo to grant his samurai plots of land and houses in the district surrounding the foot of the castle in Kōchi. Katsutoyo did grant

[18] This discussion owes much to Kären Wigen, whose work highlights the relationships between geography and the effects of human activity and policy, "The Geographic Imagination in Early Modern Japanese History"; Hirotani Kijūrō, "Tosa hansei to shoki jōkamachi."

[19] *KTK*, pp. 489–507, *Kōchi-ken shi, kinsei hen*, pp. 51–7.

his retainers fiefs but these fiefs were, with a few important exceptions among the chief retainers, composed of small parcels of land dispersed over many villages – sources of income and labor but hardly "home bases" for the samurai.[20] Samurai ties to the land were limited to receiving tax rice and laborers sent from the village. Lesser retainers, who lived on stipends of rice or cash, were also assigned residences in special wards such as Hōkōnin-machi on the perimeter of the retainer portion of the city. Other retainers, who were not granted residences, lived in nearby villages on the Kōchi plain. (see Map 2.1).

Katsutoyo utilized very similar policies to attract merchants and craftsmen. He granted plots of residential land in "townsmen wards" on the east and west edges of the retainer wards, and even stipends and the right of audience to powerful merchants and craftsmen in order to attract them to the city. Their numbers included many from outside of Tosa. Sakai-machi and Kyō-machi formed around wealthy merchants invited to Tosa by Katsutoyo. Merchants from Katsutoyo's former castle town in Tōtomi province settled in a ward named after their former home, Kakegawa-machi, having come there with the hope of maintaining established business relationships with the lord and retainers. At least ten elite craftsmen as well were granted stipends and residences to bring them from Katsutoyo's former domain, and being treated thus as retainers, they probably had little freedom to refuse. Most of these craftsmen were leaders of shops that supplied the military necessities of the Yamauchi, such as Kunitomo Shirōzaemon the gunsmith, who was granted a substantial fief worth 100 koku and a residence in Kakegawa-machi. Presumably, their many employees and servants moved to Tosa as well.[21] Katsutoyo also employed important local craftsmen, such as Oka Saburōzaemon, a master shipwright who received a fief of 18 koku in return for building ships for the lord.[22]

Shifting the commercial economy to focus on the castle town served the needs of the Yamauchi household. The Yamauchi achieved this by treating leading merchants after the fashion of retainers and granting them authority over other merchants, and by organizing other merchants into protected occupational wards. Local merchants fared far better than the Tosa samurai in the transition to Yamauchi rule. Katsutoyo actively courted their service: He

---

[20] *KTK*, pp. 472–3. *TYK*, vol. 1, pp. 570–2.

[21] Hirotani, "Tosa hansei shoki," p. 144. A full record of craftsmen in domain employ in 1626 is in ms. "Okurairi narabi ni kyūchi chō," HB, no. 7, pp. 35–55. The residence is noted in Mutō Yoshikazu, comp., *Nanroshi*, vol. 2, p. 464. An example of a chief carpenter being granted governance of other carpenters in Kakegawa is found in *KTK*, p. 429.

[22] Oka Takeshi, "Senshō Oka-ke kiroku," p. 78. Examples of papermakers, stone masons and tile makers being granted residences and or landed income rights (*kyūden*) can be found in *KTK*, pp. 571–6.

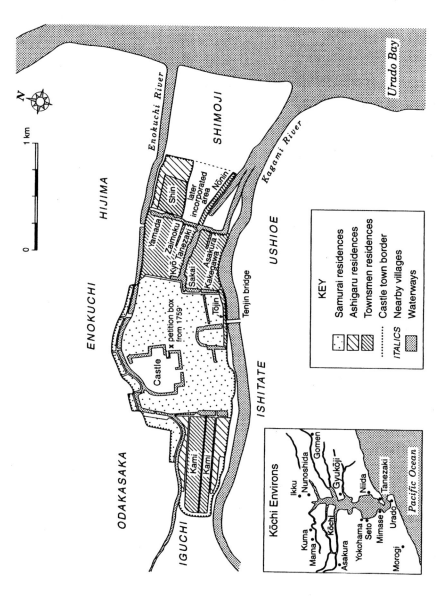

Map 2.1. Kōchi castle town, c1667. Adapted from Hirao
Michio, *Tosa-han*, p. 14 insert.

ODAKASAKA

IGUCHI

ENOKUCHI

HIJIMA

Castle

x petition box
from 1759

Kami

Kami

Yamada

Kyō Zaimoku
Tanezaki

Sakai
Kakegawa

Asakura

Tōjin

Tenjin bridge

Shin

later
incorporated
area

Nōnin

SHIMOJI

Enokuchi River

Kagami River

Urado Bay

ISHITATE

USHIOE

N

0   1 km

KEY

Samurai residences

Ashigaru residences

Townsmen residences

Castle town border

ITALICS Nearby villages

Waterways

Kōchi Environs

Ikku Nunoshida Gomen

Kuma Gyukōji

Mama Kōchi Niida

Asakura Tanezaki

Yokohama Seto

Mimase Urado

Morogi

Pacific Ocean

granted a large residence to the Harimaya, a leading merchant family of the Chōsogabe castle town of Urado, as well as the status of headman over a ward that was soon renamed after the Harimaya.[23] Likewise, the Pak family, originally Chōsogabe captives from Hideyoshi's invasion of Korea in the 1590s, were granted a ward, Tōjin-machi, to administer and a monopoly over the right to make and sell tofu in the new castle town.[24] Some of the wealthiest merchants were favored with individual marketing and purchasing privileges by the domain government, and smaller merchants had to depend upon these larger ones for protection and rights to market. The Hitsuya, for example, were a merchant family of Urado who were granted a residence and headship of the town and many favors from Katsutoyo. Their official genealogy records that the second generation Tarōemon had right of audience with the second lord Tadayoshi, and "was personally served cups of sake, and granted formal samurai clothing on many occasions. Tarōemon twice had the lord to his own residence where the lord deigned to sit." That even such seemingly inconsequential acts as serving a cup of sake or sitting down was a public event worthy of official record two centuries later reveals how the structure of public authority centered around the lord who was its highest expression. Tadayoshi also granted Tarōemon a monopoly of the purchase of foreign goods in Nagasaki. The Hitsuya were allowed to use the Yamauchi family crest on their boat, and when the Tokugawa restricted access to the Nagasaki trade in the 1640s, the Hitsuya were able to use the Yamauchi influence to maintain their privilege. In return the lord received first pick of the imports, a portion of the profits, and presents of "the strange things of foreign lands" such as tiger pelts and broad-rimmed leather hats from the Hitsuya.[25]

Merchants of lesser status who came to the castle town were forced to live in certain wards according to the grant of a special ward monopoly. For example, the merchants of Akaoka, Taruya, and Saga wards were granted a monopoly over the right to sell lumber in Kōchi and its hinterlands in reward for their financing the construction of one of the canals into the city. Thereafter, they were amalgamated into one Zaimoku-machi ("lumber ward"), and all lumber marketers had to open up stores within this ward in order to legally sell their goods.[26]

Such monopolies were given extra support by laws restricting commerce outside the castle town. Merchants in nearby market towns such as Asakura,

[23] Ms. *Hitsuya-ke monjo*, ff. 15th–16th, HB, no. 244.
[24] *KTK*, pp. 460–2.
[25] Ms. *Hitsuya-ke monjo*, ff. 5th–10th, HB, no. 244. *TTK*, vol. 1, pp. 599–601, has one of the lord's shopping lists.
[26] Hirao, *Tosa-han shōgyō*, pp. 119–20.

Tanezaki, and Yamada faced not only the decline of their traditional samurai customers of the Chōsogabe era (nearly all former senior retainers had been forced to leave Tosa), but also faced laws that prohibited them to deal in certain products.[27] These merchants and craftsmen of the regions were simultaneously drawn to the city by the opportunity to make a living purveying to the needs of the retainers and the administration. The existence of Tanezaki ward, Asakura ward, and Yamada ward testifies to the rapid influx of merchants from these outlying towns. In the mid-seventeenth century, the rulers also financed the construction of two long canals, one from the east and one from the west, to draw traffic from hinterland rivers into Tosa bay and the castle town area.[28] Because of the many policies described above, the castle town proper played from early on an immensely important role in the commerce of the domain, especially of the Kōchi plain.

The importance of the castle town within the Tosa economy can be inferred also from a glance at its population. Population statistics are unavailable for the earliest years, but in the first census in 1665 the *commoner* population of the castle town had reached 17,054 people, a full 7.09 percent of the total population of Tosa. If one adds on an estimated 5,000 members of retainer households, the castle town proper likely approached 10 percent of domainal population in the 1660s.[29] That most of the growth must have occurred in the first thirty years of the 1600s can be inferred from the growth in the number of city wards. Katsutoyo seems to have initially planned seven "townsmen wards" at the time the castle was built, but that number rose to twenty-five by the 1640s.[30] At the time of the 1665 census, there were twenty-eight wards, many devoted to the marketing of such products as fish, lumber, and clothing. The city boasted at this time 101 of the 181 sake breweries in Tosa, reflecting its dominant share in the commercial economy of the expansive domain. In this same year of 1665, a separate domain survey of the city recorded 1,070 professional craftsmen in 18 professions, including most prominently 302 carpenters, 127 dyers, 108 sawyers, and ending the list, such luxury producers as 16

[27] *Kōchi-ken shi, kinsei hen*, pp. 51–61. Not all products were restricted – at least until their economic importance was recognized. Paper was allowed to be sold freely by anyone in the town until the 1660s, when a monopoly was granted to some senior Kōchi merchants. The major exports handled by Kōchi shippers consisted of lumber products, tea, and to a lesser degree dried bonito. KTK, pp. 586–8, shows the exports of the shippers of Tanezaki village in 1602 – at that time, part of Urado castle town. Merchants of note in the town were dyers and sake brewers.
[28] *Kōchi-ken shi, kinsei hen*, pp. 131–4.
[29] No census of samurai in the castle town survives except for two years in the mid-eighteenth century. In 1749, the retainer population of the castle town was 5,784, which added to the commoner population made a total of 19,524 people. In 1762, the number of retainers and family in the castle town was 5,693 and the total, 20,351. The year 1749 in Mutō Yoshikazu, comp., *Nanroshi*, vol. 7, p. 212; 1762 from ms. *Hitsuya-ke monjo*, HB, no. 244, f. 44.
[30] Hirotani, "Tosa hansei shoki no jōkamachi oyobi zaigō machi," pp. 142, 156.

silversmiths and 5 wallpaperers.[31] Kōchi not only had a great number of permanent shops, but also provided the venue for a thriving periodic market, supplied by farmers from the nearby villages.[32]

The population of the castle town stagnated from the 1660s to the end of the domainal era (a period during which domainal population nearly doubled) at between 14,000 and 16,000 commoners.[33] Its relative importance in a growing domain rural economy undeniably declined from the eighteenth century on, which was the case for many domains, as described in Thomas Smith's excellent article on castle towns and rural development.[34] It is important, however, to recognize the castle town's continuing importance as a center of consumption focused on the household of the lord and his samurai.[35] We need also to understand the castle town at two levels. One was the administrative castle town, clearly defined and bordered by gate, fence, and law. This territory is the origin of the population statistics upon which Smith depends. The other "castle town" included the nearby sprawl outside, loosely definable as those villages containing substantial populations of individuals who had daily interaction with the city proper. Sometimes these villages grew so visibly that the official borders of the castle town were redrawn to incorporate them. In Tosa, all bordering villages continued to grow in the eighteenth century, despite the fact that the population of the castle town proper stagnated. It is likely that their growth reflected merchants and others choosing escape from castle town controls and restrictions, as argued by Smith, yet their choice of locations so near the castle town attests to the essential draw of the city on the economy. Comparison of two sets of data for seventeen proximate villages reveals that the commoner population alone rose from 9,921 in 1684 to 13,518 in 1742.[36] Various other documents reveal that these villages held very large numbers of retainer households as well.

[31] HB, vol. 9, p. 40.
[32] Hirao, *Tosa-han shōgyō*, pp. 107–15, 126–8.
[33] The year 1665 from "Okunijū shosaku demai narabi ni hitodaka tsumori," in ms. *Nanroshi yoku*, vol. 7, ff. 72nd–75th (photocopy in Kōchi Prefecture Library); 1685 from "shūmon aratame sashidashi," in *TMK*, vol. 38, ff. 83–4; 1862 from a "shūmon aratame hitodaka oboe," in Fukao Ryūtarō comp., *Onchi roku*, ff. 8–10. Hirao gives the 1665 figure as if for the year 1661 in *Tosa-han*, p. 15 but gives no source for this differing date. In addition to the above 1665 source, there is a document on domain finances entitled "Toyō kenpi roku" copied in ms. *Shūshi yoroku*, vol. 8, HB, no. 9, which gives the the year 1665 for this population figure.
[34] Thomas Smith, "Premodern Economic Growth: Japan and the West."
[35] Gilbert Rozman makes this argument for Edo in "Edo's Importance in the Changing Tokugawa Society."
[36] Documents for 1684 are the various village reports (nos. 18-37 through 18-67) surviving in the Kaganoi collection in the Kōchi City Library. Many thanks to Yorimitsu Kanji and Takahashi Shirō for providing me with photographs of these. The year 1742 comes from the domain statistical survey printed by Hirao Michio as "Tosa-han gōson chōsasho."
    The villages chosen were Ushioe, Kōda, Kamobe, Asakura, Mama, Kuma, Enokuchi, Fukui, Shioda, Ishitate, Iguchi, Odakasaka, Sōsenji, Engyōji, Ikku, Nunoshida, and Azōno.

In addition to the residential and commercial links to villages created by direct proximity to the castle town, the ports of Tanezaki, Urado, and Mimase near the mouth of the bay also can be considered part of the larger urban complex because they functioned as its port. With Tanezaki, near the former castle town of Urado, at its core, this region remained a large shipping center. It harbored 95 shipping boats in 1683. These boats linked the castle town to local ports and to Osaka. This number exceeded the 64 and 72 boats respectively of its nearest rivals for supremacy, Aki and Tano, ports twenty and thirty miles east, respectively, of Tanezaki that thrived not on the diverse trade of the castle town, but on carrying lumber to the Osaka region.[37]

In 1683, there were 55 port towns with a combined population of 37,542 (12 percent of domain population) and a total of 814 fishing boats and 807 shipping boats.[38] Some of these were located at river mouths on alluvial plains and included among their occupants many farmers and shopkeepers. Nevertheless, the distinguishing characteristics of the ports were their dependence upon fishing and shipping, and the special forms of taxation the domain placed on the residents. The ports were especially important to the Yamauchi and were administered separately by the port magistrate because only they could provide the transportation for samurai and goods to Osaka and Edo. Katsutoyo immediately forbade the sale of boats abroad, warning his administrator in 1601:

The boats of the ports are essential to everything in this country. Therefore, if shipping boats or even fishing boats are lost or sold abroad I will hold you responsible. You should exert yourself to add even one boat to the country and see that boat masters make a sufficient living because we order them to bear tough duties.[39]

From the time of Katsutoyo's arrival, boat masters were given residences and stipends and relieved of certain other duties, but their basic transport levy was great.[40] The boat owners had to send officials and official goods to Osaka at reduced rates and samurai-stipulated times, and they often complained that they could not carry on shipping trade or fishing because they were so often on call for domain duty. In the eighteenth century many people either gave up

---

[37] Hirao, *Tosa-han gyogyō*, chart on pp. 210–3. The populations of Urado and Mimase rose from 1,385 in 1710 (from a survey of the western ports in HB, no. 200, p. 67) to 1,683 in 1742 (from Hirao Michio, "Tosa-han gōson chōsasho") to 2,566 people in the mid-1840s (Hirao, *Tosa-han gyogyō*, p. 63). The population of Tanezaki fell from 903 in 1742 to 882 in the 1840s. A 1602 survey reveals thirty-five shipping boats in Tanezaki, most of which had carried lumber and tea to Osaka (*KTK*, p. 586).

[38] Hirao, *Tosa-han gyogyō*, pp. 210–3. Domain population in *TMK*, vol. 41, ff. 143–6.

[39] *KTK*, p. 474.

[40] *KTK*, pp. 636–44.

their boats or illegally registered them in other domains in order to escape this corvée.[41]

The ports were sites of control and taxation of domainal trade as well. All shipments were subject to import and export taxes. The domain kept in each port an official called a *buichiyaku*, which means a "fractioner" in reference to the fact that he was in charge of taking out as tax a fraction, usually 10 or 20 percent, of incoming and outgoing trade and fishing catches. These goods taken by the domain were then sold locally or shipped on to Osaka. The *buichiyaku* was also in charge of selling domain tax rice to the people in the ports and preventing the importation of rice in order to keep the price high, which was in the interest of the samurai. The presence of such an official distinguished the ports from the villages, which generally were allowed to be self-administrating, and expresses the great importance with which domain administrators viewed the ports.

Tosa shippers traded primarily in Tosa products and did relatively little shipping for merchants of other regions. Nevertheless, its exports were numerous, and with the likely exception of the troubled eighteenth century, shipping from Tosa crowded the Osaka landings. The number of Tosa boats ranked high among those from other provinces. A survey made for 1866 by the Osaka magistrate lists 116 Tosa boats with holds larger than 200 koku visiting Osaka that year, ranking Tosa sixth among the provinces in Japan.[42] Records of the Osaka fish market between 1817 and 1880 also reveal a similarly large proportion of Tosa cargo boats.[43] No strictly comparable reports for the seventeenth century exist, but one typhoon damage report for the Osaka area in 1687 listed the total number of boats sunk, with Tosa losing 58 of a total of 181 in the disaster, presumably reflecting a preponderance of Tosa ships.[44] The Osaka area was certainly the most common destination for exports, but Tosa shippers did not limit their activity to Osaka. Records in the 1770s show them trading even as far as the coast of the Japan Sea.[45] In Bizen Fukuyama on the Inland Sea, one

[41] From a memorandum entitled "oboe" dated *tora* (year of the tiger) 5th month written by the port magistrates. One can infer from the contents of the document that it is from 1794 and is addressed to the chief administrators (ms. in Matsunoo-ke shiryō, box of unclassified documents in the Kōchi City Library).

[42] Irish University Press, *Japan*, vol. 4, *Embassy and Consular Commercial Reports 1859–1871*, pp. 275–6. The other leading provinces were Owari, Kaga, Settsu, Etchū, and Iyo. The majority of Tosa's boats were smaller than the 200 *koku* minimum limit for this survey.

[43] Ōsaka-shi Shi Hensanjo, *Shokoku kyakukata hikae, shokoku kyakukata chō*, pp. vi–viii.

[44] *TMK*, vol. 56, ff. 39–43. In personal communication, Hirotani Kijūrō has noted that the high proportion of Tosa boats sunk may be due to the fact that many Tosa boats were large (and therefore clumsy) lumber carriers.

[45] Shikoku Minka Hakubutsukan Kenkyūsho, *Sanuki oyobi shūhen chiiki no satō seizō dōgu to satō shimegoya, kamaya (chōsa hōkokusho)*, pp. 83–4. Also see pp. 301–3 of Yunoki Manabu, ed., *Shokoku okyakusenchō*, which records more than twenty Tosa ships calling on the port of

lodging and trading house for shippers specialized in Tosa ships and recorded that 177 Tosa merchants stopped in 1791.[46] These records may be evidence that Tosa merchants increasingly diversified their destinations from the mid-eighteenth century.

The shipping industry made the ports home to the largest merchants outside the castle town. These merchants dealt in lumber, firewood, fish, charcoal, paper, sugar, eggs, and the other myriad products of the domain. When they collected enough capital, they also extended their activities beyond shipping to become sake brewers, moneylenders, and landlords to tenant farmers in Tosa. The Komeya of Tano port were one such merchant family of diverse activities. They were wealthy enough to frequently lend the domain large sums of money. They also built a lavish travel house for the daimyo for the occasions when he passed through Tano. In return, they were granted such samurai-like symbols of public authority as the right to use a family name, wear swords, and have audience with the lord, and they were also granted rights to harvest lumber on various mountains. Many other wealthy merchants were made headmen (*shōya*) of the ports as well.[47]

The main export products for most ports in the seventeenth century were lumber and firewood sent down from the mountains. This is worthy of note because the ports were affected severely when Tosa's forests declined from the end of that century. As a result, the number of shipping boats had declined from the 807 in 1683 to a mere 143 in the 1730s. When the economy rebounded (and the domain pursued policies to lighten the shipping corvée), the number revived to nearly 800 by the 1830s.[48] The new boats were much smaller in size, however, reflecting the shift away from the export of lumber to the export of such products as sugar, tea, paper, and eggs.[49]

The port towns were home to many fishermen. The most important bounty they caught were bonito. Every port in Tosa sent boats out to catch as many bonito as possible when they passed by Tosa's coast during the migratory runs of spring and autumn. In 1840, two million were caught and brought to port. These fish were processed through fermenting, smoking, and drying into a food and soup base called *katsuobushi*. It was a major export of Tosa in the nineteenth century and is one of the few domain-supported "Country Products" of

Hamada on the Japan Sea side of Chōshū in the last three decades of the eighteenth century. These ships sold two Tosa products, sugar and *katsuobushi* (processed bonito).
[46] Ms. *Kansei sannen okyaku chō Tosaya Kyūemon*, original in the Fukuyama city Tomonoura Rekishi Minzoku Shiryōkan. I used a photographic copy in the Kōchi Prefecture Library.
[47] *Tano-chō shi*, pp. 261–2, 312–3, 877–8.
[48] Hirao Michio, *Tosa-han gyogyō*, pp. 206, 220.
[49] This is nicely discussed in *Tano-chō shi*, pp. 359–65.

Tosa that is still of economic importance today.[50] The "single line and hook" (*ipponzuri*) technology of bonito fishing allowed for the decentralization of capital and organization of this kind of fishing.[51]

Whaling, at the other extreme, required many people to work in coordination and a large amount of capital investment. The industry was concentrated in two villages, and the domain was deeply involved in its support, initially inviting specialists in the seventeenth century and later providing financing, grants of income, and status to a senior whaler household in each of the two companies. One whaling company was on the southwestern cape of Tosa, Ashizuri, and one on the southeastern cape of Tosa, Murōto. This is because the two capes jutted out into the Pacific Ocean close to where the whales passed by on their migrations. When a lookout on a mountain top sighted a whale, a large number of small boats rode out to meet the whales with nets and lances. The two companies competed with each other for the largest catches. In the early nineteenth century, they caught annually twenty to eighty whales, each one bringing as much as 10 *kan* of silver.[52] Fishing and whaling were important aspects of the economy, but the ports' function as centers of sea transport was arguably more important because lumber and firewood were seventeenth-century Tosa's most important exports.

The lumber industry thrived on the resources of the inner mountain regions, administered by the magistrate of the mountains. Although the mountains were formidable barriers to travel and poor places to farm, they were at the heart of the economy of early modern Tosa because of the burgeoning urbanization that was taking place in Japan at that time.[53] In a survey of forests carried out by a retainer in 1617 in eastern Tosa, he estimated that there were over two and one-half million trees with a girth (at head height) of over eight feet.[54] These trees became increasingly valuable when in a matter of decades Osaka was built into a thriving city of three hundred thousand and became the commercial heart of Japan. In the early period of Osaka's history, Tosa was central in providing lumber and in organizing the lumber market. In the first decades of the seventeenth century, the Yamauchi dug a canal into Osaka to facilitate the unloading, storage, and sale of the lumber they and Tosa merchants exported. In return,

---

[50] Hirao, *Tosa-han gyogyō*, pp. 111–29. Kären Wigen has provided a superb study of the twentieth-century fate of the "Country Products" of Iida domain, in *The Making of a Japanese Periphery*.

[51] David Howell's *Capitalism from Within* provides a good analysis relating the influence of technology and markets on the herring fishing industry in Ezo (Hokkaido).

[52] Hirao, *Tosa-han gyogyō*, pp. 131–54.

[53] John Hall, "The Castle Town and Japan's Modern Urbanization"; Gilbert Rozman, *Urban Networks in Ch'ing China and Tokugawa Japan*. Conrad Totman discusses in detail the relationship between this great boom in construction and the razing of the ancient forests of Japan in ch. 3 of *The Green Archipelago: Forestry in Pre-Industrial Japan*.

[54] Hirao, *Tosa-han ringyō*, pp. 10–11.

Tosa merchants were given special privileges in the Osaka lumber market, such as their own wholesaler association, and they were granted an exemption from paying most of the lumber guild fees charged to all other importers. In the 1620s, the Yamauchi encountered a financial crisis, and they extensively cut and exported the forests of the expansive Shirahige mountain. This mountain's outlet was the Yoshino river, which flowed north through the domain of Tokushima and emptied into the Inland Sea only sixty miles from the burgeoning city. After paying a 20 percent tax to Tokushima domain, Tosa merchants picked up the lumber and shipped it in large flat-bottomed boats to Osaka, where they unloaded it near the Tosa Osaka compound (*kurayashiki*). The size of the mountain of lumber created there led the locals to bestow the name Shirahige Ward to the area.[55] Most other Tosa mountains fronted rivers that emptied out on the southern Tosa coast. The ports such as Tano and Aki that thrived on the export grew at the mouths of these rivers.

Despite the wealth in exportable goods, people and food were relatively scarce in the mountains. Tiny villages perched on the steep slopes here and there, but farmland was so scarce that even a village headman might boast of only one tiny paddy deep in the shadows of a narrow valley. Food was grown mostly in small mountainside gardens. These villages were subject to the county magistrate, as were those in the valleys, but much of their living was made on land controlled by the mountain magistrate. Slash-and-burn agriculture in designated forest land was quite common. In 1696, twenty-two thousand tan (six thousand acres) of agricultural land assessed by the domain consisted of slash-and-burn field.[56] Local peasants filled their food needs mainly through a mixture of this small-scale farming, hunting, and gathering. Most villagers also made cash income farming tea and paper mulberry, which grew well on the slopes, and by producing paper, charcoal, and firewood. Many also found employment harvesting wood for the domain or lumber contractors (*yamashi*).

Most of the mountain land and its trees in Tosa had traditionally belonged to the lord, since at least the time of the Chōsogabe. When the Yamauchi arrived, they also asserted ownership of large tracts of mountain land, putting it under control of the mountain magistrate. Furthermore, they declared certain valuable species of trees their property no matter whose land they grew on. The

[55] See Hirotani Kijūrō, "Genna kaikaku no ichi kōsatsu," for an excellent discussion of the early lumber policy. Also see *Kōchi-ken shi, kinsei hen*, pp. 103–6, and the classic and most comprehensive, Hirao Michio, *Tosa-han ringyō*, for Shirahige and privileges see, pp. 138–9, 165–6.

[56] Slash-and-burn fields (*kirihata*) were recorded separately from the domain totals of arable land because they produced so little and their locations shifted. Taxes were around 1 percent of 1 koku per *tan* of land. Hirao Michio, *Kōchi-han zaisei shi*, pp. 19, 22. In the 1830s the amount was 23,000 tan. See Kawashima Tetsurō, Sekita Hidesato, et al., "Kirihata keiei chitai no keizai kōzō," for an excellent study (both historical and contemporary) of the economy of a Tosa village still practicing slash-and-burn agriculture in the 1950s.

domain used corvée and hired labor to carry out its own lumbering operation or sold rights to various lumber contractors from the port towns, or those who had come from Osaka. Because the export wealth was thus controlled by merchant capital and domain law, few mountain villagers became rich off of their mountains.[57] The domain government and the merchant contractors collected the profits.

Very small plains dotted the region near or along the coast of Tosa and were the agriculturally productive heart of the domain. Mountains always dominated the view, as they dominated the economy, but most of the people, towns, and villages were in the plains. These plains were narrow river valleys usually less than a mile in width. They were intensively developed and farmed in the early modern period, and the major grains were rice and wheat. They generally lacked significant export products until the end of the eighteenth century (when sugar, eggs, and paper come to be produced there), but the plains produced nearly all of the crops for the Tosa economy, as well as the tax rice that was a central element of the income of retainers and the lord. Villagers had to pay 60 percent of their assessed crop on regular fields as taxes. Owners of these fields were also subject to heavy corvée duty. Villagers of newly developed fields were given a beneficial tax rate of 40 percent and an exemption from most corvée labor. Because the agricultural tax base was an extremely important source of income to the rulers, the Yamauchi sponsored numerous major irrigation works in addition to providing for tax breaks in order to increase cultivation of the plains. Tosa's great period of lowland agricultural development was led by the senior administrator, Nonaka Kenzan, in the middle of the seventeenth century. During this period, the plains population increased rapidly, and many new plains villages and market towns such as Yamada, Nōichi, and Gomen were created. Tosa was never known, however, as a grain-producing region, and due to population growth not enough grain was ever produced for profitable private export. Tosa people would have imported grains had the domain permitted it, but the rulers prohibited imports to keep the price high for their sale of tax rice.[58]

In the Chōsogabe era, there were a number of regional castles on the edges of plains throughout Tosa. In the Yamauchi period, most of these were abolished, but not all, and there were a few plains towns that were unusually dependent upon samurai. Because in 1600 there was still the potential of war, Katsutoyo positioned six of his chief vassals in strategic castles throughout the domain (over the next century this number was reduced to three). The castles

---

[57] For a general study of life in a mountain village see Mamiya Hisako, *Tosa-han no sanson kōzō – Mitani-ke monjo kōkyū*.
[58] *Tano-chō shi*, p. 378.

themselves were destroyed in 1616 at the order of the Tokugawa bakufu, but moated residences with minor fortifications were maintained. These retainers were required to keep additional residences in Kōchi and live there when called to service in government, but their fortifications surrounded by a number of samurai residences encouraged the maintenance of towns with merchants dependent upon the samurai. Sakawa was the largest of these; the seat of a retainer with a fief of ten thousand koku, making him the equivalent of a minor daimyo. This town had a population of around one thousand to one thousand two hundred commoners and perhaps eight hundred retainers in the mid-eighteenth century. However, even this was smaller than many of the commoner-dominated rural towns such as Nōichi and Hirooka.[59] Such towns and villages became the seats of wealthy *gōno*, entrepreneurial farmer/landlords, and *gōshi*, wealthy peasants who had the status of rural samurai. The domain frequently demanded money from these leaders to help finance bakufu duty.

Although the plains areas were agriculturally rich and full of villages, markets, temples, and schools, they were susceptible to typhoon and flood damage. River dikes were frequently breached by flood waters and needed repairs. The plains were the scene of a constant battle for the annual maintenance of fields and irrigation works. Heavy mobilization of labor for the irrigation system was not just a phenomenon of the seventeenth century, when new irrigation systems were being created to expand arable land. Even in the early nineteenth century, long after the pace of new development had slackened, the domain annually mobilized from seven hundred thousand to a million man-days of labor for the repair and maintenance of the irrigation and dike system.[60] Because the labor and expense were large for everyone concerned, the organization of dike repairs was an issue that was under constant scrutiny in the early modern period.

The relationship between the plains and the mountains was made ambivalent by the flooding. Lumber sent down the rivers from the mountains often created

---

[59] *Sakawa-chō shi, jōkan*, pp. 503–4. Retainer population is given as only 166 households. In Kōchi the average number of members per retainer household was five.

[60] Figures for the total labor mobilized are found only in the *Tōbun oboegaki*, a semiannual economic brief used by domain officials. The first figure is for 1778, and the annual labor total for *kunijū fushinpu* (domain administered construction and repair) and *denyakufu* (village and locally organized field construction and repair labor) is 778,771 man-days (GM, no. 5500, sect. 25–6). In 1800, this figure was 1,024,060 man days (GM, no. 5735 sect. 25–6). In 1804, following a year of heavy typhoons it was 1,303,881 man days (GM, no. 5540, sect. 27–8). In 1852, it was 660,486 (ms. *Kaei rokunen tōbun oboegaki*, HB, in a box of unclassified documents). Most of the labor was low-paid corvée and some was labor paid at regular wages. Total figures for earlier years are not available, but figures for domain-administered spring repairs (*haru buyaku*), which is a figure representing from one fourth to one half of the total in the above *Tōbun oboegaki* figures, are, for example: 1685 – 360,530 man days (TMK, vol. 49, f. 72) and 1694 – 154,200 (TMK, vol. 74, f. 88), showing that in the late seventeenth century as well the amount of labor was comparable.

havoc for the farmers. In a heavy rain, when the water was high, the lumber commonly jammed and breached the dikes and spilled into the fields. All villages received a standard payment from loggers to cover occasional damage, but the farmers nevertheless occasionally resisted the sending of lumber down their rivers. The office diary of the junior administrator, Mori Yoshiki, tells of how in 1798 he and many senior domain officials personally went to Ryōseki and Nunoshida villages to try to convince the villagers to permit the rafting of lumber down the Kokubu river. The villagers were not daunted by the display of rank, and the domain finally had to make many tax concessions and promise not to send lumber down when the river was full.[61] Despite this negative aspect of the relationship between mountains and plains, the plains economy itself depended heavily on some mountain products. People in the mountains grew an abundance of paper mulberry. It was the source of a mountain paper industry, but much of the raw underbark was also shipped downstream for processing into paper in plains villages such as Ino. The export of this paper was a major industry and filled an ever-growing portion of the Tosa economy.

The Yamauchi organized these four regions of Tosa to provide necessary goods and services to the Yamauchi house and their samurai. Many leading commoners were coopted into the samurai service economy through the grants of special privileges paralleling those the samurai received. The exactions required were often high, but in the face of resistance the Yamauchi could argue that their demands were necessary to finance the lord's service to the shogun. Wealthy merchants and wealthy farmers could only try to maintain their equanimity by using their acquired public status to force exactions on those lower than they were. This hierarchy is what drove much of the decision-making process concerning the Tosa economy.

Service to the bakufu in the seventeenth century

From the earliest years following the arrival of the Yamauchi clan, the people of Tosa bore numerous heavy burdens of military and construction service to the bakufu. Ieyasu ordered Katsutoyo to perform his first major construction duty in 1603–4, when Tosa provided laborers for the building of the shogun's capital of Edo. After Katsutoyo's death in 1605, his heir, Tadayoshi, had to assist the shogun in further building the cities and castles of Edo, Sunpu, Nagoya, Shinoyama, and Fushimi. Then Tadayoshi's army fought for Ieyasu in the siege of Osaka in 1614. After they burned the city and castle, they were then ordered

---

[61] Hirao Michio introduces the problems of sending lumber down the Yoshino river through Tokushima domain due to the resistance of peasants in *Tosa-han ringyō*, pp. 20–7. Ms. *Sansei nichiroku*, vol. 1 (in the Kōchi Prefecture Library), entries for 2/11/1798 and 6/12/1798.

to participate in the reconstruction. Tadayoshi also had to send an army in 1619 to oversee the confiscation of the domain from Fukushima Masanari, the lord of Hiroshima.[62] In addition to these special duties, the alternate attendance system was taking shape during this time, beginning for Tosa with Katsutoyo's first journey to Edo in 1604.[63] Not long after, in 1606, senior retainers of Tosa domain were required to send family members as hostages to Edo as well.[64]

The expense of these duties was far greater than could be paid from the regular income of this agriculturally poor domain. The Yamauchi rulers plunged into enormous debt to Kyoto and Osaka merchants. The lenders of large sums soon became aware that the accumulation was dangerously high, and by 1620, it became impossible to find lenders, and financing the duties to the bakufu became a nightmare. That year, the shogun ordered the Yamauchi to assist in the reconstruction of the walls of Osaka castle, now safely in Tokugawa hands. Tosa was unable to keep apace with other domains, and Doi Toshikatsu, the bakufu senior official in charge, called the Tosa representatives to him to explain their situation. They did so, and he retorted with an unsympathetic, "Work harder and finish it on time!" The Tosa house elders (*karō*) in charge were soon sending desperate missives to the senior administrator in Tosa. Frayed nerves over money led to accusations and pleas such as the following:

Without money, it just does not seem possible to complete construction [of the wall]. Our allotted area pours out an extraordinary amount of water, and the earth base keeps crumbling down, so the stones cannot be laid. We can only complete this on time by hiring daily two or three thousand laborers to supplement our samurai and peasants. At any rate the cost of such laborers would be about 80 or 90 kan, so we are not hiring. . . . Although we have communicated this to [the finance official Gotō] Kaemon, not even the smallest loan has been arranged. Because he has not been making enough efforts, we wonder if our portion will get completed. We wait for your directions. We think you should give a written order making Kaemon directly responsible for paying the wage laborers.

And one month later: "Because we do not have any money, things are desperate. Be it silver, be it new rice, even if you can only arrange to send it up in small amounts, send it as quickly as possible!"[65] Kaemon was already in Osaka attempting to drum up loans, but he only found one person willing to lend 10 kan, and that at very high interest.[66] Fukao Mondo was also trying with even less success.[67]

---

[62] For an exhaustive list of all the construction and military service done by Tosa for the *bakufu* between 1600 and 1656, see app. 2 of *TYK*, vol. 1.

[63] *KTK*, pp. 661–3.

[64] *TYK*, vol. 1. pp. 18–9.

[65] *TYK*, vol. 1, pp. 532–3.

[66] Ms. "Ojō haiken . . .," GM, no. 5814.

[67] *TYK*, vol. 1, p. 534.

The domain lord, Tadayoshi, feared that his domain would be confiscated unless a way were found to bear the financial burden of bakufu duty. In 1620, bakufu officials intervened, telling him that his future was on the line. With their help, Tadayoshi ordered his retainers to begin a "complete reform of everything with domain government." Tadayoshi's secretary later defined this moment as follows, "The lord of Tosa's finances were cut through, and because the lord could no longer perform duty for the shogun this meant he was in danger of losing his domain."[68] Agricultural production could not be increased rapidly. As for samurai, they were expected to be willing to give everything because they had received so much from the Yamauchi. The leaders of the domain reform wrote, "Every one of the samurai in this household has achieved success thanks to the lord, and we think it natural [that the lord should borrow some of our income]. Indeed, being such, it would not be the least strange to us if the lord took back all of the fiefs."[69] The retainers were asked to contribute 25 percent of their income to help pay off the loans, yet this was hardly enough to put more than a dent in the interest, let alone reduce the principal.[70]

Because most of Tosa's mountainous land area was at this time covered with old forests, and in close proximity to Osaka by sea, the administration created a new class of corvée duty to mobilize the peasants and retainers to spend a month cutting lumber or pay a comparable amount of money. The imposed duty was justified by appealing to examples from the Chōsogabe past in Tosa, a model of service to the overlord. "In the time of the former lord, when a duty to the sovereign [Hideyoshi] was called for, he placed extra levies on agricultural land and for lumbering on samurai and peasant alike."[71] No officials questioned the right to demand such labor for shogunal service, but they were worried about taxing the common people so harshly that they could not produce crops or might run away to another domain. Laborers stripped mountains and rafted the lumber down rivers. At the coast, the lumber was collected in such ports as Aki and Tano, and from there, shippers fulfilled their corvée by shipping the lumber to Osaka, to be sold under the supervision of officials in the new domain Osaka compound. The domain also encouraged lumbering by local private bidders and took a 20 percent portion of their lumber as tax. On the Osaka end, the administration hired a merchant to assist Tosa merchants in achieving the best prices for their goods.[72] Along the banks of "Tosa Canal" built

---

[68] Quotations from ibid., pp. 551–2. There is an excellent body of research on this reform. See Ishidori Tanehiro, "Tosa-han ni okeru Genna no kaikaku"; Takagi Shosaku, "Bakuhan seijishi jōsetsu"; and Hirotani Kijūrō, "Genna kaikaku no ichi kōsatsu."
[69] *TYK*, vol. 1, p. 603.
[70] *TYK*, vol. 1, p. 596.
[71] *TYK*, vol. 1, p. 587.
[72] Mori Yasuhiro, "Shoki no Kōchi-han Ōsaka yashiki," pp. 44–5.

by the domain in Osaka for the purpose, the lumber was piled into great hills to await bidding by lumber merchants.

Despite the enormous debt in which the Yamauchi were mired, the wealth generated from these shipments quickly repaid the loans, and the domain even had money to spare by 1627. The first financial crisis of the domain, a crisis caused by bakufu demands for service, had ended quickly with a reorganization of the domain economy to focus on exporting lumber. The domain achieved an agreement with the bakufu in the 1620s that thenceforth it would perform most of its construction duty by contributing lumber to the sites, rather than labor.[73] This arrangement reveals most clearly the direct relationship between the development of an export-oriented economy in domains and bakufu duty. The Tosa administration became dependent upon lumber to keep up with expenses, while at the same time it strove to increase agricultural production. Domain finances achieved a certain stability, and the economy of Tosa grew rapidly.

However, this growth produced many problems that developed into a crisis by the eighteenth century, a crisis that forced the people of Tosa to renegotiate their relationship with the center according to a mercantilist strategy to develop the domainal country. The next chapter will explore how a crisis developed in an economy of seventeenth-century growth.

---

[73] Ishidori Tanehiro, "Tosa-han ni okeru Genna no kaikaku"; Takagi Shosaku, "Bakuhan seijishi jōsetsu"; Hirotani Kijūrō, "Genna kaikaku no ichi kōsatsu."

3

Creating a crisis in Tosa, 1680–1787

It is astonishing to see the clear decline in our country's ability to produce wealth over the past fifty years. The agricultural tax has decreased annually, our forests have all been cut, the number of boats for commerce and fishing has dwindled.

Tosa retainer Matsuo Hikotarō, 1759[1]

By the beginning of the eighteenth century, Tosa had entered an acute period of hardship. Hikotarō's bleak appraisal of the Tosa economy at the middle of the eighteenth century linked together many strands of a complex story of developing crisis. He could have added to his list the wreck that domain finances had become, and the frequent occurrence of famine and flooding that plagued the domain. The interactions of population growth, agricultural development, deforestation, and rising taxation had produced sad conditions in Tosa by the eighteenth century. Tosa's economy had grown rapidly in the early and middle part of the seventeenth century, and this was brought about by the economy of service to the Tokugawa in which most taxes were spent by the lord outside of the domain for alternate attendance or other duty and which made the private economy of Tosa heavily dependent upon an Osaka-controlled market. The growth had been rapid, but by the eighteenth century, these same relationships had contributed to creating the problems lamented by Hikotarō and a world in which there was a widespread loss of respect for the rulers.

Tosa's population explosion

Seventeenth-century Japan witnessed a population boom in which the number of commoners rose from an estimated 10 million in 1600 to 26 million in 1721.[2] This growth was especially rapid in southwestern Japan, the region in which Tosa lay. Tosa's growth in population was especially high even within this

---

[1] *TNK*, vol. 121, f. 112th.
[2] Saitō Osamu, "Dai kaikon," pp. 172–5; Sekiyama Naotarō, *Kinsei Nihon*, pp. 123–33; Honjō Eijirō, *Nihon jinkō shi*, pp. 396–401.

region, so high that it demanded frequent attention from Tosa administrators in the late seventeenth century. Indeed, not merely Tosa officials, but those in neighboring domains as well, became concerned, because the excess sent large numbers of Tosa people flying over the borders. The growth in the number of mouths to feed rapidly outstripped the growth in production by the 1690s, and combined with a deteriorating ecological situation and more severe taxes, the early eighteenth-century consequences for Tosa were a damaged economy, society, and politics.

No Tosa census before 1665 survives, but it is worth estimating the population at the beginning of the conditions that permitted the growth, that is to say, the subservience of the domain to the Tokugawa in 1600 under the new Yamauchi daimyo. The often-used rule of thumb in Japan of calculating one person per *koku* of production provides an estimate of 200,000 people, because the first Yamauchi production assessment, in 1603, came up with 202,627 koku. A population of nearer 250,000 can be calculated if the ratio of one person per *tan* (a measurement equaling about a quarter of an acre) of agricultural land is accurate. In 1665–81, the earliest period for which we have figures, the recorded population of Tosa was indeed about one person per tan of registered agricultural land. Because there were 248,000 *tan* under cultivation around 1600, this would mean about 250,000 people. If the population growth was initiated by land development, which began at a significant pace only in the 1640s and 1650s, then it is likely that rapid growth began at mid-century and that the higher figure is more accurate as a starting point. This supposition of a mid-century start for population growth would also explain why domain administrators expressed concern over population excess only from the 1660s. We are on much firmer ground for the years after 1665.

Three types of surveys provide us with a relatively reliable group of population statistics for the period after 1665: the annual parish registry figures (*shūmon aratame*); the *bakufu*-ordered population surveys, which were collected every six years from 1721; and a separate internal domain count of households and population collected at unclear intervals. All of the surveys are in near agreement, although each type has its own problems and biases, and only the parish registry provides figures for the total domain population, including retainers.

Religious surveys were conducted in Tosa from the 1640s, as part of the bakufu's policy of suppressing Christianity, but its development into the well-known parish registry census system in Tosa was slow. Censuses of commoner males over age fifteen were taken from 1660, but censuses of the full population using this method were first taken only in 1681. The system worked annually thereafter, lasting until 1870.[3] Under the developed system, all people in Tosa were required to affiliate themselves with a Buddhist temple, and every spring the household head had to submit to the village, town, or military unit leader a list of all household members with an oath that none was Christian. These then were totaled and submitted to the domain. The domain totals included all samurai and commoners who were alive at the time of the survey. One drawback of the parish registry survey as a source for population figures is that it included people who were temporarily living abroad, as during the lord's annual residence in Edo. Furthermore, some people belonged to two temples and were counted twice. This latter problem involved a relatively minor number and was corrected subsequent to the survey of 1854.[4] A continuous annual series survives from 1681 through 1798, and sporadically for a total of fifteen later years as well.

The second set of population figures available to us were produced by the bakufu survey, which was begun in 1721 at the order of the shogun Tokugawa Yoshimune and repeated once every six years thereafter. This survey was based on reports of the number of resident commoner population by each headman of a village or town ward.[5] One limitation of this survey is that the six-year intervals make it impossible to see clearly how population responded in the short term to crop loss and other disasters. A further limitation of the bakufu survey is that it did not include retainers or their servants. Susan Hanley and Kozo Yamamura were mistaken about this, incorrectly taking these figures to encompass all the domain population except for that of the castle town. However, the bakufu order is explicit in stating that the survey should include "peasants, townsmen, shrine priests, men and women, monks and nuns, etc., and any other common people whatever. . . . You need not include retainers, their servants, and sub-retainers,"[6] which makes it clear that townsmen were

---

[3] The earliest reference I can find in Tosa for a *shūmon aratame* or *sensaku* is for the years 1641 and 1642 (*TYK*, vol. 3, pp. 148, 175), but these investigations may only have been directed at travelers and *rōnin*. The first year for which I can find orders to investigate all residents is 1650, including written submissions, although their exact nature is unclear (*TNK*, vol. 4, pp. 24, 302–3). The first year in which males over fifteen were forced to be associated with temples may have been 1660 (*TTK*, vol. 1, pp. 406–9). The next such census was in 1665 (Harada Tomohiko, ed., *Nihon toshi seikatsu shiryō shūsei*, vol. 3, pp. 562–3. Kinsei Sonraku Kenkyūkai, ed., *Tosa no kuni jikata shiryō*, pp. 360–7). The first surviving population domain total by the parish registry system is for 1681 (*TMK*, vol. 38, ff. 82–6).

[4] The domain corrected the problem of double registering in 1854–5 by requiring all people to be registered only through one temple. Matsunoo Shōko, comp., *Kaizanshū*, vol. 6, p. 477.

[5] These figures are found in Sekiyama Naotarō, *Kinsei Nihon*, pp. 136–9; and Minami Kazuo, *Bakumatsu Edo shakai*, pp. 164–85. The years 1721 and 1726 are also in *TNK*, vol. 4, ff. 32nd–37th; 1804, in *GM*, no. 5727.

[6] Hanley and Yamamura, in *Economic and Demographic Change*, pp. 48–50. The bakufu order is quoted in the basic source, Sekiyama, *Kinsei Nihon*, pp. 75–6. It can also be found in *TNK*, vol. 4, ff. 32nd–33rd. The "Domain Totals for Tosa" that Hanley and Yamamura give in their chart are

included and retainers and their household servants were excluded. Because the parish registry in some domains recorded only people above age one, or four, or even fifteen in some cases, scholars have found that for many domains the hexennial population survey provides the most reliable statistics on commoner population.[7] However, we are fortunate that the Tosa parish registry did record all living people, including infants.[8]

The internal domain survey provides us with a third source of population statistics. This survey was based on reports giving details on the economy and population of each village or town ward submitted by their headmen to domain officials. Although the individual reports contained the number of households and population of both retainers and commoners, curiously, the surviving domain totals usually omit the retainer population and give only the number of their households, thus compromising their usefulness.[9] How regularly this kind of survey was taken is also unclear. The domain totals from only ten years survive for us. The oldest population data we have for Tosa (1665) came from such an independent domain survey, although fortunately it includes the number of retainers as well.

Hanley and Yamamura have shown that in Nanbu domain, various domain statistics give widely differing numbers for population in the same year. They opted to trust internal domain totals after concluding that domain officials supplied the bakufu with population figures that deliberately exaggerated the appearance of famine in order to gain bakufu assistance.[10] In Tosa, the three sets of figures are in near agreement, and no deception is evident. All three

the parish registry totals and include retainers and their servants, and not the addition of the castle town population as they state. Their inferences concerning Okayama probably contain the same error, but this needs research.

[7] Sekiyama, *Kinsei Nihon*, pp. 124–6. Hanley and Yamamura, *Economic and Demographic Change*, pp. 42–3.

[8] The *shūmon* documents all use the phrase *tosai ijō* (those born this year and up) to describe the population counted.

[9] Kinsei Sonraku Kenkyūkai, ed., *Tosa no kuni jikata shiryō*, pp. 368–73, gives an example from the year 1670 for one village; Yamamoto Takeshi, *Kenshōbo*, vol. 7, pp. 65–6, 408–9, gives domain calls for submission of such documents. Domainwide totals survive for the years 1799, 1804, 1818, 1820, 1822, 1824, 1844, and 1852 in the succeeding year's *Tōbun oboegaki* ms. in GM, nos. 5735, 5666, 5540, 5668, 5578, 5583, and the HB box of unclassified for 1852. Also there are figures for 1818, 1820, 1822, 1824, 1826, 1828, in ms. *Kōchi-han keizai shiryō, zaisei hen (2)*, HB, no. 200, in a chart created by Hirao Michio based upon *Tōbun oboegaki* housed in the Yamauchi archives. The originals were lost in the wartime bombings. Hirao interprets these figures from these statistical briefs to represent the year of the title of the *Tōbun oboegaki*. However it is clear that population figures are for the previous year in every surviving *Tōbun oboegaki*. Therefore, I have adjusted the years in Hirao's chart in HB, no. 200, to one year previous. Also, such figures quoted in his many books are for the wrong year: for example, the household and population chart given on pp. 12–13 of his *Kōchi-han zaisei shi* states it is for the years 1819, 1829, 1843, and 1853, but in reality the figures are for the years 1818, 1828, 1842, and 1852. The surviving original *Tōbun oboegaki* for 1843 and 1853 reveal this.

[10] Hanley and Yamamura, *Economic and Demographic Change*, pp. 146–54.

surveys show similar trends, but do differ in the actual number of commoner population by as many as six thousand people for any given year. This means a maximum margin of difference of around a 1.3 percent. For example, in 1828, the population and household survey recorded 440,972 commoners, whereas the population survey for the bakufu recorded 445,473 commoners. The population and household survey for 1844 listed a total commoner population of 453,728, and the parish registry listed 459,195 commoners. The parish registry tended to give the largest figure for commoner population for a given year. This difference can be accounted for by the different methods of data collection described above. For example, the hexennial bakufu survey included only people actually present in the domain whereas the parish registry included population temporarily living in Edo. The alternate attendance system meant that the Tosa population in Edo annually alternated between fifteen hundred and forty-five hundred people, and this alone would account for a major portion of the difference in the figures of the two different surveys.[11]

The population totals of the parish survey have been used to create Figure 3.1 because they are the most complete over time and, most importantly, included the retainer and servant population, unlike the other surveys. The other two nevertheless are useful in that the trends they reveal parallel the trends in the parish survey and thus provide support for the accuracy of the data. The 1665 figure is from an internal domain survey. The dotted line between 1665 and 1681 in the chart is inferred from a set of parish registry population totals submitted to the bakufu in the 1660s and 1670s that, however, contain only the number of males over age 15.[12] These figures are thus not the total population, but they do display trends of domainwide significance, revealing an extremely rapid rise in population between the years 1670 and 1680 (1.7 percent annually) and confirming the basic accuracy of the isolated 1665 figure.

The population nearly doubled over the two centuries encompassed by the chart, from 274,731 people in 1665 to 516,545 people in 1870, but the growth was not steady. The chart reveals the eighteenth century as a period of population crisis sandwiched between two periods of sustained growth. The population grew most rapidly in the latter half of the seventeenth century, at an annual

---

[11] For example, see *TMK*, vol. 86, ff. 55–7. The alternate attendance years did not affect the parish registry trends, but did affect the hexennial survey trends if both attendance and non-attendance years were counted.

[12] Ms. *Shirin shūyō (1)*, HB, no. 355, p. 55. (1670) (99,092); *TMK*, vol. 25, ff. 79–84 (1679) (113,084); *TMK*, vol. 28, ff. 23–31 (1680)(116,970). Originals survive in Yamauchi jinja jimusho shozō monjo (a small unclassified collection adjunct to the Yamauchi Family Shrine Treasury and Archives), giving the totals for 1675 (110,050) and 1677 (111,842). The 1680 figure also gives 6,202 males for the branch domain of Nakamura, which would make the real Tosa total of males over age fifteen 128,172. The other 4 years do not include the Nakamura population.

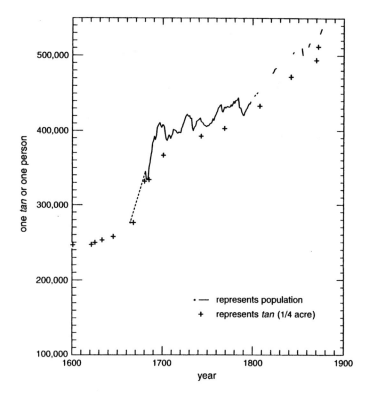

Figure 3.1. Population movement and assessed agricultural land area in Tosa, 1600–1872.

growth rate of 1.5 percent, increasing by 136,697 (50 percent) in a mere thirty-two years, from 1665 to 1697. The next fifty years were in stark contrast. The total population growth from 1700 to 1750 was zero. This was due to the appearance of recurrent famine in Tosa. The jagged shape of the population line indicates clearly that birth control and family planning were not the reason for the lack of population growth. Precipitous drops in population occurred at times of crop disaster, steepest in the years of greatest crop losses. There is much direct evidence that these declines can be attributed both to death from starvation and related illness and to the emigration of the hungry searching for sustenance elsewhere. The effect of repeated famine stopped population growth during the early half of the eighteenth century. After 1750, famine continued periodically to eat away at population, but an overall trend of population growth reappeared. This is especially visible in the period after 1790, when the population decline associated with the Tenmei famine ended. The figures after this year are incomplete, but the long-term trend in the figures, as well as incidental evidence, suggests that famine was becoming less important and that the economy had become more resilient and provided a more secure life for its people after the 1780s.

Tosa's population history differed from the history made by creating a Japanwide average, which showed essentially no population growth over the century and a half from 1721 until the Meiji period. The accepted historical explanation for no growth was once Malthusian: The economy had reached its limits of growth by the early 1700s and a regime of recurrent famine kept population from growing.[13] Since the 1970s, this view has been largely discredited by the work of such scholars as Hayami Akira, Thomas Smith and Susan Hanley, and their explanation for the low population growth for Japan has become standard. Rather than pointing to the effect of famine, they stress that various methods of population control – such as late marriage, abortion, and infanticide – came into widespread use. Furthermore, they argue that such forms of population control were not a response to extreme poverty, but rather a means of maintaining or raising family wealth and security. A transformation of family consciousness and values was at the root of the change. These scholars have in turn linked this family planning to the prosperity of early nineteenth-century Tokugawa Japan, because it was a major factor in increasing per capita wealth, preventing the population from rising at the same time that actual production and productivity were rising greatly. Many of these arguments are well-founded for certain regions and certain time periods, but it would be a mistake to envison an entire early modern Japan based on these studies.[14] The role population pressure has played in history upon the early modern archipelago cannot be wisely ignored, because its history is best understood regionally and in shorter time periods. As many scholars have pointed out, regional and time differences in population trends were striking.[15]

For many purposes of political, economic, and social history, the proper unit of inquiry should not be Japan as a whole, but rather the economic and political regions and their interrelations. Population trends in sparsely populated regions, such as Tosa, had only minor visible effect on the Japanese population average. The average population for Japan is weighted heavily toward the highly populated, wealthy centers of Japan. Their large populations actually declined slightly after the 1720s, and they were not as affected by famine as the less

---

[13] Sekiyama Naotarō, *Kinsei Nihon*, pp. 131–5; Honjō Eijirō, *Nihon jinkō shi*, pp. 399–400.
[14] Susan Hanley and Kozo Yamamura, *Demographic Change*, pp. 320–6; Thomas Smith, *Nakahara*; Thomas Smith and Robert Y. Eng, "Peasant Families and Population Control." Smith is quite cautious about the Japanwide applicability of his findings.
[15] See James White, *The Demography of Sociopolitical Conflict in Japan, 1721–1846*, for a recent exploration of population and protest with an emphasis on regional trends.

developed regions of Japan, such as Tosa.[16] The heavy weight of the population trends of these centers makes the Japan average a useless tool for envisioning or understanding the trends of many large "peripheral" regions of Japan. These regional trends, however, had major influence on local economies and policies, which in turn had influence on the rest of Japan through their political and economic ties. The origins of *kokueki* mercantilism are found in domains of western and northern Japan, and perhaps it is no coincidence that these were both areas of high population growth or instability.[17]

There was a functional relationship between the stability of the populated centers of Japan and the instability of the less populated peripheries in the eighteenth century. The central regions had immense commercial and marketing power to soften the effect of famine, but this power heightened famine in other regions of Japan. In Tosa, for example, even during the terrible famine of 1734, the domain shipped over 20,000 koku of tax rice to Osaka for sale in order to satisfy its creditors. The terrible irony is that the domain could have sold the rice at an even better price in Tosa, but local people could not provide the large advances and financial services of the large Osaka merchant houses. The domain sold the rice in Osaka knowing full well that people would be starving at home. As contemporary townsmen put it, the domain administrators presented "an unknowing face" to the problem. Ultimately, the famine proved so bad that the lord of Tosa had to borrow money from the bakufu in order to purchase rice in Osaka to ship back to Tosa for relief distribution. A scholar bitterly described the absurdity of the event:

In the seventeenth year of Kyōhō all of the fields were smitten with insects, and the crop loss was of unheard of proportions. Still the domain quickly loaded into boats more than 20,000 koku of its autumn tax rice for sale in Osaka. Because the weather was poor the boats sat for thirty days in Urado port. Finally in the middle of the eighth month the weather cleared and the whole shipment of rice arrived in Osaka at one time. Immediately, the rice was all sold together for 40 *monme* of silver per koku. From the end of autumn the price of rice rose, and those in distress numbered in the tens of thousands. Reports went [to the bakufu] from all of Japan and the shogun considered means of famine relief. But our country had sent rice for sale to Osaka and was not put on the list for consideration. When the year ended, the lord had to make requests and was granted a loan of money from the bakufu along with other lords. People frowned and muttered, 'Well, isn't it a fine thing that they let that rice sit in boats at Urado for thirty days! And what about all that time they showed an unknowing face to the reports of the local dearth of rice!'[18]

---

[16] Smith, "Preindustrial Growth," provides a stimulating thesis for understanding the decline of the urban centers.

[17] Sekiyama, *Kinsei Nihon*, charts "i" and "ro" on pp. 140–1; Arne Kalland and Jon Pedersen, "Famine and Population in Fukuoka Domain."

[18] From "[Itagaki] jike zakki," a diary miscellany by a contemporary scholar, in ms. *Nanroshi*, vol. 114, photocopy in the Kōchi Prefecture Library.

This incident reveals in an extreme form the power the marketing and credit relationships of the big cities had over the lord. The credit relationship with the Osaka merchants sustained the pattern of payment associated with the alternate attendance system, but ultimately it made the whole economy of Tosa dependent on the Osaka economy. This relationship created a center/periphery axis that, in times of scarcity, worked to the disadvantage of the regional areas. Kitamura Gosuke, a Tosa samurai, wrote a petition to the domain lord in 1759 with the following complaint:

I hear you have ordered that 20 to 30 thousand koku of rice be sent annually for sale in Osaka. . . . [Because the quality of Tosa rice is poor,] you sell it at a very low price. People from our ports who work on shipping boats then buy this cheap rice for food. Half of the rice your lordship sells in Osaka is bought and returned to the ports. . . . This naturally leads to a loss of silver from our country.[19]

The lord of Tosa sent rice to Osaka, and then his people were forced to buy it back from Osaka merchants because the lord had none to sell. The middlemen in Osaka collected profits on the whole transaction. Kitamura's resistance to this relationship took the form of a bullionist argument that was taking shape to support the goal of kokueki, reflecting that its goals were, in part, a response to this dominance of Osaka. Commoners as well as domain government were subject to this credit power. Frequently, credit relationships forced them to sell in Osaka, and often at bad prices.[20]

Life was becoming increasingly commercialized over this period due to the deepening ties with Osaka, but this did not necessarily mean an increase in per capita wealth. There is evidence to suggest that people more frequently dressed in purchased cotton cloth instead of homemade hemp or paper clothing in Tosa, but evidence like this should not necessarily be construed as an overall improvement in economic security. It is more surely just an expression of the deepening relationship between Osaka and Tosa, which could be one of subservient dependence. This dependence worked against Tosa in times of dearth to actually exacerbate hardship.

Hanley and Yamamura considered the distinction between the wealthy central regions and the less wealthy peripheral regions of Japan, and they did a study of the Morioka region in northern Japan to compare with their studies of central Japan in the hope of revealing an underlying consistency. They argue persuasively that the severity of the eighteenth-century famines has been exaggerated in some accounts. But this hardly proves that the famines were unim-

---

[19] Kitamura Gosuke (?/?/[1759]), *TNK*, vol. 122, ff. 157th–158th. This petition is undated, but by fortunate chance the submission is discussed in the diary of his friend, Mori Hirosada: ms. *Nikki*, vol. 9, entry for intercalary 7/29/1759, in the Kōchi Prefecture Library (K289/Mori).

[20] Hirao, *Tosa-han shōgyō*, pp. 237–68.

portant. With people starving to death by the thousands instead of the exaggerated tens of thousands, these were still extraordinary events. Instead, the authors choose to ignore the significance of the late eighteenth-century famines in the history of Morioka. They give greater weight to the fact that wages and standards of living in the nineteenth century were higher compared with the mid-eighteenth century, summarizing their findings as: "The economy of Morioka continued to grow during the last century and a half of the Tokugawa period." They are right, in a manner of speaking, and the historiographic context in which Hanley and Yamamura wrote prompted them to argue this point.[21] Comparing the same two points in time in Tosa would give a similar picture, but the issue of famine and periods of economic decline cannot properly be ignored by historians. Contemporaries did not live with 100-year trends; they often faced severe annual hardships, which defeated them or which they overcame. Tosa faced fifty years of instability and decline in the mid-eighteenth century. This was the trend that the retainer quoted at the beginning of this chapter felt and knew about. In order to understand the political, economic, and social history of the domains, we must take a close look at trends in population and economy in time periods significant to the people who lived in them. In most areas of Japan at some point in the seventeenth or early eighteenth century, a population excess was a problem many people faced, but which might be glossed over in an analysis of very long trends.[22] A regime of famine did dominate Tosa from around 1700 until near the end of the eighteenth century. Only after this did the economy provide more security for its people.

Because it was the imbalance between mouths to feed and the amount of food available that made famine, the population trends discussed above become more meaningful when looked at in relation to trends in production. The documents for Tosa are more problematic in this regard than those for most domains because it did not generally use a *kokudaka* system. The *jidaka* it used was a figure expressing the amount of land under cultivation rather than production. It was the agricultural land area registered with the domain office, based on occasional domain surveys and also on annual reports from village headmen. There are two major limitations to the accuracy of the figure, however. Villages had obvious reasons for underreporting, because registered land became subject to taxation. Successful underreporting would make the jidaka figure lower than the actual amount of land under cultivation. However, Tosa was much more assiduous in frequently resurveying land than most domains, some of which gave up resurveying altogether.[23] On the other hand, there was

---

[21] *Demographic Change*, Morioka study on pp. 126–60; quotation from p. 131.
[22] Hayami Akira and Miyamoto Matao, "Gaisetsu – jūshichi-jūhasseiki," pp. 58–62.
[23] Thomas Smith, "The Land Tax in the Tokugawa Period."

a factor that led to inflation of the jidaka figures over the actual amount of cultivated land. The jidaka included all land ever registered, even that which had been once cultivated and later abandoned. This is because much land was abandoned for only a few years and later recultivated. The percentage of abandoned land is a figure rarely found in surviving documents, but probably ranged from 10 to 20 percent of the total for any given year.[24] How far these two tendencies canceled each other out is unknown. Furthermore, the jidaka gave no indication of productivity or the value of production. One could assume that productivity rose in the long term due to the influence of increasing diffusion of better agricultural practices. For example, in the eighteenth century the practice of cultivating two rice crops per year spread, as well as the cultivation of the Satsuma potato, an excellent resource against famine. Counteracting influences to higher productivity existed as well. Tax records show that newly opened fields were, in the aggregate, less productive than original fields. As the proportion of the newly opened fields to the total rose, this would lead to a decline in the overall productivity. Furthermore, periods of hardship such as famine led to less careful tilling of all fields, a relationship many contemporaries commented on.[25]

The jidaka amounts should thus be taken as rough guides, significant in a general way, to the issue of how much agricultural land people had to subsist on. Their relationship to population in Figure 3.1 suggests that the seventeenth-century population boom was precipitated by land development. Between 1600 and 1646, Tosa's jidaka rose from 248,327 to 259,180, a mere 11,000 tan, but soon after this came a period of large land reclamation projects in Tosa. Under the energetic direction of the chief administrator of the domain, Nonaka Kenzan, new irrigation canals were cut across the lowlands of Tosa in the 1640s and 1650s. These canals enabled the development of great tracts of rice producing paddies in the ensuing decades.[26] As new areas came under production, most older villages increased their acreage, and thirty new villages were also created by 1699.[27] Between 1646 and 1698, the amount of registered land under cultivation rose from 259,180 tan to 368,261 tan: an increase of about 40 percent. Increased production in Tosa did not mean more food for everybody, because it was far surpassed by increased population. As noted above, popula-

---

[24] Takagi in "Genna kaikaku," p. 99, gives an estimate of 25 percent abandoned land in the 1620s, but this seems high. In 1645, it was about 20 percent (Akizawa, "Suiden seisan," p. 64). In 1740, about 349,000 *koku* of *jidaka* were planted, which when compared with the 392,000 koku of registered jidaka in 1743, suggests that 11 percent of the land was not planted, *TNK*, vol. 59, ff. 59th–64th; Roberts, "Tosa hansei chūki."

[25] Murakami Chūji (10/15/1759), *TNK*, vol. 122, f. 13th.

[26] Akizawa Shigeru, "Tosa-han shoki no suiden seisan," *Kōchi-ken shi, kinsei hen*, p. 133.

[27] Kōchi-ken Rekishi Jiten Hensan Iinkai, *Kōchi-ken rekishi jiten*, p. 380.

tion rose a full 50 percent in the mere thirty-three years between 1665 and 1697, certainly leaving less agricultural land area per person.

The uncertain relation of the jidaka figures to actual food production make their significance as a measure of available food somewhat problematic. Indeed, if land was becoming much more productive, then the dearth is illusory, and we would be forced to look for other explanations of the eighteenth-century mortalities. Some contemporaries, however, evaluated the problem of the balance between population and available food quantitatively. One unnamed official in 1665 recorded the domain's grain, bean, and potato production, giving a production value of the equivalent of 319,200 koku of rice (termed the *komedaka*), and compared this to population, calculating males at a daily diet of 5 *go* and females at 2.5 go. This comparison exposed an annual deficit of 54,300 koku. The official concluded that, with vegetables and foraging, people would get by – if administrators permitted the importation of rice during years of crop loss. A document of similar nature, created half a century later in 1723, showed a deficit of 46,000 koku, which would seem to indicate an easing of the pressure of population on production. However, this number was reached only by deducting a quarter of the population (100,000) as children, a procedure not taken in the 1665 document.[28] Without subtracting this portion (to make the document comparable with the 1665 document) the deficit would be an astounding 190,000 koku. These figures on average diet and agricultural production cannot have been precise, but the trend seen from these documents of population outgrowing production over this sixty-year period is unmistakable.

Such numerical accounts alone might still be suspect, but government officials left much evidence of severe population pressure in their laws and in records of their councils. Domain officials were keenly conscious of an excess of population in the late seventeenth century and considered many strategies to alleviate it. In 1691, the domain senior administrators ordered the county, town, and port magistrates to prevent commoners from marrying at a young age and to encourage them instead to go out as servants or find other employment. Their expressed reason was: "Throughout the whole country [of Tosa], especially in the rural districts, the number of people has increased greatly."[29] That year, the laws appended to the *shūmon aratame chō*, which was given a reading

---

[28] For 1665, "Okuni chū shōsaku demai narabi ni ninsu tsumori," in ms. *Nanroshi yoku*, vol. 7, photographic copy in the Kōchi Prefecture Library; 1723, "Oboe," in ms. *Nanroshi*, vol. 114, ff. 19–21, photographic copy in the Kōchi Prefecture Library. Yet another such document, undated but from the mid- to late-eighteenth century gives a deficit of 90,000 koku after subtracting a third of the population as "non rice eating," but it counts women as a full ration instead of as a half ration; ff. 9th–10th, in ms. *Kōgi narabi ni oie tomo mitsu shi basshō* in the Kōchi City Library (K210.5 mitsu).

[29] "Karō tsukiban kiroku," in *TMK*, vol. 68, ff. 21–2.

annually to all commoners in their villages, had two newly appended requirements: one forbidding the division of land by peasants to their children into lots too small to be self-sustaining and another forbidding all males younger than age thirty and females younger than age twenty to marry.[30] Those who wished to marry before needed to report to the county magistrate and request permission.[31]

The massive population growth led the domain to reverse its early seventeenth-century policy of discouraging emigration. During the 1610s the emigration of runaway peasants was such a serious problem for domain government and its finances that fleeing the domain was made an offense punishable by death, and even people who aided the runaway were disfigured by having their ears and nose cut off. In order to stem the outflow of peasants, and the confusion which their disappearance created, domain officials also negotiated extradition treaties with neighboring domains during the 1620s.[32] By the late seventeenth century, however, the whole foundation of policy had reversed: The domain leaders were positively relieved that many people were leaving. A letter in 1681 from the officials of the Tosa mansion in Edo to the senior administrators back in Tosa well illustrates this new mood of anxiety over excess population. It reads:

In recent years the number of people along the coast of the country has been increasing. Because people cannot make a living with what they catch, many have requested permission to go to other countries to work. Having heard that there are few people in the provinces of Satsuma and Hyūga, very many people have gone there. Because these people are making a living, we requested the Satsuma officials to allow the people to stay if they wished. Recently things have been going according to the agreement thus arranged. However this year again, Satsuma sent a message to Nakamura [branch domain] reporting that the people of Nakamura domain are going there. Reports are certainly coming in here at the Edo mansion of the lord of Satsuma about the great number of Tosa people fleeing to Satsuma.

[In your recent communication to us] you ordered us to state the following to the Satsuma mansion officials and request them to inform their domainal officials: "The country of Tosa is a place with too many people, and because those along the port areas cannot make a living many have been going [to Satsuma]. Given the above situation we are allowing those without a special prohibition to go wherever they please. Naturally, if there are any who commit offenses, inform us and we will bring them back. As for non-offenders, please let them be whenever they arrive, as our domains had agreed earlier." . . . As you noted, we will make the request informally through those of the Satsuma officials with whom we are friendly and familiar, in order to avoid as much as

---

[30] This parallels the *bakufu*'s "Bunchi seigen rei" (Law Forbidding the Partition of Farmland) of 1673, which may have been promulgated for the same reason.

[31] Yamamoto Takeshi, *Kenshōbo*, vol. 1, pp. 28–30.

[32] The problem of absconding peasants is treated in Marius Jansen, "Tosa in the Seventeenth Century," pp. 115–30. Ishiodori Tanehiro, "Tosa-han shoki hashirimono taisaku ni tsuite"; Oseki Toyokichi, "Tosa hansei shoki no josei."

possible gossip that the country of Tosa is poor and many of its people are fleeing to Hyūga in Satsuma.[33]

As this missive records, even before 1681, emigration to Satsuma had become serious enough to require official treatment; this time, however, it was not an extradition treaty but an emigration agreement. Although the officials noted that many people requested permission to leave Tosa, they also noted that many were just fleeing. Tosa domain officials were no longer worried about maintaining a sufficient population of peasants (as one imagines feudal rulers would be). Their most serious worry was that the great number of absconders would give Tosa a bad reputation and, by implication, draw bakufu censure for mishandling government. Although this document implied that the port regions were especially overpopulated, the problem was hardly limited to the ports. In the senior administrators' document of 1691 mentioned previously, the farming villages were singled out as the most overpopulated areas. In the case of emigration to Awa province, to be discussed below, the people of the overpopulated mountain regions of Tosa were fleeing. In short, all of Tosa was overpopulated.

It is worth noting that the image of Satsuma in the above document contrasts greatly with the generally held belief that it was the most closed and forbidden domain in Japan. As the agreement reveals, Satsuma welcomed the people of Tosa. A merchant of Kubotsu port in Tosa, recounting conditions in the ports in the mid-seventeenth century, stated: "People could not make a living and everyone was saying 'Satsuma is a wonderful place. People from all countries are welcome to live there and can freely pursue various trades.' After hearing this, there were many young men, and even householders who would abandon their wives and children, who would flee to that country at night."[34]

One final compelling piece of evidence of mass emigration from Tosa shows that in addition to Satsuma, many Tosa people emigrated to the neighboring domain of Awa (Tokushima). In the mid-seventeenth century, Awa province also welcomed Tosa immigrants, so that they might open up new villages on undeveloped land. Official village household registers from Kaifu county record hundreds of Tosa families involved in the opening of new village lands (Figure 3.2). These families appear clearly marked as "Tosa immigrants" in these domain surveys, demonstrating that the population movement was officially sanctioned. Emigration from Tosa to these numerous villages (now consolidated in the two large modern villages and town of Tomoura shown in Figure 3.2) was so heavy that over half of the total of new immigrants between 1632 and 1724 were from Tosa (the word immigrants in this case even included Awa people

---

[33] "Karō tsukiban kiroku," in *TMK*, vol. 37, ff. 79–81.
[34] *Nanroshi*, vol. 2, p. 42.

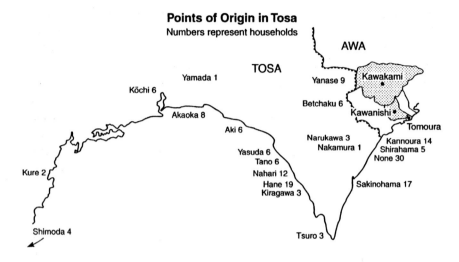

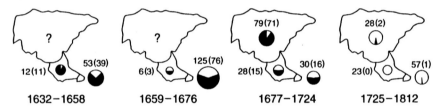

Figure 3.2. Tosa emigration to three village regions in Awa domain, 1632–1812. Based on village household registers and adapted from Minoru Kishimoto, *Hansei chūki*, diagram, pp. 22–3.

from outside these villages). They came primarily from the port towns in eastern Tosa, although some sailed from towns as far west as Shimoda and Kure. These registers suggest that immigration dwindled after 1724. This trend may have been the actual case, or it may have been due to a change in Awa domain policy restricting immigration. A change in policy would have led to the underreporting by villagers of the actual number of immigrants in such official documents as these.[35]

The possibility of continued heavy immigration is suggested by an incident that took place in the late eighteenth century on the Tosa/Awa border near the center of the island. Emigration across this border was common. In 1794, the

---

[35] Kishimoto Minoru, "Hansei chūki ni okeru Kaifugawa ryūiki no kaitaku katei."

number of Tosa residents emigrating to Awa had become so great that the lord of Tokushima ordered all Tosa immigrants, their children, and grandchildren to immediately pick up and return to Tosa. The famines of the 1780s had probably increased the incidence of Tosa immigration, and Awa, experiencing the same famine, needed no new mouths to feed. The lord probably intended to assist his own people by issuing the decree. The response, however, was the opposite of what he expected. The Awa mountain villagers organized a mass protest ready to march on the castle town to demand that the lord rescind the decree. The ōjōya (the commoner administrator of a group of mountain villages) of the region raced ahead of the protesters to the castle town and explained the situation to the domain officials:

> The Iya district has few children and is a place where they love and pity the people of Tosa. When Tosa people flee here, they are taken in. If anyone asks after them, the people hide them out for a year, or half a year until gradually they become members of the community. The fact of the matter is, that 80 percent of the people in the area are immigrants from Tosa.... If you order their expulsion, some villages will become unable to function and some will be without a soul to live in them.[36]

The clandestine nature of immigration described in his appeal reveals that the immigration was not officially sanctioned, but the number of immigrants was very large nevertheless. One must allow for some hyperbole in the district headman's description, but the whole district organized to march on the castle town, an illegal and exceedingly dangerous act, and the headman risked his own life in presenting their case to the domain. The expulsion edict clearly threatened their livelihoods. Faced with this kind of protest, the lord of Tokushima rescinded the decree.

Large numbers of people were leaving Tosa because they were poor and because Tosa was a particularly overpopulated region of Japan. In the seventeenth and early eighteenth centuries, Satsuma and Tokushima accepted these immigrants readily. No doubt many Tosa people went to the well-known immigrant regions of Osaka and Edo (one imagines more than went to Satsuma and Awa). Such cities must have been more attractive to potential immigrants than the steep mountains of Tokushima or the coasts of distant Satsuma. Just how many people went and when is not known, but Tosa must have had an extra-

---

[36] From a report sent by a Tosa border post official, Kubo Takasuke, to Nakanishi Gohei, one of the domain junior administrators; copy in the office diary of the senior administrator, ms. *Zakki shohikae oboe rui*, GM, no. 940. One of the duties of border post officials was to keep the central domain officials informed of conditions in neighboring provinces, especially *ikki* protests, because peasants in neighboring provinces would sometimes flee into Tosa to ask the lord for mercy as a means of protest against their own lord. Once such a group entered Tosa, their demands had to be heard, and complicated negotiations with the other domain would have to ensue. To avoid this the Tosa administrators tried to be informed of such potential protests and would send troops to the border to prevent entry wherever possible.

ordinary birth rate for its own population to grow so rapidly and still send out so many emigrants.

The point has thus far been argued, largely on the basis of population statistics and emigration, that Tosa was ravaged by famine in the early and mid-eighteenth century. Other direct evidence supports this assertion, revealing that the eighteenth century in Tosa was more treacherous to its inhabitants than the seventeenth century. The largest famine of the latter half of the seventeenth century was the Tenna famine (1682–3). It was caused by heavy rains that resulted in crop losses of 60,000, 25,000, and 35,000 koku, respectively, in the years 1681, 1682, and 1683. Population declined by 11,000 in three years. In 1682, domain relief in the castle town went to 6,728 people, of whom 1,133 (8 percent of the city!) were listed as "starving" in the urban commissioner's report. Just what starving meant is not defined in the 1682 document, but only those without the strength left to walk could be listed as "starving" in the reports collected from village headmen in the 1770s.[37] In the countryside in 1682, relief was given to 34,053 people.[38]

One martyr (*gimin*) of the famine was the retainer and port official, Okamura Jūbei. The populace was starving in the village he was assigned to administer (Hane port), even though the domain warehouse in the center of the village was full of tax rice. In order to use the rice to administer relief, he would first have had to travel to the castle town and present a plea to the chief administrators. After an investigation, he would probably have been granted permission to disburse the lord's benevolence (*osukui*), but this would have taken days – and maybe longer. Okamura opted instead to open up the warehouse and give the people back some of their tax rice. He then committed suicide, on his own initiative, to take responsibility for his malfeasance toward the domain government.[39] The domain leaders did not know what to do at first, but after the villagers protested, Jūbei's family were given a stipend for their welfare and his son was given the post of port official.

Conditions improved after the Tenna famine. On the whole, the seventeenth-century economy and agriculture were remarkably resistant, even to the many typhoons they weathered. Five major storms hit between 1666 and 1674, scarcely affecting the rapid growth in population at the time, although reports of some degree of famine do exist. The years 1685, 1686, and 1687 also experienced large storms that did not dim the rapid growth of population. This suggests that a reserve of production was available for the population even during most of the bad crop years. Following the Tenna famine, the population

---

[37] *Kōchi-ken shi, kinsei hen*, p. 541.
[38] From the town magistrate's report in *TMK*, vol. 38, ff. 61–3, and the rural magistrate's report in *TMK*, vol. 42, ff. 79–85.
[39] *TMK*, vol. 44, ff. 53–67.

continued to grow at a furious pace until 1697, when it reached a peak of 411,428 people.

During the fifty years following 1697, famine hit again and again, canceling out all intermittent growth. In 1749, the population was 406,812. The three worst famines of this period were the Genroku famine, the Kyōhō famine, and the Kanpō-Kan'en famine. The Genroku famine lasted from 1697 to 1708. It was worst in the year 1702 when the population fell by 12,000 people. Over the entire period, population declined by 25,000. In 1703, one official cautioned his superiors that they needed to have the relief distribution system work through the villages: "There are many people who are recorded as dying of illness, when in reality they starved in their villages." He noted that they starved because they did not want to leave their homes to go to the few available domain relief houses, because it would mean abandoning their land and homes and would condemn them to a life of shame and poverty.[40] The increasing frequency of such hardship led the domain to take his advice. In the Kyōhō famine, village headmen were given authority to disburse relief at their own discretion.[41] If such a system had been in place in the Tenna famine, Okamura Jūbei would have had an easier task. The Kyōhō famine of 1732–4 was short but unsparing, causing population to drop by 22,000 people. Two years of heavy rain and then an extraordinary insect plague in 1732 brought severe crop losses. The early months of spring, when the previous year's crops had been exhausted and the new year's crops were yet to be harvested, were the most severe months of famine. In the second month of 1732, 14,018 people received relief. This number jumped to 128,570 people in the following month.[42] A relief house for townsmen was set up in Nagahama a few miles south of Kōchi. A contemporary resident of the castle town wrote of the highway between: "I do not know how many people died on that road!"[43] The Kanpō-Kan'en famine 1743–9 by comparison was mild but long, with a decrease in population of 10,000 people over the decade. These repeated famines suggest that there was a serious problem with the agricultural economy as a whole. It had become more fragile and could not withstand as much stress, such as a typhoon, as it had been able to for most of the seventeenth century. Crop losses again forced a population decline in 1766–7 of more than 9,000 people. Famine reports from the junior administrators in the fourth month of 1766 list 8,454 people as "starving," with 754 of these coming from the castle town.[44] Continuing poor conditions meant that population recovered to above its 1765 figure of 435,787 only a decade later in 1776.

[40] *TFK*, vol. 14, ff. 6th–9th.
[41] An example can be seen in the Kyōhō famine, *TNK*, vol. 30, ff. 38th–43rd.
[42] From the county commissioners' reports to the senior administrators, *TNK*, vol. 30, ff. 36th–41st.
[43] "[Itagaki-shi] jike zakki," as quoted in *Kōchi-ken shi, kinsei hen*, p. 302.
[44] Ms. HB, no. 119, pp. 50–63.

Then in 1784–90, the infamous Tenmei famine decreased population by 24,000. It was during this last time of famine that the domain launched the Tenmei reforms.

Ecological problems

Population pressure was certainly a major factor in inviting famines at times of crop loss, but there were new ecological problems assisting the waves of mortality. Irrigation development and deforestation significantly increased the damage that storms wreaked on agricultural production. To a large extent, the famines of eighteenth-century Tosa were the product of mismanagement of the environment. The two most extensive changes in the region during the seventeenth century were the nearly complete cutting of the ancient forests and the extensive irrigation development that facilitated the expansion of rice agriculture throughout the lowland areas. These two factors increased crop losses caused by storms in the eighteenth century. The increased crop losses meant that the Tosa population, which was already stretching the limits in years of average crop production, was even more severely hurt in years of bad weather. These ecological issues in Tosa are relevant to large portions of Japan, because deforestation and extensive irrigation development were phenomena common throughout Japan in the seventeenth century.[45]

The great irrigation projects of Tosa began in the 1640s and were largely completed by the 1680s. Thanks to this development, great swaths of irrigated lowlands came to be fed by canals supplied by large rivers that did not dry up quickly in rainless weather. Compared with earlier times, when much rice farming was carried out at the edge of hills irrigated with streams and retaining pools, the water supply was more secure, sunlight was better, soil was better, and the fields could be large and more efficiently tended.

At first glance this looks very good: A larger population could be supported and tax income increased for the domain. However, in heavy rains, the rivers would flood, spread over the flatlands, and ruin crops. This occurred frequently during the eighteenth century, destroying more crops and resulting, as we have seen, in more frequent famines. The great irrigation projects of the seventeenth century raised Tosa's agricultural production but, paradoxically, helped create periodic famine. The production increase created a population boom, ultimately resulting in less food per person in Tosa. Additionally, the very lowlands that were being developed by the irrigation projects were the fields most

---

[45] Conrad Totman has argued for a closer look at the role ecology has played in Tokugawa history in *The Green Archipelago*, introduction and ch. 1; *Early Modern Japan*; and "Tokugawa Peasants: Win, Lose or Draw?"

susceptible to flood damage. The population that grew with the creation of these lowland fields was dependent on an agricultural source that was unstable on a very large scale. The construction of irrigation canals provided routes for water to enter the fields when torrents came down the mountains during a storm. Also, the construction of dikes and embankments along rivers, to facilitate lowland development, inevitably raised the level of the rivers by causing runoff soil and debris to accumulate. Without continual labor by peasants to maintain and reinforce these dikes, they became devices of potentially disastrous flooding.[46] In addition to this, the role of deforestation probably began to have an important effect in causing increased crop losses from the end of the seventeenth century.

Large forests help prevent floods by reducing runoff and maintaining soil stability, but how aware were Tosa administrators of this relationship? In late seventeenth-century Japan, Kumazawa Banzan of the Okayama area wrote of the problems for water management created by deforestation in his widely read *Daigaku wakumon*.[47] The Tosa scholar Miyaji Nakae wrote of the relationship in his economic notes of the 1810s, and in the 1840s the samurai, Chiya Hiromori, petitioned the lord to be careful about deforestation.[48] However, no evidence survives to suggest that officials in the seventeenth century made the effect of deforestation on water management an issue of discussion or policy. Even if they had, lumber sales were such an important source of income to the domain that the temptations were probably too great.

Their inaction was regrettable, because the domain owned much of the forest land of Tosa and was responsible for its management. The forest land of Tosa was divided into domain-owned forest, which was generally the best forest land, and various forms of forest that were village or privately owned. The domain also claimed ownership of all large conifers and other trees important for lumber, no matter where they might be located. Anyone wanting to cut a tree for lumber, even if it were on his own property, had to request the mountain magistrate and, if the request were approved, pay a fee. Private tree farming was encouraged, but owners had to submit to bureaucratic regulation. The domain used its own lumber sales as a staple of its income, and when its own forest land ran out, the administrators ordered surveys and claimed ownership of yet more timberland by fiat.[49] As was the case so often in domain history, the necessity of sending much of the domain's wealth to Osaka guided events.

---

[46] Conrad Totman, "Preindustrial River Conservancy."
[47] Quoted in Kanō Kyōji, *Edo jidai no ringyō shisō*, p. 443. Kanō also notes that reforestation laws were seen as part of water management even in very early Tokugawa times (pp. 446–9).
[48] Miyaji Nakae, ff. 12th–13th, in ms. *Shūwa* in the Kōchi Prefecture Library (K916/Miya); Chiya petition in ms. *Jimu ronsaku shū*, vol. 2, p. 249, HB, no. 275.
[49] Hirao, *Tosa-han ringyō*, pp. 63–71.

Lumber played its most important role in seventeenth-century domain finances. It was the major source of financing the politically unavoidable bakufu construction duty. Grain production in Tosa was low by Japanese standards, and little extra could be spared for export by the rulers. Indeed, as mentioned above, often more grain was exported than could be spared. Timber existed in abundance, however, and as mentioned in the previous chapter, the financial crisis of the 1620s led to the intense exploitation of Tosa's forest reserves in the name of bakufu service.

During the financial crisis, it was only as a temporary measure that the domain elder Nonaka Genba sent 320 musketmen (*teppō ashigaru*) into the mountains to fell trees. The musketmen were, after all, the core, if not the elite, of Tosa's fighting force. As it turned out, however the musketmen spent the next century as lumberjacks, felling the forests. One domain document in 1663 complained that most of the musketmen no longer knew how to shoot a gun (though they could swing an axe). The official response was tepid; they gave each *ashigaru* four vacation days per month, with the advice to practice marksmanship, and – if they requested it – enough shot and gunpowder to shoot four rounds on these days. The domain administrators were obviously more concerned about selling lumber.[50]

There was certainly a great amount of timber to begin with. In 1617, the domain official Okura Shōsuke went on a special tour of inspection to count the trees in Tosa. He estimated that there were more than two and a half million trees with trunks greater than eight feet in circumference. Even if fifty thousand of these large trees were cut a year, he figured, the forests would be an endlessly replenishing resource.[51] But appetites grew, and the lords of Tosa soon became known for their lavish spending. The fourth lord, Toyomasa, led to Edo an ostentatious train of retainers as large as those of domains twice Tosa's size. Rising expenditures and shrinking forests began to alarm domain officials, who in 1692 remonstrated with Toyomasa by sending him a document showing how his expenses at Edo had come to far exceed the expenses of his grandfather Tadayoshi and his father Tadatoyo. The grandfather's year's stay (from 1663 to 1664) had cost 669.205 kan (this equals 16,730.25 koku at that year's price). Tadatoyo's stay in 1666 to 1667 had cost 1,248.175 kan (24,963.5 koku), but in 1691 the costs for Toyomasa had climbed to 2,002 kan (37,782.245 koku).[52] This alarm, however, did not make the lord stem the swift rise in his Edo expenses – far from it. In the residence of 1694–5 the outlay actually

[50]   Ishiodori Tanehiro, "Tosa-han ni okeru teppōgumi."
[51]   Hirao, *Tosa-han ringyō*, pp. 10–11.
[52]   Ms. *Tadayoshi-sama, Tadatoyo-sama, Toyomasa-sama gozaiEdo oirime zōgen hikikurabe oboe*, GM, no. 5824.

doubled to 4,492 kan (74,866.6 koku), and in 1696–7 expenses rose from even this astronomical figure to 4,882 kan (81,366.6 koku).[53] The forests appeared endless to Shōsuke in 1617, but they were not. Realizing that trouble was on the horizon, the domain administrators instituted rotation cutting schedules in the 1660s. The planting of seedlings was encouraged in many ways, and control of lumbering became increasingly detailed, culminating in a great mountain survey in 1683.[54]

The beginning of these efforts at planned forestry were auspicious, but in reality, things went downhill. Abundant amounts of lumber continued to be floated down the rivers for shipment to Osaka, and soil increasingly washed down the mountain slopes, clogging the waters. One reason the schedules did not work as planned was the bakufu's many demands for large amounts of lumber that, for political reasons, the domain could not refuse. In the seventeenth century, demands for lumber contributions came on thirty-six occasions, in eight years exceeding fifty thousand trees.[55] The bakufu ordered in 1661 over two hundred thousand pieces of lumber to be sent to rebuild the imperial palace in Kyoto. Cutting schedules were abandoned, and the merchants of the domain were conscripted into full cooperation.[56] This event strained the domain so badly that it has been interpreted as the indirect source of the fall from power of the renowned administrator, Nonaka Kenzan, in 1663. He was accused of abusing the people for "selfish reasons," but in reality it was the enormous cost of service to the bakufu that caused his excessive tax demands on the populace.[57] Despite the obvious link, people in the seventeenth century did not often verbalize their discontent with foregoing care of the domain to fulfill bakufu duty or to serve the lord's lavish ways in Edo perhaps because of fear, perhaps because they were only just becoming aware of the deleterious side of the relationship with the bakufu. In the eighteenth century, however, people began pointing a finger at Edo life and bakufu duty as sources of domain poverty, and kokueki thought played an important role in the articulation of the point. Another reason why the domain continued overcutting the forests was debt. In the face of a stoppage of loans from the merchants of Osaka, alternate attendance duty could not be performed. This made it relatively easy to cut just one more mountain, instead of working to preserve the logging schedule.

---

[53] From a finance officer's report in *TMK*, vol. 88, ff. 84–90.
[54] In Tosa, this is a critical period in the intensification of the kind of forest protection described as "the negative regimen" by Totman in *The Green Archipelago*; surveys in *NRSCS* reels 23–4.
[55] Hirao, *Tosa-han ringyō*, pp. 4–9.
[56] *TTK*, vol. 1, pp. 431–8.
[57] Ishiodori Tanehiro, "Nonaka Kenzan shissei makki" and "Kanbun no kaitai ni kansuru ichi kōsatsu."

All surviving documents point to mountains becoming increasingly bare between 1660 and the second decade of the eighteenth century. Domain profits from logging slid from 705 kan of silver in 1682, to 500 kan in 1709 and 200 kan in 1733.[58] Over the same period, the value of the kan decreased by over 50 percent in terms of rice, a basic price indicator, which meant that domain income from forests had declined at least 80 percent in real terms. One mountain official's report from 1689 notes: "In recent years the domain-held mountains have been deforested and even the mountains open to private cutting are becoming scarce."[59] A domain administrator's report in 1701 stated: "The mountains with timber have been cut clean. A few remained in one area, and to relieve financial difficulties we leased it out to a merchant from Awa, but the timber is of poor quality and brings a bad price."[60] The emphasis in these documents was probably on stands of old timber. Reforestation was encouraged (with unknown success) as early as the 1660s, but the removal of most of Tosa's old-growth forests in a short half-century certainly created problems of water runoff and soil erosion. The water of storms would have rushed quickly down the mountains into the plains, and the soil runoff would have collected in the diked rivers and irrigation system of Tosa, raising the water level and further increasing the frequency of flooding.

The amount of crops ruined by storms increased dramatically between 1660 and 1760. Domain storm reports survive in relative abundance beginning in the 1660s. The format of these detailed documents changed little over time. They provide a constant view of storm damage, including among their many categories the amount of crop and field lost, the extent of irrigation ditches needing repair, and the number of houses destroyed, boats sunk, and people drowned. These documents reveal that the latter half of seventeenth century experienced many large and devastating storms, a fact one would not surmise from the records of famine. Five major storms hit in succession between 1666 and 1674 and five more between 1681 and 1687. This compares with a cluster of five storms between 1700 and 1707 and nine between 1736 and 1744. The seventeenth-century storms averaged annual losses of 44,000 koku: much less than the average annual loss of 72,000 koku for the eighteenth-century storms.[61] Further evidence of the growing seriousness of the effects of storm damage on

---

[58] For 1682, ms. "Omakanaikata tsumori mokuroku," in *Tenna monjo, Tenna gannen*, the Kōchi Prefecture Library; 1709, ms. "Okurairi omononari narabi ni shounjōgin tomo honbarai ōzumori," in *Hōei monjo*, the Kōchi Prefecture Library; 1733, *TNK*, vol. 32, f. 104th.

[59] *Kōchi-ken shi, kinsei hen*, p. 342.

[60] *TFK*, vol. 4, f. 107.

[61] These averages are calculated from storm reports in the following: 1666, *TTK*, vol. 2, pp. 490–511; 1669, *TMK*, vol. 1, ff. 105–7, 158; 1671, *TMK*, vol. 10, ff. 43–5; 1673, *TMK*, vol. 12, ff. 34–40; 1674, *TMK*, vol. 14, ff. 66–73; 1681, *TMK*, vol. 32, ff. 102–18; 1683, *TMK*, vol. 40, ff. 44–64;

the economy is that, during the seventeenth century, these storms did not dim the extraordinary pace of land development and population growth, but in the eighteenth century, storm periods inevitably precipitated famines and even general production declines.

Although the vicissitudes of weather are certainly important in the history of Tosa, the context in which the weather occurred was more important. Deforestation, the development of flood-prone plains, and overpopulation all played a fateful role in creating hardship for the people of Tosa. There was yet one other human source of the tragedy: The domain was increasing the tax burden.

Rising agricultural taxation

In the face of rising expenditures and declining forestry income, domain officials struggled to locate new sources of income from the populace. The domain continuously strove to enlarge the agricultural tax base through further land development. In the late seventeenth century, they used various means to raise agricultural tax rates. After the failure of this policy in the early eighteenth century, official agricultural tax rates as such actually declined, but this decrease was illusory. It was more than offset by the appearance of huge special levies exacted from the populace from the beginning of the century. The size of these levies grew substantially until the last quarter of the eighteenth century, after which, because of Tenmei reform policies, they declined. In the long run, the severity and the corrupt nature of the special levies helped to make the mid-eighteenth century a time of political crisis as well. The population was able to get angry with the rulers in ways it could not with the rains. The special levies will be discussed in more detail in the following chapter. The focus in this section is to show how taxation of agriculture became increasingly severe until the early eighteenth century, when the special levies took over. Needless to say, this increased taxation had a limiting effect on the local economy and harmed people's livelihoods.

The agricultural tax burden was increased in the late seventeenth century through three methods: (1) raising the tax percentage of the crop produced; (2)

1685, *TMK*, vol. 48, ff. 28–35; 1686, *TMK*, vol. 52, ff. 1–4; 1687, *TMK*, vol. 56, ff. 34–49; 1701, *TKF* vol. 6, ff. 35th–41st, 51st–56th; 1702, *TFK*, vol. 11, ff. 83rd–87th; 1703, *TFK*, vol. 13, ff. 77th–81st; 1704, *TFK*, vol. 16, ff. 86th–190th (earthquake and tidal wave); 1736, *TNK*, vol. 41, f. 65th; 1737, *TNK*, vol. 47, ff. 1st–3rd; 1738, *TNK*, vol. 50, ff. 1st–20th; 1739, *TNK*, vol. 53, ff. 81st–96th; 1740, *TNK*, vol. 59, ff. 19th–21st; 1741, *TNK*, vol. 64, ff. 39th–64th; 1742, *TNK*, vol. 67, ff. 94th–97th; 1743, *TNK*, vol. 73, ff. 23rd–26th; 1730, 1731 in ms. *Hanshi naihen*, vol. 24, ff. 75–77, in Kōchi University Library. (The disastrous insect plague of 1732 was not calculated into the average.) The increasing tendency of crop losses can also be inferred from Figure 4.1.

raising assessments of yield per land area; and (3) having peasants produce strains of rice with higher market value. The agricultural tax was collected at a separate rate for two types of fields. Fields created and first surveyed before 1600 (termed *honden*) were required to give up 60 percent of production in taxes. This tax rate was also applied to new fields surveyed by the domain inspector, Murakami Hachibei, before the year 1626 (termed *Murakami shinden*). This tax rate was not altered throughout the Edo period. There was a separate tax rate for fields created and surveyed after 1626 (termed *shinden*), which were taxed at 33.3 percent until 1690. The lower tax rate on "new fields" was given to encourage participation in land development. In 1690, however, officials declared an increase in the rate on new fields to 40 percent of production, a rate they continued despite the famines that came at the end of the decade. Furthermore, soon after rate increase, in the face of vigorous village protests, officials conducted a vast resurvey of agricultural land in the 1690s to uncover hidden new fields and reassess productivity.[62]

Domain efforts to increase agricultural tax income through resurveys focused on discovering unregistered fields and on raising the amount of taxes paid per tan of land. The former quite simply increased the size of the tax base. The latter required reassessment of the amount of production per tan of already existing fields. In a basic assessment, each field was surveyed in midsummer by the tax inspectors and assigned various grades of productivity, ranging from "very poor" (*gege*) to "high" (*jō*). By raising the estimate of productivity on any field to a higher grade, the actual amount of tax per tan rose accordingly. Such upgrading and resurveying were occasionally carried out on a massive scale, such as in the resurvey of the 1690s, and at other times were carried out locally. These surveys produced significant direct financial benefits for the domain. In the seventeenth century, taxes collected per unit of land area increased steadily. Domain officials estimated the average amount of koku collected per tan from the total of "original fields" in Tosa to be around .3 koku in 1602. This remained the case in 1622, but rose to higher than .45 koku in 1665 and .56 koku in 1696. This was almost a doubling of the tax per land area over the course of the century, meaning that productivity increases were being substantially absorbed by the domain. The average amount of koku collected from shinden ("new fields") is not known for periods before the 1680s. In the period between 1682 and 1686, the amount was .291 koku, and between 1696 and 1698, it had risen slightly to .296 koku.[63] Figures are scarce, but a look at the period around 1700

---

[62] *Kōchi-ken shi, kinsei hen*, pp. 239–40, 294–6.
[63] See sources for income cited for Figure 4.1 and 1602 estimates in *Kōchi-ken shi, kinsei hen*, pp. 50–1; 1622, *TYK*, vol. 1, pp. 596–7 and; 1665, ms. "Jidaka kome ginsu honbarai mokuroku," Kaganoi-ke shiryō, no. 16-30, Kōchi City Library.

Table 3.1. Effective tax rates on demesne land.
Koku collected per *tan*

Years	Honden (old fields)	Shinden (new fields)
1682–6	.537	.291
1696–8	.555	.296
1733	.519	.234
1768–9	.474	.221
1778	.524	.218
1800–2	.519	.220
1842–4	.550	.209

in Table 3.1 shows that taxes per tan at this time were at their highest. Much of the increase in productivity of the land encouraged by the diffusion of better agricultural methods was thus collected by the domain tax officials. As with the timing of the raising of the percentage of crop collected from new fields described above, the aggressive reevaluation of the productivity of fields occurred during the most severe stage of the population boom and is an example of how the tax burden was often increased with little sensitivity to the adverse effects on the people of Tosa. Tax policy thus put limitations on the economic reserves of peasants and played a role in creating the eighteenth-century disaster. This policy was counterproductive in the long term. Despite domain attempts to keep taxes high, an increased frequency of crop damage, undercultivation of many fields, and a rise in the extent of abandoned land due to flood damage, poverty and famine led to the lowering of the amount of tax collected per tan in the mid-eighteenth century as seen in Table 3.1. Poverty often meant unkempt fields, as described by Murakami Chūji, a *rōnin* scholar living in the village of Gomen, in a petition to the domain lord in 1759:

In recent years the benevolence of your lordship has not been reaching the common people. The peasants have been weakened and have become unable to take care of their fields as they wish. Each year crop losses increase, and annually tens of thousands of koku of crop loss are recorded. With the continuing crop losses, the finances of your lordship and retainers have worsened, and then peasants do not have enough food to eat. As a result, the following year they are unable to put the proper energy into cultivation of the fields and each year the crop losses continue.[64]

Detailed tax information from the village of Satokaida reaffirms the authenticity of this interpretation of effective tax rates gained from the admittedly incomplete domain figures. Satokaida was a large and stable village situated in the

[64] Murakami Chūji (10/15/1759), *TNK*, vol. 122, f. 13th.

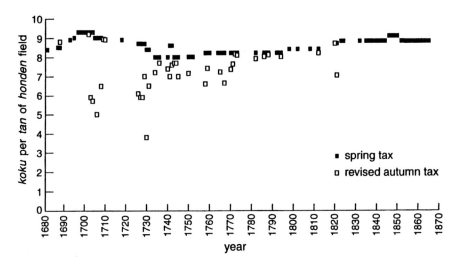

Figure 3.3. Spring and autumn *honden* tax rates in Satokaida village, 1680–1865. Adapted from table in Nangoku-shi Hensan Iinkai, *Nangoku-shi shi, gekan,* pp. 199–205.

heart of Tosa's most productive plain. In Figure 3.3, tax records for the village show in greater detail trends that parallel those described above. Tax-per-tan rates on honden fields rose like a roller coaster approaching the top of the hill in 1700, where they slowly peaked and began a slide accelerating downward into the 1750s and 60s. Between 1725 and 1780, rates of tax per land area were lower than at any time on record, before or after. Even with these lower rates, the villagers frequently asked for special autumn reassessments to further reduce taxes in response to the loss of crops to rain damage. Such requests were mainly limited to this period, making it appear that crop damage in Satokaida was most frequent and extensive during the mid-eighteenth century than at any other time. Although there is much evidence to suggest that this interpretation has truth in it, one cannot ignore, together with these declines, the simultaneous appearance of the special levies to be discussed below. The desire to help offset the impact of the special levies (on the villages and themselves) might have made officials more easy to bribe to lower tax rates. After 1780, tax-per-tan rates began to ascend again, but slowly, presumably reflecting improved conditions in the village, as well as the decline of the special levies. This shift also parallels the averaged trends evident for the whole domain.

The argument presented here is primarily to understand the development of Tosa, but some comment is perhaps due concerning trends on the whole archipelago. Thomas Smith has presented the argument that it was the samurai fear of peasant protest, more than peasant hardship, that prevented a rise in tax rates in most domains after the first two decades of the eighteenth century. The evidence presented here is for one domain in southwestern Japan and does not disprove Smith's argument, which was based on research covering central and northwestern regions. Although Smith considers the issue of population pressure, he concludes that it was not a factor, after noting that there are frequent reports that farm laborers were scarce in the eighteenth century. This evidence is suggestive, but it is neither direct nor time-specific enough to discourage reinvestigation of the issue of population pressure on the decisions of rulers not to raise tax rates in the mid-eighteenth century. Furthermore, as Smith mentioned, many domains resorted to special levies and other sources of taxation, which need to be studied. On the other hand, Tosa's example may be an isolated case, or only relevant to southwestern Japan.[65]

One final example of how taxation policies aggravated hardship for the peasants deals not with taxation rates, but with the strains of rice collected. Domain leaders attempted to collect in taxes varieties of rice that had higher market value in Osaka. In the 1670s, they launched a program to encourage a shift away from the cultivation of a sturdy strain of red rice of poor market value (*taimai*) to the cultivation of a strain of fine white rice (*kichimai*) that sold at higher prices. The problem created for the peasants was that the kichimai was less resistant to weather extremes. Taimai was better suited to poor soil conditions and more resistant to flood damage.[66] Many peasants preferred the security that the cultivation of this reddish rice offered. The domain program was encouraged regardless, and the amount of white rice collected in taxes increased from 15,550 koku in 1677 to 37,080 koku in 1690. However, because peasants protested that it left them much more vulnerable to crop losses, the policy of increasing the percentage of white rice in taxes had to be abandoned in the 1690s.[67] As with higher tax rates and resurveys of productivity, this policy, too, adversely affected peasant security during the era of most severe population excess and at a time when increasing flood damage might have encouraged a return to taimai, but immediate financial necessity and a focus on sales in the Osaka market were driving domain officials.

Although agricultural tax rates began declining in the early eighteenth century, the overall tax burden on peasants likely did not. This was due mainly to the appearance of special levies. In the eighteenth century, the administrators often needed to locate quick sources of income to prevent the collapse of finances. There was a decline in the capacity of the forests to produce lumber, which was the traditional guarantee against loans in Osaka. In 1704, the domain

---

[65] "The Land Tax in the Tokugawa Period."
[66] Saitō Osamu, "Daikaikon, jinkō," pp. 182–7.
[67] *TMK*, vol. 69, ff. 53rd–64th; *NRSCS* reel 45, "Genroku yonenbun oboegaki," vol. 1, f. 5.

defaulted on a large amount of loans. When loans from Osaka merchants were no longer forthcoming, the domain was unable to fulfill its construction duty to the bakufu. This emergency situation led domain officials to force retainers and the populace to pay special levies to the domain. As had been the case with new exactions during the Genna reforms of the 1620s, the rulers justified the levy by stating that it was for bakufu duty. Furthermore, these levies were advertised as temporary, and there were promises of repayment, which made them more palatable initially than direct tax increases. However, repayment promises were broken, and officials used these levies with ever greater frequency, and the amounts demanded grew larger from the period around 1710 to the 1770s.

There was growing awareness over this time that the increasingly immoderate use of these special levies destroyed the social foundations of government, even while it prevented the short-term bankruptcy of the domain. However, officials often felt that their only choice was to continue levies or see the domain become unable to pay for the alternate attendance trip to Edo. Only after a long period of criticism and protest had seemingly threatened to destroy the very foundations of rule, did the domain carry out the serious belt tightening and reorganization of priorities that were necessary to abolish the levies.

Chapter 4 will look at the finances of the domain spanning the whole early modern period. A crisis in domain finances was developing from the late seventeenth century, closely related to the economic troubles described in this chapter. The economic and financial troubles led to an erosion of older values and ideals that were the basis of the political system. The latter half of the book will focus on how people in Tosa extricated themselves from this crisis, and the next chapter will set the scene for our understanding of this recovery, by exploring the steady recovery of domain finances after the 1780s.

4

The decline and restoration of domain finances

Finances have reached this level of hardship and many years of impoverishment because We have passed the time thoughtlessly and inattentively. We are extremely dissatisfied. We declare a cut in expenses in Edo and the country to within the level of our income beginning now. Furthermore, We have requested to the shogun that We may live at a status of 100,000 *koku*. If this reform does not succeed, then We do not deserve being granted this country and can do nothing other than give it up. Know our heart: All, high and low, must accept this together.

Domain lord Yamauchi Toyochika, eighth month 1787[1]

The financial condition of Tosa domain worsened steadily over most of the eighteenth century. Because seventeenth-century finances were so dependent on lumber income, the disappearing stands of forest devastated finances as directly as they harmed the Tosa environment and economy. Furthermore, because overpopulation problems contributed to crop losses and difficulties with tax payment, they also troubled financial officials. *Bakufu* demands for labor duty in the eighteenth century became standardized as a monetary contribution for almost all domains, Tosa included, but the sudden calls for money inevitably sent domain finances reeling.[2] Furthermore, normal Edo expenditures continued to grow: a by-product of the culture of conspicuous consumption in which the lords and their families lived. When lumber was plentiful in the seventeenth century, the lords of Tosa were very well off and could afford to be insouciant. As the forests declined, continuing dependence upon Edo and Osaka rendered the rulers careless of their debt – and of the pain their expenditures caused back in Tosa. Instead, domain officials resorted to extraordinary measures to gain quickly needed income. They collected special levies from retainers and the populace, and they coerced loans from the populace, knowing well that they did not have the means to repay them. The frequently offered justification that such measures were needed to support the lord's service to the Tokugawa became less and less palatable. People became

---

[1] Yamamoto Takeshi, *Kenshōbo*, vol. 1, p. 143.
[2] Ōhira Yūichi, "Kinsei no daimyō 'kōmu' to sono hōkai."

increasingly resentful and distrustful of government, which led to a crisis of confidence in the rulers.

Political troubles and financial troubles peaked in the 1780s in Tosa. Protests, rampant corruption, and an absence of lenders to the domain led the lord Toyochika to begin what became known as the Tenmei reform in 1787. If the period up to the 1780s was a descent into disorder, the Tenmei reform was the beginning of a steady ascent into a new stability. By the eve of the American arrival in 1853, Tosa finances were in better condition than they had been for nearly two centuries, perhaps one reason why Tosa was able to play such a crucial role in the decades that followed.

A survey of the whole history of domain finances highlights the miserable situation sandwiched in between. Circumstances were much better before and much better after, making the middle of the eighteenth century a severe dip within the longer history. The crisis period fostered, perhaps required, the search for a new orientation in government. Without having begun a fundamental reorientation toward government in Tosa, as augured by the increasing use of the term *kokueki* in public discourse, the recovery of the nineteenth century would not have happened. Kokueki thought provided an admirable ideological tool to inspire and justify the changes in taxation policy to remove special levies, foster policies encouraging commercial production, and limit expenditure outside the domain, all of which were crucial to the turnaround. Because so much of the new policy was related to taxation and expenditure, an understanding of the changing finances of the domain will better situate us to interpret the arguments and fresh perspectives of the people of the mid-eighteenth century, which we will explore in the succeeding chapters of this book.

An outline of domain income sources

Let us begin our exploration of finances with a summary of the sources of income for the domain. It is possible to classify the vast and complex array of domain income sources into six main groups: corvée, lumber sales, agricultural tax (feudal rent), special levies, domain-run businesses and lending, and commercial taxes.[3] The survival of documents for all of these groups is sporadic, making reconstruction of a complete picture of changing domain income impossible. However, enough documents survive to allow us to see most of the important shifts.

[3] The best general work to date is Hirao Michio, *Kōchi-han zaisei shi*. Akizawa Shigeru provides a lucid discussion of finances over the first half of the Edo period in Tosa in "Kinsei zenki han zaisei shi."

Corvée, encompassing all of the labor duties owed the domain by the populace is one of the most difficult sources of income to quantify accurately, because of poor document survival. The corvée was usually remunerated with very low pay not sufficient to cover the transportation and food costs incurred by the laborer. Most participants found it onerous. Many forms of corvée were commutable into cash payments, and the domain used this money to hire laborers at a higher wage. Under corvée, fields and the irrigation system were repaired, lumber was harvested, and officials and goods were transported on roads or by vessel. Field and repair corvée alone could exceed a million man-days a year. In addition to this, there was the transportation corvée, for which no domainwide totals exist. The county of Hata used 65,427 days of transportation corvée labor in 1685 and 64,857 days in the following year. Extrapolating on the basis of population would give an estimate for the whole domain of nearly 400,000 man-days at this time.[4] It was commonly agreed, and bitterly complained about, that the amount of transportation corvée continued to grow throughout the Edo period. Village records suggest the scale of the burden on peasants. In the nineteenth century, one village of fifteen hundred people situated along a domain highway – which gave it a particular burden – reported a year's total of 15,104 man-days plus 708 horse-days of labor.[5] The heavy amount of transportation corvée provoked frequent resistance. It was blamed for the poor care of crops by peasants, unsuccessful commerce by shippers and bad catches by fishermen. Lesser retainers such as musketmen and *yōnin* business officials invited criticism for abusing the system for personal benefit. Repairs corvée as such was rarely criticized, although many people criticized its mismanagement, which translated into greater cost and labor for the peasant. Corvée was a significant part of domain income even though it cannot be put in the table on domain income that follows (Table 4.1).

Table 4.1 represents income figures divided into the major categories listed above for the years 1681, 1709, 1778, and 1852. It is based upon modified budgets for the first two years, and income records for the final two years. The table should be viewed as a general guide to income, because domain financial documents are complex and, for some matters, untrustworthy. The first two budgets tended to leave some cash income unrevealed. The figures for the latter two years are, however, presumably complete except for income in gifts, bribes, and possibly money lending. The table reveals important shifts over time in the relative importance of income sources.

---

[4] Ms. "Hata-gun uttae sho shina mokuroku," photographic copy in the Kōchi Prefecture Library, (Ken shi shiryō, no. 304), p. 47. Constantine Vaporis discusses the effects of the transportation corvée on villages in central Japan in "Post Station and Assisting Villages."

[5] "Sashidashi" from Noneyama village in *Kōchi-ken shi, kinsei shiryō hen*, pp. 509–10.

Table 4.1. Sources of domain income in *koku* equivalents

Year	Total	Land tax	Lumber sales	Domain business and lending	Commercial	Special levies	Other, casualties	Conversion rate *monme* per *koku*
1681	109,847	56,630	27,272	10,000	11,909	0	4,036	55
%		*(51.5)*	*(24.8)*	*(9.1)*	*(10.8)*	*(0)*	*(3.6)*	
1709	140,299	82,600	16,666	ca. 10,000	11,500	16,200	3,333	60
%		*(58.8)*	*(11.8)*	*(7.1)*	*(8.1)*	*(11.54)*	*(2.3)*	
1778	168,219	108,410	1,952	16,963	5,096	27,838	7,960	75
%		*(64.4)*	*(1.1)*	*(10.0)*	*(3.0)*	*(16.5)*	*(4.7)*	
1852	177,911	132,831	5,116	18,425	8,644	205	12,690	115
%		*(74.7)*	*(2.9)*	*(10.4)*	*(4.9)*	*(0.0)*	*(7.1)*	

Lumber played a central role in early seventeenth-century domain history, and the eighteenth-century decline in the importance of lumber as a source of domain income, which Table 4.1 reveals, is astonishing. Unfortunately, no figures survive from the 1620s to the 1660s, the heyday of lumbering activities in Tosa, but the early days of that period were a time when, as the official domain history of the period states: "The sending of lumber to Osaka was like the sending of rice for other domains."[6] As late as 1681, lumber sales still provided around 25 percent of revenue. This fell drastically to a mere 1 percent in 1778. Even these figures do not fully state the extent of diminishing income from forestry. The commercial taxes received in 1681 were primarily paid by private exporters of lumber and firewood. Duties from other products such as paper, eggs, and sugar were almost nonexistent in the figure for 1681, but these industries later expanded to provide the bulk of commercial taxes in 1852. The decline in the proportion of lumber earnings was primarily a reflection of an absolute decline in lumber income, but resulted in some degree from the growth of other sources of income.

Revenue from the agricultural tax heads the list of this growth. Rising expenses and the decline in income from forestry spurred officials to enlarge income from agricultural taxes. The agricultural tax (*kurairi mononari*) was the most important source of income for domain finances at least from the 1680s and probably earlier. In Table 4.1 the growth appears steady, but in reality, like the changes in population, it too followed a pattern of initial rapid growth, subsequent stagnation and later moderate growth. Figure 4.1 records these trends in detail, displaying the available data on annual totals of land tax received by the domain. The double bars on the graph are the averages given for those periods in domain financial documents. The figures for 1603, 1625, and 1627 are calculations based on information given in financial documents, and they represent an estimate of average income for those periods. All other figures are actual for the year as given in the tax official's annual reports. Domain officials achieved the trend of growth visible in the chart in two ways: one was by raising the amount of taxes collected from each plot of land – as described in the previous chapter, and the other was by increasing the amount of demesne land itself. The land for which cultivators paid taxes directly to the domain was called the *kurairichi*. This demesne land could be enlarged by registration of new land development and by confiscation of the retainers' fiefs and incorporating them into the kurairichi.

Unlike many domains in Japan, which reduced all of their retainers to stipendaries during the seventeenth century, Tosa never wholly abandoned the

---

[6] Quoted in Hirotani Kijūrō, "Genna kaikaku." The source is ms. *Hanshi naihen* held in the Kōchi University Library; Mori Yasuhiro, "Shoki no Kōchi-han Ōsaka kurayashiki."

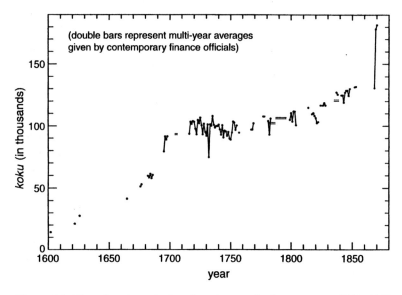

Figure 4.1. Tosa domain agricultural tax income for known years, 1600–1871.

fief system for retainers.[7] As late as the start of the Meiji period, over four
hundred senior retainers received income directly from their fiefs. This land
was free from direct domain taxation. The residents paid taxes directly to their
samurai fief holders.[8] Nevertheless, much land was confiscated from retainers
during the first century of Yamauchi rule. When Yamauchi Katsutoyo arrived in
Tosa in 1600, he gave out the lion's share of Tosa's agricultural land in fief to his
retainers. Of 240,000 *tan* he kept only 45,000 for direct domain income. This
favoring of retainers over domain income was a common tendency of many
lords until the early Edo period. Constant warfare required them to disburse
significant tracts of land to their warriors in order to keep a large and loyal army
at hand. However, with the fall of Osaka castle in 1615, the advent of peace
meant that retainers with military talents were no longer as necessary, and a
small demesne proved insufficient for the unexpectedly large expenses of a
peacetime daimyo. In Tosa, after the financial crisis of 1620 had created a keen
awareness of the importance of control over domainal sources of income, a clear
tendency developed for the administrators to reduce fief amounts at times of
inheritance, when the opportunity presented itself. The number of senior

[7] It was generally the large peripheral domains that maintained true fief systems. John Morris has
given the most thorough explorations of early modern fiefs in his studies of Sendai and Nanbu
domains in his *Kinsei Nihon chigyōsei no kenkyū*. The fact that these domains also produced
kokueki thought in its earliest manifestations, may be more than coincidence.
[8] Hirao, *Kōchi-han zaisei*, pp. 75–82.

retainers with large fiefs was reduced drastically. Retainer offenses were punished severely, leading to fief reductions and the extinction of many lineages.[9] By 1698, the land held in fief by retainers had been reduced to 110,000 tan, and 85,000 tan of the confiscated fief land had been incorporated into the demesne. Together with newly developed agricultural land, this made the demesne total 197,723 tan, or almost five times the amount possessed by Katsutoyo in 1605.[10] In addition, a large portion of the demesne was gained by the fortuitous return to the Yamauchi of the 30,000-koku branch domain of Nakamura which had existed within the bounds of Hata county.[11] The increase in land tax income shown in Figure 4.1 between 1695 and 1696 is due to the return of this branch domain, which brought 13,000 koku of revenue in 1696. The lord Toyomasa, so lavish in all his behavior, celebrated the return of Nakamura by disbursing gifts that year equal in cost to half the income derived from Nakamura's holding.[12] After the 1690s, however, only very small amounts of land were added to the demesne in this way. Paralleling trends in the bakufu's policy toward daimyo, Tosa lords became increasingly reluctant to confiscate land from retainers.

Land development continued to increase the demesne, but as we have noted, it was most rapid in the period from 1640 to 1690. The chief domain administrator Nonaka Kenzan saw to it in the 1640s and 1650s that the domain directly sponsored the development of great tracts of land in order to increase income. Private land development was also encouraged by granting the status of rural samurai, or *gōshi*, to a man who developed more than 30 tan of land. Initially, this status was limited to those who could show samurai family origins, then those of peasant origins were included, and by the mid-eighteenth century, even people of lowly merchant origins could apply.[13] By 1685, there were 747 such rural samurai, possessing as fief 23,498 tan of developed land.[14] After 1700,

[9] A history of the retainer corps of Tosa in the seventeenth century, written by a domain scholar-retainer in the 1830s, reveals the drastic changes of the period; Mutō Yoshiharu, ms. *Shokaikyū kakushiki no kongen*, held in the Tokyo University Historiographical Institute. Also see "Okachū hengi" (Mishaps in the Household) (no author), a catalog of crimes, confiscations, and punishments of retainers in Tosa, printed in *Tosa shidan*.

[10] Calculated from ms. "Okurairi mononari mokuroku," in *Genroku monjo, Genroku jūichinen*, Yamauchi Shrine Treasury and Archives; also copied in *TMK*, vol. 91, ff. 61–3; *Kōchi-ken shi, kinsei hen*, pp. 76–82. I have written an unpublished paper on the fate of retainers and their fiefs in the seventeenth century entitled, "Political Centralization and the Weakening Retainer in Seventeenth-Century Tosa."

[11] This domain had been confiscated in 1689 by the shogun Tsunayoshi when the lord of Nakamura (a younger brother of the Tosa lord) refused to become a junior elder in the *bakufu* on the grounds that he could ill afford it and that he was a *tozama*, an outer lord, not customarily considered eligible or bound to hold post in the bakufu. *Nakamura-shi shi*, pp. 399–400.

[12] *TMK*, vol. 83, ff. 51–99.

[13] Jansen, *Sakamoto Ryōma*, pp. 26–32.

[14] Ms. *Kōgi narabini oietomo mitsushi basshō*, the Kōchi City Library (K210.5 mitsu), f. 37th. Ms. *Doyō kenpi roku* (in HB, no. 9), pp. 27–8 gives 1,061 such rural samurai for the earlier year 1665. The number may have gradually declined after the fall of their governmental patron, Nonaka Kenzan, in 1663.

progress in land development slowed, but from the middle of the eighteenth
century until the Meiji period, new land continued to increase the tax base at a
pace that averaged out to a still substantial 780 tan per year. By 1852, the total
demesne had risen to 331,485 tan of land. Many domains elsewhere in Japan
were unable to increase their tax base after the mid-eighteenth century, either
because the limits of land development had been reached or because they were
unable to effectively register newly developed land due to opposition from the
populace.[15] The Tosa administration was thus comparatively fortunate that
registration of newly developed land added increments yearly and because it
had the administrative capability to carry out resurveys from time to time.[16]

At the beginning of the previous chapter the retainer Matsuo Hikotarō is
quoted as saying in 1759 that agricultural taxes had been declining for fifty
years. Figure 4.1 bears him out at least for the thirty-five years preceding his
statement. This can be linked to the increased incidence of crop loss, most
notably the terrible Kyōhō crop loss of 1732.[17] As we have seen, these repeated
crop failures led to a cycle of declining productivity, because starvation in one
year meant ill-tended crops the next. The phenomenon of declining agricultural
production was real enough to contemporaries, although it must be noted that
the decline in land tax income may also be due some extent to locally and
illegally arranged compensation for the increasing severity of the special levies.
The two primary forms of special levies in Tosa were *kariage* and *goyōgin*.

In some domains in Japan, kariage was collected only from retainers, and the
people were spared a direct imposition of this tax.[18] In Tosa, however, administrators were able to exact kariage from all people of the domain. Samurai
contributed a percentage of their income from fiefs, townsmen a frontage tax,
fishermen a net tax, and peasants a percentage of their agricultural production
after tax. One document from 1825 suggests that the burden fell heaviest on
samurai, who bore 79.5 percent of the total, whereas peasants bore 20 percent,
and townsmen and fishermen together bore less than 0.5 percent of the total.[19]
It should be noted that the peasants on samurai fief land probably also bore a
percentage of the samurai total, but this would not appear in domain records.
Townsmen and fishermen, it is clear, were let off lightly. This kind of levy was
first imposed in 1704. Initially, the rate of the levy was 10 percent of fief income
or, for peasants, what remained after taxes, but this rate steadily increased until
it reached a peak of 50 percent in the 1760s. As the word for the levy, kariage

---

[15] Nagano Susumu, "Hansei kaikaku ron," pp. 202–11; Thomas Smith, "The Land Tax."
[16] *Kōchi-ken shi, kinsei hen,* pp. 294–6, 602, 612–4, 860.
[17] For storm reports, see Chapter 3.
[18] Takahashi Tsutomu, "Chūki Akita han no shakuchi seisaku ni tsuite."
[19] Kusunoki Oe, *Hiuchi bukuro,* vol. 9, pp. 17–8, provides a record of 33 percent of the levy actually
     returned to the payers.

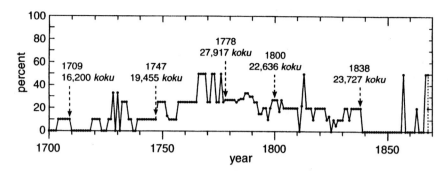

Figure 4.2. *Kariage* special levy amounts, 1700–1868. Percentage of income or agricultural product after taxes, collected from retainers and commoners, with actual amounts collected by domain and calculated in terms of rice for some years.

("loan to a superior"), indicates, it was ostensibly a loan from the people to the domain. In reality, very little of this "loan" was ever returned. The domain carried out a rectification of names in 1789 when it renamed the levy *demai* ("a portion of rice taken out").

In time, people protested more and more against kariage, but the domain persisted in its collection because kariage had become an essential source of income preventing financial collapse. It was first imposed to help pay for construction duty for the bakufu on the Tone river. The state of domain finances was such that creditors in Osaka were wary. The domain could not borrow the money in Osaka, so it ordered the collection of 10 percent after taxes from retainer fief income and peasants' assessed agricultural product. Townsmen paid rates on the frontage of their house and fishermen on the size of their boats.[20] Tosa was in the midst of a famine in 1704 and, as part of governmental relief duties, the domain was disbursing relief rice with one hand, while adding this extra imposition with the other. The situation was somewhat absurd, but bakufu demands could not be easily refused within the existing structure of authority. This first impost lasted for six years. A nine-year hiatus followed, but the levy reappeared in 1719, after which, as Figure 4.2 reveals, a nearly incessant sequence of levies followed. During the 113 years between 1726 and 1839, kariage was imposed in all but six years and was most frequently collected at a rate of 20 percent to 30 percent of income after taxes. The period of kariage's most rampant use was from 1766 to 1776, during seven years of which the levy was collected at 50 percent. Although initially the levy had been used to pay for bakufu demands, it quickly came to be used to make payments on Tosa's

---

[20] Yamamoto Takeshi, *Kenshōbo*, vol. 3, pp. 43–9.

increasing debt to Osaka merchants. It was devastating for a commoner to have to pay from one third to one half of his income in taxes and then have as much as half of the remainder taken away by the special levy. To add insult to injury, the domain failed to keep its promises of repayment.

In the early years of the use of kariage, people were not pleased, but on the surface at least they consented to its being a part of their duty to the lord. Initial criticism was mild and poked fun at the sudden dearth in which people found themselves. Such an episode occurred in 1748 when the domain was forced at bakufu order to improve the dike and irrigation system of the Ōi river in the Tōkaidō region. To meet expenses, the domain declared that for the next five years a kariage would be levied at a rate of 25 percent. Soon after, an anonymous retainer wrote and circulated parodies of poems from the well-known *Ogura hyakunin isshu (Hundred Poems of a Hundred Poets)*. He took Ki no Tsurayuki's "I know not the hearts of men, / but the plum blossoms of my home village / still have their old familiar smell" and changed it to the less fragrant: "I know not the hearts of men / but my ravaged pockets / still have their old familiar smell" in reference to his futile search for cash. Ōe no Chisato's reflective "As I look at the moon / and ponder my endless troubles / I am not the only one experiencing autumn" was given a more prosaic rendition: "As I look at the moon / and brood over the things in my arms / I'm not the only one in the pawn shop."[21] As the levies became a permanent fixture in people's lives, angry criticism replaced humor. With a boldness born of frequent disappointment, a *rōnin* teacher in a village school, Murakami Chūji, wrote the following bitter comments in a petition submitted to the domain lord in 1761:

> Ever since the time of our last lord, special levies have been collected from the castle town, villages and ports with increasing frequency. When you order levies the officials proceed from village to village, announcing with great clarity and severity, 'Come the end of this year, or in early next spring, the lord will order the return of the levy amount with added interest! Therefore everyone, contribute with all of your ability!' People contribute but when the stated period comes there is not the slightest word, and the loan drifts unpaid, until at some point you order that there will be no return of the money. Or, another time, the officials said that all of the money would be returned on a ten-year payment schedule and that all should rejoice and be thankful. Indeed, the first year payments were made beautifully, but after that, time just slithered away and nothing was done. How often this has happened! And because government does not keep its promises, people have lost trust in it. Your officials are faithless, and the way of your government is unjust. Certainly all of this has been kept from you by officials, but the hatred of all of the people focuses on the single person of your lordship.[22]

Other petitions reveal that Chūji was not alone in thinking domain officials faithless and unjust, nor was he the only one openly expressing anger over the

---

[21] Parodies in *TNK*, vol. 87, ff. 68th–71st; originals with notes and modern translation in Kaneko Takeo, *Ogura hyakunin isshu no kōgi*, pp. 59–61, 91–4.
[22] Murakami Chūji, Gomen-machi ni makari aru rōnin, (9/3/1761), *TNK*, vol. 130, f. 33rd.

levies in the 1750s and 1760s. However, officials continued to use the levies, and conditions became even worse. By the 1780s many people had come to see the levies as the source of all the social ills of the time: corrupt officials, poverty, breakdown of the status system, and economic decline. By then, voices had risen to the point where they could not be ignored.

Vociferous resistance by both commoners and retainers at first succeeded in forcing the domain to reduce the amount of kariage collected and finally managed to stop collection of this special levy altogether in 1839. The mercantilist logic of kokueki played a supporting role in the development of this outcome, because of its emphasis on keeping money within the domainal country and its de-emphasis of the performance of duty to the bakufu. It was partly through decreasing ties with Edo that finances improved sufficiently to allow a reduction of the levies. Although some might interpret the defeat of the special levies merely as the domain's weakened authority over its people, the fact is that the domain was able to reduce the amount, and then finally abolish kariage, without going into further debt, highlighting the essential financial solvency of the domain in the nineteenth century.

Trends in the use of the other special levy, goyōgin, reveal a similar peak of use during the eighteenth century and a decline in the nineteenth century. This forced loan of money from the populace was sometimes repaid in part, but more often it just accumulated in domain hands. Goyōgin (more commonly called *goyōkin* by scholars today because that was the name used by the bakufu and many eastern domains) was another form of special levy in Tosa, which required that commoners and rural retainers lend cash to the domain at no interest. It was not a voluntary loan, and despite early promises, there was little hope of repayment, especially in the eighteenth century. After determining the amount of cash it needed to borrow, the domain then divided that sum among the regions of Tosa and directed the local officials and people to decide who would pay. It complemented the unequal distribution of the collection of kariage, by focusing on people who possessed cash. The burden seems to have been borne disproportionately by the wealthy merchants of the various regions, but many people of low status and income paid as well. Some people argued that the wealthiest commoners escaped the levy because they were all village and ward officials, a tax exempt status.[23] A document of 1853 reveals the total accumulation of goyōgin unrepaid by the domain.[24] The document divides the total sum into the amounts collected in each era (*nengo*). Of the goyōgin collected between 1751 and 1800, 7,521.982 *kan* still remained unrepaid in

[23] Kihei (8/21/1759), SB, no. SP 6, ff. 91st–120th, especially ff. 108th–09th.
[24] *Kaei rokunen tōbun oboegaki*, HB box of unclassified, printed in the second edition of Hirao, *Kōchi-han zaisei*.

1852. This and other documents reveal that in the late eighteenth century, goyōgin had been collected almost annually, and most repayment attempts were unsuccessful.[25] The money collected went to repay the domain's loans to Osaka merchants or to pay directly for bakufu construction duty. This sudden removal of so much cash certainly hurt the local economy. The burden was heaviest at the beginning of the Tenmei reforms in 1787 and was perceived as a major problem to be corrected by this reform. The reform produced significant results, because between 1801 and 1852, the amount of goyōgin that remained unrepaid was less than one tenth that of the previous half-century, only 749.679 kan. Almost all of this later amount came from one occasion of bakufu duty in 1813. Goyōgin was collected less frequently in the nineteenth century; 1813, 1822 and 1831, each time on the occasion of bakufu construction duty. Furthermore, most of the latter two levies had been repaid by 1852.[26] The declining dependence on goyōgin in the nineteenth century parallels almost exactly the decline in use of the kariage, indicating obliquely that the severe financial needs of the eighteenth century had been overcome.

The restoration of financial health after 1787

This indication of a revival contradicts most descriptions of domain finances in Japan, which talk about perpetual difficulty or a steady worsening up to the end of the Edo period. The current picture of the finances of domains in Japan is one in which most domains were in nearly continual financial trouble starting in the Genroku period (1688–1703). Tosa's miserable condition certainly was part of this picture, at least until the 1780s, and the information presented above says nothing about other domains – all of which possess their own histories. Yet many scholars of Tosa domain finances have pictured either a steady decline or a continuous state of subpar performance up to the Meiji period. The chief authority on Tosa's finances, Hirao Michio, has stated that finances were probably continuously in the red.[27] He also did not attach fiscal significance to the reduction and the consequent disappearance of the use of kariage, although the list he created reveals these facts.[28] Ikeda Norimasa concluded that the abolition of kariage in 1839 was implemented as a means to counteract worsening

[25] *An'ei hachinen tōbun oboegaki*, GM, no. 5500, sect. 22.
[26] Yamamoto Takeshi, *Kenshōbo*, vol. 1: 1813, p. 213; 1822, p. 240; 1831, pp. 266, 268. Each was a direct result of bakufu construction duty. *Goyōgin* was also collected in 1857 (p. 388) as Tosa geared up for war.
[27] Hirao, *Tosa-han*, pp. 29–34; *Kōchi-han zaisei*, pp. 35, 40–2, 121–6.
[28] Hirao, *Kōchi-han zaisei*, pp. 100–3.

samurai poverty, without considering the fiscal factors that made this possible.[29] In general, domain finances have been described as proceeding from one reform (*kaikaku*) to the next: each reform preceded by a financial crisis, and no reform making more than a temporary improvement in a bad situation.[30] Here the task will be to bring more evidence to prove that finances did improve steadily after the 1780s.

The domain frequently spent more than it earned. Budget deficits at the end of the year were covered by borrowing extra money from the wealthy merchants of the "three cities," Osaka, Kyoto, and Edo. Much of the borrowing, called *tokigari*, was a natural part of the flow of goods and cash to pay for the expenses of alternate attendance in Edo. The expenses of the journey and residence could be covered with loans and then paid off within the year by selling domain goods in Osaka or by shipping cash earned in the domain, but when expenses continually exceeded income these loans accumulated. On occasion, the debts grew too large to envision regular repayment, and then domain officials had to reschedule the interest and payments. In the worst cases, the domain even canceled its debts. The lord very rarely canceled debts to outside merchants because of the several problems they could cause. First, when mistreated by the domain, they could stop lending to Tosa and instead lend elsewhere. Secondly, they could take the problem to bakufu court and invite the possibility of a reprimand by a shogunal official.[31] Even canceled loans remained in domain records, however, and the state of loans as seen in documents is probably the best indication of the health of finances.

Income and expenditure records exist for only scattered years, but their comparison with accumulated debt totals gives a good indication of the domain's relative financial well-being. Table 4.2 gives a comparison of the total debt to income for representative years in the Edo period. These loans do not include the goyōgin and kariage amounts discussed above, and so provide an independent verification of similar trends. The loans are primarily from merchants of the three big cities of Japan. The amounts are given in the table in terms of both silver kan and rice equivalents based on the rice prices in the documents. A comparison of the years 1709 and 1852 demonstrates why it is necessary to consider both measures. The debt expressed in kan for both years is not very different, but, in terms of rice-equivalents, the 1709 debt is more

---

[29] Ikeda Norimasa, "Tenpō kaikaku ron no saikentō – Tosa-han o chūshin ni shite," pp. 26–7; "Tosa-han ni okeru Ansei kaikaku to sono hantai ha," p. 24.
[30] Also see Matsuyoshi Sadao, *Tosa-han keizai shi*, pp. 47–51.
[31] On the other hand, Tosa merchants were captive lenders and had no right to use bakufu courts for redress against their own lord. Toward them, the domain was more often remiss in repayment. They became adept at pleading a lack of funds, and often the domain had to coax loans from them with promises of providing commercial monopoly privileges.

Table 4.2. Domain indebtedness as a percentage of annual income

Year	Total indebtedness[a]	Income	Percentage
1620	2,500–2,600 *kan* (75,757–78,759 *koku*)	400 *kan* (12,121.2 *koku*)	650
1681	3,722 *kan* (68,581.8 *koku*)	5,182.5 *kan* (94,227.2 *koku*)	72.78
1709	12,961 *kan* (216,016.6 *koku*)	7,438 *kan* (123,971.6 *koku*)	174.24
1759	16,338.846 *kan*	?	
1778	29,184.081 *kan* (389,121 *koku*)	12,690.45 *kan* (169,206 *koku*)	229.96
1804	20,330.002 *kan* (282,361.1 *koku*)	11,418.83 *kan* (158,594.9 *koku*)	178.03
1852	11,162.916 *kan* (97,068.8 *koku*)	20,459.86 *kan* (177,911.87 *koku*)	54.56

[a] These totals do not include *goyōgin* amounts

than twice that of the 1852 debt, because the value of the kan had declined. As a percentage of domain annual income, the 1709 debt is more than three times larger than in 1852.

Table 4.2 reveals that the domain took a serious plunge into debt in the first two decades of its existence, after which it extricated itself from this burden and stayed in relatively good financial health until the 1680s. Subsequently, debts accumulated steadily until the 1780s. In 1778, debt had risen to more than twice domain annual income. After the 1780s, the level of debt was steadily reduced, reaching very low levels by the mid-nineteenth century. In 1804, despite a substantial drop in total income, the percentage of debt to income still had been reduced significantly. By 1852, the year just prior to the arrival of Commodore Perry, debt was down to half of annual income. The actual amount of loans in terms of rice had been reduced to one fourth of the amount in 1778. This pattern indicates that after the 1780s, domain finances improved steadily, at least until the eve of Perry's arrival.

The consistency of these trends regarding domain loans versus income, in comparison with trends in kariage and goyōgin strongly supports the conclusion that the domain faced its biggest financial crisis during the period from Hōreki to Tenmei (1750–89), after which it gradually but steadily improved until the 1850s. It could be said that finances in 1852 were better than they had ever been. The health of domain finances in the mid-seventeenth century had depended upon cutting Tosa's forests at a nonreplaceable rate, and doomed the domain to troubles when the forests ran out. Finances in 1852 were based on agricultural taxes, a scaled-down but replenishable forest industry, and a diversified base of commerce and industry as will be discussed in the final chapter of this book. The special levies that had been used in the eighteenth century were no longer needed. The decline in income from special levies was supplemented by a slow growth in the effective agricultural tax rate, presumably because of a decline in corruption, a rebound in the agricultural economy, and a reduction in the amount of abandoned land.

In a certain sense, the argument that domain finances were constantly on the border of difficulty until the end of the Edo period is true. Certainly, the lords and domain officials of the nineteenth century frequently described finances as either being in failure or needing reform. Officials implemented a number of government reforms in the nineteenth century, and each reform was precipitated by some perceived financial crisis. Reading their statements, one would conclude that domain finances were in terrible shape until the end of the Edo period. Certainly no government official in the nineteenth century rested comfortably with a sense of excess wealth. How can this paradox be explained?

When examining domain finances over a long period, it becomes clear that the definition of what constitutes a crisis serious enough to institute reform changed over time. Standards of success were clearly getting higher. In the mid-eighteenth century, reforms were first felt necessary when the domain could find no way to borrow or pay for its most necessary expenses, such as retainer stipends or the alternate attendance journey. By contrast, after the Tenmei reforms, domain officials aimed for the abolition of the need for special levies. When they saw loans starting to accumulate they began reforms, and to make people feel the need for the reforms they used the rhetoric of financial crisis. Further evidence exists showing that after the 1790s loans from Osaka merchants were all repaid according to schedule up to the 1850s and no new debts piled up even after the final abolition of the kariage levy in 1839.[32] Domain officials were achieving their goal of fiscal solvency.

---

[32] Section on loans in ms. *Kaei rokunen tōbun oboegaki*, HB unclassified, also printed in Hirao, *Kōchi-han zaisei*, pp. 158–61, with minor mistake of repeating the first and second lines of p. 159 as the third and fourth lines.

The office diary of Mori Yoshiki, one of the junior administrators (*shiokiyaku*) of the domain, reveals this new attitude of reducing domain expenditures in order to eliminate the need for special levies. In 1800, thirteen years after the beginning of the Tenmei reforms, he argued energetically with the other top officials of the domain to attempt administrative cost cutting by instituting a stringent measure called *kingai itchi* that would reduce the number of domain staff. This would mean having only one official fill at the same time (1) posts devoted to the service of the lord and the Edo residence (*kin*) and (2) posts devoted to the administration and defense of the domain of Tosa (*gai*). In the following passage, Yoshiki records his arguments to the other leaders of government. He was quite aware that the reforms had been thus far successful, and he listed their successes one by one, but in his mind the single most important issue of the kariage special levy remained to be solved:

1800/1/4: If when this ten year reform ends [in 1806] we are unable to rescind the better part of kariage, then things cannot go on this way much longer. . . . The way things are, I cannot see how we will be able to put a stop to kariage in the seven years we have remaining in this reform program.

1800/2/2: I called everyone from the finance office and asked them if when the ten year reform is over, we ought to be able to rescind the kariage. They all responded, 'Rescinding kariage is out of the question! We will probably have to raise the amount.'

1800/2/6: [He records his argument to the other senior officials.] True, it is difficult to say that finances are in trouble. Indeed everyone thinks finances are well off. Generally they now flow smoothly. For one, before the reform [1787] we had no rice to disburse for stipends in the spring and had to purchase it in town. Now we have over 10,000 koku in store. Two, we now have over 20,000 koku in unhulled rice stored up [for relief] in the domain and port warehouses and this can be used in an emergency. Three, we have been able to acquire great numbers of new armaments yearly. Four, we have made two new warships. Five, we have been able to deposit over 100 kan a year into the military reserve fund. Six, when last year we had to do service for the bakufu, we acquired the 1,200 kan necessary in Osaka. Seven, we are now collecting only one tenth the amount of goyōgin as before the reform started. All seven of these things are a great improvement over conditions before the reform. However, every official in the country is certain to know that finances have improved and will tend to spend more, and then loans from Osaka will increase, and we cannot use for basic expenses the money we use to pay for loans, and then it will be very difficult to stop collecting kariage. I can see this happening.[33]

Yoshiki's efforts to have the cost-cutting measure of kingai itchi adopted by the senior administrators failed. The one senior administrator who said he agreed with Yoshiki repeatedly managed not to show up at the councils, and the others asked Yoshiki to wait a year or two before taking drastic measures in order to see how things developed. Yoshiki was later relieved of his office, promoted to the position of guardian of the young lord-to-be, Toyonori, and the

[33] Ms. *Sansei nichiroku*, vol. 2, ff. 46th–47th, 56th–57th, 65th–66th in the Kōchi Prefecture Library.

stringency measure was not carried out. As Yoshiki predicted, at the end of the ten-year reform, kariage could not be rescinded. Yoshiki perhaps achieved final victory when the lord Toyoteru finally ended the uniformly hated levy in 1839. Certainly it was the efforts of officials like Yoshiki who restored finances, while reducing the burden on the populace and retainers.

The decline of the Tosa economy and the waning trust in domain government in the eighteenth century were a result, in part, of the effects of the population boom and the ecological changes. Changes in population and the ecology were the unforeseen effects of forces set in motion by the Tokugawa settlement and the alternate attendance system. These created the financial burdens that prompted the domain to cut the forests and expand production of rice. Such actions created a short-lived prosperity and, as we have seen, were the sources of the eighteenth-century disaster. Furthermore, the alternate attendance system geographically organized the Japanese economy into one in which the functions of marketing and financing were centered in Osaka, and production of marketable agricultural and forestry materials for export was delegated to the domainal regions. As the problems that developed from these relationships increased, they were further aggravated by increased levels of taxation and the imposition of levies. Even the satisfaction that the taxes might restore domain finances was denied: The financial muddle worsened. The middle years of the eighteenth century marked a period of crisis in Tosa history. The economy was weak and in decline. People were fleeing the borders in great numbers. Many people ceased believing that the government was worthy or capable, and both protest and corruption increased. By the 1780s, most samurai were arguing that the special levies were eroding traditional morals of obedience, public service, and duty to the lord, and that the lord's benevolence was not reaching the people. The samurai perceived frequent popular protest and official corruption to be signs of this malaise. Because they believed that the righteousness of the lord and his officials preserved the peace of the country, government was seen as basically a moral affair. The decline in the morals of commoners and officials was a terrifying signal of the decline of government itself.

Given the many seemingly intractable problems of the decades before, it is surprising that after 1787 we see such a clear and steady recovery to stability and soundness. In reality, it was the result of ideological and institutional changes that were beginning to take place in the 1750s. The perceived crisis forced the people of Tosa to search for answers. The one bright spot of the low period from the 1750s to the 1780s, visible only in retrospect, was that, intellectually, this troubled time was the preparatory ground for the Tenmei reforms, which began in 1787 and changed the goals of domain rule. A process of dialogue between the rulers and the ruled helped provide new answers to the problems of rule. There were ways for the ruled to be integrated into government which allowed them at times to suggest the answers to the problems facing Tosa. In the time of crisis they forced the rulers to better integrate their desires into government.

In the late eighteenth century, the people of Tosa began to overcome this crisis by redefining their relationship with the Tokugawa and with Osaka. Kokueki thought played an important role in this redefinition by making the development of a nonsubservient, vigorous domainal commercial economy a priority. The people and rulers strove to make the Tosa economy less dominated by the Osaka market. The lord's relationship with shogunal authority was slowly redefined to be less subordinate. After the domain government clearly embarked on these policies in the late 1780s the economic and financial crisis was steadily resolved. The severity of the crisis itself suggests why the samurai administrators at last became willing to implement new and potentially dangerous policies. The next chapter will look at the political crisis facing the rulers, the response, and the opinions many dissatisfied residents expressed via the petition box.

5

Voices of dissatisfaction and change: The petition box

Although I am of base birth and have never received your munificent bounty, I am nonetheless a man of this country. At a time when high and low will sink or swim together, I think it would be dishonest of me to hold back in my criticism. This is not a time to stop being angry. As long as my spirit holds out, I will set my fear aside and tell you what I think of your government.

Kihei of Kuma village, 1759[1]

The villager Kihei wrote a severe set of criticisms of domain government in a letter to the lord, Yamauchi Toyonobu, late in the year 1759: Officials were embezzling government funds and had not improved their ways since the call for reform made a few months earlier. Samurai children were vandalizing crops just for fun, and there was a general lack of respect and care for *hyakushō* that made many wish to leave their status. Village headmen and other local officials were not doing their jobs well. Corvée labor was undercompensated and mismanaged. People were blaming the immorality of government officials for recent weather disasters and the fire that destroyed Yōhōji, the temple devoted to the lord's ancestors. The domain needed to better educate its officials.[2] The criticisms in this epistle go on and on. Numerous petitions surviving from this era show that Kihei was not alone in his criticisms.

People certainly had sound reasons to be dissatisfied with their rulers in the middle of the eighteenth century. To review some of the main points made in the earlier chapters: Tosa domain finances were spiraling downward deep into debt. Administrators had begun in the early part of the century to occasionally force the populace to lend the government money and rice. After the late 1730s, these exactions became annual, and grew steadily in size, affecting all of the people of the domain. These "loans" assisted finances but made people cynical:

This chapter was originally published in slightly different form as "The Petition Box in Eighteenth-Century Tosa," *Journal of Japanese Studies*, vol. 20, no. 2 (Winter 1994), and is presented here with permission.
[1] Kumamura jūnin Kihei (11/1/1759), *TNK*, vol. 122, ff. 58th–59th.
[2] Kumamura jūnin Kihei (11/1/1759), *TNK*, vol. 122, ff. 52nd–73rd.

It not only emptied their pockets but advertised repayment plans were never carried out in fact, and to heap insult on injury, the corruption of officials flourished even while feeding on this new and irregularly managed source of income. Bribery was common among officials, perhaps justified in their minds by the fact that they, too, had to give up large portions of their own fief income to the domain as part of the forced loan program.[3]

The government financial debacle was the broken crown of an economy that was itself troubled. Tosa suffered in the early eighteenth century from the long-term effects of massive deforestation and overpopulation. Many mountains were bare of trees, which had been shipped as lumber to the market of Osaka in order to pay for the lavish costs of the lord's alternate year residence in Edo. By the early eighteenth century, the decline of the forests had ultimately left behind a declining shipping fleet with little cargo to carry, and the agricultural economy was buffeted by a marked increase in the incidence of flooding. Large crop losses were common, and horrible famine repeatedly ate away at the population that had grown in the boom years of the late seventeenth century.

The economic and financial troubles in the middle of the eighteenth century had begun to deeply affect people's trust in government, such that the *rōnin* Murakami Chūji, quoted in Chapter 3, could write to the lord in 1761, "Your officials are faithless and the way of your government unjust." The lord read these petitions, but meted out no punishments for insolence, because Chūji, Kihei and others had submitted these letters via a petition box (*sojōbako*, *meyasubako*), a special system of direct appeal to the domain lord himself. The Tosa petition box system was begun in 1759 and was used continuously until 1873. The lord encouraged any person in Tosa, regardless of social status, to write signed petitions for any of three purposes: (1) to offer suggestions for improving society or government, (2) to give complaints and information concerning current officials or policies, and (3) to present legal appeals to the lord concerning court cases that the petitioner felt had not been fairly dealt with. The box itself was large and wooden, with a small opening in its lid to receive petitions. Monthly, it was locked and sealed by the chief inspector (*metsuke*) of the domain and placed across from the main castle gate inside the *ōkoshikake*, which was a small building where people could sit while waiting for permission to enter the castle on business. This location was deep within the samurai part of town, at the very foot of the castle, and it probably took courage for a commoner to approach the area. The box was removed from the waiting house only once each month and was opened by the chief inspector. He then took the sealed petitions to the senior councilors, who forwarded the sealed petitions to the lord himself to open and read.

[3] Marius Jansen gives an excellent discussion of Tosa in these days in "Tosa During the Last Century of Tokugawa Rule."

Although the petition box functioned for over a century, most of the petitions have unfortunately been lost. Transcriptions of petitions survive in greatest abundance from the decade after the box's inauguration. One hundred and forty-nine transcribed petitions from the years between 1759 and 1771 survive in the archives of the descendants of the lords of Tosa. This is because house historians transcribed many originals in the first half of the twentieth century into the massive collection known as the *Yamauchi-ke shiryō* (Yamauchi house documents). This collection largely escaped the aerial bombings of World War II, but only two of the original petitions survived.[4] Because of the loss, we cannot know the full extent to which the petition box was actually used. It is clear, however, that the existing transcriptions are but a small fraction of the total that survived into the early part of this century: The only person to write about the petitions in prewar times was one of the house historians, Fukushima Ōba, who noted that at that time there were "thousands."[5]

This special system provided a one-way verbal link from the commoners and samurai to the domain lord. The link was not only direct, but was also the most honest form of communication permitted. As the examples noted above demonstrate, many people expressed their opinions in an unconstrained fashion, and the authors were nearly (if not absolutely) safe from punishment. The surviving petitions are thus rare and fascinating windows into the political life of eighteenth-century Tosa. The authors of these petitions wrote in ways that make them rich and extensive documents bearing on not only the political, but the social and economic history of Tosa as well. One farmer wrote a petition of agricultural advice, in what amounts to a farm manual to give to his lord. Another village doctor worried about sexual transgression, recorded how women are vulnerable to rape when their husbands are in the fields and also expressed his opinion that in cases of adultery the husband should kill the offending wife on the spot.[6] There is enough evidence within the thousands

---

[4] The two surviving originals are in an unclassified box in the HB collection held in the Kōchi City Library. The largest body of full transcriptions is the volumes of *TNK*: vol. 111, ff. 35th–47th; vol. 121; vol. 122; vol. 127; vol. 130; vol. 134, ff. 217th–225th; vol. 135, ff. 66th–104th; vol. 139, ff. 33rd– 100th; vol. 144, ff. 13th–25th; vol. 148, ff. 22nd–101st; vol. 153, ff. 3rd–27th; vol. 154, ff. 77th–85th. *TCK*: vol. 2, ff. 126th–136th; vol. 11, ff. 106th–123rd. Two are missing from the final draft versions of the *TNK* and *TCK* but exist in the rough draft transcriptions, which are bound in the rough draft volumes – the *fukuhon*: *TNK*, Hōreki kyūnen kūgatsu oyobi zassai no kan, ff. 24th–57th, and *TCK*, Meiwa rokunen shōgatsu-jūnigatsu no kan, foliation unknown but within the section entry entitled, "Kono tsuki Yusuhara-mura kagebyakusho. . . ." All of the above total 130 petitions. A dozen or more samurai petitions are copied in later volumes – most importantly, many for the Tenmei period. Also forty-three complete transcriptions are in SB, nos. SP 3, SP 5, SP 6, SP 7, SP 8 and SP 9. Eighteen of these are also in the *TNK* and *TCK*, and two are officials' reports not counted as petitions; in SP 3, one by Doi Hachiemon, and in SP 7, one by Kawada Matasuke.
[5] Fukushima Ōba (Nariyuki), "Hōreki no ijin." For some additional information see my "'Tosa-han sojōbako no seido to kinō."
[6] Kamigun Akaoka-ura hyakushō Shinbei (2/3/1760), *TNK*, vol. 127, ff. 20th–32nd. Gomen-machi sumioru ishi Tateda Kachū (1759/11/26), *TNK*, vol. 122, ff. 87th–90th.

of pages of these very diverse epistles to be of substantial use to many kinds of historians. In this chapter, however, I will use the petitions and other sources to explore how the petition box system itself was created and used in Tosa. I make the following arguments: First, social unrest and widespread demand played an important role leading to the creation of the petition box itself. Second, men of various statuses and regions of Tosa society considered the petition box useful and actively utilized the system once it was created. Third, many of the petitions indeed became the origin of important domain policies.

Because the petition box system provided the core of the surviving documents relating to *kokueki* thought among commoners, it is important to grasp the nature of the petitions and the system that produced them. Since one of the central arguments of this book is that kokueki thought was primarily the creation of merchants and townspeople and was adapted by samurai officials, this chapter provides an explanation of the kinds of communication that existed to facilitate the transmission of ideas. Petitioning, through regular channels to middle-level officials and through the more special petition box that sent opinions directly to the lord, was a device to integrate opinions of those outside of the government hierarchy into the decision-making process of the rulers. Finally, this chapter makes evident the fact that early modern patterns of rhetoric that exalt samurai and government officials hide from history an important degree of commoner input into government and may help explain why the commoner contribution to kokueki thought has thus far gone unrecognized by scholars.

The history and historiography of petition boxes

Petition boxes were well adapted to elite bureaucratic rule, because they encouraged vertical communication and reserved the power of decision for the rulers. The most ancient reference to a petition box comes from second-century B.C. Han-period China, where one local official used a petition box to garner accusations in order to root out corruption.[7] The first imperial petition box was created in the year 686 by the Empress Wu, and this system functioned regularly thereafter at least into Sung times. In Japan, the use of a petition box by an emperor may have begun even earlier. The *Nihon shoki* records that the Emperor Kōtoku had instituted a petition box for the Japanese court in the year 646.[8] The Japanese imperial petition box later disappeared, but institutions of

---

[7] *Shih-chi*, ch. 122, pp. 3,149–50. A similar example from the second century A.D. is in *Han shu*, ch. 76, pp. 3,200–1. Thanks to Prof. Ron Egan for translating these sources for me.
[8] I owe my knowledge of the Chinese system to Prof. Denis Twitchett and also give thanks to Prof. De Min Tao who aided me in document translation. The major Chinese source is pp. 956–9 in

similar spirit were created sporadically through medieval times.[9] Sengoku period daimyo in the mid-sixteenth century, such as Imagawa Yoshimoto and Takeda Shingen, used petition boxes as well.[10]

Domainal rulers in the Tokugawa period were often conscious of these examples, both Chinese and Japanese, when they ordered the creation of petition boxes in their domains. Petition boxes were used by a large minority of domains in Tokugawa times, and their use generally increased over time. This is reflected in Table 5.1, which gives the dates for the establishment of various petition boxes in early modern Japan. The list is based upon a survey of local histories and other scattered references. The survey is necessarily incomplete, yet reveals a great spread in the dates of creation, extending from the beginning to the end of the Edo period. Yet how did these boxes really influence domainal rulers?

The petition box created by the daimyo of Okayama domain, Ikeda Mitsumasa, serves as an illustration. In response to social problems exacerbated by flooding in his domain, he created a petition box in 1654. He placed above it a placard written with a humility engaging in a feudal autocrat, "Because I, my senior officials and magistrates make proclamations which are not always for the best, we should borrow the wisdom of the whole country. Therefore, I am creating a remonstrance box (*isamebako*), and people ranging from senior officials down to the least individual may write on any topic, and submit anonymously their petitions into this box." Mitsumasa's personal diary after this time is replete with references revealing the many roles of the petition box within his government. A group of counterfeiters were nabbed thanks to the petition box, revealing that it functioned to collect secret accusations and root out corruption. Other petitions were filled with commentary on society and government, and some of these so impressed Mitsumasa that he made efforts to meet the authors. Mitsumasa also had his aide, the famous scholar Kumazawa Banzan, carry petitions around the countryside to investigate the issues the petitions raised. It is clear that, as Tanaka Seiji has argued, the petitions played a role in suggesting policies.[11]

T'ang hui yao. See Nemoto Makoto, "Tōdai no tōki ni tsuite." Also a glance at the words *ki* (character no. 2639), *kōtō* (no. 28144), *shōin* (no. 40902.1), and *bōboku* (no. 35817.31) in the Morohashi *Dai kanwa jiten* is instructive. For Emperor Kōtoku, see Inoue Mitsusada, editing translator, *Nihon shoki*, vol. 1, pp. 349, 353–5 and the valuable endnotes.

[9] Sugawara Michizane, *Ruijū kokushi*, pp. 442–3. I owe much information to an extraordinary reference work, the *Kōbunko* of Mōzume Takami. See entries for the words *meyasu*, *soshō*, and *uttae*.

[10] Ishii Susumu, Katsumata Shizuo, Ishimoda Shō, *Chūsei seiji shakai shisō, jōkan*, pp. 206, 506–7; *Kokushi daijiten*, vol. 13, p. 776.

[11] Tanaka Seiji, "Hansei kikō to kashindan"; Fujii Shun, Mizuno Kyōichirō, Taniguchi Sumio, eds. *Ikeda Mitsumasa nikki*, pp. 247, 278, 302–4, 307, 318, 327, and so forth (quotation is from p. 247); Ishii Ryōsuke, ed., *Hanpōshū*, vol. 1, pp. 652, 671; John W. Hall, "Ikeda Mitsumasa and the Bizen Flood of 1654."

Table 5.1. Petition boxes in Japan

Authority	Year of creation	Other	Authority	Year of creation	Other
Imperial court	646		Mito domain	1749	g
Imagawa Yoshimoto Sunpu	1550's		Nakatsu domain	1751	
Amagasaki domain	before 1636		Minaguchi domain	1753	
Ōgaki domain	1636		Nagoya domain	1753	c
Aizu domain	1644		Tottori domain	1758	e
Hiroshima domain	1645	a	Takamatsu domain	1759	
Okayama domain	1654		Tosa domain	1759	
Hiroshima domain	1712	b	Kii domain	1778	
Kii domain	1711–15		Kaminoyama domain	1783	
Sado magistrate	1716		Tsugaru domain	1784	
Bakufu—Edo	1721	c	Shirakawa domain	1784	
Matsumoto domain	1721–23	d	Kaga domain	1785	a
Hagi domain	1721		Aizu domain	1788	
Hikone domain	1721		Kumamoto domain	1788	
Kokura domain	1726	e	Fukuchiyama domain	1789	
Bakufu—Osaka, Kyoto	1727	c	Yonezawa domain	1791	
Tawara domain	1728		Himeji domain	1791	
Fukuoka domain	1733	a	Komono domain	1798	
Matsuyama domain	1733		Bokata village council, Hida no kuni	1804	
Uwajima domain	1734		Fukue domain	1809	
Hamamatsu domain	1735		Shimoaizuki village council, Echizen no kuni	1831	
Bakufu--Sunpu, Kōfu	1736	c	Takada domain	1838	
Osaka Inspector	1736		Amagasaki domain	1842	
Shirakawa domain	1737	a	Takatomi domain	1850	
Nanbu domain	1739	f	Bitchū Matsuyama domain	1850	
Fukuyama domain	1742		Nagoya domain	1855	h
Takada domain	1743		Imperial government	1868	
Kurume domain	1749		many *han*	1868–71	

a soon abolished

b 14 county locations, reduced to three in castle town in 1759

c not open to use by retainers, box set out only on specified days

d open only to retainers

e includes county locations as well

f permitted no legal appeals, only suggestions and opinions

g permitted anonymous petitions

h only open to retainers, to supplement system for commoners

The best studied example of the petition box is the one created by the shogun Tokugawa Yoshimune in 1721, and it provides the occasion both to discuss what historians have made of the petition box system and to explore a little more the general character of petition boxes before launching into the distinct story of Tosa. Yoshimune was the first of the shoguns to use a petition box, and as was the case with most domains, its introduction was associated with troubled times and reform. Yoshimune was daimyo of the Tokugawa branch house of Kii domain, when he was called in to be shogun after Ietsugu died heirless. The economic fortunes of the bakufu and samurai in general had been declining in the face of the rapid commercialization during the Genroku period (1688–1703), and on his arrival Yoshimune launched a series of reforms. The idea for the petition box was based on Yoshimune's earlier experience using one while daimyo of Kii domain. Tsuji Tatsuya notes that the box served to strengthen Yoshimune's hand against officials in the bakufu, something he needed because of his outsider origins and the disruptive nature of his policies. Tsuji also discusses the importance of the petition box as a means for the shogun to garner social and political commentary and policy suggestions.[12] Ishii Ryōsuke and other legal historians have argued that Yoshimune created the system to control the problem of *osso*, which were illegal direct appeals to high officials, and of *sutebumi*, which were unsigned petitions left anonymously before the gate of the high court, often containing secret accusations against officials. The petition box system legalized direct appeals to the shogun with a view to putting order and control on the activity and limiting the harm they often occasioned.[13] Sone Hiromi has noted that use of a shogunal petition box for a legal appeal (as opposed to use for social commentary) was nevertheless risky and difficult. Many formal criteria, insuring that the petitioner had tried to use proper legal channels first, had to be met for the appeal to be taken up by the shogun, and even then the case could be lost and the appellants punished.[14]

This perhaps gives an image of the petition box as serving merely the needs of the rulers. However, this one-sided view does not explain why, as we shall see clearly in the case of Tosa, there was such popular clamor for the system. Petitioners had their own uses for the petition box as well. Immediately after the shogunal box was installed in front of the bakufu high court (*hyōjōsho*), it was used by bold critics of government, such as the masterless samurai, Yamashita Kōnai, who deposited a trenchant epistle that soon became famous. His well-known petition, along with others, was copied and passed around

---

[12] *Kyōhō kaikaku no kenkyū*, pp. 119–24.
[13] Kobayakawa Kingo, *Kinsei minji soshō seido no kenkyū*, pp. 50–5; Ishii Ryōsuke, *Shogun no seikatsu sono hoka*, pp. 77–86.
[14] Sone Hiromi, "Kyōhō ki no sosho saibanken to uttae – Kyōhō ki no seiji to shakai."

throughout Japan. One graffiti wag in Edo quickly put Kōnai on a list of "Odd things" and the petition box on a list of "Things that won't last long."[15] Despite this dour prediction, the Tokugawa actually created additional shogunal petition boxes to be placed in other major shogunal cities such as Kyoto, Osaka, and Sunpu, and they all were used until the downfall of the Tokugawa in 1868. The earliest scholar of the petition box, Mikami Sanji, noted that there were social policies, such as the development of the Edo fire brigades and the creation of the shogunal hospital at Koishikawa, that find their origins in these petitions.[16] Many people used petition boxes to deliver social and political commentary to the ruler, hoping to change government, and these are usually the most fascinating documents. Kenjo Yukio has explored aspects of the political thought of peasants and rulers, through his thoughtful commentary on one petition of a peasant from present-day Gumma Prefecture.[17] Kenjo notes the tension in the peasant's use of language, where he wavers between direct statements of criticism and defense of the hierarchical structure of political authority. Perhaps this was just self-protection on the part of the sender, but perhaps the language reflected a wider ambivalence in Japan over the question of who had legitimate political knowledge.

Yoshimune's shogunal petition box was influential for other domains thereafter, but the later domains did not merely copy the shogunal example as has been contended.[18] People in Tosa, for example, were conscious of different examples. One Tosa samurai, urging that his lord create a petition box, especially noted the tradition in the histories of ancient China and Japan.[19] Mito domain permitted anonymous petitions and was likely imitating the ancient example recorded in the *Nihon shoki*. Furthermore, there is some regional clustering of dates evident in the table, such as for Shikoku in the 1730s and 1750s and Tohoku in the 1780s, suggesting that the activities of neighboring domains were in many cases more important than following the shogunal example. Most importantly, a reading of the sources upon which Table 5.1 is based reveals that the rulers were usually responding to local and regional conditions of unrest. The example of Tosa makes abundantly clear how extensively local people were involved in the creation of the petition box itself.

[15] Graffiti from "Kyōhō rakusho" in Yano Takanori, ed., *Edo jidai rakusho ruijū*, vol. 1, p. 124.
[16] *Edo jidai shi*, vol. 5, pp. 80–5.
[17] "Edo bakufu meyasubako e no ichi sojō bakumatsu ki aru rōnō no bakusei hihan."
[18] *Kokushi daijiten*, vol. 13, p. 776; Mizuki Sōtarō, *Gikai seido ron*, pp. 258–9; Kodama Kōta and Kitajima Masamoto, eds., *Monogatari han shi*, vol. 8, p. 337. A forthcoming work by Professor Ōhira Yūichi of Ritsumeikan University will discuss the results of his extensive research on petition boxes in the early modern period and this should correct many misconceptions.
[19] See, for example, the quotation from Fukuoka Zusho's petition below, where he mentions "examples in ancient Japan and China." Another Tosa individual knew of Hōjō Tokiyori's petition bell: Miyata Bunsuke (alias) (2/?/1760), *TNK*, vol. 127, ff. 72nd–82nd.

The creation of a petition box in Tosa

The lord acted to create the petition box in Tosa in response to pressure from many parts of Tosa society, high and low. Village protests in the 1750s played a direct and crucial role in stimulating anger at government officials, and bystanders placed blame for the emergence of protests squarely in the government's lap, arguing that it was not listening to its people. Such commoners' complaints caught the ears of many lower officials, some of whom then carried the ideas into government. The general accusation that government officials were not responsive had meaning for, and originated from many samurai as well. As a class, samurai were as (or more) assiduously prevented from carrying out political discussion than commoners were. Only samurai who were government officials had the reins of power, and these officials had become widely perceived as being corrupt. One samurai complained in a telling metaphor, "There is a castle built against communication."[20] Documents record that in 1759 commoners and samurai specifically requested that a petition box be created to break open this barrier.

The first step in the events directly leading to the creation of the petition box concerned domain commercial policy. After the lumber-based industries of the mountains declined, many people in the mountain villages came to produce paper as a source of livelihood.[21] The domain administrators tried to profit from the growing paper industry, and this provoked an incident with far-reaching consequences. In 1751, the government devised a plan to gain income by selling to merchants monopoly rights to purchase paper from the village producers. The monopoly meant that villagers could legally sell their paper only to their prescribed merchant. The merchant was thus able to pay very low prices and make much more money when he sold the paper on the lucrative Osaka market. In 1755, the residents of the mountain village, Tsunoyama, presented a petition to their district administrator complaining that their monopoly merchant was paying unfairly low prices for their goods. He did not respond, and the villagers determined to march on the castle town, hoping that if the domain lord knew of the injustice, he would set things right. The domain leaders sent troops to break up the protest and arrest the organizers, who were put in prison and tortured. Their leader, Nakahira Zennoshin, was arrested, but he bravely continued his protest for two years from prison. General opinion held that the merchant was in the wrong, but the domain, nevertheless, beheaded the gadfly Zennoshin on the twenty-sixth day of the seventh month in 1757 – a fateful day on which an enormous typhoon struck and ransacked Tosa. It tore roofs from

---

[20] Miyaji Haruki (8/?/1759), *TNK*, vol. 121, ff. 64th–66th.
[21] Made from the underbark of certain varieties of cultivated shrubs.

houses, flooded fields, sank ships, and severely damaged the castle, sending the proud finial tiles of the keep tower crashing down on the pavement below. One samurai exclaimed in his diary, "They say there hasn't been a wind like this for seventy years."[22]

Hirao Michio has shown that popular interpretations of the event placed responsibility for the disaster on the rulers. The government had incurred heaven's wrath by permitting injustice, said those invoking Confucian beliefs. Others felt the domain had wronged Zennoshin and thus created a vengeful spirit. Hirao notes that the storm was called *Zennoshin kaze*, or the Wind of Zennoshin. The disaster itself grew to mythic proportions in the popular memory. In the lore of later years, an earthquake and a tsunami were remembered as having occurred at the same time, an event of such unnatural coincidence that it could only signify heaven's punishment. According to another tradition, Zennoshin's severed head rose up into the storm and flew about in the winds. Finally, it was seen flying off to the castle and wrenching the finial tiles from the roof of the keep with its teeth. Yet another rumor had it that after the storm, the lord of Tosa himself created a shrine in the castle grounds to appease the avenging spirit of the wronged hero.[23]

Some of these stories are of later years, but contemporary comments also show that many people were certain that heaven was punishing a corrupt and undeserving government with disasters. Commoners in Tosa were familiar with the proverb of political wisdom that expressed the social contract implicit in the theory of heaven's mandate, "Heaven has no voice, so it speaks through the mouths of the people." Heaven's will was only expressed in the voice of the crowd. Kihei of Kuma village had something to say about the punishment and used his own variation of this proverb in his criticism sent to the lord in 1759. He wrote:

> On the day Zennoshin was executed a great disaster befell the castle town and environs. All of the people despised the evil activities of the merchant of the Country Products Office. The government is to blame for the punishment [of Zennoshin]. People say that heaven looked with contempt on the state of affairs and inflicted an incalculable financial loss on the domain. 'Heaven has no voice, and the people say that recent events make their hearts bitter.'[24]

This was written two years after the incident, and similar commentary in yet another of the petitions of 1759 indicates that the Tsunoyama episode was still

---

[22] Ms. *Nikki*, vol. 7, entry for 7/27/1757, held in the Kōchi Prefecture Library (K289/mori).

[23] Hirao Michio, *Tosa nōmin ikki shi kō*, pp. 14–23. Hirao gives the name as Zennojō, but the accepted reading is Zennoshin, as in Hirotani Kijūrō, "Tosa no gimin denshō." Anne Walthall discusses the tradition of spirit appeasement for commoner martyrs in early modern Japan in "Japanese Gimin: Peasant Martyrs in Popular Memory"; Yokoyama Toshio, *Gimin denshō no kenkyū*.

[24] Kihei, Kumamura jūnin (11/1/1759), *TNK*, vol. 122, f. 53rd.

a lively topic of discussion and reflection. The event had come to symbolize in people's minds the many injustices and corruption of domain government. The above evidence suggests that the government was losing its aura of sacredness. Heaven was on the people's side, and, as one samurai noted, using the Chinese term then current in contemporary Japanese political philosophy, the ruler was losing "heaven's mandate".[25] In a practical sense, this use of the notion of heaven freed people to think critically about government.

Disillusionment with the course of rule was widespread, and the Tsunoyama incident only symbolized – it did not in itself cause – the many frustrations that many people had with government. As seen in the petitions that have survived, many petitioners were exasperated with the collection of special levies, the presence of uneducated officials, mismanagement of corvée, the creation of monopoly privileges in commerce, and officials who used public office for private ends. Many people felt that officials were seeking only to increase their own power and authority and were not interested in listening to the complaints and concerns of common people. Indeed, the most frequent complaint in the petitions is against officials who do not listen to pleas.[26] This focus on communication is why the appearance of the petition box should claim pride of place in any history of Tosa in the 1750s.

The scholar Miyaji Haruki described the widespread frustration succinctly in a petition to the lord in 1759: "The reason your government is in such bad condition is none other than the damming up of the avenues of speech. Nothing causes the decline of government more than the obstruction of communication. The fact that many laws need correcting is an issue peripheral to your main problem: [Proper communication has been obstructed, and] government is in a terrible state." Miyaji then presented a long litany of how officials smothered suits, pleas, and ideas, turning people away repeatedly unless they brought bribes. "The people must receive [these rejections] as if they were precious lumps of gold. . . . They become quiet, as they must, but not a few become unsettled and go through life hating those above them." And then Miyaji ended ominously, "Of old it was said, 'Rebellion has roots in places where hatred collects.'"[27]

---

[25] In relation to this, see Matsumoto Sannosuke's suggestive article, "The Idea of Heaven: A Tokugawa Foundation for Natural Rights Theory." Relevant petitions are Tokuhiro Shirozaemon (10/1/1759), *TNK*, vol. 121, ff. 141st–147th; Miyaji Haruki, ibid., ff. 63rd–80th.

[26] In addition to the petitions specifically noted in the previous and following paragraphs, there are Hirabayashi Chōshin (Autumn/?/1759), *TNK*, vol. 121, ff. 61st–63rd. Matsuo Hikotarō (9/?/1759), ibid., ff. 107th–114th. Risuke of Susaki-ura (10/5/1759), ibid., ff. 147th–151st. Kitamura Gosuke (10/15/1759), *TNK*, vol. 122, ff. 1st–12th. Kihei of Kumamura (8/21/1759), SB, no. SP 6, ff. 91–120, especially the end.

[27] Miyaji Haruki (8/?/1759), *TNK*, vol. 121, ff. 64th–66th. Original rough draft now held in the Kōchi Prefecture Library, ms. *Kikō: keizai zakki, jōsho an* (K122/14/25/Miyaji).

Miyaji and others were demanding action from the lord to ensure greater responsiveness in a government where the hierarchy had ceased to provide the illusion of a link to the lord. These people included the Tsunoyama villagers who were trying to make a direct appeal to the lord by going to the castle town. The wide expression of the belief that corrupt officials were getting between the lord and the people can be seen as a spur for the creation of the petition box, which would link the lord to his people directly. The origins of the petition box in popular protest can fortunately be traced yet more clearly, although the story must begin at the top of the samurai hierarchy in the domain. In the seventh month of 1759, one of the senior administrators of the domain, Yamauchi Genzō, wrote a memorial to the lord describing the crisis in finances and the problems of corruption and disillusionment that were increasingly making it impossible for government to function. He urged the lord to institute a general government reform to save money, cut corruption, and increase morale, and specifically proposed that the lord set up a petition box in the waiting house by the main castle gate, so that all people might submit petitions directly to the lord.[28]

At Genzō's behest, the lord Toyonobu called for a reform, but he resisted the idea of the petition box. Instead, in the following month he issued a directive encouraging only retainers to submit petitions with ideas "for the lord's benefit."[29] They were to write their opinions and give them in sealed form to the chief inspector of Tosa, who would pass them on to the lord unopened. This in itself was a significant change in policy concerning political expression. Hitherto, only senior officials had held the right to directly submit writings to the lord. Suddenly, nearly 18,000 retainers – including samurai, footsoldiers, relatives, and servants involved in every menial task of government – became able to address the lord directly in writing.[30] This decision was received with great acclaim by retainers, who wrote petitions full of praise to the daimyo for "opening up the channels of communication" that had become blocked by an entrenched hierarchy. Only five of these retainer petitions from the short month before the petition box itself was created survive, but three of these recommended further increasing avenues of communication with the lord. The samurai Shibuya Kizaemon wrote, "I fear to suggest this, but you should speak directly to samurai, certainly, and even directly to the common people."[31]

---

[28] *TNK*, vol. 119, ff. 86th–87th.
[29] The order can be found in the diary of Mori Yoshisada for intercalary 7/19/1759 (ms. *Nikki*, vol. 9, Kōchi Prefecture Library [K289/mori]).
[30] Male members of a retainer family also often submitted petitions via the *metsuke* and seem thus to have held the right. The figure for all retainer family males over fifteen years of age nearest in year to 1759 for which data survives, is 18,776 for 1694 (TMK, vol. 90, ff. 83–5).
[31] Shibuya Kizaemon (intercalary 7/28/1759), *TNK*, vol. 121, f. 19th. Ikoma Sadayū (2/25/1760), *TNK*, vol. 127, f. 52nd.

Most notable among these petitions was that of a low-level retainer, Kawatani Keizan, who was a scribe and astronomer for the domain. His own grandfather had been a commoner, a village head in the port of None, and he himself had close ties to the craftsmen in Kōchi.[32] From this perspective of a scholar situated between the world of commoner and retainer, Keizan wrote a broad-ranging criticism of government, in which he proposed that the lord set up petition boxes in many convenient places, allowing even anonymous writings. These conditions differed significantly from Genzō's proposal and would have made the petition box more accessible and less intimidating to the user. Keizan closed his suggestion with the phrase: "I am only writing what I have heard the people talking about, which is that if you set up a petition box, then the conditions and feelings of the low will reach you and the people will submit [to your government]."[33] Keizan states clearly that the petition box was an issue being talked about widely among the people and implied that if the lord did not set up a petition box, the people would remain disobedient.

It is necessary here to consider how commoners and samurai in Tosa might have known about petition boxes, and how communication between the oft-segregated groups might have occurred. Only five months earlier, the neighboring domain of Takamatsu had created one. Other neighboring domains such as Matsuyama and Uwajima had been operating petition boxes for twenty-five years. Copies of the placard from the Matsuyama petition box exist in the Tosa lord's archives and in the documents of senior Tosa retainer families, as evidence of interest in neighboring systems. These examples must have been known to Tosa officials and commoners who traveled on business and played a role in Tosa's adoption of the system. Communication of opinions and ideas from commoners and samurai even to officials who might have remained within the domain could have taken many forms, most commonly from townsmen to low officials, such as Kawatani. However, other methods can be imagined. One highly placed retainer avidly recorded local graffiti in his miscellany, and the diaries of other retainers record popular forms of political expression such as street singers and graffiti, although I have found nothing relating to the petition box in Tosa.[34]

It is easy to understand why commoners and samurai would request a petition box, but why would senior officials have urged its creation as well? One reason certainly was to help defuse tension. Another memorial from Fukuoka

[32] Ms. *Osamurai chū senzōsho keizu chō (ka,wa)*, vol. 8, in the Kōchi Prefecture Library, entry for Kawatani Yoshikichi.

[33] Kawatani Teiroku (intercalary 7/20/1759), *TNK*, vol. 121, ff. 63rd–68th.

[34] The high-status retainer (a *chūrō*) Yamauchi (Maeno) Akinari recorded local political graffiti in his personal miscellany, *Yōsha zuihitsu*, in the 1810s and 1820s. Kattō Isamu, "'Yōsha zuihitsu' ni mieru Teshima jiken." Mention of a political street singer and more graffiti are found in the diary of retainer Kusunoki Ōe, *Hiuchi bukuro*, vol. 7, p. 67.

Zusho presents other useful evidence on this matter. Zusho was one of two senior councilors newly appointed to be in charge of the reform Genzō had called for. On the one hand, his memorial suggested the great pressure Zusho felt from the people of Tosa for better communication in government. On the other hand, he felt it would be a useful "tool of government," effectively reasserting the lord's position in the domain. Curiously, Zusho requested in his petition that the fact of his suggestion be forgotten.[35] Instead, he wished that the petition box would appear as if it had been the lord's inspiration. In writing this, Zusho was not fawning and cultivating the favor of the lord. He was an astute politician who realized that, if the box were widely perceived as originating from someone less than the lord, it would then be open to criticism that it might be serving selfish ends. The lord was synonymous with "public" (*kō*) and the individual least assailable of harboring "selfishness" (*shii*), the two polar concepts in the continuum of legitimacy in the political language of the day. Zusho's proposal serves as a concrete illustration of how this belief worked to cloak political activity in the rhetorical guise of lordly preeminence, and this point has relevance to the way the system is remembered and recorded in documents:

I respectfully submit that setting up a petition box is the thing that is needed at this time. It is the natural thing for government. There are examples in ancient Japan and China, and I have investigated this and submit this information in a separate report. Although no example can be found in this country [of Tosa], looking at the mood and behavior of the times the petition box seems essential. I submit that with the awe it will inspire in the people, it will naturally become a tool in governing the country. . . . [Because if the petition box is seen as originating from someone below the lord it will be criticized,] I speak these my thoughts to you in the utmost secrecy. Certainly the fact of my suggestion should be forgotten, and [the petition box] should be received as if originating from your lordship.[36]

The daimyo Toyonobu, who as we have seen, had initially hesitated, finally gave in, and on 8/16/1759, the senior administrators circulated the memorandum informing the people that the lord wished to create a petition box:

It has recently been ordered by the lord that a petition box be placed in the waiting house in front of the castle gate. People who wish to convey appeals or their thoughts and ideas directly to the lord, regardless of their status, should write them down without any reservations whatsoever, together with the date, their address and name, and seal and place the petition in the box. Ultimately it is the lord's wish to reform public morals, straighten out corruption and be informed of the feelings and conditions of the common people.[37]

---

[35] Zusho seems unaware of Kawatani's proposal and, perhaps even, of the fact that Genzō had actually proposed the box earlier in writing, although he is aware of Genzō's support of the idea.

[36] *TNK*, vol. 119, ff. 71st–72nd.

[37] Yamamoto Takeshi, *Kenshōbo*, vol. 1, p. 78.

This order made explicit the lord's wish to know his subjects and hinted at the problems of corruption and lack of communication that were afflicting government at the time, but its rhetoric was, like most public documents of the day, reticent about the agitation for more responsive government that ushered in this order. This has relevance to the way we as historians must look at the documents of the day.

The creation of the petition box was the product of specific and general demands of many people, including commoners, but these origins of the system are part of neither scholarship nor the earlier cultural memory in Tosa.[38] The elitist psychology of politics affected patterns of verbal expression in the documents of the Tokugawa period, creating an illusion of the autonomy of the ruling elite: The petition box was created by a wise and benevolent lord, Toyonobu. Years after the box's creation, in 1812, the renowned local man of letters, Emura Yasa, wrote that the petition box had been created by the daimyo Toyonobu after learning of the system from the lord of Uwajima domain via an exchange of letters.[39] A myth recounting elite origins had taken root, paralleling in its emphasis on elite paternalism the commonly propounded myth that the shogun Yoshimune had invented the petition box in 1721. The integration of the political activity of the ruled into government was not publicly recognized in much of the rhetoric of the day, because of the ideology of paternal rule. The ideology meant that a challenge to an official's greater wisdom could be viewed logically by a contemporary as a challenge to his very right to rule. This made the operation of the petition box at times a ticklish business.

The usage of the petition box

The assertiveness of people in Tosa society in the face of the social and political debacle did not stop with the inauguration of the Hōreki reforms nor with the creation of the petition box. Suggestions for better government poured into the box from all over Tosa, and much of this advice ultimately worked its way into policy. Petitioners immediately recommended improvements in the petition box system itself. The condition that the name and place of residence of the petitioner had to be written received the most criticism, and most detractors recommended (as Kawatani had initially suggested) that for people to use the

---

[38] Fukushima Ōba (Nariyuki), "Hōreki no ijin." Hirao Michio has dealt with the petitions concerning the paper monopoly in "Hōreki kokusangata shihō to nōmin." He does not describe the creation of the petition box as related to protest, but does relate how many people used the petition box to cause the end of the monopoly.

[39] Emura Yasa (2/9/1812), *TSK*, vol. 17, ff. 26th–27th. No such actual evidence exists, and the placard proclamation that Emura appends to his letter and ascribes to Uwajima domain is in reality from Matsuyama.

system free of fear, anonymous petitions had to be licensed.[40] One petitioner wrote that the lord should listen to the very logic of his own announcement:

Your lordship created the petition box because for many years the conditions and feelings of the common people have not been communicated upwards.... However, you ordered that petitioners must sign their names. The people have many things they want to say, but the conditions and feelings of the common people are exactly that they do not want to sign, for fear of troubles which may arise later. By all means, do not require people to sign their names![41]

He punctuated his point by leaving his own memorial unsigned. People heard rumors that unsigned petitions would be burnt unopened. Although the domain did not change the regulation publicly, in reality the domain seems to have tolerated anonymous submission of petitions. Proof of this is that many un-signed petitions were housed together with the others in the domain lord's archives.[42] Other petitioners criticized the fact that there was only one box for all of Tosa and suggested that boxes should be provided for more distant areas. Yet another criticism of the system was that the lord himself did not personally open the box, compromising the safety of the petitions.[43] The fact that the inspector and senior councilors handled the petitions on the way to the lord meant that the possibility of tampering existed, although I have found no direct evidence of its occurrence.[44]

Despite these criticisms of the system, people received the petition box with great acclaim and used it extensively. Petitions were submitted in large num-bers, and their contents speak of hope for better government. Now, I will discuss usage of the petition box based on the surviving transcriptions of 149 petitions from 1759–71. As has been noted, these surviving petitions are but a small fraction of the total that existed into the twentieth century.[45] Even this

---

[40] Murakami Chūji (10/15/1759), *TNK*, vol. 122, ff. 12th–38th; Tateda Kachū (11/26/1759), ibid., ff. 73rd–107th; Anonymous (?/?/1761), *TNK*, vol. 130, ff. 126th–141st.

[41] Anonymous (2/1/1760), *TNK*, vol. 127, ff. 18th–20th.

[42] Thirteen of the 149 petitions currently surviving from the period 1759 to 1770 were anonymous. The origin of this belief is that the bakufu system administrators publicly burnt anonymous petitions unopened. Kobayakawa Kingo, *Kinsei minji*, pp. 50–5.

[43] Emura Yasa (2/9/1812), *TSK*, vol. 17, ff. 26th–27th; Tateda Kachū (11/26/1759), *TNK*, vol. 122, ff. 106th–107th; Kumamura jūnin Kihei (11/1/1759), *TNK*, vol. 122, ff. 58th–59th.

[44] "Oboe" within ms. GM, no. 5499, is a memo listing the petitions in the box when it was opened, which accompanied the petitions on the way to the lord. It reveals the intermediaries, and by chance, it additionally proves that obviously spurious petitions were passed on to the lord.

[45] Eighty-seven mostly partial transcriptions of petitions also exist in the HB collection in the Kōchi City Library, nos. 42, 76, 134, 200, 211, 213, 282, 207, 208, 274–5, 362, 368, 369, 382. I have excluded these from treatment in Map 5.1 and Table 5.2, because it is difficult to determine the nature of some of these, and their selection is biased by his search for specific contents. They, nevertheless, contain many fascinating petitions that I have used elsewhere in this book for their content. Petitions for later periods survive sporadically in many collections. These total perhaps seventy more documents, but they are not a representative group as they are almost all from retainers.

limited sample, however, demonstrates that the system was used by a very broad social and geographical spectrum of males.

There is suggestive evidence that the surviving petitions can be considered a roughly representative sample. The document collection in which the transcriptions survive, the *Yamauchi-ke shiryō*, was organized chronologically around events of significance to the history of the Yamauchi family or the domain. The petitions are mostly collected in the sections directly pertaining to the creation of the petition box. Examples of section headings read, "On 8/19/1759 Toyonobu orders the creation of a petition box. The number of respondents is extraordinarily large"; or "This year too (1760) the number of commoner and samurai petitioners is very great." Thus the interest of the compilers was in representativeness, and the body of petitions themselves reveals to the reader no obvious pattern of selectivity. The primary editor and transcriber, Hirao Michio, was an extraordinary scholar of wide-ranging interests. Hardly an area of early modern domain history exists in which his eminent writings are not represented. Given his eclectic interests, the problem of his having been prejudicially selective was probably minimal.

Petitioners came from throughout Tosa, except for the distant Hata county to the far west.[46] Map 5.1 portrays the geographic origins of petitions (where known) divided by Tosa's seven counties and by port, village and castle town. The geographical trends appear to be a natural distribution, when considered in light of such factors as easy access to the petition box, literacy, and familiarity with government. Of the 132 petitions whose place of origin is known, 68 – just over half – come from the castle town. If one includes petitions from the surrounding Kōchi plain area, the number rises to 95. The remaining 37 come from more distant ports and villages, some more than a day's journey away deep in the mountains. This distribution probably arises from the following conditions: Samurai and other retainers lived primarily in the castle town area, and they were the group most likely to be literate and interested in central politics. Townsmen, too, were more likely to be literate than their rural counterparts, and the proximity of central government and officials in their daily lives probably made government seem more approachable to them than to the villagers. Similar reasons can be given for the relative preponderance of petitions from people of the ports over villager petitions.

All of the surviving petitions are from males. No petitions from women or, apparently, children are extant. (However, one samurai noted much later, in 1853, that some children once put "awful things" into the box for a prank,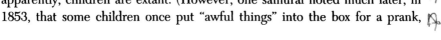

---

[46] It should be noted that one Hata county petition, transcribed in the Hirao bunko collection mentioned above (HB, no. 200, pp. 163–4), is not part of this sample.

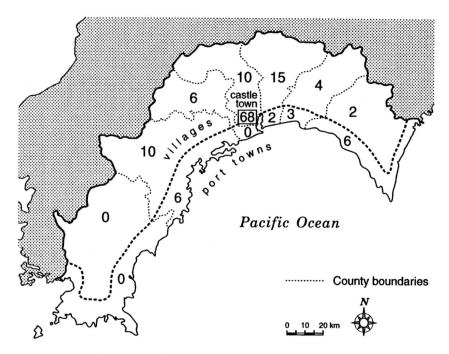

Map 5.1. Tosa domain. Number of petitions by region. See Chapter 5, note 4 for sources.

"greatly chilling your lordship's enthusiasm!"[47]) Although women and children were not expressly prohibited from using the petition box, social pressures made it likely that they rarely (if ever) submitted petitions.[48] Yet among the adult male population, the social range is quite diverse, the only obvious absence being members of the outcaste group. Petitioners included, for example, the collective household heads of a mountain village, a merchant living in a port town, a group of fishermen, a well-to-do peasant, a landless peasant, a tea merchant, a foot soldier (*ashigaru*), a domain scholar, a commoner literatus of the castle town, a scabbard craftsman, the leaders of the carpenters guild, samurai, a village doctor, a pair of former tenant farmers trying to make a go at commerce in the city. Table 5.2 plots the petitions by the social group of the petitioner.

[47] From a petition of Okunomiya Sōsai (10/?/1853), Okunomiya bunko, ms. no. 5-5, in the Kōchi City Library.
[48] I have seen an instance of a woman using the shogun's petition box. *Miharu-chō shi*, vol. 2, pp. 116–18.

Table 5.2. Petitions by status of petitioner

Status	Social group	Number
Retainer	Samurai	17
	Scholars	21
	Low official (*Yōnin, ashigaru* etc.)	12
	Rural retainer (*Gōshi*)	8
Semi-retainer	Stipended craftsmen	5
	Masterless samurai	12
Townsman	Townsmen	16
Port resident	Port merchants	6
	Fishermen or farmers	7
Villager	Village doctor	5
	Village elder or headman	3
	Villagers as a village	9
	Villagers as individuals	13
Priest	Priest	1
Anonymous		13
Unknown		1
Total		149

Source: Based on documents in Chapter 5, footnote 4

Townsmen and port merchants are well represented. They make up 16 percent of the surviving petitions of known origin, although together they comprised less than 10 percent of the population. This is, of course, related to their proximity and ease of travel to the petition box, and also to the fact that their professions made them literate. Furthermore, they tended more than villagers to request the kind of aid that only the lord could grant, arguing for domainwide policies concerned with importing and exporting, utilizing the rhetoric of kokueki thought. Such policies could only be implemented at the highest level. In contrast, village concerns expressed in petitions were more often related to taxes, corruption of headmen, and local land and water use. With the exception of transportation taxes and corvée, the geographic scope of these concerns meant that they were usually addressed to the rural magistrate – only appeals would need to go higher up.

Although villagers and non-merchant portsmen represented 80 percent of the population of Tosa, their petitions make up 27 percent of the total. Given the conditions of their immediate interests, lower literacy, and the greater inconvenience of traveling to the petition box, this percentage might be considered an impressive record of their participation. Most upper-level male villagers had village government responsibilities that made them reasonably literate, but the average villager probably could not write. No evidence exists to suggest that paid scribes were used by any of the 149 petitioners, although the fact that the petitions are in modern transcription denies us the possibility of judgment based on writing styles. Many villager petitions were corporate, where all the villagers affixed their seals to the petition, or the village representatives affixed their seals on behalf of the village collective will. Such petitions were either pleas to have their village headmen chastised for corruption, or requests for projects affecting the whole village, such as the planting of a forest or the starting of a sake brewery.[49] Their collective support was probably a main criterion for judgment, since the domain officials wanted to make sure that local peace was preserved. Collective petitioning was a tactical move related to the nature of village government and governance. When the petitions did not directly affect the life of their own village, that is, when they were personal petitions or general commentary, villagers wrote as individuals and with confidence and character.[50] One villager named Shinbei, eager to provide his thoughts on rural administration and farming lore to the lord, heard rumors about the box and went to the village elder to see the government order. The village headman had taken two months to circulate the order, perhaps fearing that some complaints might concern himself.[51]

Retainer-scholars made up a very small portion of the population of Tosa, but they figure largely in Table 5.2. True to their training in Confucian thought, they sent the daimyo many petitions advising him on how best to run government. Many felt confident of their ability to help or even to run the realm better than "uneducated officials," an epithet frequently sliding from their brushes.[52] Indeed, the visibility of scholars in the petitions occurred at a time when they were becoming prominent in domain political history. In the ensuing decades, individual scholars were chosen to fill posts of government precisely because

[49] For example, Ōtaki-mura hyakushō sōdai (9/6/1759), *TNK*, vol. 121, ff. 151st–155th; Ōtaki-mura sōbyakushō (10/6/1759), ibid., ff. 155th–158th; Hane-ura kumigashira, urabito sōdai (10/13/1759), ibid., ff. 163rd–170th, and so forth.
[50] See, for example, Chūnoshin of Ue-mura (8/30/1759), *TNK*, vol. 121, ff. 53rd–61st; and Rokurōemon of Kamiyakawa-mura (10/28/1759) SB, no. SP 8, ff. 18th–22nd.
[51] Two petitions of Shinbei of Akaoka (both dated 2/3/1760), *TNK*, vol. 127, ff. 20th–32nd.
[52] A good English language discussion of the ideological foundations for scholars acting as remonstrators in China can be found in Charles O. Hucker, "Confucianism and the Chinese Censorial System."

the lord had enjoyed their petitions. For educated samurai, the new right to petition the lord directly opened up paths of advancement and altered the nature of samurai politics. One such beneficiary was Kyūtoku Daihachi, a retainer of very low rank who, after submitting a petition the lord greatly liked, was raised to samurai status and put in charge of domain finances in 1787. Today, transcriptions of his petition can be found in many collections in Tosa, no doubt copied by retainers pondering the secrets of his remarkable elevation.[53] Petitioning was intimately related to the oft-noted phenomenon of the increasing use of middle- and low-level samurai in many domain governments during the latter half of the Edo period.[54]

The number of petitions from masterless samurai (rōnin) is also quite large. They, too, were primarily scholars who were confident of their knowledge – and furthermore in need of a position. The most flamboyant was certainly Murakami Chūji, quoted previously as informing the lord of how much his people hated him. He boasted in his petitions of having lectured in earlier days to lords in Edo and imperial aristocrats in Kyoto. At the time of his petitions, however, he was instructing children in his cottage in the rural town of Gomen. He submitted five petitions to the domain lord between 1759 and 1763. These unreservedly criticized the many failings of government policy and officials and gave suggestions for improvement.

Chūji wanted the chance to be personally in charge of setting things straight in the domain, noting that if the lord wished to employ Chūji's talents he should make him a junior administrator and grant him a fief worth 1,000 *koku*, or perhaps even a head of government with a fief worth 3,000 koku. He disclaimed interest in wealth and status, but noted those things would be necessary to gain respect so that he might effectively carry out his job, and concluded blithely, "After 10 years I will have put government back in order. Then I would like you to grant me leave, so that I may move to Edo and Kyoto and strive to return Japanese studies (*wagaku*), Japanese poetry (*waka*) and Japanese prose (*wabun*) back to their pristine, ancient form." Despite his boast of great governmental talents, he confided to the lord that his real desire was to simply continue private studies, concluding with painful grandiloquence, "If you do not hire me, I will consider you merciful to me, but I have not the kind of unfaithful heart that would think of my own selfish interests while gazing upon

---

[53] Early modern ms. copies can be found in GM, no. 7968, Mori-ke monjo (unclassified), the Taoka bunko (K253/10) (these latter two in the Kōchi Prefecture Library), and Chikamori bunko no. 0542 (Kōchi City Library).

[54] Saigō Takamori is a famous example of a menial retainer being lifted from obscurity because the lord admired his petition. Chuck Yates, *Saigo Takamori*, p. 28; Inoue Kiyoshi, *Saigō Takamori, jōkan*, p. 42.

your possible benefit."[55] Perhaps the lord revealed his renowned benevolence to Chūji, who was never offered the chance to rescue the domain. Although Chūji submitted at least one petition later in 1763, he then left Tosa for employment in Okayama domain.[56] In his later years, he indeed taught poetry in Edo and Kyoto and published a number of literary commentaries, showing that some of his boasts were not empty.[57]

Nonscholarly retainers, high and low, are also well represented in the surviving petitions.[58] The comments of many samurai, the top 10 percent of all retainers, show that they were primarily interested in issues of how well people performed duty to the lord, the state of public morality, and whether or not the lord's benevolence was being actually expressed to the people. Their proposals thus focused on corruption, proper education, and choosing men of talent for government office. Others merely had bones to pick concerning the behavior of individual samurai, writing lists of names followed by their failings. On the other hand, many of the low-level retainers, such as *yōnin* (a low-level administrative status) and ashigaru, were in posts involving the day-to-day implementation of government policy and often had proposals for policies to improve the actual workings of government. A number of these people were of merchant family origins (status at this low level was quite fluid), and all were in frequent contact with townsmen and commoners. The way some of these low retainers thought and expressed themselves was more similar to that of townsmen than that of the senior samurai retainers.

Finally, anonymous petitions merit special comment because they highlight the nagging issue of how freely people could express themselves. Thirteen petitions without name currently survive. Some may have been wrapped in envelopes with signatures and dates that have since been lost and so were not originally anonymous, but many of the petitions were deliberately

[55] Murakami Oribe (1/1/1761), *TNK*, vol. 130, ff. 1st–10th. The first quotation is from f. 10th. In the same volume are found a second petition submitted at the same time as the above, "to be read only if your lordship wishes to hire me" and signed "Sannin Minamoto Kagemo," ff. 11th–18th, and another undated one signed Murakami Chūji, ff. 26th–52nd. Two others are one dated 10/15/1759 in *TNK*, vol. 122, ff. 12th–38th, and one dated 7/26/1763 signed Murakami Chūji in *TNK*, vol. 139, ff. 72nd–74th.
[56] Yamamoto Takeshi, *Kōchi-ken no rekishi*, p. 126.
[57] Kōchi-ken Jinmei Jiten Henshū Iinkai, *Kōchi-ken jinmei jiten*. His works are listed in the author index volume of the *Kokusho sōmokuroku*, p. 887.
[58] Retainers actually had two possible routes for submitting their petitions: They could either submit them directly via the chief inspector or use the petition box. There is clear evidence that retainers used both routes, but in many cases the route is not known. Because both systems began within a month of each other, because both had the same purpose and function, and because both routes ultimately passed through the hands of the inspector, they are treated together in Map 5.1 and Table 5.2. For convenience, I sometimes refer to this group as all being submitted through the petition box. All *rōnin* and commoner petitions would by necessity have utilized the petition box.

anonymous.[59] One petitioner signed the alias "Miyata Bunsuke" (Bunsuke means "the writer's helper") on the envelope because he was afraid that if his petition had no signature, it would be burned before the lord saw it. He would not sign his petition, he stated, because he was afraid of punishment. This is surprising because his petition was neither more nor less critical of government than many of the signed petitions and, in fact, serves as a good illustration of the type of comments found in a typical nonscholarly petition.

Bunsuke's petition contained the following suggestions and comments: The retainers in Edo did too much cavorting in brothels and this represented a great drain on Tosa's gold and silver bullion; commoners should be allowed to use parasols in the castle town [where it was a sign of samurai status]; foreigners [i.e. non-Tosa people] should not be required to pay the fee at ferry crossings because "It is a shame for the country" [presumably because they should be treated as guests]; the number of laws had proliferated too much; the lord should not hunt on designated days of prayer; the petition box was wonderful because it kept corrupt officials fearful; and the number of dogs in the castle town should be limited, because they made it dangerous for women and children to walk the streets at day, and for men to walk the streets at night.[60]

The criticisms and suggestions in this anonymous petition were similar to many signed petitions and apparently not worth the fear of punishment. Refusal to sign, however, reflected the fear and distrust engendered by a general pattern of suppression of political discourse in Tokugawa society. People could be punished severely for daring to comment on government away from the petition box. Some petitioners who signed their memorials wrote that they did so with trepidation and often took great pains to emphasize that they had discussed their ideas with no one, not even family members. Such comments were presumably to spare friends and family from possible punishment, or they might have functioned to reassure the lord that the individuals were not fomenting political discussion. Some anonymous petitions spat venomous accusations at specific officials, and to protect themselves from reprisals, their authors chose to keep their names hidden. The petition box itself was thus not absolutely safe to use, although it was by far the safest method of engaged political expression available. As we have seen, the shogun's petition box had many

---

[59] For example, one petition appears without a name in the *TNK* version and, from its contents, appears to be from a village doctor or rural samurai. However, it is copied in SB, no. SP 5, preceded by what is apparently a copy of the writing on the envelope "Amaeda mura Konagawa Shōhaku." There is indeed a lineage of village doctors named Konagawa later given official status as doctor by the domain; third lineage in ms. *Ishi nenpu*, in the Kōchi Prefecture Library (K288–44). It is conceivable that some of the thirteen "anonymous" petitions were also simply ones in which only the covering envelope was signed. The novelty of the petition box system led to a great variety of document formats, because nobody knew the "correct" form.

[60] Miyata Bunsuke (alias) (2/?/1760), *TNK*, vol. 127, ff. 72nd–82nd.

stipulations for use, which if not adhered to, left the petitioner open to punishment. Some domains, such as Takamatsu domain, had similar stipulations, whereas others, such as Matsuyama domain, made a point of promising no punishment. Tosa was vague on the matter, giving no indication either way. Because of the ambiguity, perhaps, the bolder petitioners were extremely blunt, whereas the more timid wrote indirect criticisms or concealed their identities.

There was reason for fear; the petition box certainly disturbed some officials in Tosa, who disliked receiving criticism from commoners. The villager Kihei submitted a very critical petition in 1763 touching on the domain's policy of selling the tax rights on land to merchants, forcing loans from the populace, methods of annual tax payment, and many more issues in detail. In 1765, a junior administrator, Kawada Matasuke, reviewing the petition at the request of the lord, wrote a scathing response that, ignoring most of the arguments, made a great point of Kihei's daring to criticize government despite his humble birth:

This base Kihei . . . says he is of the lower vulgar orders, and thus his crime in criticizing your government is no small thing. . . . He writes, 'It is a terrible pity that it is easier for a commoner to look up, than for the elite to look below.' This is the utmost in insolence! He is terribly criminal to make light of his superiors in writing this way. If we let him be, the officials in your service will not be able to carry out your work. He is a criminal against the government, and I would like you to order that he be thoroughly investigated.[61]

This document makes clear that the way some commoners used the petition box was threatening to the traditional beliefs of some samurai – and highly placed ones – and that to be too critical could be quite dangerous. Documentary limitations prevent us from knowing whether or not an investigation was approved or carried out.

Punishment for criticism in the petitions did exist, but was likely very rare. The above petition that sparked the official's ire was Kihei's fourth and not his most virulent. Other critics were permitted long careers of petitioning as well, probably because, given the public mood, the lord had more to lose by punishing petitioners than by ignoring them. Also their criticisms may have seemed as reasonable then as most of them do today. Some petitioners in Tosa recommended to the lord that he never punish any petitioner for what was written, noting that if he did so, the common people would stop informing him of their true feelings and desires, which was, after all, the main purpose of the petition box.[62] In general, it seems people were given great freedom in the petitions. In

[61] SB, no. SP 7, ff. 27th–50th.
[62] Fukutomi Hanjō (12/?/1785), *TCK*, vol. 44, f. 4th of section entitled "Kono tsuki rusuikumi Fukutomi Hanjō . . .''; Anonymous (?/?/[1761]), *TNK*, vol. 130, f. 130th.

only one case is it known that a petitioner was punished for what he wrote. A yōnin was shown to the border and banished from Tosa in 1809 for something he wrote – the contents are unknown – and submitted through the petition box. The punishment was light in that it did not extend to his family, and his son remained in domain employ at the Tosa mansion in Edo, the city where the man came to live. Tragically, the son died a few years later, and the father was occasionally seen haunting the gravestone, upon which he had inscribed his own name as well.[63]

Another case is especially interesting because it reveals a public space of political discussion that could be communicated to the lord by the accumulation of a number of individual petitions. In 1759, the representatives of the Tosa carpenters' guild wrote that the members of the guild would continue to work inefficiently on official domain projects, and skip work to do better paying jobs when they were available, until they received fair pay. Their petition was in effect declaring a form of craftsmen's strike against the domain. In response, they were punished (the nature is unclear) by the domain. The punishment made support for the carpenters' cause potentially dangerous. Despite this judgment, four petitions were submitted from noncarpenters who voiced support for the carpenters' side.[64] A village doctor, Tateda Kachū, pointed out the immorality of the domain policy and its actions toward the carpenters:

Samurai and commoners pay carpenters in cash as is ordered by government. Carpenters thus work energetically because they are able to make a living. The government itself, however, pays carpenters in rice [at a poor exchange rate and with delays]. . . . Recently this has put the carpenters in financial distress and they petitioned you. Your lordship did not accept their appeal and instead punished them. If they had not been in financial hardship and made an appeal, then it would indeed have been insubordinate, but I think to punish people who petition because of unbearable poverty is not kingly government.[65]

These petitions in support of the guild suggest that people communicated with each other even on politically dangerous topics. The structure of a one-way communication route from individuals to the lord facilitated by the petition box was consistent with the strategy of political atomization embodied in prohibitions of political discussion. Yet in reality, by permitting individual petitions

---

[63] From the diary of a contemporary, Kusunoki Ōe, *Hiuchi bukuro*, vol. 1, p. 33, and vol. 3, p. 75.

[64] The carpenters' petition (9/16/1759) is in *TNK*, vol. 121, ff. 116th–120th; Murakami Chūji (10/15/1759), *TNK*, vol. 122, ff. 31st–32nd; Tateda Kachū (11/26/1759), ibid., f. 102nd; "Nōfu" (8/?/1761) SB, no. SP 5, ff. 50th–51st; Umi Rampei (this month/this day/1761), *TNK*, vol. 130, ff. 125th–126th. This last one might possibly be an alias, because the name is so odd and neither the date nor home village nor town is given. It argues diverse problems seemingly from the standpoint of a man of a port town near the mouth of Kōchi bay.

[65] Tateda Kachū, *Gomen-machi ni sumioru ishi* (11/26/1759), *TNK*, vol. 122, ff. 102nd–103rd.

discussing common themes to accumulate before the lord, the petition box created a new route with which to convey the important topics of public discussion. Furthermore, there were petitions authored by two or more people, as well as petitions representing corporate interests such as those from the carpenter, village, and fishermen organizations.[66]

The following examples of common topics from these thirteen years illustrate the kind of political issues that were under public discussion. The domain should restrict its use of transportation corvée because it harms the villages (eight petitions).[67] The rulers should stop granting merchants monopoly privileges and abolish the Country Products Office (*kokusan yakusho*) (eleven petitions).[68] The lavish life of the lord's concubine, Ni-no-maru, should be restrained because it hurts the people (four petitions).[69] Special tax levies harm the populace and consequently the domain itself, and should be reduced or abolished (nine petitions).[70] The lord should pursue policies to more actively support education and learning, especially amongst officials (twelve petitions).[71]

[66] Okada Heisuke and Shinoda Monbei (7/27/1760), *TNK*, vol. 127, ff. 95th–98th; Yosōemon (tea merchant) and Heijō (smithy) (10/6/1760), ibid., ff. 102nd–103rd; Nasu Ben'emon and Norōyama Yogenji (4/26/1763), *TNK*, vol. 139, ff. 33rd–35th.

[67] Chūnoshin of Ue-mura (8/30/1759), *TNK*, vol. 121, ff. 53rd–61st; Murakami Chūji (10/15/1759), *TNK*, vol. 122, ff. 12th–38th; Kihei of Kuma-mura (11/1/1759), ibid., ff. 52nd–73rd; Kubozoe Chūnoshin a rural samurai (1763/7/13), *TNK*, vol. 139, ff. 67th–72nd; Kidenji of Momikiyama-mura (8/12/1763), ibid., ff. 74th–78th; Kihei of Ikku-mura (8/22/1763), ibid., ff. 78th–88th; Ichirobei, Umeya of Tōri ward (1/?/1764), *TNK*, vol. 144, ff. 15th–17th; Johei of Nijūdai ward (11/29/1765), *TNK*, vol. 148, ff. 97th–101st.

[68] Hirao Michio has dealt excellently with petitions concerning this issue in "Hōreki kokusangata shihō to nōmin." The eleven petitions I have noted are: Kaemon, Izumiya of Tanezaki ward (8/25/1759), *TNK*, vol. 121, ff. 41st–48th; Zenpachi, scabbard maker of Sakai ward (9/3/1759), ibid., ff. 96th–106th; Tokuhiro Shirozaemon, of Kami ward yonchōme (10/1/1759), ibid., ff. 141st–147th; Murakami Chūji, rōnin teacher of Gomen town (10/15/1759), *TNK*, vol. 122, ff. 12th–38th; Tateda Kachū, doctor of Gomen town (11/26/1759), ibid., ff. 73rd–107th; Nakayama Sazō, ibid., ff. 135th–148th; Murakami Chūji (1/1/1761) and (?/?/1761), *TNK*, vol. 130, ff. 1st–10th, ff. 26th–52nd; anonymous (2/13/[1762]), *TNK*, vol. 135, ff. 68th–71st; Tokuhiro Ichizaemon and Hamasaki Magodaiyū, Nōchi-mura *gōshi* (8/23/1759), SB, no. SP 6, ff. 120th–131st; Kichibei, Mizutōrimachi Komiya (10/13/1759), SB, no. SP 5, ff. 103rd–106th.

[69] Miyaji Haruki (samurai scholar) (8/?/1759), *TNK*, vol. 121, ff. 76th–77th; Kihei (villager) (11/1/1759), *TNK*, vol. 122, ff. 53rd–54th; Nakahira Heizaemon (younger brother of a rural samurai from the mountain village of Yusuhara) (10/21/1761), vol. 130, ff. 66th–68th; same person (5/4/1765), vol. 148, ff. 78th–79th. Yoshimoto Toichi is noted as having criticized Ni-no-maru in a petition no longer surviving (*TNK*, vol. 123, entry for 9/27). Also note in text below the mention in Mori Yoshisada's diary of another such petition.

[70] Andō Yazenta (8/13/1759), *TNK*, vol. 121, ff. 30th–32nd; Kitamura Gōsuke (10/15/1759) and undated, *TNK*, vol. 122, ff. 1st–12th and 148th–168th; Murakami Chūji (?/?/1761), *TNK*, vol. 130, ff. 26th–52nd; Ueki Kōsai (12/26/1761), ibid., ff. 95th–120th; Umazume Giemon (2/28/1762), *TNK*, vol. 135, ff. 73rd–97th; Asada Jūrōemon (6/?/1763), *TNK*, vol. 139, ff. 43rd–57th; Nakahira Heikaku (1765/5/4), *TNK*, vol. 148, ff. 57th–93rd; Johei, of Nijūdai ward (11/29/1765), ibid., ff. 97th–101st. Kitamura Gosuke (11/15/1759), SB, no. SP 8, ff. 30th–36th.

[71] Andō Yazenta (8/13/1759), *TNK*, vol. 121, ff. 32nd–33rd; Anonymous (9/?/1759), ibid., ff. 33rd–38th; Matsuo Hikotarō (9/?/1759), ibid., ff. 107th–114th; Tokuhiro Shirozaemon (10/1/1759), ibid., ff. 141st–147th; Kihei of Kuma-mura (11/1/1759), *TNK*, vol. 122, ff. 59th–73rd; Horiba

Many of these, and other, suggestions affected a wide range of policy in the ensuing couple of years, from structural issues of the management of commerce and taxes to symbolic issues of dress codes. It cannot be merely coincidence that so many of the following changes in policy occurred soon after the submission of proposals in the form of petitions. A very important issue of economic policy was the abolition in 1763 of monopoly commerce, the system that had led to the Tsunoyama disaster. Numerous petitions denounced this system on economic grounds as harming the "prosperity of the country," or on moral grounds as theft by the lord of the people's rightful profit, and only two petitions were in support, one of these written by a merchant with privileges under the system.[72]

Also of great importance to government and education was the institution of the domain school, Kōjukan, which opened in the first month of 1761. This, too, followed a great number of petitions encouraging domain sponsorship of education and denouncing the uneducated state of officials.[73] Kihei of Kuma village suggested on 8/21/1759 that the lord send a tour of inspection around the domain. On the first day of the tenth month, such an order was given.[74] Domain officials reformed the unpopular transportation corvée system after receiving many complaints. The prolific Kihei thanked the lord for this improvement in his next petition.[75] The importation of raw and spun cotton was prohibited in an attempt to foster local production. At first, twelve merchants were given a privilege, and then in response to further petitioning free local trade was permitted.[76] Another petition argued that if the domain opened up the lord's highway over the mountains to the north to freer use by commoners for pilgrimages, more money would flow into Tosa. This highway was opened up to commoners on 8/27/1763, with the stated purpose of increasing commerce.[77] The exclusive privilege of samurai to wear parasol hats in the castle town

Shōzaemon (11/28/1759), ibid., ff. 107th–120th; anonymous (2/1/1760), *TNK*, vol. 127, ff. 18th–20th; Minami Ihei (12/?/1760), ibid., ff. 103rd–105th; Murakami Chūji (?/?/1761), *TNK*, vol. 130, ff. 26th–52nd; Ueki Kōsai (12/26/1761), ibid., ff. 95th–120th; Umazume Giemon (2/28/1762), *TNK*, vol. 135, ff. 73rd–97th; Kataoka Chūjirō (3/30/1765), *TNK*, vol. 148, ff. 22–57th.
[72] The petitions against are cited above in footnote 68. The two in support are Konagawa Shōhaku (2/28/1760) in SB, no. SP 5, ff. 3rd–17th, and Gihei, Kurei-ura sanbutsu tonya (9/2/1759) in SB, no. SP 5, ff. 92nd–102nd.
[73] Tokuhiro Shirozaemon (10/1/1759), *TNK*, vol. 121, f. 145th, specifically demands the creation of a school. Other petitions on education are cited above in footnote 71. *Kōchi-ken shi, kinsei hen*, pp. 505–6.
[74] Kihei of Kuma-mura (8/21/1759), SB, no. SP 6, ff. 82nd–120th.
[75] Petitions are cited above in footnote 67. The reform can be found mentioned in the petition of Kihei (8/22/1763), *TNK*, vol. 139, ff. 78th–79th.
[76] Ms. *Hitsuya-ke monjo*, in the Kōchi City Library, HB, no. 244, p. 49. Relevant petitions are Kan'emon, Shin'ichimachi Chōjiya (8/27/1759), *TNK*, vol. 121, ff. 48th–49th, and one anonymous petition in opposition, (2/13/[1762]), *TNK*, vol. 135, ff. 71st–73rd.
[77] Zenpachi, son of scabbard maker Heizaemon of Shinyōhōji ward (9/3/1759), *TNK*, vol. 121, ff. 96th–106th. The order for opening up the highway can be found in Mutō Yoshikazu, comp., *Nanroshi*, vol. 7, p. 229.

became an oddly significant topic of resentment, probably expressing deeper frustration with the inequities of the class system. Commentary in the petition of the person who used the alias "Miyata Bunsuke" has already been noted, and another petitioner warned that "it is not a sign of benevolent government to have your people roast under the hot sun." Quite early in 1760 permission was granted to commoners to use parasol hats in the castle town like samurai.[78] In addition to these examples from the realm of policy, the petition box functioned to uncover crimes. The villages of Hane-ura and Notomo were both able to rid themselves of corrupt village headmen by placing accusations in the petition box.[79]

The mechanism by which petitions affected policy was that they fostered discussion within the government structure. Surviving office memoranda show that petitions were copied and passed around within the administration for review and comment.[80] Copies of over thirty petitions survive in the collection of the Gotō family, who supplied many of the senior administrators of Tosa domain.[81] The office diary of the junior administrator Mori Yoshiki in 1798 records his comments on the petition of a retainer concerning the domain's commercial policies for soy sauce, cotton, paper, currency, and irrigation system repairs.[82] Records also reveal that many petitioners received recognition for their comments through an official message of praise from the lord.[83] The petitions even worked their way into the education of the lords of Tosa. In the

---

[78] The petitions are Tokuhiro Shirozaemon (a townsman scholar, sometime low official) (10/1/1759), *TNK*, vol. 121, f. 144th; Tateda Kachū (a village doctor) (11/26/1759), *TNK*, vol. 122, ff. 78th–79th, 104th–105th; Miyata Bunsuke (alias) (2/?/1760), *TNK*, vol. 127, ff. 74th–75th. The decree is in Yamamoto, et al., eds., *Kenshōbo*, vol. 1, p. 80.

[79] These incidents are introduced by Takahashi Shirō on p. 6 of "Kitagawa-gō sōdō to Sukumō ryōmin ikki." The original source is the unclassified and untitled diary in the keeping of the Kōchi Prefecture Library and referred to as "Fukushima Heitabei nikki." The Notomo village suit (12/21/1759) still survives in *TNK*, vol. 122, ff. 126th–132nd. The Hane village suit does not survive. This article also introduces the petition box suit of Kitagawa-gō villagers: a suit against their headman, which they lost.

[80] I have seen five memoranda from the senior administrators concerning the passing around of petitions. One is on f. 74th of *TCK*, vol. 53. One 1769 petition on paper currency together with commentary by officials is in HB, no. 208, pp. 123–8. The other three are GM, nos. 6179–12, 6174–16, and 6204–14. Many more memoranda are sure to exist in the GM collection but I have not had the time to do a full survey.

[81] GM, nos. 5189, 5192, 5197, and 7966–8000.

[82] Mori Kanzaemon Yoshiki, ms. *Sansei nichiroku*, vol. 1, entry for 9/6/1798, the Kōchi Prefecture Library; see also 9/14/1798.

[83] Nakahira Heizaemon's petition (10/21/1761) notes the praise he received for an earlier petition, *TNK*, vol. 130, ff. 52nd–83rd; Fukutomi Hanjō received similar praise in 1785, *TCK*, vol. 44, on f. 11th of section entitled "Kono tsuki rusuikumi Fukutomi Hanjō . . ." The *Seyō nikki*, apparently written by a merchant-cum-gōshi named Fukushima Heitabei of Tanoura port, mentions many people receiving praise, ms. held in the Kōchi Prefecture Library (K212/40/Taoka), vol. 1, f. 30. One of those mentioned in this document, Yoshimoto Toichi, is noted in a domain document as having received praise in late 1759 from the lord, *TNK*, vol. 123, entry for 9/27.

1830s some of the copy books of the young lord-to-be, Toyoteru, contain his transcriptions of petitions of retainers, and he himself composed an essay on the importance of keeping open the "paths of communication."[84] Many collections of local retainers also have copies of petitions written by non-Tosa people to the shogun of Japan, revealing that reviewing other people's petitions was a means of staying on top of the broader political world of Japan and played a role in spreading political ideas throughout the islands.[85]

We can imagine how important this new means of political activity was to people at that time by peering into three months of the personal diary of the samurai Mori Hirosada. Only days after the lord called for retainer petitions in 1759, Hirosada's friend, Kitamura Gosuke, visited to discuss submitting a petition he had written seventeen years earlier, but which he had been unable to have sent up the ladder of hierarchy, a fact he resented. Almost a month later, Gosuke, another samurai, and some lower non-samurai retainers were called to the government office concerning their petitions, all of which had recommended the circulation of paper currency within the domain and had prompted discussion among the senior council. The councilors had decided to consider issuing such currency from the second month of the following year. Gosuke had a short-lived moment of vindication. Two days later, he and the other retainers were again called to the residence of a senior councilor, where they were told that the lord himself had ordered the plan for using paper currency be scrapped: This was because Tosa had had a particularly bad experience with paper currency in the 1690s. Although this instance ended in unsuccess and reminds us of the ultimate authority of the daimyo, it reveals how the petitions had fostered debate within government.

Hirosada's younger brother Nōemon submitted a petition to the lord on 8/17. Two weeks later, Hirosada, as family head, was called to the house of the senior councilor in formal dress. There he received written praise for the petition from the lord to pass on to his brother. Two weeks after that, the rural retainer Kichimoto Toichirō was raised to the status of attendant (*koshō*) "because he had written a petition critical of the lord's concubine and other things." On 10/10 the senior councilors called Morio Hikotarō and Adachi Mohei to receive official commendation for their petitions. On 11/27 Hirosada himself and other samurai unit leaders gathered to discuss economic poverty among retainers and jointly composed a petition asking for aid to the senior domain officials. One of the senior officials was shown this petition "unofficially," and he responded that they should not submit the petition at this time because there was nothing the

---

[84] Ms. *Kōseshi ogakusoku* (ya 150/28), *Hocho taii* (ya 150/61), and *Suigyō* (ya 150/29) in Yamauchi bunko collection in the Kōchi Prefecture Library.
[85] GM, no. 7967; and a document in the Kōchi Prefecture Library, (K250/26/Miyaji).

domain could afford to do. They were called the next day, however, and told that the domain would consider making loans available to retainers in financial distress.[86]

These examples come from a mere three months of a single samurai's diary and reveal in a succession of events how the right of direct petition directly affected policy discussion and preferment. They reveal the extensive participation of samurai in the system and illustrate how acts of petitioning functioned to encourage political communication between individuals, influencing their lives. The examples here show that Hirosada was directly involved only in the last instance, but he knew about the contents of, or was even consulted about, many others. The petition box increased the extent of political discussion within the domain.

Commoners played a broader role in the political processes of early modern Japan than the elitist rhetoric of most documents of the day reveals. The Tosa populace played active roles in protesting a bad governmental situation and in the creation of the petition box system. Thereafter, a broad social range of men in Tosa used the system to make legal appeals, denounce corrupt officials, propose new policies, and criticize current institutions and social conditions, leading to many changes in Tosa. Officials made use of many petitions, accepting advice from commoners despite their consciousness of superiority. Lower samurai were the best positioned to benefit personally. They found that the petition box opened up new possibilities of advancement. The rise of government by scholars that is seen toward the end of the eighteenth century in Tosa may very well be related to their ability to directly appeal to the lord after the year 1759.

Petitioning in all forms was a major means of integrating the interests of the ruled and the rulers. It facilitated the incorporation of new policies and ideas into the administration of government, despite the fact that government was controlled largely by a hereditary samurai elite. It provided government with a means of adaptation and thus served to maintain the legitimacy of samurai rule over centuries of change. Petitioning gave those out of political power access to the ears of the rulers and a legitimate avenue of political expression. Allowing people to petition with suggestions for government was by no means a symptom of democratic ideology. However, as has been noted, a limited amount of political discussion was encouraged inadvertently by the petitioning process.

The increasing use of petition boxes throughout Japan in the late Edo period does suggest an intensifying search for new ideas.[87] The context of domainal

---

[86] Ms. *Nikki* (K289/mori) in the Kōchi Prefecture Library, vol. 9, year 1759, intercalary 7/21, 8/17, 8/21, 8/24, 9/4, 9/8, 9/27, 10/10, 11/27, 11/28, 12/7.
[87] Hirakawa Arata, "Chiiki keizai."

crisis inspired some officials to be more receptive to new ideas expressed in petitions. Kokueki thought was at this time more firmly embedded in the rhetoric of townspeople and others involved in commerce than in the petitions of samurai of this era. Over time, petitioners would succeed in inserting a merchant-defined kokueki into samurai discourse. The next chapter will look at the kokueki thought expressed in the petitions and consider how it was finally adopted by the samurai.

6

Imagined economies: Merchants and samurai

In the year of the rabbit [1759] you ordered that all people high and low should submit petitions with ideas to benefit the prosperity of the country.
Ichirōbei, head of the merchant house Umeya in Tōri-machi, first month 1764

[I have seen your order] deigning to open up the paths of speech to all below, to give whatever thoughts they might have for your benefit.
Matsuo Hikotarō, [upper samurai], ninth month 1759[1]

The petitions of the petition box are a rare window into the political and economic thought of many types of people in Tosa. These petitions reveal that merchants and not samurai were the primary force behind the spread and development of *kokueki* thought, and that kokueki thought emerged earlier than previously has been thought. A second agenda of this chapter is to argue that kokueki was gradually adopted by the samurai rulers because it allowed them to justify limiting their devotion to the "economy of service," articulate reasons for supporting commercial enterprise, and thereby strengthen the foundation of their rule in the face of the changes and crisis that the economy of service engendered. My purpose in this and the next chapter is to reveal the diverse class interests that led to the origins and spread of kokueki thought, and to link these to the specific historical context of the mid-eighteenth-century domainal crisis as defined in the previous chapters.

The research to date that deals with the origins of kokueki thought is that of Fujita, who states that kokueki thought was created in the Hōreki/Meiwa period (1751–71) by domain financial bureaucrats. The earliest examples of kokueki he provides are the 1755 writing (which has the logic of kokueki, if not the term) of the samurai doctor, Tatebe Seian, and the 1765 petition (which contains the first apearance of the term) of Hayashi Shihei written to the lord of Sendai domain. However, most of his research discusses kokueki thought and related

---

[1] Ichirōbei, Tōri-machi Umeya, (1/?/1764), SB, no. SP 2, ff. 33rd–35th; Matsuo Hikotarō, (9/?/1759), *TNK*, vol. 121, ff. 107th–114th.

policy in the nineteenth century. Research by other scholars, such as Amano Masatoshi, that deals with kokueki thought provides no earlier examples than Fujita's and also focuses on the period after the 1780s.[2] This research gives – rightly, I think – the impression that the nineteenth century was the heyday of the use of the rhetoric of kokueki in domains. It also shows convincingly that from the last quarter of the eighteenth century, the rhetoric and thought of kokueki were being understood and utilized by samurai officials in many domains. However, the assumption that it was therefore created, or primarily spread, by these officials at that time is not correct.

My argument is based on temporal primacy (although, as will be noted below, this issue is complicated by the earliest survival of the term "kokueki" in some Tosa samurai-generated documents) and on consideration of the differing class cultures of samurai and merchants. These documents reveal that merchants, by whom I mean not only townsmen (*chōnin*) but also port merchants and other people significantly engaged in commerce, had already explored a wide range of ideas through the rhetoric of kokueki thought. The term kokueki appears commonly in the petitions of townsmen, even in the earliest petitions of the year 1759, playing a key role in an extensively developed rhetoric imagining a commercial economy for the domainal country of Tosa within a Japan of many countries. Using the rhetoric of kokueki, they argue variously for import protections, development of exports and import substitutes, the creation of a transportation and marketing infrastructure outside of the domain, the ecouragement of tourism, and even free trade economics, in short all of the basic elements of kokueki thought as defined by Fujita, and then some. This is in contrast to the petitions of samurai, who use the word "kokueki" less often and, when they do use it, primarily associate it with issues of loyalty to the lord, education of officials and cutting corruption issues more directly related to a domainal economy of service. When samurai stress the bullionist aspects of kokueki thought, it is usually in terms of the prohibition or limitation of "luxuries" that waste precious money and corrupt morals. It is as if they used a popular term as a new container for old Confucian wine. The economic vision of the samurai was conditioned by their essential dependence upon their lord's household. The difference between the samurai and merchants can also be seen as a contest of governmental values. As one anonymous samurai angrily exclaimed in a petition to the lord, "If you rule only with silver, you might as well give up the whole country to townsmen!"[3]

---

[2] Fujita, *Kinsei keizai*, pp. 35–9; Amano Masatoshi, *Awa ai keizaishi kenkyū* and "Kishū-han bakumatsuki no keizai shisō."

[3] *TNK*, vol. 121, ff. 33rd–38th. The content of this anonymous document makes it clear that the author is a samurai.

Because these petitions come either from, or just before, the period identified by Fujita as the beginnings of the development of kokueki thought in Japan, a few conclusions may be reached. First, merchants were much more "in tune" than samurai with kokueki thought and its intellectual and ideological possibilities. Second, the early date of these documents, in or before the period suggested by Fujita as originary, makes it unlikely that the merchants of Tosa were adopting kokueki thought from bureaucrats outside of the domain. Third, the highly developed nature of the kokueki thought of the merchants and the widespread usage of the term suggest earlier origins than the 1750s. Finally, comparison with proclamations issued by domain administrators in the 1820s reveals that, by that time, the samurai were expounding a form of kokueki thought similar to the kokueki of the merchants back in the 1750s. The merchants' kokueki had already become adopted and adapted as a part of the ideology of the Tosa state.

The aspect of my argument based on temporal primacy is complicated by the survival of two samurai-generated documents that use the term kokueki decades earlier than the petition box petitions, and in a manner justifying domainal involvement in the development of local industries. The earliest known use of the word anywhere is in a 1728 document associated with an early abortive attempt to develop sugar production in the domain. Hamaguchi Jinzaemon, the headman of Niida village, grew sugar cane and tried to manufacture sugar in the 1720s. When the *bakufu* inspector and herbalist Uemura Saheiji toured Tosa in 1728 he asked about this, and Jinzaemon said that he had purchased the shoots from Satsuma. Tosa officials said that the Country Products Office had received some shoots from merchants in Osaka and, because "it was a product which would in time be for the kokueki, the officials ordered the headman of Niida to plant the cane." The word kokueki is clearly associated here with export development, but whether it meant "government profit" or "prosperity of the country" cannot be fully surmised from the context. A separate document records that when another Tosa farmer asked to be shown how to make sugar from Hamaguchi, domain officials refused to show him the "secret manufacturing methods." This seems to imply that kokueki meant "government profit." The whole project soon ended in failure.[4] The next significant appearance is in a document of 1742, relating to the closing down of a domain-supported project to manufacture iron, an incident that I will discuss in detail below.[5]

---

[4] Hirota Kōichi, "Tosa-han kansho", p. 58; Hirao, *Tosa-han kōgyō*, pp. 142–3.
[5] *TNK*, vol. 69, ff. 28th–29th. The only other pre-1750s usage of the term I have found is in the 1739 memorandum of a junior administrator who argues that if the chief officials are sincere about reform, this will be copied by lesser officials and work for the *kokueki*, *TNK*, vol. 53, ff. 17th–18th.

Use of the term is, nevertheless, rare in pre-1759 samurai documents. In contrast to samurai-generated documents, merchant petitions from this period do not survive in any significant numbers, and therefore no direct comparison can be made. Furthermore, as argued in the previous chapter, the rhetorical patterns of samurai-created documents tend to obliterate commoner identity and action. By chance, enough documents relating to the iron production effort of the 1730s survive to suggest that an iron merchant was the source of the kokueki rhetoric justifying the project. My argument that merchants' petitions to domain officials were the likely source of the rhetoric and focus on the country's commercial economy rather than on the lord and government is most clearly evidenced in the surviving petition box petitions, which have miraculously survived and give us a fair basis for comparison of the thought of commoners and samurai in the early stage of the development of kokueki thought.

Samurai and merchants spoke decidedly different versions of "kokueki" in the 1750s. A number of samurai used the word kokueki, although to a lesser extent than merchants, but when they did, it was to argue that dutiful service to the lord and moral behavior were the root of the prosperity of Tosa. Judging from samurai documents alone, the thought associated with the term kokueki had not, by the 1750s, acquired consistent mercantilist and economic-nationalist assumptions. Merchants writing in the 1750s, however, filled their documents with kokueki, and gave mercantilist arguments containing the assumption of a "national" economy. Only a few samurai, generally of a peripheral status ineligible for office, argued policies in a similar fashion. It seems clear Tosa government officials and samurai were just beginning to adopt kokueki thought from commoners during this era.

The **kokueki** *of the merchants*

Kokueki was a word of Japanese origin, having no counterpart in Chinese.[6] During the 1750s when this new word was coming into popular use in Tosa, it was used most commonly by townsmen and people from the ports: a fact that, in itself, suggests that they were its natural reservoir. More than any other class in Tosa, they were reminded in their daily experience of the intangible fact of "country." When they exported or imported, they paid taxes for no other reason than crossing an invisible border. They were forbidden to deal in certain goods across borders. It was, for example, illegal to export rice or horses and illegal to import rice, sake, or many luxury items. Regional capital and many goods were scarce because the lord appropriated and exported so much to pay for expenses

---

[6] *Kokushi daijiten*, vol. 5, p. 616, Fujita's entry on kokueki.

outside of the domain. Local finance markets became constricted and domain merchants became bound by financial ties to rich Osaka merchants. Many of these merchants with new projects asked for help from the domain government, enticing it to cooperate with appeals to the benefit of the realm's economy.

One of the first petitions to be submitted to the petition box illustrates a merchant's use of kokueki thought. This case also permits an exploration of how the thought then became transmitted to domain administrators, because related documents survive. The petition was from Kaemon, the head of the merchant house of Izumiya in Kōchi.[7] It was a petition that gave many suggestions for economic policies, ranging from freeing the paper market of privileged merchant control to the creation of a special Tosa Products wholesaler in Osaka. Among his many points, Kaemon argued that the domain should revive the attempt it had made at bog iron production several years previously that was canceled midway. This topic was dear to his heart, because he had been the merchant in charge of the project in the 1740s.

The argument for domain support was cast in terms of "prosperity of the country." He noted that the domain had canceled the project because the cost of moving the production facility away from its test site to an area rich in forest (for charcoal) was too high for the *kokusangata* (Country Products Office). He argued that the iron produced at the test site was considered to be of high quality by local smiths and by the wholesale merchants in Osaka. If only the domain had continued support of production, it would have been making profits by the time of his petition. He closed that section of his petition with a bullionist argument in support of the project:

This country is [on] an island and more than most places imports a great amount of iron from other countries. If you ordered the local production of iron, the silver used to import iron would not leave our country for others. Furthermore, if the iron were exported to Osaka, then the silver of other countries would flow into the country and be an extraordinary source of the prosperity of the country.

Even if for example the government lost a little money in the process, the production of a treasure inside the country from dirt and sand would forever work for the prosperity of the country. An old man like me thinks it so regrettable to see such a thing just thrown away that I am petitioning.

If you appointed a chief wholesaler for the products of our country in Osaka, in the manner of the lord of Satsuma, it would be a great benefit to the prosperity of the country. I placed a petition at the Country Products Office in the third month of 1753 and have twice since then made follow-up appeals but received no response. Therefore I presented a petition to the town government on 7/28.[8]

---

[7] Kaemon, Tanezaki-chō Izumiya (8/25/1759), *TNK*, vol. 121, ff. 41st–48th. Kaemon's petition is quoted fully in Hirao, *Tosa-han kōgyo*, pp. 56–8.

[8] *TNK*, vol. 121, ff. 46th–47th.

Kaemon's petition contains many aspects of kokueki thought. The bullionist logic of the argument is meaningful to Kaemon because he saw Tosa as a single economic unit whose economic health was dependent on the state of the export/import trade. His focus on "country" rather than "lord" is also evident in that he tendered the possibility that the domain should work for "the prosperity of the country" even if it meant a little loss of money to domain finances. Kaemon indeed implied that working for the "prosperity of the country" by supporting commercial and industrial projects would in the long run improve domain finances, but it reflects a shift from an emphasis upon the lord's benefit (*otame*) to the welfare of the commercial country.

As it happens, one of the earliest uses of the word kokueki is in the 1743 document of a junior administrator, who argued in a memorandum to the lord that domain-sponsored iron production would work for the "prosperity of the country" in time, but was presently costing the administration money, and that during a domain fiscal stringency drive (*shōryaku*) this was unacceptable.[9] The argument that the production had the potential to work for the national prosperity in time shows that kokueki had been the ideological justification for the project, although now outweighed by other concerns. When the domain began its iron production project in 1741 Kaemon was appointed the merchant representative. A probable scenario of why the domain used this justification is that, in the 1730s, Kaemon had petitioned the Country Products Office to support iron production with the phrasing of kokueki. One could argue the converse, that Kaemon had learned the rhetoric of kokueki from a domain official involved in the project. Hirao Michio credits the domain finance official of the time, Baba Yagoroku, with initiating the project.[10] But there is evidence suggesting that this is unlikely.

This evidence survives in a document written by Baba Yagoroku himself. Baba was an official very supportive of many mining projects in Tosa. When he retired in 1743, just as the iron production project was being cancelled, he wrote a long account of his work and the reasons why he thought that mining was so important.[11] This cogent and often eloquent argument never once used the term kokueki and was very lord-centered in its rhetoric. Yagoroku defined the benefits of the mines as a new source of wealth for the lord to replace the declining income from the depleted forests of his domain. Yagoroku may have been the originator of the project as Hirao notes, but he was certainly not the originator of its justification in terms of kokueki. Government officials such as

---

[9] Ibid., vol. 69, ff. 28–29th. "Kokueki" may refer here to domain government profit rather than the more general prosperity of Tosa. The context makes it difficult to decide.
[10] Hirao, *Tosa-han kōgyō*, pp. 15–21.
[11] Found in Mutō Yoshikazu, *Nanroshi*, vol. 4, pp. 35–51.

Yagoroku were at this time wrestling with an extremely bad financial situation, which made them reluctant to give financial support to projects but susceptible to arguments of profit. It is more likely that Yagoroku did not originate the project (this ascription may be merely due to patterns of Edo period rhetoric that ascribe origins to elites), but rather enthusiastically supported a project initiated by Kaemon. As is clear from remarks in Kaemon's 1759 petition, he repeatedly petitioned his ideas despite a cool reception. Kaemon was a persistent and political man. He had given this petition to the Country Products Office once and, after getting no response, submitted it twice again. After receiving no response even then, he submitted it to the city government, which also failed to answer him. He then wrote a petition directly to the lord. He was, in short, a man very interested in getting his ideas across to government.[12]

Yōemon of Tei port was an indigo merchant who, like Kaemon, used arguments concerning the economic prosperity of the domainal country to appeal for government legal support for his own project. Yoemon's petition began by calculating that four or five shiploads of indigo were imported from Awa domain (the famed producer of this product) into Tosa a year, representing an outflow of 25 *kan* of silver annually. He then noted that he had earlier employed some indigo producers from Awa domain to teach him the method of production. Because Awa domain did not allow its specialists to teach the production techniques to foreigners, he had to arrange for their departure from Awa through a long stay at Osaka before they could make their way to Tosa. After producing the indigo, he nevertheless had difficulty selling it in competition with the reputation of the imported Awa product. He requested that the domain order explicit support for his project to teach many people the means to produce indigo and grant him a privileged sales region in eastern Tosa. Then the native production of indigo would increase. Yōemon capped this argument with the phrase, "If our needs are produced within the country it will continually work for the prosperity of the country."[13]

Yōemon cast the argument of his petition in a fashion similar to that of Kaemon: not in terms of "the lord's benefit," as Baba Yagoroku had done, nor in traditional terms of maintaining his job (indeed, he was traditionally an indigo importer and wanted to change this role). He justified his request for government aid by identifying his project with the "prosperity of the country." Large domains had three forms of support they could effectively offer merchants: financing,

---

[12] Although Tosa merchants were not able to be active in the realm of published economic tracts, there is a similarity between the petitions and the economic tracts in early modern England analyzed by Joyce Appleby in *Economic Thought and Ideology in Seventeenth Century England*, a work to which I owe some inspiration.

[13] Yōemon, Tei-ura (11/22/1759), SB, no. SP 6, ff. 73rd–79th.

organization, and legal authority (especially control of the border).[14] Middling merchants such as Kaemon and Yōemon felt they could gain something by asking for these things. Kaemon requested financing and organizational support, and Yōemon's request was for legal support to protect his fledgling industry and restrict imports. Under kokueki thought, such forms of support were described as tools to help organize and improve the economy in general.

Whether the users of the rhetoric sincerely believed that their projects were for the benefit of the domainal country is not a crucial issue. What is important is that they thought arguments based on appeals to kokueki would be persuasive and seem reasonable. The issue of self-interest is important. The fact that kokueki thought could be used to argue for the self-interest of such merchants and, at the same time, appear to many as a convincing understanding of economic relations is what gives it ideological importance. Reading between the lines of the petition of Kaemon the iron merchant, it is clear that he was short of capital. Having the domain support the project would not only have provided him with financing, but would have given him government authority and the ability to use its facilities on the Osaka market. While arguing for the interest of the country, he was clearly arguing for his self-interest as well. The potential to argue that their activity was of a public nature which was denied them in Confucian economic thought and for the common good made kokueki suitable as an ideology of the merchants.

Kokueki thought was of course not always used for self-interested manipulation. It became a way of understanding the world for the people who used it. Like Kaemon, Yōemon argued in his petition for other projects unrelated to his personal interest in terms of prosperity of the country. For example, he noted that if the domain encouraged the planting of linseed in unused land in Tosa it "would continually work for the prosperity of the country." He even extended the discussion to wild wax berries, which he argued Tosa peasants were allowing to fall and rot instead of collecting and exporting to Osaka. Other merchants and townsmen were also writing petitions with suggestions supported by the logic of kokueki thought, and often these suggestions had nothing to do with personal profit. This breadth of application of its concepts indicates that kokueki thought was gaining wide acceptance among such commoners as a view of economic relations.

The scabbard maker Zenpachi's petition gives another example of how this thought was not merely a means of arguing self-interest, but was a convincing

---

[14] The issue of financing by an "impoverished" domain is complex. The checkered history of domain support for iron production reveals that the domain might have managed to gather enough support for a project in the hopes of future returns. One problem of the period before the 1790s was domain inconsistency.

way of understanding the economy and the lord's and people's roles within it.[15] Not one of Zenpachi's ten suggestions had personal economic interest at stake, yet most were inspired in whole or in part by bullionist concerns and phrased in terms of kokueki. He argued that all domain commercial monopolies should be abolished because they discouraged production and, ultimately, exports. All merchants should be allowed to deal in whatever products they wished and be allowed to export freely, whereupon they should pay taxes on this commerce. In addition, he noted that free commerce would save the lord many policing costs. Zenpachi also urged the lord to promote religious tourism to Tosa's famous Godaisan temple by making entry into the country easy for foreigners at the temple's festival time. If this were done and the pilgrims increased, "every year great amounts of foreign gold and silver would drop into the country, working eternally for the prosperity of the country and providing all of the people with a living."

It is not inevitable that a scabbard maker should be so concerned with, as he says, "thinking of ways in which to have foreign money drop into Tosa," or that an indigo importer should work so hard to have it produced locally or care whether Tosa people should be aware of the export value of certain wild tree seeds. What was common to these and many other petitions was a vision of Tosa as a single economic unit, the welfare of which was dependent mainly upon commercial concerns – most often export industries – and cash flow within the domain. Their vision of government was that it should work to protect and develop industry within an international market.

Just a few of the other projects argued by merchants and townspeople in terms of benefit to the kokueki should be mentioned: Risuke of Susaki port encouraged silk production, and the planting of new forests.[16] Suga Sōzaemon, chief domain smith, hedged his bets using both traditional and newer rhetoric, arguing that if the domain did not give smiths more support, this would not only make it difficult for them to maintain their time-honored jobs, but would also be bad for the kokueki.[17] Kihei of Aki port argued that the construction of a large harbor at Aki would increase trade and the prosperity of Tosa, and that there-fore all boats of Tosa could reasonably be taxed to finance the project.[18] Jihei, an elderly palanquin bearer and lover of arithmetic scaled to the size of Tosa, wrote a petition calculating that 2,160,000 *kin* of tobacco was smoked in the country annually and reasoned that this was bad because tobacco was not food and its

---

[15] Zenpachi, Shinyōhōji chō sayashi Heizaemon no segare (9/3/1759), *TNK*, vol. 121, ff. 96th–106th.

[16] Risuke, Susaki–ura (10/5/1759), *TNK*, vol. 121, ff. 147th–151st.

[17] Suga Sōzaemon (3/19/1760), *TNK*, vol. 127, ff. 85th–89th.

[18] Kihei, Aki-ura Higashi hama (9/24/1759), *TNK*, vol. 121, ff. 124th–126th.

production deprived Tosa of 7,200 *koku* of rice production. He then noted, rather inconsistently, that if cotton were produced on this tobacco land, this would work for the kokueki. Jihei then rationalized that if every smoker in Tosa purchased a tobacco pipe and pouch annually, this meant 251 kan of silver going out of the country to the Osaka area for "unprofitable items." He therefore urged the domain to prohibit all people currently under the age of fifteen from ever taking up tobacco smoking, fining those who did and using the money to develop new farmland that would "be for your lordship's benefit and ever work for the prosperity of the country."[19] Umeya Ichibei urged that the domain place no taxes at all on domainal exports to encourage production and sales but that the domain should conversely place high tariffs on imports of luxury items.[20] The merchant Hirōya Magohei urged the domain to promote the export products of the mountain regions such as tea, as "this would enhance livelihoods of people in the mountain regions and work for the prosperity of the country." Magohei records a persistence in petitioning activity equal to that of Izumiya Kaemon, writing, "I am fifty-six years old, and for thirty years I have thought of ideas to benefit the prosperity of the country and petitioned with plans repeatedly over the years. However your lordship has not utilized any of my foolish thoughts. Certainly, I have never requested anything out of personal desire."[21] These suggestions range from development of anything commercial to dividing economic goods into traditional categories of useful plain goods and wasteful luxurious goods, yet are all within the economic sphere and closely tied to the import/export market. Their very volume reinforced the view that the purpose of government was to protect and foster industry within an "international" market.

Although many merchants and townsmen utilized similar kokueki arguments to support their suggestions, this did not mean that they agreed on all specific proposals. There was, in general, a tendency to stress protection of local industries against imports and some advocated outright import prohibitions to protect local industries. Others, however, used kokueki thought to argue for a free market. The scabbard maker Zenpachi, for example, argued that the prohibition of imports of soy sauce was not very productive. He noted that foreign merchants who brought soy sauce to Tosa always filled their boats with Tosa tea to take back to sell in their home countries. The prohibition on imports thus hurt Tosa exports. He wrote that prohibitions on imports were bad because they lead to highly priced products of poor quality, such as was currently the case with local soy sauce. His argument was based on kokueki but not upon the

---

[19] Jihei, furukagohiki (9/23/1759), HB, no. 282, pp. 50–4.
[20] Umeya Ichihei, Tōri-machi (1/?/1764), *TNK*, vol. 144, ff. 15th–17th.
[21] Magohei, Shinmachi toshiyori Hirōya (intercalary 9/24/1767), *TNK*, vol. 154, ff. 82–84th.

simple bullionism expressed by many of his contemporaries, "Merchants who go buy soy sauce or iron in Bizen load the tea of our country to sell there when they arrive. Because commerce is made up of such reciprocal interchange, [imports] do not necessarily mean a loss to the prosperity of the country."[22] One anonymous petitioner (internal evidence suggests a townsman) cited the same prohibition as the wrong way to go about encouraging local production of soy sauce itself.[23] He wished to see soy sauce produced locally, but with the prohibition, the local producers could get away with making a bad product "in which larvae thrive and which spoils." He argued that the lord should allow free imports of Bizen soy sauce, because currently the Tosa merchant with the monopoly was able to produce a bad product at a high price. Free trade would encourage him to make a good product at a competitive price. The petioner wrote, "In an example from former years, both vinegar and noodles were imported from other areas, but both items of good quality came to be produced locally at a price cheaper than the imports. Naturally the imports declined and enough of these products are produced locally." His postscript shows that his standpoint was that of a small retailer or a consumer. One can sense between the lines that probably the local soy sauce producer did not use small retailers. "If you order things as I have described all small shop owners, peddlers, and those who purchase soy sauce . . . will be happy and grateful." The domain did not respond to this petition, no doubt because the monopoly merchant was a great contributor of *goyōgin*, or special monetary levy, to the domain.[24] Seventeen years later, in 1787, the actions of a peddler against the privileged soy sauce merchant sparked the worst castle town riot in domain history.

The arguments of the merchants and townsmen are very readable to a person today. Their arguments seem understandable and relatively familiar because, ideologically, they were budding economic nationals, but this does not mean that they seemed so reasonable to all their contemporaries. Reading the petitions of the samurai puts the contemporary distinctiveness of the townsmen's and merchants' kokueki thought in relief.

The samurai economy of service

This year is the 150th anniversary of the death of [the first lord] Katsutoyo. If you order rites in honor of this in the Edo compound and in this country, making sure that the ceremonies are carried out, that all retainers mourn properly and visit the grave site with

---

[22] Zenpachi, Shinyōhōji-chō sayashi (1759/9/3) *TNK*, vol. 121, f. 104th.

[23] Anonymous (5/23/(1760)), *TNK*, vol. 127, ff. 92nd–94th.

[24] Mutō Yoshikazu, comp., *Nanroshi*, vol. 7, pp. 257, 260, 263–4, finds the soy sauce producers Tatsumiya and Toraya as the two top contributors of *goyōgin*.

faithful hearts, then our country will naturally become wealthy and prosperous and your wives and descendants will flourish![25]

These lines from the petition of the samurai Nagahama Seizaemon at first glance strike the modern reader as strange or even perhaps illogical, but his thought was meaningful to a large body of people, and he was arguing his economic interests and vision as effectively as the merchants were arguing theirs. The key to unravelling the meaning of Seizaemon's thought and to gaining an understanding of kokueki thought is understanding the assumptions that their proponents held. Neither kokueki nor Seizaemon's thought was meaningful without a body of supporting assumptions.

In arguing kokueki thought, the merchants were making assumptions that an increase in the flow of money into certain sectors of the realm would in turn encourage buying, lending, and investment to ultimately benefit all involved in commercial activity and themselves. Furthermore they were assuming that most people were involved in commerce significantly enough to be affected and convinced by this argument. The import/export issue was integrated into a body of behavior that they had in the back of their mind. Without these assumptions backing him up, Yōemon's argument that the export of gathered wild wax tree seeds would work for the prosperity of Tosa also seems rather ludicrous.

Nagahama Seizaemon made a number of assumptions common to most of his fellow samurai. He probably expected that the worship would serve as a reminder to all of the great debt they owed the lord, that they would then repent their selfish ways and work with greater effort and diligence for the Yamauchi house. Most samurai knew that peculation of tax funds weighed heavily on domain finances. Bad finances in turn led to more extraordinary tax impositions, which in turn led to more corruption. Corruption seemed to feed on itself and was a serious problem affecting finances, the economy, and ultimately the social bonds of government. Bad examples by officials bred bad behavior in all. Good examples by superiors bred good behavior. If people could be made a little more self-sacrificing for the lord, then that energy would accumulate for the benefit of all and ultimately "naturally" help the economy. If people were reminded of the fact that they owed everything to the lord, they would become spiritually renewed, sincerity would flourish, and honesty would prevail. Under the conditions of such a moral revival, how could the economy and finances not improve?

Such a view made sense to the samurai, no doubt in part because they were fully dependent upon their lord. Not only were their fiefs and stipends received

---

[25] Nagahama Seizaemon (9/15/1759), *TNK*, vol. 121, ff. 114th–116th.

directly from the lord, but they were prohibited from gaining other forms of income.[26] Furthermore, their life was imbued with rituals repeatedly emphasizing this dependence on the person of the lord and their obligation to him for all they possessed. The ultimate expression of this dependence was the fact that if their lord were attaindered by the shogun, all of the retainers lost their incomes, posts, and even residences. Conversely, lords were often attaindered for problems they did not create themselves, but for problems created by retainers, such as domainal mismanagement or retainer factional fighting (*oie sōdō*). This gave lords and officials in high position reason constantly to reaffirm and reinculcate the samurai's sense of obedience and duty. The feeling of limitless debt to the lord, made service (*hōkō, goyō*, or *yaku*) hold a strong moral valence, and the performance of service not merely an honor but a public activity.

Unlike many petitions from samurai, commoners' petitions frequently made a clear demarcation of the interests of the lord and the people (or the country). An example of this is the petition of the scabbard maker Zenpachi, who gave a petition of ten articles to the lord with the postscript, "Of the ten, one is for your benefit, seven are for the benefit of the people and two concern things which harm the people."[27] In kokueki thought the people and the country were often synonymous terms. Arising from this was the suggestion that the prosperity of the country could be an end in itself and was not necessarily the result of working for the lord. The direct emphasis the merchants had on country was quite different from the direct emphasis on the lord evinced by many samurai. This difference in emphasis had implications for the policies each group conceived and suggested. Because of the centrality of the lord, samurai tended to link the prosperity of the lord and the people, tending to make the lord's prosperity be seen as the source of the people's prosperity. Sacrifice for the lord was, in a sense, sacrifice for all. Within the discourse of kokueki thought, the same kind of conceptual merging of the interests of the economic country and the people existed. The potential for a conflict of interests between this abstract country and the people was obscured. The country was primary, and the prosperity of the people and even that of the lord tended to flow from that. The country's prosperity was defined in terms of the state of commercial and industrial activity, and kokueki thought served ideologically the interests of people situated to benefit from this realm of activity.

To turn once again to Seizaemon and the samurai, most samurai envisioned an economy of service that centered on the lord. This highly influenced their

---

[26] Along this line of thinking, it is tempting to believe that one reason why *gōshi* rural samurai in Tosa were so insubordinate in the *bakumatsu* period was because they were not economically dependent upon the lord.

[27] Zenpachi, Shinyōhōji-chō sayashi (1759/9/3), *TNK*, vol. 121, f. 104th.

interpretations of kokueki, making economic well-being arise out of devotion to the lord. Shibuya Kizaemon wrote in 1759 that, "If the lord places greatest care on issues of public morals and people's hearts, it would be the most important thing affecting the prosperity of the country. . . . If people had pure hearts then costs of 100 kan would drop to 70 or 80 kan. Averaged out over the whole country, this would be an enormous savings and work eternally for the prosperity of the country." The country that existed in Kizaemon's imagination consisted of samurai officials instead of merchants or consumers.[28] The petition of Mabuchi Sagorō also argued, with typically samurai usage of the term kokueki, that if the lord continually urged people to reform their ways, "in time people's hearts will reform and this will work ever after for the prosperity of the country."[29] The rural samurai Kubozoe Chūnoshin argued a more pure vision of economic service when he wrote, "At a time when all know your lord's finances are in distress, if you order a half of all rural samurai income given up in *kariage* . . . they will still be able to provide you with full military service."[30] Another rural samurai, Hamada Seisaku, suggested that the lord take all retainer fief income for three years and provide retainers with a mere subsistence stipend, and he added that rural samurai should receive no stipend as they could fend for themselves, "except, of course, in the event of fire or other calamity when we would request your munificent benefaction."[31]

Although limitless service and the importance of frugal ways were an influential ideal, this kind of morality seemed hard to come by for many samurai in the mid-eighteenth century. Shibuya Kizaemon lamented that he thought retainers and the people did not have the spiritual stamina of "the great people of days of old." The great peace that Ieyasu had provided had weakened their character. Therefore, even when the lord declared fiscal stringency measures and moral reform, all too soon people reverted to their old selfish ways.[32] "Though you may order that all live frugally as in former days, because of this weakness of spirit it is unlikely to take hold. Your lordship's economizing becomes ineffective and therefore the lower people become impoverished as well. This time if you pay most attention to improving public morals it will do more than anything else can for the prosperity of the country" (f. 16th). Similarly, Mabuchi Sagorō noted his worry over corruption and its effect on the realm: "If you order someone with skill in finances to give a severe accounting and if people's hearts and

[28] Shibuya Kizaemon (intercalary 7/28/1759), TNK, vol. 121, ff. 15th–21st.
[29] Mabuchi Sagorō (intercalary 7/28/1759), TNK, vol. 121, ff. 21st–25th.
[30] Kubozoe Chūnoshin, Ikku-mura (7/26/1763), TNK, vol. 139, f. 71st.
[31] Hamada Seisaku, Ueda-mura gōshi (9/2/1759), TNK, vol. 121, ff. 95th–96th.
[32] Shibuya Kizaemon (intercalary 7/28/1759), TNK, vol. 121, ff. 16th–21st.

public morals gradually improve toward the way of Good, then this would work eternally for the prosperity of the country."[33]

These latter two quotations from samurai used the term kokueki, but in a context quite different from the townsmen's petitions. Samurai considered the root of prosperity to be moral behavior and service to the lord. For Sagorō and Kizaemon, the main problem of the era was one of morality. They thought that poor finances and an unstable economy were caused by people tending to live indulgently, selfishly, and with little serious sense of duty to the lord. One despondent samurai wrote, "The fact that you do not see people following your order and example shows how much in these times people are not honest about morals."[34] Many encouraged policing and strict accounting to root out corruption and luxury. In the context of decline of morals, however, this had its limitations. Shibuya unwittingly revealed the bankruptcy of his thought when he, in effect, encouraged the lord to order the people to be more sincere about following his orders.

This emphasis on service and frugality made samurai not so much opposed to commerce as not deeply reliant on it. No samurai argued that commerce as such was a bad thing, but many emphasized that without the guiding force of morality all the wealth in the world would not rule a country. Andō Yazenta elaborated this view of wealth at the head of his petition to the lord:

I think that practicing virtue and restricting one's needs are the two foundations of government. When there is not enough wealth to fill the needs in a country, then the government will not keep the people in peace. All people are disturbed to hear that your heart has been troubled by financial impoverishment for many years. However wealth is at the periphery and virtue is at the center (of government). If the center is upright then the periphery should naturally become well off. Even if for example the country were brimming with wealth and treasure, if the way of governing virtuously and restricting needs were not clear, that wealth would instead become the source of extravagance and disastrously ruin moral customs. No matter how poor in wealth one might be, practice virtue and the country will be safe and secure.[35]

Morality was essential to rule, and samurai were the guardians of the country's morality. Merchants and other commoners could only be moral in nonpolitical ways. For them, moral behavior was to carry out their jobs to gain a living sufficient to raise a family and to obey the rules of filial piety. Merchants contributed to immorality when they gave money to government or became officially recognized by the lord. One anonymous petitioner, clearly a samurai, argued that wealthy merchants were getting better treatment from the lord than faithful samurai. Merchants, he argued, were immoral because they had no

---

[33] Mabuchi Sagorō (intercalary 7/28/1759), *TNK*, vol. 121, ff. 21st–25th.
[34] Nagao Kurozaemon (8/11/1759), *TNK*, vol. 121, ff. 25th–30th.
[35] (8/13/1759), *TNK*, vol. 121, ff. 30th–33rd.

sense of duty. He criticized the lord on this point for the lord's lack of support of the moral value of selfless duty and wrote, "If you rule only with silver, you might as well give up the whole country to townsmen!"[36] A *rōnin*, Tanaka Gisuke, saw the merchants as fine, but fit them squarely into the economy of service, writing, "Merchants do not mix with warfare, flood and fire, but think daily of profit and cutting costs. They live in comfort with food, clothing and housing and store up money. When the country has a large expense, they contribute money to the lord. This is the way of the merchant."[37]

As a result, samurai interest in the economic potential of commerce and commercially inspired industry was mixed. For example, many samurai were clearly attracted to the idea of bullionism, but used it to argue points of frugality rather than productive expansion. Many argued that imports of "luxuries" should be forbidden, because they led to an outflow of gold and silver to pay for morally corrupting vanities. Nakayama Sazō felt that the idea and projects for developing new products in the domain were nothing but a plot of greedy officials deceiving the lord and harming the people.[38] In contrast, Hara Takazaemon liked the idea of products development, but wanted to place a 25 percent tax on them to be used to pay off samurai loans and create a cash reserve for domain duty to the bakufu.[39] He saw new products as fulfilling the same place in the economy of service as rice production.

Among people of samurai status, the most attuned to issues of trade and the economy were peripheral types such as rōnin and younger brothers. Unbound to the lord economically or by the rituals of life, they reveal greater diversity of thought. Yet their petitions also reveal the influence of their class identity. Kataoka Chūshirō was the younger brother of a samurai household head. He argued that the lord should order all samurai men and women to wear nothing but cotton, so they would not order luxurious clothes from Osaka. This would prevent the "wasteful" outflow of bullion from the country and bring prosperity so that all samurai would have money prepared for a sudden order for bakufu duty, he said.[40] Although Chūshiro had the same bullionist understanding of the economy as Kaemon and Yōemon the merchants, his samurai biases are evident in his focus on members of his class, his describing the major benefit of the savings as being better prepared for bakufu duty, and his emphasis on cutting luxurious consumption rather than on developing new exports. An unenfeoffed son of a samurai, Teshima Jungo, had a greater sensitivity to the economic

[36] Anonymous (9/?/1759), *TNK*, vol. 121, f. 36th.
[37] Tanaka Gisuke (11/1/1759), SB, no. SP 6, ff. 80th–90th, quotation from f. 85th.
[38] Nakayama Sazō (12/?/1759), *TNK*, vol. 122, ff. 135th–148th.
[39] Hara Takazaemon (12/15/1759), *TNK*, vol. 122, ff. 120th–126th.
[40] Kataoka Chūshirō (3/30/1765), *TNK*, vol. 148, ff. 22nd–57th.

needs of the populace in general. Although he did not use the concept of kokueki, his petition reflected a strong sense of the importance of exports to the livelihood of the people of Tosa. He argued, on the one hand, that samurai should be encouraged in ways of frugality and military training, whereas on the other, that the domain should end its commercial monopolies and in general permit free trade and an unregulated lifestyle to commoners who would prosper best by this policy. He also believed in the benefits of free trade to both merchants and consumers. Yet, the publicly important end of this pro-commerce policy was that rich merchants would arise who could give the lord money when called for duty. Jungo's market-oriented thinking did not ascribe a public value to commerce, but was guided by the notion of the economy of service. He noted that commercial monopolies meant that:

> products of the country decline and people within the country become poorer. It means fighting for profit with the people, and is not a means of raising and nourishing the people. . . . If you collected a small tax on major items of export and allowed all other items to be traded freely with other countries, then our country would flourish, and merchants of talent would become rich. Wealthy people who could be of great service to you would emerge, who would have no difficulty in serving at unexpected calls for duty, and I think it would thus even be for the benefit of your lordship. . . .
> Item. You have granted a monopoly of the production of soy sauce to one person, Tatsumiya Somebody, and prohibited the importation of soy sauce from Bizen. This is said to be for the benefit of the country by preventing bullion from leaving to other countries, but I think this is not good for the people of the country. The notion of preventing bullion from flowing to other countries is just armchair theorizing. There are good reasons for sending bullion out. Money is something which if you do not move, does not increase. If you allowed free flow of cash, then merchants of talent would become very rich. Because you prohibit the import of Bizen soy sauce, the merchant boats of Urado and Tanezaki which go to Bizen [to sell Tosa goods] have no goods to carry back.[41]

Like other samurai, Jungo relied heavily on the neo-Confucian conception of the moral behavior of the lord. He thought of the populace as being under

---

[41] The contents of Teshima Jungo's petition, which was submitted on 12/3/1759, unfortunately survive only in part. According to Hirao Michio, who copied sections into one of his notebooks (HB, no. 207, pp. 37–8, 44–50), the original was extremely long. Furthermore, on pp. 39–44 of Hirao's transcription notebook is a transcribed section of the petition of the rural town doctor, Tateda Kachū, which is written without attribution and has unfortunately been mistakenly attributed to Jungo by Hirao in his published writings (beginning with "Hōreki kokusangata shihō to nōmin") and cited from there in *Kōchi-ken shi, kinsei hen*, pp. 494–5, and by Irimajiri Yoshinaga, in *Tosa-han keizai shi kenkyū*. The petition written by Kachū is relevant, because he uses the term kokueki a number of times, although to mean "government profit," which he opposes to "people's profit." He then, like Jungo, chastises the ruler for "fighting for profit with the people." Kachū is another example of a person of peripheral status showing influence of both samurai and neo-Confucian thought on the one hand and commoner attitudes on the other. Kachū's petition (11/26/1759) exists in two separate full transcriptions, so there is little doubt about the accuracy of my present note of correction. *TNK*, vol. 122, ff. 73rd–107th (misattributed portion on ff. 96th–101st), and SB, no. SP 6, ff. 23rd–55th (ff. 45th–49th).

the personal care of the lord. The lord should not "fight for profit with the people" but merely collect from those who could give what he needed to fulfill his duty.

Some of the very lowest ranks of retainers such as *gedai* and *ashigaru* and some household members of rural samurai, where the borderline with commoners was very fluid, were more clearly interested in products development. Their social peripherality enabled and encouraged their eclectic approach. Nakahira Heikaku was the younger brother of a rural samurai who used the import-export-focused logic of kokueki. Heikaku encouraged the lord to permit peasants to plant tobacco and cotton in rice fields, because cotton and tobacco were more profitable, would enrich the village, would restrict the outflow of bullion from Tosa by discouraging imports of these products, and would provide villagers with hard cash to pay taxes.[42] One anonymous petitioner, who identified himself as a *karuki mono*, or low-level retainer, urged the domain to order all farmers to raise chickens for eggs as a local industry, to control exports over the mountains so that the domain merchants would profit, to reduce product taxes in order to increase local production, and to reconsider the import restriction on ginned cotton, because an insufficiency of local ginning meant that people were importing more finished cloth, leading to an outflow of bullion.[43] Ozaki Kōsuke, retainer in charge of the weights and exchange house, urged the domain to reduce taxes to encourage production and to purchase local products even if they were more expensive than foreign products because it would keep money in the domain and boost the local economy.[44]

The rōnin doctor Horiba Shōzaemon also argued for many policies inspired by kokueki thought. His petition is especially fascinating because it highlights the contrast between the link of lord-centered consciousness with moral behavior, first, and the link of country-centered consciousness with commercial issues second. His petition neatly divides into the first arguments, centered on education, military arts, and moral issues and the latter arguments centered on trade. The first half urges the lord to continue garnering people's suggestions; to enforce respect of status, age difference, and frugal ways by making all people wear clothing revealing their status and by restricting the luxury of women in particular, as they lead in corrupting the rest of society; and to encourage learning by promoting children's education, by hiring a famous scholar from Kyoto, by encouraging competition among domain teachers, and finally by encouraging military studies among retainers. These proposals extend for over five folios (more than half of the petition), but Shōzaemon uses the

[42] Nakahira Heikaku (5/4/1765), *TNK*, vol. 148, ff. 57th–93rd.
[43] Anonymous "oboe" (2/13/1762), *TNK*, vol. 135, ff. 68th–73rd.
[44] Ozaki Kōsuke (9/30/1759), *TNK*, vol. 121, ff. 131st–135th.

word for country only four times. The emphasis of the sentences and thought is clearly on the lord. In the last half of the petition, Shōzaemon begins by noting that the well-being of the house depends on the enrichment of the country, and furthermore that the enrichment of the country depends on the balance of trade. His policy suggestions were that the domain should buy Tosa products even if they were more expensive than imports in order to keep the money flowing within Tosa; abolish domain-approved merchant monopolies and allow free commerce; invest in local production projects; and prohibit doctors and monks from studying outside of Tosa to prevent a bullion drain; and deliberately purchase local goods above market price to encourage production. This last section is comprised of only four folios (less than half of the petition), but Shōzaemon used the term country no less than sixty-five times.[45] Within the context of Edo period morals and education, the lord was a significant entity. Within the context of the commercial economy, the country was the significant entity. This contrast of linkage suggests that it was the experience of interdomainal trade that heightened the country-oriented consciousness and, therefore, that those involved in this activity would develop such a consciousness.

Most samurai had a vision of a lord-centered moral economy that affected their use of the term kokueki and their interpretation of the implications of bullionist thought. In general, their use of the term kokueki had nothing new to it. The samurai Shibuya Kizaemon and Mabuchi Sagorō could have expressed their points without any reference to kokueki. The merchants Izumiya Kaemon and Yōemon of Tei port could not have dropped the logic and phrasing of kokueki without ruining their arguments. This indicates that the seed-bed of kokueki was with the merchants. It was transplanted from them to domain samurai who were desperate for answers to new problems. The reason for the adaptation was a crisis in economy and values.[46]

Kokueki thought permitted people to conceive of rule and government in a significantly different fashion from the neo-Confucian tradition. Much of the ideology of rule in the eighteenth century focused on the person of the ruler. Kokueki thought focused on identification with one's geographic country as an economic entity. Within traditional thought, the lord was in a sense the source of the welfare of the country. His immoral behavior could bring disasters of flood and famine to the realm. His moral fiber and will were transmitted to his servants and people as the behavior of parents affects their children. Within the

---

[45] Horiba Shōzaemon, Horiba Chisa oji, rōnin (11/28/1759), *TNK*, vol. 122, ff. 107th–120th.
[46] Tetsuo Najita posits a "moral crisis" in eighteenth-century thought leading to just the kind of practicality and eclecticism seen in the behavior of Tosa samurai bureaucrats. "The Conceptual Portrayal of Tokugawa Intellectual History," pp. 18–23.

discourse of kokueki thought, the lord became a policymaker. His decision to support an industry or not had no immediate bearing on people's moral behavior. Heaven would not judge the morality of his decision. The only climate to be affected was the business climate, and his actions were either effective or ineffective, not moral or immoral. This conceptual division is idealized here to point out the forces that the language of kokueki thought embodied. The reality is that the concepts of the moral economy of service centered on the lord and of the international economy of the archipelago were often used together in the same breath. The next chapter will look at the gradual appropriation and development of kokueki thought by the government.

7

Declining service

People say that 80–90 percent of domain expenses are in Edo and the remaining 10–20 percent of expenses go for this country. And they say that of the needs in Edo a large portion go as presents to *bakufu* officials. Why do you use up such an enormous amount of money? . . . If 80–90 percent of the money which daily goes out of the country were used for country expenses, and you used that to make prosper the samurai of the household and all lesser people, then each of the four classes would not be poor in clothing, food, and housing.

Fukutomi Hanjō, 1785[1]

The petitions of the 1750s inspired a rapid succession of projects and reforms affecting commerce. The rural samurai Fukushima Heitabei noted in his diary, "This year [1760] the officials of the Country Products Office started many new projects."[2] Johei of the castle town described the frenetic activity more critically in 1765 when he wrote in a petition, "In recent years your lordship has begun many new projects in response to petitions, but they do not clearly bring prosperity for the country. You must investigate and beware that if these new projects do not last into future generations, it will be unprofitable."[3] In 1763, the domain officials opened up the northern highway to encourage trade, and most importantly, they abolished the monopoly system of commerce and allowed the producers of Tosa to sell to any merchant they pleased, including foreign merchants who were also allowed access to the market. The leaders maintained export taxes to garner income, but the main purpose of the change was to encourage economic development in the service of lord and country; "Officials

Material for portions of this chapter concerning the 1787 protests and the petition of Imakita Sakubei previously appeared within "A Petition for a Popularly Chosen Council of Government in Tosa in 1787," *Harvard Journal of Asiatic Studies*, vol. 57, no. 2 (December, 1997), pp. 575–96.
[1] (12/?/1785) *TCK*, vol. 44, ff. 150th–161st, quotation from ff. 153rd and 155th.
[2] Ms. *Seyō nikki*, f. 34, in the Kōchi Prefecture Library (Taoka/K212/40).
[3] Johei, Nijūdai machi (11/29/1765), *TNK*, vol. 148, ff. 97th–101st.

and village headmen should energetically encourage each industry. . . . All common people should remain frugal and work ceaselessly at industry, to work for the lord's benefit and the prosperity of the country."[4]

Yet this first attempt at internal free trade had a short life of only three years because it came into conflict with service to the bakufu. Protecting the *kokueki* could easily put the lord at odds with shogunal duty. There was no greater cause of the outflow of bullion from the domain than the alternate attendance system or payments of cash to the shogun to finance construction and development projects outside of Tosa. After the decline of the forests and the ruination of finances, the latter impositions invariably translated into a call for duty, *goyō*, from the populace in the form of money, *goyōgin*. This in turn disrupted the local economy and increased its ties with Osaka as local merchants scrambled for loans from the big financiers. The interests of the lord, his closest retainers (*kinshū*), and family who primarily lived in Edo were served well by structuring the economy in this fashion, which funnelled more than half of domain regular income into their life abroad, as were the interests of samurai whose fiefs and public authority came from their position within this economy. Nevertheless, the system was approaching a crisis and the lords increasingly felt their position was threatened. The crisis hit with fullest force in the protests of 1787, shocking the domain officials into making an important and long-lasting change in policy to begin a process of divorce between domain governance and bakufu service.

Naming the problem

In 1765 the bakufu ordered the lord of Tosa to dredge out the moats of Edo Castle, and the associated expense sent the domain officials into a flurry. Extra money could not be borrowed from Osaka merchants because accumulated debt had become prohibitively high. Additionally, the domain could not guarantee shipments of its products to prospective Osaka lenders because of the experiment with free trade begun in 1763. There was widespread hatred of the *kariage* levy, but the domain officials saw no other way to pay for the bakufu duty than to raise the kariage levy amount from 25 percent of income to an unprecedented 50 percent for a period of four years.[5] An earlier commentary in 1763 by one official found a silver lining in such a dark policy: From the standpoint of a government encouraging morality, the sudden loss of 50 percent of all people's income gave them no choice but to practice frugality with

---

[4] *Kōchi-ken shi, kinsei hen*, p. 509; Mutō Yoshikazu, comp., *Nanroshi*, vol. 7, pp. 227–9.
[5] *Kōchi-ken shi, kinsei hen*, pp. 513–5.

sincerity.[6] More people, however, were convinced that special levies encouraged forms of avoidance and corruption.[7] Seen locally, the bakufu demand was another disaster. In addition to noting in his diary drought, epidemic, mysterious fires and the birth of triplets in his town as signs of the unsettled times, Fukushima Heitabei also records the domain officials scrambling to find the 100,000 *ryō* for the project, only to discover that the cost has risen to 150,000 ryō.[8]

When the domain abolished the commercial privileges granted to wealthy merchants and allowed free commerce, it lost an important source of emergency income because these merchants became reluctant to give goyōgin. In effect, merchants had used gifts of goyōgin to the domain in order to gain commercial privileges. In the year the domain abolished the granting of privileges, it thus had to resort (for the first time in its history) to selling land tax collection rights on new fields to gain emergency cash.[9] This was one more embarrassing sign of the decline of the old order, and it reduced the amount of taxes collected by shrinking the tax base. By 1779, over 13,000 *koku* of annual tax rights had been sold in this manner.[10] The amount needed for bakufu service in 1765, however, was so great that it could not be acquired through the sale of tax collection rights and the higher kariage combined.

Thus, the kariage levy was quickly followed by a revival of the commercial monopoly system in 1766 and recourse to goyōgin impositions.[11] The domain officials were aware of public resistance, and in the order for re-creation of the monopoly, they urged that all transactions between licensed wholesale merchant and producer be at a "mutually agreed price." The order made it illegal to sell to a nonlicensed merchant, however. Those with licenses gained substantial leverage over the village producers, and they bought products at very low prices. Friction concerning the revival of monopoly trade arose again, bringing back the old tensions that had existed before the Tsunoyama disturbance of 1755. However, the monopoly system allowed the domain to reap income from trade. When new bakufu demands and a fire destroying the residence in Edo confronted the domain officials, they again could and did order a substantial amount of goyōgin to be collected in 1771, 1772, and 1776 from all the regions of Tosa, especially from the castle town. The largest merchants of the town –

---

[6] From a memorandum ("oboe") from an anonymous official (6/?/1763), probably the Finance Chief (*kanjōgashira*), TNK, vol. 139, ff. 64th–67th.
[7] Fukutomi Hanjō (12/?/1785), TCK, vol. 44, ff. 150th–161st; Asaka Seieimon, Nikawa Tohei, Maeno Mōnai (2/23/1787), ff. 48th–66th in TCK, vol. 53.
[8] Ms. *Seyō nikki*, ff. 47–9, in the Kōchi Prefecture Library (Taoka/K212/40).
[9] *Kōchi-ken shi, kinsei hen*, pp. 511–13; Kawada Matasuke (12/?/1765), SB, no. SP 7, ff. 39th–40th.
[10] Ms. *An'ei hachinen tōbun oboegakai*, sect. 21, GM, no. 5500.
[11] *Kōchi-ken shi, kinsei hen*, pp. 515–22.

such as the Tatsumiya and Toraya, who were granted a licensed monopoly in soy sauce production, each contributed the ample sums of 9.5 *kan* on the first occasion, 15 kan on the second occasion and 18 kan on the final occasion.[12] Furthermore, large amounts of goyōgin were collected directly from the domain Country Products Office: in 1778 200 kan, or twice the amount collected from the all castle town merchants combined.

In this first crisis after the beginning of the Hōreki reforms, the domain had chosen to revert to demanding money from the people to fulfill its place in the economy of service centered on Edo. But fewer people were supportive than before. Many eighteenth-century Tosa petitioners attributed the enfeeblement of their economy to the cost of bakufu duties, not only because of its impact on domain finances but with regard to the problem of outflow of bullion from the domain. For example, Nakahira Heikaku, the younger son of a rural samurai and, significantly, one of the peripherals noted earlier as having a clear interest in kokueki thought, expressed a growing skepticism, unmasking the politics beneath the rhetoric of the economy of service when he wrote in a petition to the lord:

Recently you have been assigned duty to dredge the muck out of the moats of Edo castle. It is such an important duty that I would like to give my congratulations. But really! This would just be fawning and following the form of what people are supposed to say. The reason is that in response to the extreme warfare of the time, and in order to build a secure foundation for his progeny, Ieyasu . . . knew that in the long term wealthy lords great and small would become ambitious at an opportunity. Thus, it has become standard policy and a long term military consideration to assign expensive construction duty to each daimyo in turn to weaken their finances.[13]

Heikaku judged that the bakufu assigned duty to daimyo who appeared to be the most well-off, but it did not intend to totally ruin their households. He therefore proposed the ingenious, if naive, solution that the lord should have some family treasures sold on the streets of Edo in order to have gossip of the lord's financial straits reach the bakufu senior council. This would, he argued, prevent Tosa from being assigned duty for a while.

He wrote many suggestions to avoid bakufu duty in his petition. In one significant linkage, he noted that alternate attendance and special duties to the bakufu led the domain to post special levies on the populace, which in turn led to the decline of public morals and trust in government (f. 74th). He also argued that the young daimyo-to-be should not perform alternate attendance until absolutely necessary because of its deleterious effect on finances (ff. 89–90th). Heikaku named clearly the conflict between care of the country and service to

---

[12] Mutō Yoshikazu, *Nanroshi*, vol. 7, pp. 257–67.
[13] Nakahira Heikaku (5/4/1765), *TNK*, vol. 148, ff. 57th–93rd, quotation from ff. 66th–67th.

the bakufu. I wonder whether he realized how shocking his suggestion to peddle family treasures on the streets of Edo must have been to a lord involved in the ostentatious displays of power and wealth among the daimyo.[14]

The Tenmei *protests*

Despite the profligate imposition of taxation and levies, and the reestablishment of hierarchically organized commerce so that merchants could "contribute money up to the lord when the country has a large expense," special expenses and further hardships accrued debts that pushed finances to the brink.[15] In 1772, the primary domainal residence in Edo went up in flames – less than a decade after having been slowly rebuilt from the fire of 1756. In 1776, the bakufu ordered Tosa to help with the rebuilding of Tōeizan (Kan'eiji) temple, a temple dedicated to the Tokugawa clan. In the 1780s weather took a downturn and crops repeatedly failed, reducing domainal income. A famine commenced in 1783, causing the population to drop by twenty-five thousand over the next seven years.[16]

Resentments and frustrations coalesced in the midst of the famine. In the autumn of 1786, the chief retainer Andō Genzō, who ruled a large autonomous fief in the Sukumō area of Hata county, left his mansion to go hunting. What happened next is recorded in the diary of a contemporary:

He found no peasants appearing outside at all. He thought it strange that, unlike a normal day, no one should appear outside, and when he asked the reason he was told 'No one is going outside because we have an important request.' Then two or three peasants down at the river's edge blew conchs, and from all around came a great number of peasants bearing hoes, spears and staves saying that they wished to make a request. 'We have no hatred of your lordship, but you must replace all of the officials including Ōme [Saburōzaemon] and those below him. We wish a halving of taxes this year, and a lowering of the per unit area tax rate to that of previous years. . . . We have resolved to flee the domain, if you do not grant us these requests.'[17]

From the river's edge they proceeded to Ōme's residence and destroyed it, and then broke apart residences of three townsmen and one peasant who refused to join the protest. The Hata county magistrates, Aki Gonshichi and Oike Danzō, heard of the riot and arrived to quiet the situation. They were

[14] I know of no literature on the expenses of display for lords. With his usual acuity, the historian Takagi Shōsaku once laughed to me when I spoke of the increasing resistance to *bakufu* construction impositions, "Gift giving and status competition among lords. Now *that* was the real Edo duty!"

[15] Tanaka Gisuke (11/1/1759), SB, no. SP 6, ff. 80th–90th, quotation from f. 85th.

[16] Ms. *Okuni nendai ryakki*, entries for appropriate years, in the Gest Library, Princeton University. Also refer to Figure 3.1. Crop loss amounts are given in *TCK*, for appropriate years.

[17] From the diary of a contemporary, Umazume Gonnosuke, as quoted in *Kōchi-ken shi, kinsei hen*, pp. 557–8.

aware that by targeting officials and not just merchants, this protest expressed a loss of faith in government. In the same month, Aki and Oike received word from the Kōchi senior councillors that they could administrate the county in any way they saw fit and carry out a reform. Many officials within the Sukumo fief as well as some domain officials were relieved of office soon after and punished.[18] They reduced many taxes and also rescinded the licensed commercial monopolies within Hata county.[19]

Over the next few months, protests spread throughout Tosa. In the second month of 1787, more than seven hundred mountain villagers from the paper producing region of the upper Niyodo river fled en masse across Tosa's border into Matsuyama domain, and begged the lord of Matsuyama domain to allow them to live there. This was probably not their ultimate objective, but rather a bargaining tactic. They wanted abolition of the paper monopoly, lessening of corvée duty, and fairer payment procedures for government tax transactions. They had petitioned for this earlier but without response. The peasants' actions resulted in great embarrassment for the rulers of Tosa. The domain wanted the incident dealt with as quietly as possible and enlisted the help of village headmen (*shōya*) in the area to resolve the situation. As they sat in council, one of the headmen wrung his hands and noted the predicament the domain was in, "Although the law states that, even if the lord is in the wrong, such resistance is punishable by death, you can't just go in with a calm face and shoot down eight or nine hundred people." After more than a month of fruitless negotiation, the domain ultimately gave in to all of the peasants' demands and gave a promise (which it would later break) that no one would be punished.[20]

This second incident had only just been settled when, throughout the domain, villagers in Kusaka, Mimase, Tanezaki, Akaoka, Yamada, Sōsenji, and Morogi and the people of the castle town carried out various protests. The castle town protest began with a riot sparked when a peddler noticed that Toraya, the wealthy privileged soy sauce merchant, was using wheat to make soy sauce right in the midst of the famine. The peddler strolled into the front garden of the merchant's house, jumped up on the front entry veranda, and snatched the store's account book. He lay down on the veranda, using the account book for a pillow and began shouting "This house is breaking the law!"

---

[18] A contemporary official account of the incident can be found in ms. "Sukumō hyakusho totō ikken," GM, no. 5706. The punishments of officials are found in ms. "Sukumō no kerai Ōme Saburōbei nado batsu oboegaki utsushi," GM, no. 7820.

[19] Yamamoto Takeshi, *Kenshōbo*, vol. 3, p. 363; for all policies of the Hata reform see vol. 1, pp. 127–35.

[20] Hirao Michio, *Nōmin ikki*, pp. 32–61. Anne Walthall, *Social Protest*, pp. 41–2, 74–7, 90–2. Ultimately, two of the leaders were executed and the village had to pay for many of the costs borne by the domain during the incident; quotation from Luke Roberts, "Tenmei shichinen," p. 24.

The frightened servants tried to give the peddler sake in order to quiet him down, but a crowd had already gathered. The home of the merchant and that of another were destroyed by the angry mob, despite attempts by the town police to stop it. A vast crowd had formed, and led by packhorse drivers who knew where rice was hidden, they marched to the bay and removed rice stored by the wealthy in boats. The food riot continued all night, developing into a more serious political protest. The next morning, the town officials found a great crowd gathered on the river plain in the middle of town. The officials tried to learn the reason for the gathering, but the crowd refused to respond. Instead they chanted repeatedly, "A bridge of money has been built!" presumably in reference to bribery and corruption in government. They said they would talk only with domain representatives, not mere urban officials. This incident was resolved only when domain leaders ordered the dismissal of all of the chief town officials and the domain town magistrate.[21]

Even in areas that did not break out in protest, the level of disillusion with government was very high. In 1788, one district headman (*ōjōya*) of a group of mountain villages, which had had not been involved in the protests, wrote the lord concerning conditions in his village in the previous year:

> After the peasants of Ikegawa village fled the domain last year, the hearts of the people did not rest, and they did not listen to the directives of government. When the county magistrate proceeded through the land and gathered village headmen, village elders, and group leaders, etc., to a reading of the laws and proclamations, the headmen and elders were respectful, but the group leaders and all below could not have cared in the least. They yawned and slept in a completely unlawful manner and, on their way home, made all sorts of jokes and insults. They said things like, 'I went to a ballad performance today, but the chanter was so poor we were all bored to death!' Or they reviled the reader, 'He stopped and started and was most boring. He certainly needs more practice'. They did not have the slightest fear of their superiors. I heard all the people saying, 'As strange as the world is today whatever we say to the rulers is of no use. The only thing to know is that it is most important to look out for oneself'. This was unbearably alarming. The thing that worried me most was that perhaps the annual rent would not come in smoothly. I was so distressed I could not happily eat or sleep.[22]

The situation in Tosa was clearly far beyond a pure rice riot disturbance associated with famine. Famine was important in creating discontent, but in each of the above cases, the discontent focused on domain officials and the corrupt nature of rule. There was a pervasive atmosphere of malaise, more intense than during the period of protests in the 1750s.

This mood was not confined to Tosa. Many people throughout Japan believed that the man in charge of bakufu government, Tanuma Okitsugu, was leading

---

[21] Hirao Michio, *Nōmin ikki*, pp. 62–71; quotations from the diary of a scholar who lived near the castle town, published in Roberts, "Tenmei shichinen," p. 24.

[22] From ms. *Tenmei shichinen hinoto hitsuji doshi Seitokuin-sama on oboegaki, zen* (K253/14), in the Kōchi Prefecture Library, and quoted fully in *Kōchi-ken shi, kinsei hen*, p. 564. The author is Yoshimoto Sotokichi (Mushio), the headman of Motoyama district.

the land down a road of immorality with his profligate use of bribery and disrespect for traditional rights. The Tosa scholar, Nomi Reinan, recorded in his diary in 1787 many of these widespread protests in Japan and added the invective, "It can all be called the poisoned breath of Tanuma!"[23] A massive rice riot hit Edo that spring, continuing uncontrolled for three days and ultimately led to the downfall of Tanuma and to the beginning of the Kansei reform under Matsudaira Sadanobu in 1788. Even some of the Tosa domain warehouses run by merchants in Edo were looted. The domain lord, Toyochika, was in Edo at the time and what he saw there no doubt influenced his interpretation of the messages from Tosa detailing the many disturbances. He became keenly aware of the severity of the situation and was ready to institute a thorough reform.

The mood of exploration in the wake of the crisis of the 1780s also was not limited to Tosa. Some trends in the rest of Japan should be noted in order to put the Tosa reforms into context. Many of the domains in northern Japan instituted petition box systems during this period, and domains throughout Japan carried out diverse reforms. Matsudaira Sadanobu, the leader of the bakufu Kansei reforms, repeatedly stressed the need to "open up the paths of communication" in the reform movement. Conversely, the previous era became castigated as one in which only "money talked," and Tanuma Okitsugu was reputed (truthfully or not) to have prevented the bakufu petition box from reaching the shogun. Sadanobu was supposed to have revived the petition box to its proper functioning.[24] Tetsuo Najita notes that just before becoming bakufu senior councillor, Sadanobu went to the Osaka merchant academy Kaitokudō to listen to lectures by its merchant scholars on political economy. It is symbolically significant that he went to the merchant school instead of calling them to Edo. The Kaitokudō scholar, Nakai Chikuzan, then gave Sadanobu a solution to the problem of daimyo finances that seems to be typically merchant inspired: The amount of alternate attendance time should be reduced, and the daimyo should sell their Edo residences to merchants, who would run them efficiently as hotels for the lords when they visited Edo on alternate attendance. He also suggested that the status ranking of the lords should not be based on the *omotedaka* (public assessment of agricultural productivity), which was, after all, based on outdated surveys from the 1590s, nor on the question of their allegiance at Sekigahara. Rather, the lords should be ranked according to their fiscal solvency

---

[23] Roberts, "Tenmei shichinen," p. 23; John Hall in *Tanuma Okitsugu* (pp. 63, 74–83), has correctly noted that Tanuma was one of the most procommerce leaders ever in charge of the bakufu. Yet Tanuma wanted commerce in the service of the bakufu, and he consistently suppressed domain interests, commercial and otherwise (Bolitho, *Treasures*, pp. 192–8). Anne Walthall has most excellently explored the Tenmei period protests which occured throughout much of the Japanese islands as a crucial turning point in the pattern of protests in *Social Protest and Popular Culture*.

[24] Aoki Michio, *Kindai e no yochō*, pp. 24–5.

and, if necessary, treated in ways to bring them out of debt. All samurai should be relieved of their fiefs and stipends, be chosen by talent, and paid according to the value of the office they held. Almost needless to say, Sadanobu did not adopt these startling suggestions in his reform, but he listened to them without incident, and Nakai later published his recommendations in his widely read *Sōbōkigen*.[25] In Tosa, the lord Toyochika would receive startling suggestions from other quarters.

The Tenmei reform leadership

Yamauchi Toyochika returned to his domain of Tosa on 6/16, not long after the spring protests. He quickly began receiving information on the situation in the domain through officials' reports and through the petitions of retainers and commoners. Numerous people in Tosa wanted a change, but there was a lack of confidence in whether an effective reform could be carried out, so many previous reforms had ended fruitlessly. Many writers of petitions felt that the behavior of officials had become thoroughly corrupt.[26]

Ten days after the return of the lord, one samurai, Imakita Sakubei, handed in a petition that expresses most deeply the pervasive loss of confidence in contemporary government. Sakubei argued that official corruption had made a rift between the rulers and the ruled so deep that it could not be repaired by further admonitions from the lord to improve morals. He suggested a change in the structure of government. The way to "bring high and low together" was to have the people of Tosa select a group of "faithful people" to sit in council next to the lord and advise him on the problems of government:

> If you wish to improve public morals, then you should select faithful people from throughout the country regardless of high or base birth, place them at your side and have them discuss and investigate everything. . . . Faithful people strive to reject profit and carry out what is righteous. They strive to abandon self-interest and carry out the lord's public will. Such people are without ambition for fame or fortune. . . . Now, because faithful people are of a will different from the mass of people, they cannot be chosen in the ordinary way. You should order all of the people of the country to choose such people, and if you order a careful investigation then such people will be found. . . . Even in these times there are good people living in this country.[27]

Councils of government chosen by a public did not exist in Japan except within some villages. This petition suggesting a popularly chosen council for

---

[25] Tetsuo Najita, *Kaitokudō*, pp. 171–80.
[26] Ōtani Genai (7/26/1787), *TCK*, vol. 53, ff. 74th–123rd, especially ff. 76th–77th; Kyūtoku Daihachi (9/13/1787), *TCK*, vol. 52, ff. 65th–89th, especially ff. 65th.
[27] *TCK*, vol. 54, Imakita Sakubei (6/26/1787), ff. 65th–74th. I have published this document fully in an article, "Tosa-han shi Imakita Sakubei."

high government including members regardless of class was, for its time and place, extraordinary and suggests the depth of Sakubei's sense of crisis. Sakubei's aim was to restore a sense of unity and public morality within the domain by improving communication. In order to achieve this, people needed to feel they were being listened to, and the lord had to have direct access to the common peoples' feelings and desires. This had, of course, been the purpose of the petition box, but Sakubei had noticed, "It is very difficult to learn the details of the conditions and feelings of the low only through writings. You must talk directly to the people who live in these conditions. Common people know all about what is right and wrong with government and what is profitable and unprofitable for government." His final statement contradicts the contemporary Japanese neo-Confucian political assumption that only the samurai were disinterested and noble enough to manage government.

Sakubei's "living petition box" was not a repudiation of hierarchical rule. His "faithful people" were what samurai were supposed to be in Japanese neo-Confucian doctrine, but were obviously failing to be: individuals who by their moral character were above private or partisan interests. Only fine character would make them able to perceive the conditions and feelings of the people and to sensitively include this awareness in their council deliberations. Because he believed impartial rule was possible, he expected the council to give its consensus to the lord for his consideration.[28] The extreme form of Sakubei's remedy points to the profound loss of confidence in the traditional means of rule and suggests why the government, despite its fundamentally elitist ideology, was increasingly responding to change in the domain by incorporating popular opinion on a limited basis. A petition such as Sakubei's helps us understand why the Tenmei reforms did indeed result in a signficant break from tradition.

After assessing the situation, the lord began choosing the people to carry out a thorough reform. There are two distinguishing characteristics of the reform leaders: Most were scholars, and many were promoted from very low status. The central role of domain scholars helped give the reform its special character. The two county magistrates who had begun reform efforts in the semi-independent Hata county in 1786 after the Sukumo disturbance were appointed as junior administrators of the domain and placed in charge of the domain-wide reform announced on 8/3/1787. One of these was the literary scholar, Ōike Danzō. The lord also selected Tani Mashio and Minoura Senpachi, lecturers at the domain school, to be chief inspectors of the domain,

---

[28] Sakubei's idea of the council and the oligarch's idea of the early Meiji period Diet are very similar. Despite their hopes for unity of opinion, the Meiji Diet quickly formed parties representing differing interests (W. G. Beasley, *The Modern History of Japan*, pp. 131–3); Robert Scalapino, "Elections and Political Modernization in Prewar Japan," p. 255.

in charge of police and controlling corruption. Umazume Gonnosuke, a scholar and poet who gave lectures to the lord, was made successively inspector of lord's pages, grand inspector, and castle town magistrate.[29]

When Toyochika declared the beginning of a reform, he did not replace the senior councillors, but neither did they play a significant role in the reform, suggesting that a change in the structure of political power was taking place beneath the surface. Power had shifted to the posts of junior administrator, chief inspector and the newly created post of finance magistrate.[30] Furthermore, people of a status beneath those eligible for these positions were raised in status to enable them to fill the posts. Some were chosen because petitions they had written caught the lord's eye. Imakita Sakubei was one of these. Toyochika did not implement Sakubei's suggestion of a popularly chosen council; as Sakubei himself predicted, it would have threatened too many vested interests. Toyochika did recognize Sakubei's talents and fidelity, however, and chose him to fill ever more important posts in the domain, despite his low status. Sakubei had been near the bottom of the *rusuikumi*, the lowest unit to be conferred with full samurai status, but less than two months after submitting his petition, he was appointed Magistrate of Finance and became a leading member of the Tenmei reform. Another retainer of even lower rank, but also with a rising star, was Kyūtoku Daihachi. This scribe and scholar submitted an elegantly written petition, entitled *Asaji no tsuyu* (Dew in a Reed Waste), urging financial retrenchment and moral reform. The lord greatly admired Daihachi's petition and chose him to serve as Magistrate of Finance together with Sakubei. After two weeks in his new post, Daihachi composed a petition (which Sakubei also signed) with further detailed plans for improving domain rule.[31] In 1789, Daihachi was appointed junior administrator of the domain, an appointment unprecedented for one of such lowly origins. Daihachi's fortune was envied, and a not-so-elegant contemporary critical verse has "Useless Daihachi taking the reins of government because of something he wrote."[32]

An important factor in the reform was the domain school, Kōjūkan, completed in 1761. The intensification of scholarly values played a role in the

[29] *Kōchi-ken shi, kinsei hen*, p. 566, mentions most of these and highlights the scholar orientation of the reform as a break from the past. It does not mention Umazume Gonnosuke in this context, which is surprising because the volumes from the *Toyochika-kō ki* portray Umazume as possibly the leading member of the reform.
[30] The kanjōgashira had been a low-status post chosen from sub-samurai retainers until the Tenmei reforms. With the Tenmei reforms, the post was raised in status and authority, renamed *kanjōbugyō* (Finance Magistrate) and chosen from among the low-status samurai retainers (although likely candidates from sub-samurai status such as Kyūtoku Daihachi could be raised in status to fill the post).
[31] *Kōchi-ken shi, kinsei hen*, pp. 556–7, 570–1.
[32] Anonymous verse quoted in Teraishi Masaji (Masamichi), *Nangakushi*, p. 717.

greater fluidity of status in government. Although most scholars preached respect of status, they argued more persuasively for placing honest and able retainers in high positions in government regardless of their status within the samurai hierarchy. Kyūtoku Daihachi's petition argued these points, and Sakubei's petition took this to a greater extreme by suggesting extending eligibility beyond the retainer class to all of the people of Tosa. The world of scholarship was socially fluid, and its many members were of diverse origins because the standards of good scholarship often overrode issues of status.[33] Some samurai were threatened by the new value placed upon scholarship. Ikoma Sadayū wrote to the lord that because values and morality were part of the natural order of things, people who did not favor learning could still be as upright and useful as the learned, and that an excessive emphasis put on learning would just make people craftier with words.[34]

Because respect for status was an integral element of the early modern order, mobility was threatening to the social order. One petitioner in 1765 argued that doctors and monks destroyed both "family governance" and government of the country because they came from a mixing of classes.[35] The separation of classes was a powerful element binding government and family life. The domain school was open to commoners if they wished to attend, and one of its four teachers, Tobe Sukegorō, had been raised to that position in 1759 by the lord from the almost sub-commoner caste of actor.[36] This caused a great stir in Kōchi, and a flurry of petitions was sent to the lord both against and in support of Tobe's appointment. This freedom from the basic status orientation of society did not go unnoticed and threatened some people.

The scholars who attained powerful positions in government were intent on improving the quality of domain rule and were less concerned with bakufu relations. Most scholars who ended up in high positions in Tosa government served in positions such as port, county, or forest magistrate, administering the day-to-day business of commoners, and some of them associated with commoners in their intellectual activities. This gave them the opportunity to benefit from commoners' ideas. The town magistrate Umazume Gonnosuke participated in literary circles with townsmen and was very active in local

---

[33] Ronald Dore, "Talent and the Social Order"; Thomas Smith, "Merit as Ideology."
[34] Ikoma Sadayū (2/25/1760), *TNK*, vol. 127, ff. 46th–57th.
[35] Nakahira Heikaku (1765/5/4), *TNK*, vol. 148, ff. 57th–93th, especially f. 80th.
[36] *Kōchi-ken shi, kinsei hen*, p. 946; *TNK*, vol. 127: Tani Mashio (1/?/1760), ff. 2nd–8th; Chūnai, Nakauchi Rokudayū ninan, Kitahōkōnin-chō nichōme sumu (2/18/1760), ff. 32nd–46th; Anonymous (3/1/1760), ff. 82nd–85th; Minami Ihei (12/?/1760), ff. 103rd–108th, and so forth. The socially conservative Tani Mashio was thoroughly appalled at Tobe's appointment. The original draft of his petition of protest survives in Rikkyō University, Department of National History. They kindly provided me with a copy of the petition by mail; listed in Rikkyō Daigaku Nihon Shi Kenkyūshitsu, ed., *Tani Jinzan, Tani Kanjō ke monjo mokuroku*, doc. no. 1080.

government. Umazume even became a student of the Shingaku philosophy created by Kyoto townsman Ishida Baigan. It is surprising, perhaps, that eight years after Matsudaira Sadanobu's prohibition of heterodox studies, Umazume was commended by the lord for this study of Shingaku.[37] These scholars brought into the higher reaches of government much practical experience and contact with commoners, and their education in the principles of government gave them the confidence to attempt drastic change. They increasingly envisioned the purpose of rule to be government of the country of Tosa and not service to the bakufu. This made them predisposed to resist bakufu imposition when it harmed Tosa welfare.

Another aspect of the attitudes that the scholars brought to their work was imperial loyalism, and this gave scholars another means of resisting the bakufu. Toyonobu officially favored the emperor-focused Nangaku branch of the Kimon school of neo-Confucian studies when he created the domain school. One startling example of the imperial loyalism exhibited by this school of thought in Tosa occurred in 1762. The shogun had ordered that the mourning period for the recently deceased Momozono emperor be limited to only three days, so that the shogunal accession ceremony did not have to be delayed. Three Tosa scholars residing in the Tosa residence in Edo were up in arms over what they saw as the impudence of the shogun. Traditionally, the mourning period for an emperor had lasted from forty days to one year, they argued, and expressed their objections in petitions to their lord, also in Edo at the time.[38] One of them, Miyaji Haruki, wrote, "There is no doubt that you have received from the emperor your title of Fourth Rank Protector of Tosa. It is thus clear who is the lord and who is the retainer. Nevertheless, the glory and power of the shogun's house has risen and the emperor's glory has declined. It is a pitiful and base world we live in when the people think that the shogun is the lord and the emperor is nothing more than a living god (*ikiru kami*)." Such loyalist attitudes among many who gained leadership within domain government often included hostility to the bakufu. Although unrelated in origin to kokueki thought, increasing loyalism at this juncture in history reinforced the developing attitude of resistance to bakufu dominance.[39]

---

[37] Ms. *Hitsuya-ke monjo*, ff. 27th–28th, HB, no. 244. This was in 1799. Conservative leaders regarded Shingaku as fine for commoners but not for samurai. In later years in Tosa, however, the official Mabuchi Kahei was punished a number of times for his interest in Shingaku. Mabuchi was nevertheless a favorite of the lord Toyoteru, who used him in leading posts in government.

[38] *TNK*, vol. 134: Tani Tannai (8/12/1762), ff. 217th–219th; Minoura Ugenta (8/13/1762), ff. 219th–220th; Miyaji Haruki (9/6/1762), ff. 220th–225th. Miyaji began his petition, "There are not two suns in heaven and there are not two lords on earth."

[39] Further reading on the nuances of eighteenth-century loyalism can be found in Bob Wakabayashi's *Japanese Loyalism Reconstrued*, where he argues that the loyalist attitudes of the mid-eighteenth century were not restorationist, although they formed a rhetoric with which the policies of shogunal government officials could be criticized, see especially pp. 52–64.

Toyochika, himself, became far more active in domain government than he had been since his accession in 1768. He frequently appeared at the deliberations of senior officials at the government council building, a practice that had not been characteristic of previous lords. Between 2/11 and 7/17/1788, when he should have been in Edo, but had delayed by pleading illness, he went to such meetings seventeen times. He also required all senior officials to come to him on the twenty-seventh of each month for council.[40] He not only reiterated the invitation his father Toyonobu had made in 1759 for retainers to submit petitions, but he also occasionally called groups of retainers to his room to personally ask each one their thoughts and ideas concerning government.[41] Because many petitions from retainers begged his involvement, he knew that his taking part would build morale for everyone. He also visited personally a number of irrigation system construction sites, in order to note their progress and encourage the project with his presence.[42]

Toyochika was young but frail, and he died at age thirty-nine late in 1789. Perhaps intimations of his own mortality led him to strive for continuity in the reform by training his heir Toyokazu to take on the responsibilities of direct rule and not become the proverbially stupid and pampered "daimyo's son." He had the scholar-official Umazume Gonnosuke instruct Toyokazu. Gonnosuke recorded in his diary, "I went to the lounging room in the sleeping apartments and approached his young lordship. I said again and again, 'The rule of a country depends above all else on putting energy into the study of letters and the military arts. Although now you say you wish to become a good ruler, you must give up raising little birds and the like, and from this very moment put your attention to ruling the country.'"[43] These efforts were successful, and Toyokazu carried on his father's reform efforts and personal involvement in domain rule.

Although the selection of well-educated retainers to run administration did not occur without criticism and comment, the practice continued to be a part of the operation of domain government. Each notable administration in Tosa thereafter was formed around a group of scholars. One might speculate that this was related to the increasing care given to daimyo education. It also might have resulted from the success of the Tenmei group of reformers. One critic around 1780 wrote in a comic verse, "All the scholars have finally gathered, making a mess of their novel projects!"[44] Their projects were often novel, but within a decade, few could argue with the success.

[40] *TCK*, vol. 60, ff. 29th–30th; *TCK*, vol. 59, f. 7th.
[41] *TCK*, vol. 59, ff. 5th–6th, records thirteen retainers called that day.
[42] *TCK*, vol. 52, ff. 116th–117th. *TCK*, vol. 53, ff. 28th–34th.
[43] *TCK*, vol. 53, ff. 3rd–4th.
[44] Anonymous verse quoted in Teraishi Masaji (Masamichi), *Nangakushi*, p. 717.

Tenmei reform policies toward Edo

Reform policies focused on cutting expenditures, reorganizing the local tax system, fostering the private economy, and restoring faith in samurai leadership. Some policies could not have been carried out without cooperation or tolerance from the bakufu. In the same month that the Tosa reform began, the troubled bakufu declared its own reform under the leadership of Matsudaira Sadanobu. This was fortunate for Tosa, because as Harold Bolitho has pointed out, Sadanobu generally pursued policies favorable to domain interests. He represented the preferences of many lords in the bakufu who were threatened by the centralizing policies of Tanuma Okitsugu. He loosened bakufu control of domainal activity on the Osaka market, allowing them more room to maneuver with their own policies.[45] His encouragement of frugality and austerity in ceremony coalesced with the desire of domainal officials to cut the costs of Edo life. The Tosa reformers felt that Sadanobu could be counted on to support their policies.

In the ninth month of 1787, Toyochika sent to the Edo mansion a draft of a formal request to the bakufu to allow Tosa to perform all ceremonial duties and gift giving at the half-status public assessment of 100,000 koku for a period of ten years. Toyochika pleaded poverty and asked for a reduction in the frequency of bakufu impositions of special duty, but promised to perform bakufu duty at full status and maintain performance of central duties to the bakufu as before. Officials of the Tosa residence in Edo compared notes with the Hosokawa clan of Kumamoto domain, who had earlier asked for and received a halving of status. They changed the request to be more similar to the precedent and also included the various branch families of the Yamauchi in the status change. Then Hazama Jūzaemon, the Edo residence representative of the domain, carried the request to the representative of one of the senior councillors of the bakufu. He called on the representative almost daily for twenty days until the senior councillors approved the request in the twelfth month.[46]

With this major matter arranged, other similar moves cutting Edo-related expenses followed quickly. The lord instructed the branch house of Yamauchi Toyoyasu to have no New Year's greeting ceremony, so that it might avoid ceremonial costs and the expense of giving and receiving gifts.[47] The number of retainers sent to Edo with the lord was reduced.[48] The budgets of all of the

---

[45] Harold Bolitho, *Treasures*, pp. 198–205.
[46] *TCK*, vol. 52, ff. 118th–135th.
[47] *TCK*, vol. 55, f. 37th.
[48] For example, the troop of accompanying foot samurai (*kachi*) was reduced from seventy members to forty members. *TCK*, vol. 57, ff. 1st–2nd.

lord's dependent relatives (*ichimon*) in Edo were limited, including a 50 per-cent cut in the expenses of the young heir.[49] Also, gifts to other daimyo and bakufu officials were reduced, and at times the lord of Tosa refused even to accept gifts from other lords, because return gifts would have been in order.[50]

This cutting of expenditures was ostensibly a special ten-year reform meas-ure, but it became the standard of the domain relationship with the bakufu thereafter. In 1797, when the ten years were over, the domain again asked for a ten-year extension. The senior councillors granted the extension with the self-interested exception that gifts to bakufu officials should be given in accordance with Tosa's regular 200,000 koku status![51] In 1806, the domain requested and received yet another ten-year extension, and in 1809 asked for permission to reduce its gifts to bakufu officials over five years.[52] In 1816, the domain returned to regular status, but reconsidered the following year when it requested and received once again permission to serve at reduced status.[53] These extensions not only saved money in themselves, but had the effect of continually reminding the bakufu senior councillors that Tosa could not bear the burden of many construction projects and so served as a way to lighten the burden of duty requested by the bakufu.

Furthermore, when the bakufu called the Yamauchi to perform shogunal service, they went at it less than dutifully, with a mind to cut costs. In 1788, the journey to Edo for alternate attendance duty was delayed by four months at Tosa's request, ostensibly because of the lord's illness, but in reality to save expense. Interestingly, this was done with the full knowledge of the relevant bakufu officials, who suggested to Tosa the convenient and "proper" excuse of illness.[54] Later, after the lord Toyochika arrived in Edo, the bakufu requested that he make a pilgrimage to Tōeizan (Kan'eiji), one of the gravesites for the Tokugawa clan. Toyochika, however, declined on account of his continuing illness. Then, late in 1788, the bakufu requested all domains to contribute money for bakufu construction projects at a rate of 51 ryō per 10,000 koku. Tosa responded by asking for a delay in the payment time. In 1789, the bakufu ordered Yamauchi Toyoyasu, a branch house of Yamauchi, to perform guard duty at Sunpu castle. The Tosa lord noted his priorities when he wrote in his diary his recommendation to Toyoyasu, "Be sure that all is done in a way to cut

---

[49] *TCK*, vol. 52, ff. 113th–115th; *TCK*, vol. 59, ff. 40th–42nd.
[50] See for example, *TCK*, vol. 63, ff. 39th–40th; *TKK*, vol. 1, f. 62nd.
[51] *TKK*, vol. 31, ff. 72nd–80th; vol. 32, ff. 52nd–59th.
[52] Ms. *Otōke nendai ryakki* held in the Gest Library, Princeton University; *TSK*, vol. 3, ff. 39th–44th. *TSK*, vol. 4, ff. 116th–122nd.
[53] Source is the *kōbun* (Contents) volume for the *TSK* series of volumes. The *TSK* volume in which the transcribed documents should be located, *TSK*, "ichigatsu-gogatsu," is missing.
[54] *TCK*, vol. 58, ff. 7th–76th.

expenses, and do your duty faithfully with a full heart," that is, go with a full heart but a half-empty purse. When the time came for service, Toyoyasu declared sickness in order to delay his departure for Sunpu by two months beyond the deadline.[55] This performance set a pattern for later years when domain lords would frequently plead illness in order to delay or avoid execution of duty. In another example, in 1808, the bakufu ordered Tosa to contribute funds for the reception of the Korean embassy. Tosa responded by asking to be allowed to make the payment in installments over the next fifteen years, because of its "extreme poverty."[56] In the same year, the domain officials also began considering how much to cut the number of retainers in Edo, including "reducing the number of retainers serving on the fire brigade ordered by the bakufu."[57] Another example is seen in the 1830s and 1840s, when the retired daimyo Toyosuke repeatedly sought and gained permission from the bakufu to stay at home in the domain. The grounds for his requests were that he needed the cure of a salubrious hot springs in Tosa for his illness. Aside from the fact that this made him appear to be in ill health for decades in succession, the reason was even more curious because Tosa is one of the few regions in all Japan without a natural hot springs. The reality was that he wished to avoid the expenses and duties of living in Edo. In lieu of enjoying Edo life, the retired Toyosuke became a forceful presence in domain rule right into the Meiji period.[58] It was not extreme poverty of the kind the domain had experienced in the 1770s that urged the domain to take these measures. As we have seen in Chapter 4, domain finances improved greatly throughout this period. In the 1800s the domain did not want its tentative financial success threatened by bakufu-related expenditure.

Kokueki thought played an actively destabilizing role in the realm of domain-bakufu relations. Duty to the bakufu, and full participation in Edo life were almost invariably seen as harming the prosperity of the country, because they represented both an outflow of bullion on a grand scale and the reason for government abuse of its taxing authority. It was possible for people to ignore this conflict, but unlike performance duty to one's own domain lord, no one could argue that performance of bakufu duties worked for the kokueki.[59]

[55] *TCK*, vol. 64, f. 88th.
[56] *TOK*, vol. 2, ff. 36th–53rd. Furthermore, when the bakufu ordered Tosa to assist in Kantō area construction in 1813, Tosa asked the bakufu for a three-year reprieve on its payments for the Korean embassy (*TSK*, vol. 25, f. 10th).
[57] Ms. *Bunsei sannen nigatsu yori ometsuke yaku yori dasu bun kakitsuke*, GM, no. 5552.
[58] Personal communication from Prof. Akizawa Shigeru of Kōchi University, who is familiar with the documents of Tosa official requests to the bakufu. Toyosuke was in reality a very healthy man who outlived his sons and survived the Meiji Restoration and the abolition of the domains. Toyosuke's father Toyokazu also did the same thing in 1812 (*TSK*, vol. 19, ff. 7th–30th).
[59] Fujita Teiichirō, *Kinsei keizai*, pp. 203–15; and in his "Kansei ki jōkamachi shōnin," pp. 373–84.

The payoff for Tosa

The most important change in local government made possible by the reduction of service and expense outside of the domain was a commitment to reduce the amount of special levies made on the populace. Cutting expenses and the amount of bakufu duty helped to eliminate the need for the collection of goyōgin. The domain also reduced the need for goyōgin levies by restoring its borrowing power with Osaka merchants. This was not an easy task because outstanding loans exceeded 30,000 kan, or more than two years' total domain income. A number of chief officials, including Kyūtoku Daihachi and Imakita Sakubei, traveled to Osaka in order to convince the merchants to reschedule the loans by instituting an extremely long-term (one hundred years), low- or no-interest repayment plan.[60] Surprisingly, this measure soon restored Tosa's borrowing power. Thereafter, the domain was able to faithfully repay all new loans, while paying back the rescheduled loans steadily at a much slower rate. By 1854, the domain had paid off 83 percent of its rescheduled debt and had achieved the more noteworthy feat of having accumulated no new rescheduled debts over the sixty-seven years since 1787.[61] The opinion in Osaka quickly came to hold that Tosa domain was good for its loans. Therefore, in 1799, when the bakufu ordered Tosa to contribute for repairs to the shogun's palace, the domain was able to borrow money in Osaka, diminishing need for goyōgin. Goyōgin had been collected in great amounts in the 1760s, 1770s and 1780s, but the junior administrator Mori Yoshiki was able to tell his fellow officials in 1800 that "the collection of goyōgin and *demai* has been reduced to one-tenth of pre-reform levels."[62] Subsequent records, discussed in Chapter 4, reveal that goyōgin was collected on only three occasions until 1853 and that most of this amount had been repaid. This reduction in special impositions not only aided the local economy, but also helped restore trust in the government.

Because people had gradually come to feel that the levies were at the root of many of the social ills of the time, decreasing the levies had become an impor-

---

[60] Yasuoka Shigeaki has presented the writings of a scholary contemporary, Kusama Naokata, concerning the widespread defaulting on loans by daimyo in Japan at this time. Tosa is mentioned on p. 180 ("Kansei Bunka ki ni okeru hanseki shōri ni kansuru Kusama Naokata no iken.").

[61] *TCK*, vol. 59, ff. 58th–64th. Inspection of the sections on borrowing from *Tōbun oboegaki* (primarily in GM) show that no new loans were defaulted on after this point. See also Hirao, *Kōchi-han zaisei shi*, pp. 123–26, who notes that at the abolition of the domain in 1871, all unpaid Edo period loans were from before 1788. The amount remaining was about 2,000 *kan* (recorded as 19,965 *ryō* in the text), which shows that over 90 percent of the original 30,000 kan had been repaid by this time. The gradual decrease in the loan amount can be seen in the various *Tōbun oboegaki* from 1800 to 1854; 1854, in Hirao, *Kōchi-han zaisei shi*, pp. 158–61.

[62] *TKK*, vol. 46, ff. 1st–7th; Mori Yoshiki, ms. *Sansei nichiroku, niban*, entry for 2/6/1800, in the Kōchi Prefecture Library.

tant project for government officials. The extensive use of kariage, reaching heights of 50 percent in the 1770s, was widely hated. It had harmed commoner and samurai economic conditions and morale to the point of the rebellious conditions of 1787. Many samurai developed the theory that special levies encouraged corruption and, ultimately, the ruin of government. The samurai Fukutomi Hanjō wrote the lord in 1785, beginning with a cautionary statement:

> The country does not belong to one person.... Although your lordship is great and stands above the four classes of people, you cannot stand without them.... However, finances have recently been in trouble causing you to order special levies. Retainers and all of the people alike have become impoverished. Retainers of high status have cut the number of their servants from ten to seven or five people. Retainers of low status have not enough to provide their families with food, clothing and shelter. Therefore some do handicrafts to fend off the cold – but they cannot pursue the study of letters or military arts. Instead they learn base customs and come to pursue selfish profit. Officials become untrustworthy and only wish to use office to collect bribes.... This occurs because people are short of food, clothing and shelter. One cannot punish them severely for this.[63]

Immediate abolition of kariage was impossible, but it became a long-term goal of the administration. On 8/18/1789 the lord declared a 50 percent reduction in the surplus special levy (then called demai, a 10 percent surcharge on top of the 25 percent kariage) from 10 percent to 5 percent of income after taxes, "Although We do not really have at the moment the means to express Our benevolence, We ignore worry about the future and the past, and order a fifty percent reduction in the surplus special levy."[64] In 1793 the 25 percent kariage was abolished per se and replaced with a 15 percent levy called demai, thereby reducing the levy by two fifths.[65] Renaming of the levy from kariage (loan up to the lord) to demai (rice given out) publicly recognized that the "loan" terminology was inappropriate and unified terminology with practice. This was a step toward reducing public cynicism. The renaming was not an attempt at giving the levy permanence. In many years in the nineteenth century, half of the amount of the special levy was reprieved or returned in cash both to the

---

[63] Fukutomi Hanjō (12/?/1785), *TCK*, vol. 44, ff. 150th–161st. Fukutomi was rewarded by the lord for his petition. Later, Fukutomi's petition was included in the 1830s compilation of petitions entitled *Shinmin kigen* ("The Origins of the New People"), Chikamori bunkō, no. 0542, in the Kōchi City Library. See also the petition from the three chief inspectors to the lord on 2/3/1787 (Yasuzumi Seieimon, Nikawa Tōbei, and Maeno Mōnai, *TCK*, vol. 53, ff. 48th–65th).

[64] *TNK*, vol. 64, ff. 123rd–125th.

[65] *TKK*, vol. 19, ff. 82nd–101st; *TKK*, vol. 24, ff. 17th–19th.

commoners and retainers. Thus, the actual amount collected declined steadily over the years until its abolition in 1839. The average rate shifted from 45 percent of income after taxes during the period 1766–77, to about 20 percent in the period 1787–1822, and 10 percent in the period 1823–38.[66]

In order to further reduce the need for special levies, the domain created a special reserve of money to support payments for bakufu duty. This fund was created by annual contributions from the domain's more profitable offices – the Mountain (forest) Administration and the Finance Administration. In the seventeenth century, a similar reserve based on the then-immense forestry income had been kept in preparation for bakufu duty, and it had helped prevent the use of special levies. In 1707 the reserve became virtually defunct until its revival in 1790.[67] Sources for the reserve expanded in 1817 to include contributions from the commercially oriented Shipping Administration (*funakata*) and later yet from the revived and reformed Country Products Office (*kokusan yakusho*).[68] This reserve was used for emergency expenses and resulted in less pressure on domain finance officials to depend upon kariage and goyōgin. The reduced need for special levies allowed the domain a freer hand at managing commerce in the domain, because it became less dependent on contributions from licensed merchants.

Another important change in the domain supports the general interpretation of the broader meaning of kokueki thought as given by Fujita, who argues that it gradually replaced a notion of the economy and governmental responsibility based on the lord's duty of famine relief (*osukui*).[69] Osukui was one of the traditional mainstays of the relationship between the lord and the common people, and was designed explicitly to maintain commoners in their prescribed occupations (*hongyō*). These occupations were obligatory, but the lord had a duty to keep commoners from becoming unable to perform them due to famine or other natural hardship. The mutual responsibilities of the ruled and the ruler defined their heirarchical relationship. When people asked for relief they did so by saying that they could no longer continue in their occupation or, in a transfer of the paternalistic ideology, that they could no longer take care of their families – the people entrusted to their care.[70] Osukui was an ideology appropriate to an

---

[66] See Figure 4.2.
[67] *Kōchi ken-shi, kinsei hen*, pp. 262–3 for decline; revival from ms. "Gokuhi kakidome" (GM, no. 5837).
[68] *TSK*, vol. 4, f. 136th; *TSK*, vol. 46 f. 78th. HB, no. 372, pp. 48–50, has document from 1861, including Country Products Office.
[69] Fujita Teiichirō, *Kinsei keizai*, pp. 6–7.
[70] Fukaya Katsumi, "Hyakusho ikki"; Irwin Scheiner, "Benevolent Lords and Honorable Peasants," pp. 39–62, especially pp. 51–2.

agricultural economy subject to the vicissitudes of weather. Ideally, taxes were to be used wisely and benevolently by the lord to fend off famine among the people in years of crop loss.[71]

One monolithic ideology never replaced another – the rhetoric of kokueki and the lord's famine relief coexist in many documents – but the general tendency implicit in Fujita's argument that kokueki ideology replaced osukui ideology is evident in the following occurrences in Tosa. In the early eighteenth century, famine increased greatly, and the domain's finances worsened. The domain not only became unable to provide sufficient relief, but also taxed people more heavily and worsened their economic condition.[72] This was evident to many people and created a great amount of cynicism toward government. By the mid-eighteenth century, the lord was publicly announcing time and again his inability to carry out famine relief as he would wish.[73] With the Tenmei reforms, the government immediately began urging villages to bear some of the burden of their own famine relief by creating relief warehouses under village organization (*gisō*). Finally, in 1838, at the time the domain finally stopped using the special levy, the domain ordered villages to use the rice thus saved to run their own relief houses.[74] Because the burden of operating relief for the village was clearly less than the amount of special levy, this likely was attractive to villagers. Yet within the limits of this arrangement, the government was making itself irrelevant. By publicly giving up (in what was after all a public recognition of a de facto situation) a large amount of its relief duties, the domain lost an important part of the rhetoric of its relationship with the peasants.

However, over the same period, the domain officials increasingly issued proclamations describing their work for the prosperity of the country: drawing bullion into the country, aiding the economy, and providing new livelihoods for the people of Tosa. The role and usefulness of government had in this aspect changed, and the language of its relationship to the people had changed as well. Its duty had come to be defined as working for the kokueki. This rhetoric could justify government support of commercial activity in ways that belief in the duty of famine relief and in prescribed occupations could not. New industrial and commercial projects could be described abstractly as working for the prosperity of the country and local conditions of finance, and even concretely as providing alternate forms of work for the people. These projects, however, were sometimes disturbing to the economic lives of villagers. One petitioner wrote the lord

---

[71] Stephen Vlastos makes an excellent argument concerning the declining meaning of lordly relief for villagers in northern Japan whose lives were becoming increasingly dependent on sericulture income rather than agriculture (*Peasant Protests*, pp. 42–91).

[72] As noted in Murakami Chūji (9/3/1761), *TNK*, vol. 130, ff. 32nd–36th.

[73] Yamamoto Takeshi, *Kenshōbo*, vol. 1, pp. 83, 90, 104, 110, 113, 114, 120, 122.

[74] Yamamoto Takeshi, *Kenshobō*, vol. 3, pp. 131–5, 142–3, 180–2.

with exasperation, "Because so many of the lord's commercial projects are changing all the time . . . the people have become unsettled."[75] It was difficult to urge a peasant to change his crop from soy beans to sugar cane using the ideology of maintaining the peasants in their prescribed occupations. They could always respond that they were able to perform their occupation quite well already. With kokueki thought the domain could argue to the peasants that the change to sugar was necessary to improve the balance of trade, improve the local economy and provide new means of making a living.

Kokueki thought was an ideology tied not to the maintenance of agriculture but to the regional protection of commerce, and it shifted the "center" of ideology from the lord to the country. But, unlike the case with the shogun, kokueki did not often specifically deny or openly conflict with the concepts of osukui, *hōkō* and *on* as related to the lord. Concepts of famine relief or duty to one's lord could easily be seen to be working for a loosely defined kokueki, because the country and the lord's realm could in most instances be thought of as the same thing. The lord Toyosuke justified the imposition of a special levy in terms of goyō and *on*, and commercial production projects in terms of kokueki.[76] To give an example, in 1824, the senior officials appealed to both sets of terms in a call for support of a reform, and the ideologies worked together without conflict:

Our former lord [Toyochika] ordered a reform [in 1787] out of his grave concern for affairs. Although his will was indeed carried out, it was nevertheless necessary to extend the reform. Even so, expenses seemed to grow and in the recent year of the dragon [1820] a complete renewal and return to the conditions of the first year of the reform was ordered. Each administrative office was required to bear a percentage reduction in expenses to take on this heavy responsibility.
    Increasingly the castle and roads and bridges have been receiving repairs. Agricultural land has been resurveyed, wasteland has been developed, the mountains have been resurveyed to work eternally for the lord's benefit. Furthermore corruption has been punished and people's hearts placed on a straight foundation. Each administrative office has been instructed to fill its needs only with products made in this country and to restrain luxury. Doing this we can prevent silver and coins from leaving to other countries and thus maintain a healthy flow of cash and financing in this country. The first and most important thing for the prosperity of the country is that even day laborers can make a living. It is essential to take to heart each of these wishes of the lord, as his wishes have indeed gradually been realized.
    Therefore in the past year of the lamb [1823] the lord ordered a disbursement of supplemental money to all retainers and commoners despite the low current price for rice and grains.[77]

[75] Juhei, of Nijūdai ward (11/29/1765), *TNK*, vol. 148, f. 98th.
[76] Yokogawa, "Bunseiki," pp. 293–5, gives many examples of the use of the term *kokueki* and contrasts this to the lord's use of "the lord's benefit" (*ontame*). For an example of "*goyō*," see Yamamoto Takeshi, *Kenshōbo*, vol. 1, pp. 266–8.
[77] Untitled single folio memo dated year of the monkey, first month, and beginning with the phrase "Osendai sama atsuki oboshimeshi o motte . . ." held in the Yamauchi Shrine Office collection.

This document reflects the merging of a lord-centered ideology with a strong mercantilist view of the economy. Although the language is traditional, in that it has all of these policies originating from the lord, the emphasis on the welfare of the people down to those who live on day wages (*hiyō*) as the main indicator of the prosperity of Tosa is surprising. Their inclusion here in linkage with "prosperity of the country," as well as the emphasis on the state of credit and cash flow in Tosa, reveals how much the economy had become "national" in the administrative imagination. Kokueki thought thus strengthened the ruling hand of the daimyo of larger domains, while subtly altering the foundations of government. This is most visible in the realm of commercial policy and enterprise, which will be explored in the next chapter.

8

Cooking up a country: sugar, eggs, and gunpowder, 1759–1868

The fruits of this wild wax tree [can be used] to make hair oil and candles for the needs of the country. . . . The lord has recently opened up the demesne mountains in the eastern six counties to allow mountain guards to collect the fruits which we buy at a good price, and this should work for the prosperity of the country. . . . Until now in this county [of Hata] these seeds have been allowed to fall and rot upon the ground!

From order by Hata county government, Motoi Gennojō, 7/30/1839[1]

The reforms of 1787 were an important turning point in Tosa history. The most easily identifiable result of these reforms was the restoration of the stability of domain finances. Cost-cutting measures were made possible by a new domainal government desire to limit the costs of Edo life and *bakufu* duty. The reduced burden on the local economy immediately allowed the people to enter a new period of growth, which focused on increasing the exports of traditional Tosa products and the development of new sustainable industries. The rhetoric of lordly rule remained dominant, but to the degree that the government decreased its role in the pyramidal economy of service centered on the shogun, it increased its role, both in actuality and in rhetoric, in the "internationally" conceived commercial economy.

The scholar Yokogawa Suekichi has surveyed a major collection of domain proclamations and has noted the great surge in the administration's use of *kokueki* thought in the Bunsei period (1818–29). He characterized the government's use of kokueki thought at this time as embodying a more enthusiastic support of commercial projects than previously. He summarized his argument, writing:

The Country Products policies of the Bunsei period included many new projects. These were labeled 'a lord's initiative' (*oshukō*) or 'a lord's experiment' (*otameshi*). In a feudal society given to reaffirming tradition, the support for these new projects appears very progressive. Furthermore, the domain claimed 'kokueki' – enrich the country – to rally

[1] Yamamoto Takeshi, *Kenshōbo*, vol. 3, pp. 460–1.

177

the energies of the realm's people to support the growth of independence of the domain economy.[2]

Commercial policy indeed became more complex, adaptable, and supportive of the export industry. There are three important features of policy after 1787. First is the appearance of a two-pronged approach to industrial development: The domain supported the well-developed industries such as paper by freeing restrictions on merchants and producers, but it continued granting monopoly licenses to merchants in minor and developing industries. The domain government invested more of its own money and energy into sponsoring those new industries, such as the production of sugar, eggs and gunpowder, that displayed export potential or had value as an import substitute. The second main feature is a shift away from a fiscal dependence on monopoly license fees (*myōgagin*), levies on monopoly merchants, and taxation of cottage industrial product as a supply of goods to the lord's household toward a dependence upon sales taxes and export taxes. This shift permitted the domain to continue profiting from industry while letting go of the pyramidal organization of commerce.

The third main feature is that the new industrial and commercial projects are not best characterized as government-led, top-down enterprises, but are better understood as the product of dialogue between many parties. This dialogue is often obscured in surviving documents by elitist patterns of rhetoric rooted in the paternalistic ideology of the public role of the samurai. I emphasize this last point because the introduction of growth-oriented and export-oriented policies has a very government-originated image in the literature, like common descriptions of the cameralist or Colbertian version of European mercantilism. Historians' interpretations have not changed substantially since Tōyama Shigeki described the mercantilist policies of the large domains in the 1840s as "having very little initiative and power from below. Rather rulers began the reforms in response to their own troubled finances. It was a thoroughly top-down venture."[3] The various interests involved in new kokueki policies can best be understood, however, by focusing on the dialogic nature of its creation.

The paper industry

On 3/10/1787, in the midst of the Ikegawa protest, the domain abolished all merchant monopolies and declared the sale and export of any product to be free to any merchant, as it had done in 1763. Furthermore, on 3/27/1787, the domain agreed to temporarily stop collecting most commercial taxes from

[2] Yokogawa Suekichi, "Bunseiki Tosa-han kokusan shihō no kenkyū," p. 301. The collection of proclamations is the *Kenshōbo*, which I liberally use in this chapter.
[3] Tōyama Shigeki, *Meiji ishin*, p. 33.

villages and ports, as a relief measure for the people of the domain.[4] Income from commercial taxes were 195 *kan* in 1781, but after the reform, only some imports and the export of tea provided taxes amounting to 33 kan in 1800.[5] These two policies limited domain income, but contributed to economic and political stability by making exportable items such as paper much more profitable to producers. The domain further encouraged sales outside of the domain by allowing foreign shippers to export any Tosa item freely. This was a change of policy reflecting the shift in emphasis from the protection of certain local shippers to the encouragement of the export products in general, and characterized the government's relationship to established industries thereafter.[6]

Papermaking was a well-established, decentralized, and relatively high-technology industry, which bound much of the Tosa region together. The history of this industry illustrates many of the nuances of the transition from what may be called feudal policy to commercial-state policy. As in many regions of Japan, paper had been produced in Tosa since ancient times. It is recorded as a tribute item from Tosa to the emperor Daigō in the early tenth century.[7] At the beginning of the early modern period, new technology was learned from neighboring Iyo province and spread throughout Tosa, thriving especially in Agawa county along the Niyodo river. The impetus for this expansion includes the increased demands both of the Tosa market and, later, of the export market that were created by the development of the early modern political economic order.

In contrast with tea, which was also a major export subject to domainal taxation and, at times, monopoly control, paper production inspired far more protest against domain policy. This is because paper producers were more affected than tea producers by the market. The consciousness of the producers was affected by the increasingly complex market organization of paper production. The main raw material was paper mulberry shrub, grown on Tosa's steep mountain slopes. Its branches were cut semiannually and steamed in large barrels, so that the recent year's annual growth of as-yet-unhardened wood could be peeled off like a skin. This skin was cleaned of the bark and defects such as insect damage. Then it was dried and baled for shipment to paper-producing areas. Preparation was a common activity in mountain villages

---

[4] Mutō Yoshikazu, *Nanroshi*, vol. 7, pp. 274–5.
[5] For 1778 it was 189 *kan*, ms. *An'ei hachinen tōbun oboegaki*, sect. 37, GM, no. 5500; 1781 was 195 kan, Mutō Yoshikazu, *Nanroshi*, vol. 1, p. 468; 1782 was 164 *kan*, "Okuni sanbutsu okuchigin chijime" in *TCK*, vol. 36, f. 148th; 1800 from ms. *Kyōwa gannen tōbun oboegaki*, section 39, GM, no. 5735; 1802 from ms. *Kyōwa sannen tōbun oboegaki*, sect. 38, GM, no. 5534; 1804 from ms. *Bunka ninen tōbun oboegaki*, sect. 40, GM, no. 5540.
[6] Mutō Yoshikazu, *Nanroshi*, vol. 78, pp. 278–9.
[7] Listed in the *Engishiki*, as quoted in Hirao, *Tosa-han kōgyō*, p. 98.

throughout Tosa. As we have seen, many mountain villages produced substantial amounts of paper as well, but much of the raw material was sent to plains villages such as Ino. At the site of paper production, this raw material was boiled in an alkaline solution of water and wood ash or, increasingly, purchased lime. After boiling, it was beaten to separate it into hair-thin fibers and then whitened by bleaching in running water and sunlight. The fibers were then placed in a large tub of water thickened with starch from the root of a special variety of hibiscus called *tororo aoi*. Then the papermaker used a carefully made boxed screen to draw out and strain a portion of the solution. The strained fiber residue on the screen was the paper. This paper was then moved to a growing stack of wet paper, then pressed in the stack and dried individually on large boards, and cut and bundled for sale. Because the technology was complex, most producers had to purchase the raw materials, the large boiling pot, the lime, the screen, the knives, the brushes, and the drying boards. This made them aware of, and very sensitive to, the selling price. The account book of one village producer reveals this clearly. He recorded his costs carefully, noting the initial capital required to purchase tools of production as well as raw material. At the end of each year, he recorded his profits or losses, which amounted to the earnings for his labor, "1784 .35 *monme* loss, 1785 109.14 monme profit, 1786 66.43 monme profit, 1787 56.80 monme profit, 1788 121.65 monme profit."[8] This consciousness affected not only producers but all marketers as well. Paper was a product used and exported in such quantities that a great number of merchants and shippers depended on its production for their livelihood. Monopoly licensing was often criticized in petitions by merchants whose interests were adversely affected.[9] Producers and merchants increasingly made demands based on their awareness of the costs of production.

Paper became a significant export only in the eighteenth century, but it was collected by the domain as a tax item from very early in the seventeenth century, paid primarily by mountain villagers as part of their casualties taxes (*komononari*).[10] The villages of Ino, Naruyama, and Umekubo along the Niyodo river were famous for the high-quality paper they produced, and developed a special relationship with the government. The domain assured them a supply of raw materials, took a portion of the paper as tax, and purchased some of the remainder.[11] The finest of this paper was chosen as a gift to the shogun, whereas

---

[8] *Kōchi-ken shi, kinsei hen*, pp. 534–7. The calculation does not include the expense of his own labor.

[9] See, for example, the petition of Izumiya Kaemon (8/25/1759), *TNK*, vol. 121, ff. 41st–48th.

[10] *TYK*, vol. 1, pp. 697–8, shows the casualties paid by one mountain village, including such items as paper, charcoal, deerhides, and millet.

[11] Hirao, *Tosa-han kōgyō*, pp. 100–7; *Kōchi-ken shi, kinsei hen*, pp. 374–5. Yamamoto Takeshi, *Kenshōbo*, vol. 3, pp. 329–31 contains a summary of domain policy from the year 1600 to the year 1737.

most was used in domain offices or sold to domain samurai. Private sales of the paper people produced after paying their tax quotas did not attract domainal attention, except for a general prohibition of the export of paper. The lack of attention can be assumed to reflect the relatively small scale of private sales within Tosa rather than explicit government recognition of free-market rights.

Control by a commercial monopoly first occurred in 1662 when, under the direction of the chief administrator, Nonaka Kenzan, who was looking for income to pay for a large bakufu imposition, the private sale of four important domain products – paper, tea, lacquer and oil-bearing seeds – was licensed to wealthy merchants of the castle town. Free commerce in these products was banned throughout the domain, and violators were fined or thrown in prison. This system was enforced severely enough that it inspired the protest that contributed to Kenzan's fall from power in 1663.[12] The following administration quickly abolished the monopoly and recognized the right of all merchants to deal freely in the four products within Tosa. Exports of paper, oil-bearing seeds, and lacquer were prohibited as they had always been. Tea continued to be a major export item and was taxed at the border.[13]

The domain did increase thereafter its control of the paper industry in Ino and Naruyama, however. This included quality control and price fixing of the raw materials as well as of the final product. Traditionally, the domain had ordered mountain villages to supply the raw paper mulberry underbark directly to the licensed producers in Ino and Naruyama. However, from the 1660s the domain began sending an official around to the mountain villages to purchase the underbark at a fixed price. He also was assigned to instruct villagers in the planting, harvest, and preparation.[14] In 1685, the domain issued improved quality standards and a price list for all of the varieties of paper to the producers in Ino and Naruyama.[15]

In 1704, government officials asked five town merchants to export paper, cloth, cotton, rope, and edible ferns to Osaka. It is highly unlikely that there was a great volume of trade in these products, especially as Tosa was generally a net importer of cloth and cotton. Three merchants of the castle town took the lead in 1709 in increasing the amount and quality of paper production in the mountain villages of Tosa. They hired specialist teachers from central Japan whom they sent around to the villages, and they lent capital to producers. These merchants acquired a licensed monopoly of the right to sell to the government, retainers, and temples, but sales to commoners were still uncontrolled. In 1714, the domain set up for the first time a Country Products Office (*kokusan*

[12] Hirao Michio, *Tosa-han kōgyō*, pp. 112–4.
[13] Yamamoto Takeshi, *Kenshōbo*, vol. 3, pp. 319–21.
[14] Ibid., pp. 329–30.
[15] Hirao Michio, *Tosa-han kōgyō*, pp. 101–5.

yakusho) and took over control and financing of the operation. It appointed seven merchants as its representatives and ordered many villages to fill production quotas that they would have to sell to domain purchasing agents at officially declared prices. The domain named all paper thus handled *kuragami* (storehouse paper), for the place where it would be stored for sale: the now little-used Nagasaki goods storehouses. The domain also employed low-level retainers as officials to travel around Tosa, instructing producers, checking quality, and keeping track of production amounts. This paper was sold locally and for export to Osaka. Fiscal difficulties led to the closure of the office in 1728, but kuragami quotas and purchases seem to have continued. The kuragami system was a burden on mountain villages because the declared purchase price was lower than the market price. The only relief for the producers was, as we have seen, that all production over quota was ignored by the domain – in effect allowing free sales of surplus paper to any merchant.

This policy changed in 1752 when the domain tried to monopolize almost all commerce in Tosa by once again setting up a Country Products Office, which managed the assignment of licensed monopolies to merchants in various products. A paper monopoly was created to control all production in excess of the kuragami quota. Under this system, producers were unable to make a profit on any of their paper. This situation quickly led to the Sakawa and the Tsunoyama protests described in Chapter 5. Many other villagers reduced production, sold on the thriving black market, or individually absconded across the mountains in hopes of a new life in Awa domain. The lordless samurai, Murakami Chūji, described this situation in a petition in 1761, writing: "Because the domain buys up these products at an unreasonably low price, it is much more profitable to sell on the black market. One can get three or four times the price on the Osaka market, and many people, therefore, become criminal and smuggle their goods."[16] Thanks to protests and such petitions, the monopoly was relaxed in 1761 and abolished in 1763. Paper over kuragami quota production was allowed to be sold and exported freely and was designated by the term *hiragami*.

Although, as we have seen, this policy lasted for only three years, it was a significant precursor of later policy that officially encouraged production for private sale. Because the domain taxed the private sales, it thus opened the way for the government to benefit fiscally from private exports as well.[17] Therefore, exports of paper were encouraged as a means of increasing the kokueki, rather than prohibited, as in the seventeenth century. The domain approved for the first time not only exports through the ports, but also those across the domain's

---

[16] Murakami Chūji (1/1/1761), *TNK*, vol. 130, f. 3rd.
[17] Yamamoto Takeshi, *Kenshōbo*, vol. 3, pp. 345–7.

mountain borders. As most mountain villages were near the borders, this gave producers more freedom from the control of purchasing agents by increasing their options.[18] In this way, we can see that villager protest worked to expand government recognition of the logic of market relationships.

When once again some wealthy merchants were granted monopoly control of hiragami during the fiscal crisis of 1766, the new system of control over the paper industry was doomed to failure. As in the 1750s, the focus of the protests by the mountain villagers in 1787 was the paper industry. The villagers of Ikegawa protested that the licensed paper merchant Kyōya Jōsuke was paying poor rates, which prevented them from making any profit, "If we could sell to merchants from other countries we could sell at 2 monme 3 or 4 *bu* per bundle. When we sell to the licensed merchant's buyers we get 1 monme 5 or 6 *bu* for the same thing!"[19] The villagers of Nanokawa who joined the protest also pointed out that the coercive kuragami purchasing rates had by this time become a mere one third of the market rate, writing, "Please purchase the paper at an agreeable price."[20]

The domain's response to this protest embodied many progressive policies, but also some conservatism, leading to the creation of three separate categories of paper administration: (1) A quota of kuragami was purchased from designated mountain villages at confiscatory rates; (2) hiragami could be freely bought and sold (after 1805, subject to sales and export taxes); and (3) an amount of hiragami was purchased using domain agents. The domain re-created the hiragami category by rescinding the licensed monopolies on paper and other products. Only weeks later, it also stopped collecting taxes on the export of paper and most other products as a measure of relief, and closed down the Country Products Office once again.[21] However, the domain tried to strengthen the system of kuragami collection by arguing that it was a form of tax (*jōnō*). As a concession, they reduced the quotas of production for kuragami by a small amount, but did not raise the abysmally low purchasing price.[22] This was to maintain an inexpensive supply of paper for domain and samurai use, and to gain a supply of paper for export to Osaka.

The domain also developed the third category of treatment because the quota of kuragami paper was not enough to secure the amount of loans the domain needed from merchants in Osaka. By abandoning the practice of granting licensed privileges to merchants, the domain lost control over the destina-

[18] Yamamoto Takeshi, *Kenshōbo*, vol. 3, p. 336, shows that, in 1761, export over mountains was still prohibited. In 1763, mountain and port exports were permitted, pp. 340–1.
[19] *Kōchi-ken shi, kinsei hen*, pp. 558–9.
[20] Irimajiri Yoshinaga, *Tosa-han keizai*, p. 102.
[21] Yamamoto Takeshi, *Kenshōbo*, vol. 3, p. 370.
[22] *Kōchi-ken shi, kinsei hen*, pp. 574–5.

tion of the exported hiragami paper and could no longer use guarantees of paper sales to gain loans in Osaka. The domain responded to this problem by purchasing hiragami at the prevailing private-market rate and exporting this paper to Osaka so that "the lord's conditions of financing in Osaka will improve." In 1789, all village headmen were ordered to purchase paper from producers at the market price, "just as any other merchant would purchase it. . . . The paper price should be determined in the same way as townsmen purchasers and you should not decide the price yourself."[23] Because the domain initially had no money to lend, they ordered the village headmen and some other village grandees to use their own capital to purchase the product. The policy also attempted to encourage production through providing marketing assistance to producers and the infusion of capital. The domain recommended to the village headmen and other purchasers, "There are some people who wish to increase their production of paper but cannot because they cannot acquire the capital. Lend capital to these people at no interest and collect the paper when it is made in payment."[24] The domain paid, presumably from profits, the participating headmen and others substantial fees in return for acting as purchasing and capital-lending agents. In Hata county, seven purchasers were paid 30 monme (82 monme = 1 *koku*) and two were paid 150 monme for their services in the year 1795.[25] The paper bought and sold through this system was called *shogunshi*, and sold on the Osaka market. Sekita Hidesato has pointed out that, unlike the monopolies or kuragami, the purchase of shogunshi was not coercive in nature. By competing with other merchants on their own terms, the domain was, in effect, acting as a private commercial company within this sphere of activity. Although the shogunshi undoubtedly served to help gain loans in Osaka, the domain also advertised itself as aiding the livelihoods of all producers. The price of the main raw material, paper mulberry, for example, became a very sensitive issue to the domain in the nineteenth century. As paper production increased, the price of paper mulberry rose, and it became difficult to acquire. The domain tried many different measures to control price fluctuations, often because "paper producers are in distress," and it asked its shogunshi purchasers to lend capital to producers.[26] This system had a public significance, because it added one more government affirmation of the commoner's right to produce and sell their product according to market rules.

[23] Sekita Hidesato, "'Hiragami' no hatten to 'shogunshi' no seiritsu," p. 80; Yamamoto Takeshi, *Kenshōbo*, vol. 3, pp. 377–9.
[24] Sekita, "Hiragami," p. 80.
[25] Yamamoto Takeshi, *Kenshōbo*, vol. 3, pp. 381–2. Sekita Hidesato points this out but misquotes the amount in "Hiragami," p. 81.
[26] Yamamoto Takeshi, *Kenshōbo*, vol. 3, pp. 399–400, 420–2, 435–6.

The three-tiered system lasted from 1787 until 1860, but the kuragami collection steadily declined and finally became untenable. Around 1820–1, total paper production known to the government was valued at 3,990 kan, equivalent in value to over 44,000 koku of rice. Eighty-five percent was free-market hiragami, including 4 percent bought by domain agents. Kuragami represented 15 percent of Tosa production.[27] A glance at domain profits and taxes from the paper industry reveals that kuragami was the most profitable, yielding 23 percent of the 362 kan collected. Producers complained that they could not profit from kuragami production, but the domain argued that kuragami was a kind of a tax (using the word jōnō) that should be borne as a responsibility, not as a profit-making activity. Producers subverted the kuragami system in a number of ways: They produced thin, poor quality paper;[28] they included too few sheets per bundle;[29] they absconded from villages with a kuragami quota to settle in other villages, or even outside of the domain.[30] These various forms of resistance made enforcement expensive, and because paper quality was low, it often brought a bad price in Osaka relative to the free-market paper. In 1836, the domain began raising the rates that it paid to producers as a temporary relief measure.[31] This was not enough, and in 1838 the domain reduced village kuragami quotas by 20 percent for five years, while raising the price paid to producers by 20 percent.[32] When this five-year period was up, one domain official wrote about the kuragami system in a report to the senior administrators,

Because all producers lose a great amount of money [on kuragami sales] they have been put in terrible distress. For many years numerous villages submitted petitions concerning this, but this did not receive the slightest investigation. Finally [in 1838 the quota was reduced from 150,000 bundles to 132,000 bundles a year for a period of five years, and the price was raised by thirty (sic) percent. Now that period is over.] People in the countryside have piled up great losses of money because of the kuragami system. Kuragami has been a source of decline for the people of the country.[33]

This severe assessment, long expressed in petitions, had become the common opinion among officials. After 1838, the domain reduced by two thirds the amount of kuragami paper it sent to Osaka, and instead used kuragami in government and for sale at a reduced price to retainers. Hirao Michio notes in

[27] Hiragami figures are for 1820, calculated as twelve times the taxes collected, HB, no. 200, pp. 21–3. Remainder for 1821 is from a financial document copied in ms. *Obugukata kenbunroku*, unclassified document in Mori-ke monjo in the Kōchi Prefecture Library.
[28] Yamamoto Takeshi, *Kenshōbo*, vol. 3, p. 395.
[29] Ibid., pp. 384, 393–4.
[30] Ibid., pp. 413–6; Irimajiri, *Tosa-han keizai*, p. 102.
[31] Yamamoto Takeshi, *Kenshōbo*, vol. 3, pp. 448–9, 455.
[32] Ibid., pp. 456–9.
[33] Ms. (untitled and unsigned – internal evidence suggests that it is a report from the rural magistrate circa 1843), GM, no. 5704–2.

his research that between 1817 and 1859 the amount of kuragami paper collected fell from 197,109 bundles to 134,740 bundles, and the value of sales fell from 529 kan to 291 kan.[34] Comparing this to hiragami production in 1860, shows that kuragami had declined to less than 5 percent of total production of paper in the domain.

Finally, in 1860, the domain abolished the kuragami system altogether and allowed the free sale of all paper.[35] The chief administrator of the time, Yoshida Tōyō, wrote his perception of the problems of the system in the proclamation abolishing kuragami:

> Over the years a great gulf has developed between the market price for paper and the kuragami price. All producers have had great difficulty, and they have submitted petitions for many decades. Kuragami has been a means for the administration to get by its short term (financial) troubles, but its existence makes it difficult to sustain government. People strive to make this paper in order to care for their parents and children and to give themselves a safe living. Retainers receive stipends and status in order that they may protect and care for the welfare of peasants. Instead, we are receiving this paper bought at an unfairly low price. It is truly something about which to hold our heads in shame. Therefore we will abolish kuragami distribution from the first of next month.[36]

Yoshida's assertion that the kuragami system "makes it difficult to sustain government" (*oseitai aitachinikui gi*) reveals the deep ideological shift that had taken place. People no longer accepted the subjection of their commercial production to a tax-in-kind and a service to the lord and his household. Government had to base its rule upon acceptance of the commercial rules of exchange, because (especially in the paper industry) its people had become so dependent on commercial relationships.

In contrast to the decline in kuragami production, the production of free-market paper in Tosa expanded greatly after the abolition of the monopoly in 1787. For seventeen years, this production went untaxed, as a measure of relief to producers. However, in 1805, the domain revived the export tax and created an internal sales tax on many products including paper.[37] The tax rate for paper was one-twelfth of the sale value. Because the paper industry continued to expand rapidly, the paper sales tax became the single most important source of domain cash income by the 1840s. Producers continued to be permitted to market to whomever they wished, but village headmen were entrusted with keeping records of all sales and shipments from the village, in order to administer the tax system. This sales tax system was strengthened over time. Yoshida Tōyō, for example, made the sales tax system much more thorough than before

---

[34] Hirao Michio, *Tosa-han kōgyō*, p. 117.
[35] Ibid., pp. 118–20.
[36] Ibid., p. 119.
[37] Yamamoto Takeshi, *Kenshōbo*, vol. 3, pp. 386–9.

Table 8.1. Domain income from paper industry sources, expressed in *kan*

Year	Kuragami			Hiragami (free market)	
	Osaka marketed	Domain marketed	Profits	Taxes	Estimated total production
1776	502	166	148	64[a]	768
1781	355	178	80	64[a]	768
1800	336	124	77	none	
1802	317	114	104	none	
1818	459	107	58	110	1320
1820	392	104	?	270	3240
1842	137	164	?	362	4344
1847	133	195	?	372	4464
1852	138	127	?	457	5484
1859	113	127	?	?	
1860	none			478	5736

[a] under monopoly control

at the time he abolished the kuragami system.[38] Production continued to rise to an average of 6,822,373 bundles of paper in 1864–6.[39] In the first years of Meiji, around 1870, Osaka officials noted that Tosa was exporting about 100,000 *maru* of paper to Osaka, which far exceeded the 20,000 maru of its nearest rival Chōshū and amounted to 60 percent of the paper sent to Osaka from all of Japan.[40]

Table 8.1 illustrates the gradual increase in the importance of free-market paper over kuragami paper to domain finances from the 1770s to the 1860s. The amount of profit from kuragami sales fluctuated over time, but taxes from free-market sales of paper rose steadily in the nineteenth century. To the right of the free market taxes in Table 8.1 is given a column of the estimated total production of free-market paper, based upon the one-twelfth tax rate. Because avoidance of taxes was common, the amount is surely an underestimate of the actual

[38] Hirao Michio, *Yoshida Tōyō*, p. 121.

[39] Figure for 1864–6 from ms. *Kōchi-han shi, bussan rui*, vol. 1, f. 13th, held on microfilm in the Kōchi Prefecture Library.

[40] Ōsaka Shōkō Kaigisho, *Ōsaka shōgyō shi shiryō*, vol. 2, f. 119. Because the number of bundles (*soku*) per *maru* differed for each type of paper, it is impossible to convert this into bundles. A common size of paper, *ōhanshi*, took 240 sheets to make a bundle and 40 bundles to make a maru, or 9,600 sheets. Around 1804, a paper merchant estimated total Tosa production, including exports, to be about 60,000 maru (Miyaji Nakae, ms. *Shūwa*, [K916/Miya], Kōchi Prefecture Library, ff. 6th–7th).

free-market production, possibly a vast underestimate if the sugar industry, to be discussed below, is any indication.[41] Even with this limitation, Table 8.1 shows the great expansion of the value of free-market production of paper in Tosa relative to kuragami production. The words of the many petitioners of the 1750s and 1760s, claiming that the abolition of monopoly control would increase exports and work for the kokueki were prophetic. Over time, domain income from taxes of this free-market paper improved, while income from the more coercive kuragami system stagnated and declined.

The domain purchases of free-market paper are not reflected in the documents that provided the basis of Table 8.1, and unfortunately, documents revealing the scale of the system are scarce. One detailed financial document from 1821 shows that 33 kan of paper were purchased as shogunshi by village officials for the domain and 124 kan were purchased otherwise (probably in the castle town). Sales of this paper after costs reaped a profit of only 6 kan for the domain, but the major function of the system was to gain loans from Osaka merchants by funneling produce to the merchants in payment, and in this it was successful.[42] Furthermore, the free-market paper was of better quality than the kuragami paper and was sold at a better price in Osaka. A separate document shows that in 1821 paper prices on the Osaka market were depressed and that the kuragami sales were made at a loss to the domain, whereas the paper purchased on the open market still managed to make a small profit, probably the 6 kan quoted above.[43] It seems reasonable to conclude that in good years as well, the latter was more profitable. This would explain why, in 1838, the domain finally decided to restrict exports of kuragami to the Osaka market and sell most of it locally, where it served to provide cheap supplies to domain offices and retainers.

In sum, after 1787, paper production could not be returned to the control of licensed monopoly merchants for fear of protest by producers. Popular protest was crucial in forcing changes, because much was at stake for the domain in an already well-established industry like paper. Wealthy merchants who provided the domain with *goyōgin* had to be appeased, through more infrequent calls for the money and more faithful paybacks. New means of securing Osaka loans had to be found, such as through the shogunshi system. New means of taxation of commerce had to be developed to assert control over an abstract "national" market, such as through the creation of an internal sales tax. The domain responded reluctantly and with many mistakes, but it ultimately did develop workable answers.

---

[41] Yamamoto Takeshi, *Kenshōbo*, vol. 3, pp. 399–400.
[42] Ms. *Obugukata kenbunroku*, unclassified document in Mori-ke monjo in the Kōchi Prefecture Library.
[43] Sekita, "Hiragami," p. 81.

Less was at stake for both producers and the domain in the newer industries, and the domain government embraced kokueki thought energetically and vociferously in the nineteenth century. It provided capital, marketing capabilities and legal control of the border of Tosa to foster the development of many new industries in Tosa aimed at increasing exports or reducing imports. Producers also were, initially at least, less troubled by monopoly control of these newer products. In the next section, some of the new domain projects such as the production of sugar will be examined.

Sugar, eggs, and gunpowder: New projects

The domain embarked upon many new commercial and production projects in the nineteenth century, in order to create jobs, cut imports and expand exports. Officials repeatedly exhorted the people with phrases like, "Only import things that are absolutely necessary. If you use as much as possible products made in this country, then the lord's intentions will be fulfilled."[44] Production and commerce envisioned at the level of the country were becoming, in effect, a public affair. This is not to say that the domain officials are best understood as leaders of these enterprises. The sugar industry at first glance looks like a prime example of a top-down project, bestowed by enlightened bureaucrats upon the realm. However, the process of creating a formidable sugar industry in Tosa in a few short decades illustrates how the energy of the domain authorities and monopoly merchant interests was quickly outpaced by expansive commercial activity among the rest of the populace.

The headman of Niida Village, Hamaguchi Jinzaemon, attempted sugar manufacture in the 1720s, likely with the direction of the Country Products Office, but this project ended in unsuccess.[45] In 1788, the domain official and scholar Umazume Gonnosuke was in Edo on duty when the lord ordered him to learn about the making of sugar from the lordless samurai Ikegami Tarōzaemon, who produced sugar in the nearby post station village of Kawasaki. When Gonnosuke returned to the domain, he attempted to make sugar. Ikegami's production method was written out, and copies were made available to the senior domain officials to enlist their support.[46] Early on the project met with little success.

The turning point came in 1797 when Gonnosuke became the castle town magistrate and gained the cooperation of the wealthy merchant Tamuraya Gen'emon. Hearing of the project, a sugar specialist named Araki Sahei from outside Tosa showed up at the Tosa border one day to offer his assistance.

[44] From a proclamation of 1819 or 1820, Yamamoto Takeshi, *Kenshōbo*, vol. 3, p. 401.
[45] Hirao, *Tosa-han kōgyō*, pp. 142–3; Hirota Kōichi, "Tosa-han kanshō," pp. 48–50.
[46] An untitled copy survives in GM, no. 2448.

Border guards were ready to turn back this foreigner without a passport, but after being notified, Tamuraya overcame opposition by arguing that if Araki helped the project succeed, "the lord's wishes will be fulfilled and it will work for the prosperity of the country."[47] Sahei was granted entry, and on his recommendation, the merchant Amagasakiya Matabei imported sugar cane shoots for planting and began experimental production in the Niida coastal region. The domain began supporting expansion of the project in 1803 by declaring it a lord's initiative and announcing that it would accept petitions from anyone wishing to manufacture sugar using Araki Sahei's method – a far cry from its attitude in the 1720s. The domain also offered to sell sugar cane plants to anyone who wished to plant them, and offered to lend the capital to prospective planters.[48] The domain provided 70 percent and Tamuraya 30 percent of the purchasing capital for the enterprise. The merchants were granted 5 percent of sales as a fee, but from 1803 to 1805 both the domain and Tamuraya lost money annually.

In 1806, the project finally began making profits, and Tamuraya and another merchant, Mokuya Yōemon, were appointed monopoly wholesalers of sugar in Tosa. Retail merchants had to purchase sugar from these two wholesalers, and free sales of sugar by producers were prohibited. The Osaka sugar market was booming, and it was very easy in most years to make profits. Sugar production in Tosa expanded rapidly to become, in only a few decades, the second most important export product after paper. Tosa production grew so quickly that Satsuma domain, the traditional producer of sugar, filed a suit with the Edo bakufu to limit sugar production in Tosa and other domains because it was creating unfavorable competition.[49] For its part, the bakufu was worried about the effect on rice prices in its cities and responded to the rapid spread of sugar production in Shikoku with a decree prohibiting the cultivation of sugar cane on traditionally rice-producing fields.[50] However, Tosa officials had little reason to enforce these proclamations in coastal rice fields of marginal productivity. Sugar made money for the domain and provided coastal farmers with a hardy crop less susceptible to typhoon damage than rice. Furthermore, it gave the people of Tosa new livelihoods, and unlike Tosa rice, sugar was so exportable it worked for the "prosperity of the country."

In 1820 exports had grown sufficiently that the domain applied export and sales taxes. Of course, the bottom line was money, and income to the domain from sugar rose swiftly, reflecting the rapid growth in production. In 1824,

[47] Hirao, *Tosa-han kōgyō*, p. 145.
[48] Yamamoto Takeshi, *Kenshōbo*, vol. 3, pp. 383–4.
[49] Shikoku Minka Hakubutsukan Kenkyūsho, ed., *Sanuki oyobi shūhen*, pp. 82–3.
[50] Hirao, *Tosa-han kōgyō*, p. 149.

sugar sales generated 26 kan in taxes. This rose to 75 kan in 1845 and 122 kan in 1860.[51] The domain justified placing these taxes in terms of its long-term financial support for sugar production and its determination to work for the prosperity of the country:

Since [the 1790s] the lord ordered the production of sugar, but the product was of poor quality and for many years money was lost. However it was decided that in time production methods would be refined and product quality would improve. More than anything it was hoped to work for the prosperity of the country and in time become a source of export taxes. Therefore all effort was made regardless of the cost. Recently the lord's wish has been fulfilled and production has increased annually. The sugar sells profitably on the Osaka market and these days villagers and people in the ports have been able to pursue sufficiently good livelihoods.[52]

As in the language of many domain documents the sugar industry is depicted as a thoroughly top-down enterprise in this statement. The language is a blend of lord-centered ideology and kokueki ideology, where the lord asserts his labors for the kokueki. Although in the case of sugar, domain initiative was apparently more important than in many industries, there was significant involvement from many quarters by merchants and peasants that disappeared from this government-produced text.

As with the domain, merchants also based claims for licensed privileges on their efforts to promote the prosperity of Tosa. The domain government designated Tamuraya Gen'emon and Mokuya Yōemon the wholesale merchants to Osaka in 1814, granting Tamuraya 80 percent of the market and Mokuya, 20 percent. But production had already risen to sufficient amounts that in 1815 Tamuraya used his influence with some retainers who had access to the lord to discuss the limitations of expansion on the Osaka market and the potential profit in Edo. In Tamuraya's words, "The lord favorably received the argument that this would work for the prosperity of the country," and ordered the setting up of a retail outlet. Tamuraya requested to sell one third of exported Tosa sugar through the Edo store of the Tosa merchant Tatsumiya Kōzaemon. However, Tamuraya was granted only 30 percent of wholesale rights to the new Edo market, the lion's share going to Mokuya. He wished for more and wrote the domain a petition, "Ever since the production of sugar was initiated in this country of Tosa, I have given it my all, thinking of nothing but the prosperity of the country."[53] Although his request was not successful, his means of asking was significant. As a merchant with already neat ties to the lord, he could conceiv-

---

[51] For 1824, Hirao Michio, "Bunsei nenkan sanbutsu okuchigin hyō," in HB, no. 100, p. 23; 1845 Hirao Michio, "Kokusangata sashidashi hyo," in HB, no. 200, pp. 41–2; 1860 Hirao, *Tosa-han shōgyō*, pp. 220–1.
[52] Yamamoto Takeshi, *Kenshōbo*, vol. 3, pp. 402–4.
[53] Hirao Michio, *Tosa-han kōgyō*, pp. 160–4.

ably have described his part in sugar production as service to the lord with terms such as *hōkō* or *goyō*, but instead he chose to justify his effort in terms of economic nationalism. Tamuraya is clearly a precursor of the Meiji industrialists who justified their activities in the same way.[54]

The control of the monopoly wholesalers and the government weakened in the face of enormous expansion by producers throughout the domain. Because the sugar industry was so profitable, this did not create serious problems. Every year the domain, the monopoly merchants and the producers saw greater income in the expanding market. In 1838, the domain was able to raise the export taxes on sugar with confidence, "In recent years the price of sugar on the Osaka market has risen enormously. This will certainly work for the prosperity of the country. However the previous tax scale is low compared to the current prices, and we have decided to raise the amounts accordingly."[55] The interest in the export tax arose because the government was not controlling a large amount of the sugar production through its merchant monopoly system. In 1840 for example, the amount of sugar under production and purchased by the domain was listed in official documents as 266,797 *kin*.[56] Calculating from export taxes, however, gives a figure of nearly one million kin.[57] General port taxes were more successful at gaining income from the sugar trade than the monopoly itself. Because, as with all products, many sales escaped the tax system, this itself is surely an underestimate of production. In 1848 the domain did make an attempt to incorporate new producers and new local marketers of sugar into its system, but this attempt met with little success.[58] In 1868, Tamuraya gave an estimate of Tosa production at 270,000 kin writing "of course I have no idea how much this over- or underestimates production, and all is increased by 20%" showing that he believed at least 20 percent of production was escaping his purview.[59] Records created by Osaka merchants concerning sugar imports from all of the domains of Japan in the same year, however, show that he was short by no less than a factor of ten. They record that 2,700,000 kin (1,620,000 kg.) of sugar were imported into Osaka from Tosa. This represented only the amount shipped to Osaka. Because sugar was shipped to other parts of Japan and was consumed locally, the actual production was certainly much higher. Other early Meiji period figures corroborate the higher estimate and reveal that the vast

---

[54] Byron Marshall, *Capitalism and Nationalism in Prewar Japan*, pp. 39–40; Fujita Teiichirō, "Kinsei Nihon ni okeru 'kokueki' shisō no seiritsu to sono tenkai katei," pp. 22–3.

[55] Yamamoto Takeshi, *Kenshōbo*, vol. 3, p. 459. Although the tax rate remained constant, this rate was applied to a standard price rather than to actual sales prices.

[56] Hirao, *Tosa-han kōgyō*, p. 150 (1 *kin* equals about 0.6 kg.).

[57] Shikoku, *Sanuki oyobi*, p. 83.

[58] Yamamoto Takeshi, *Kenshōbo*, vol. 3, p. 478 for producers, p. 481 for marketers. A document on p. 506 shows that, in 1856, the domain was still trying to control marketers.

[59] Hirao, *Tosa-han kōgyō*, p. 150.

majority of the supposedly monopolized Tosa sugar industry was escaping the system.[60] Because sugar had so quickly become an important element in the lives of Tosa people and because it was so oriented to the export market, it is likely that if the domain had seriously tried to control all production it would have created social problems of the order that it created with the paper industry in the late eighteenth century. Instead, it tolerated the private enterprise and attempted to gain income through a strengthening of the port tax system.[61]

The case of salt production in Tosa is a well-documented example of the tendency to ascribe origins of industries to samurai leadership, where the real impetus came from commoners. The samurai scholar Tani Mashio is credited with beginning the Shimizu salt works in 1780.[62] In reality, the people of Shimizu had heard of the potential lucrativeness of salt production from foreign shipping merchants who traded there. The people of Shimizu port repeatedly requested domain port officials for capital to create the salt works but were turned down a number of times. When Tani became the port official and toured in 1778, he accepted their idea and approved domain support for the project to produce salt, in order to fix the problem that "twenty to thirty thousand koku of salt are imported annually into this country," and that it would provide a livelihood for locals. In time, the Shimizu salt works produced an average of over seven hundred koku of salt per year. In Tani's own memorandum on the project written in 1784, it is not so much that he inserts his own name into the origins of the project as that he obliterates the petitioning of the people of Shimizu.[63] From this beginning, it was not long until he was remembered as the founder.

In contrast with salt production, which needed much capital, chicken eggs could be produced by anyone. They became a surprisingly important export to Osaka, given Tosa's distance by sea. In 1762, one anonymous petitioner suggested that the domain order all villages to produce eggs and collect a small tax.[64] The record of domain support for egg production in the ensuing decades is scanty, but an initiative seems to have been made by the castle town government to export eggs. In 1820, the domain began taxing exports at 5 monme of silver per one hundred eggs. In the same year, it encouraged the exports of eggs by releasing previous restrictions on which port they could leave from.[65] There-

---

[60] Shikoku, *Sanuki oyobi*, p. 116; Hirao, *Tosa-han kōgyō*, p. 150.
[61] It is rather fascinating that a domain survey of all production in Tosa for 1864–6 inexplicably does not include sugar; ms. *Kōchi-han shi, bussan rui*, vols. 1–3, held on microfilm in Kōchi Prefecture Library.
[62] *Tosa Shimizu-shi shi, jōkan*, p. 581, and more generally on the local salt works, pp. 581–7.
[63] *TCK*, vol. 28, ff. 5th–24th. The relevant points are on f. 5th and f. 10th.
[64] Anonymous (2/13/(1762)), *TNK*, vol. 135, ff. 68th–71st.
[65] Yamamoto Takeshi, *Kenshōbo*, vol. 3, pp. 402–4.

after, taxes fluctuated from 20 to 30 kan per year, showing that in a good year over six million eggs were exported. Exporting the eggs was no easy business, requiring careful packing in woven straw bundles. The domain scholar Miyaji Umanosuke was on his way to Edo when he witnessed in 1832 the terrible fate of one ship laden with eggs in rough seas. The ship pulled out of Murōtsu port bound for Osaka, but

the wind was blowing strongly. The ship threw out its anchor but the rope broke and the boat was carried up and broken upon the coastal rocks. The four sailors were able to climb up to the shore sustaining only small injuries. A great crowd of old and weak, men and women swarmed like maggots on the shore, lifting the ship's cargo out of the water as it washed upon the rocks; 240 bundles of Nosayama pottery and 280 bales of eggs – 10,550 eggs – and many other things they say. I could not bear to watch it![66]

The ship Miyaji described was also carrying pottery, another recently encouraged export. Its history rather eloquently illustrates the shift away from the importance of Edo life in domain rule. Odoyaki pottery had been made in Tosa since the middle of the seventeenth century. It had been produced as high-quality ware mainly for use by the domain lord for gift giving to other daimyo lords and chief retainers. In the seventeenth and eighteenth centuries, most commoner pottery in Tosa was imported from domains with large pottery industries such as those in Kyūshū. The changed attitude of the domain in the nineteenth century led it to order the potters to stop producing lordly gift ware and begin producing ware as an import substitute and for export. The lord placed the potters under the jurisdiction of the castle town government, which moved the kilns to a new location at Nosayama in 1822 where production could be expanded. An attempt was then made to find the raw materials locally, instead of importing some necessities as had been done before. This, however, had the deleterious effect of reducing product quality, and soon Osaka exports declined. The solution the town magistrate proposed, and gained approval for, in 1837 was to make the pottery work as an import substitute, a solution characteristically linked to a strong kokueki consciousness. He suggested that the lord encourage the Kōchi pottery wholesalers to send the pottery to all of the Tosa ports without being subject to tax (foreign pottery was subject). They would then "try as much as possible to sell at a price lower than imports from other countries. Then naturally people will begin using only domestically made pottery, and this will work eternally for the prosperity of the country."[67]

In addition to assisting the development of other products such as camphor, iron, lime and others too numerous to deal with here, the domain worked

[66] Ms. *Edo nikki, Tenpō san, ichi*, f. 5th, held in the Kōchi Prefecture Library (K122/19/Miyaji).
[67] Hirao, *Tosa-han kōgyō*, pp. 170–2. See also Yamamoto Takeshi, *Kenshōbo*, vol. 3, pp. 464–5.

generally to aid marketing of products outside Tosa.[68] Domain support of exports on the Osaka market and its prohibitions of some imports affected the marketing privileges of Osaka merchant organizations. Sometimes those merchant organizations reorganized themselves to accommodate domainal changes, and sometimes they resisted these changes by going to court or did their best to thwart domain initiatives through use of their market power and lending power. In the eighteenth century, the domain had successfully supported its firewood exporters in the court of the Osaka magistrate a number of times to preserve the market rights of the Tosa firewood industry.[69] It set up wholesalers in towns other than Osaka to prevent flooding the Osaka market and depressing prices.[70] It arranged for sales of Tosa products in the lucrative market of Edo and supported legal cases there in defense of its marketers.[71] With the Ansei reforms, inaugurated soon after Perry's arrival, the domain set up the Kaiseikan, a domain management office centering on an aggressive industrial development program.[72] Although legal support for domain products was not a new phenomenon of the nineteenth century, the shift of emphasis away from Osaka in these endeavors was new and was at times threatening to the interests of Osaka merchants who then complained to the bakufu.

Interdomainal trade and aggressive export marketing policies increased in many domains from the mid-eighteenth century on, and this has long been recognized by historians as a thorny problem for the bakufu.[73] On the one hand, the bakufu wanted domain lords to be strong enough to rule their domains, yet on the other hand, domain economic activities increasingly disrupted the Osaka-centered market order that benefited the bakufu. Depending upon who had the reins, the bakufu sometimes expressed support for domain economic

---

[68] Hirao Michio's many books contain superb institutional studies of the many industries of Tosa.

[69] Hirotani Kijūrō deals with a 1715 legal case in "Osaka ni okeru Shōtoku gonen no maki kakarime soshō mondai." Yasuoka Shigeaki deals with a 1770s case in *Nihon hōken keizai seisaku shi ron*, pp. 45–78. Once again, the domain supported its producers against Osaka merchants in 1842 (Yamamoto Takeshi, *Kenshōbo*, vol. 3, p. 467). See also Tano-chō Shi Hensan Iinkai, *Tano-chō shi*, pp. 301–6 for the use of lending power to thwart domain initiatives.

[70] Yamamoto Takeshi, *Kenshōbo*, vol. 3, p. 407, for the creation of a wholesaler for Tosa products in Kaizuka in 1822. One was also instituted in Hyōgo (lord's diary copied in ms. *Hakuyō nichiroku*, HB, no. 72, pp. 110, 127). Hirao, *Tosa-han shōgyō*, pp. 237–68.

[71] For example, the case of sugar above. Also the domain gave the Edo merchant Mitsui Tomojirō a substantial sum in reward for his aid in a legal case called "The Country Products Sales Incident" ("okokusan urisabaki ikken"). From lord's diary copied in HB, no. 72, pp. 173–5. I have unfortunately been unable to locate the records of the case.

[72] Marius Jansen, *Sakamoto Ryōma*, pp. 246–7, 308–9; Morita Norihiko, "Kaiseikan shihō no tenkai to sono genkai."

[73] Yamaguchi Tetsu, "Bakuhansei shijō," p. 234; Fujita Teiichirō, "Bakuhanseiteki shijō kōzō no hōkai – Tenpō sannen Kata-ura shokoku sanbutsu kōekisho ikken."

projects, and at other times, it used prohibitions and other limitations to aid the merchants and townsmen of shogunal territory, most especially Osaka, and to strengthen bakufu authority.[74] In the 1770s, the wielder of bakufu authority, Tanuma Okitsugu, a well-known centralizer, tried suppressing domain marketing activities in Osaka to give the Osaka merchants the upper hand.[75] In the 1840s Mizuno Tadakuni abolished outright all domain marketing facilities and organizations in the futile hope of lowering prices.[76] Yet suppression was ultimately doomed to failure. The economy of service centered on the shogun was being rejected, and domains that embraced mercantilist strategies to develop and protect themselves flourished.

Although the weight of this book has focused on the creation of something new, it should be stressed here that the old order of samurai supremacy and their values remained dominant in most spheres of activity. The domain officials, as samurai, were always concerned with morals, selfless duty, seating arrangements and military affairs. As soon as finances rebounded with the Tenmei reforms, the government spent money to build two new naval vessels and purchased new arms – selling the old ones to needy retainers at low rates.[77] This had more to do with bolstering self-image in a time of doubt than with practical military matters, but when the fracases with the Russians and British brought increasing pressure for coastal defense in the early nineteenth century, the domain began doing its best to manufacture locally guns and gunpowder. Early on, production of "the country product most important for defense" was fully controlled by the domain, but because production lagged behind needs, officials began encouraging anyone to produce what they could.[78] After Perry's arrival made battle become an imminent prospect, commoners saw a new opportunity to appeal for their public worth. The wily residents of Satokaida village argued in 1856 that, if only the domain would permit them to set up a market place with ten stores in front of their temple, "we could best service the signal fires and troops stationed in our area."[79] The Western nations brought immense commercial and military pressure to the archipelago – an entity that

---

[74] Horie Yasuzō has focused on forms of *bakufu* support for domain projects in *Kokusan shōrei*, pp. 32–42.

[75] Takeuchi Makoto, "Kansei kaikaku," pp. 4–5.

[76] Ōguchi Yūjirō, "Tenpō ki no seikaku," pp. 341–2; Ono Masao, "Bakuhansei seiji kaikakuron," pp. 322–9; Yoshinaga Akira, *Kinsei no senbai seido*, pp. 222–4.

[77] Ms. *Sansei nichiroku*, vol. 2, ff. 65th–66th, in the Kōchi Prefecture Library; *TKK*, vol. 31, ff. 83rd–84th. For a delightful criticism of the used-arms sale and other policies of the reform, see *Heso no tanuki*, written as a *gesaku* style parody (ms. *Hakuwansō*, vol. 28, photographic copy in the Kōchi Prefecture Library)

[78] Hirao, *Tosa-han kōgyō*, pp. 200–29; Yamamoto Takeshi, *Kenshōbo*, vol. 3, pp. 393, 432–4, 461, 463–4, 496, 499–501.

[79] Ms. "Ukagai tatematsuru kōjō oboe," no. 2052 in the Uka-ke monjo collection held in the Kōchi Prefecture Library.

the Westerners called a closed country and proponents of kokueki saw as an international economic order. The country of Tosa was soon to lose its identity, absorbed into the newly developing nation-state of Japan, but domains like Tosa happened to have found one ingredient of the national recipe.

9

Conclusion

People in government and commerce responded to their eighteenth-century problems more effectively with the premises of *kokueki* thought than was possible with arguments from traditional modes of thought. Ideologies of service to one's superior gave little justification to avoid performance for the shogun. The bullionist concepts of kokueki thought, however, supported any tendency to restrict official expense outside of the domain, and the rhetoric of kokueki had nothing within it to condemn lack of service to the shogun. Policies of resistance to *bakufu* duty and Edo life reduced the need for excessive taxation. Emphasis on balance of trade encouraged the domain to choose its markets more freely and to decrease its dependence on Osaka loans. At the level of the individual person, kokueki thought condoned commoners' pursuing a variety of livelihoods or changing one profession for another that was more profitable. This was very unlike the concept of *hongyō* ("hereditary profession"), which encouraged preservation of the status quo in production arrangements. In this way, kokueki thought was used to argue for economic diversification. It also provided a rationale for protecting livelihoods in Tosa that had become inexorably tied into the export market. The government's involvement in activities to benefit the kokueki became a justification for the extension of its commercial and export tax system. The development of this kind of taxation allowed the domain to respond to increasing commercialization with a variety of policies, no longer as dependent on the provision of commercial privileges to certain merchants in order to gain substantial income from commerce.

I have situated the development of kokueki thought within the context of the single realm, or country, of Tosa, because the rhetoric of kokueki carried ideological significance scaled to the domainal country, and not to the size of the whole archipelago of Japan. This approach has allowed me to delineate the various economic and political interests influencing the development of policy and rhetoric, and come to a number of novel conclusions concerning the nature and import of kokueki thought. Although these findings have implications for the understanding of some other situations outside of Tosa, I have generally left out comparative comment in the main text. In the Conclusion, I wish to say a few words on the following three questions not permitted by this approach: (1) What relationship does this study have to the history of economic thought among Edo period scholars in Japan? (2) How did kokueki thought fare in other domains? and (3) How did the Meiji government make use of kokueki thought?

Dazai Shundai (1680–1747) is regularly credited with being the first scholar to display a positive attitude toward government support of commercial and industrial development, and the beginnings of a separation of morality and economic analysis.[1] This appears first in his *Keizairoku shūi*, written sometime around 1741–4. He favorably cites the examples of numerous domains augmenting finances through commercial monopolies and argues that lords should purchase at a good price all of the useful goods that the people of the realm produce, sell this locally and then sell the remainder from the domain warehouses in Osaka, Kyoto and Edo.[2] Yet, despite the image of his thought as originating a new framework for discussion extending beyond the economic thought of his teacher Ogyū Sorai (1666-1728), it seems to me that *Keizairoku shūi* can be best interpreted as an example of a scholar learning from ideas that were becoming prevalent in the world around him and trying to incorporate them into his larger body of scholarly theory and knowledge. One can sense Shundai's difficulty in making lordly commerce fit his theories, as he writes nostalgically:

In these days of decline, it would be a great good if as in the past we could lessen the amount of money, have countries [i.e., daimyo] live within their means and so not cause inconvenience to samurai and commoners, but without a renewal of the structure of government in Japan and without improving public morals it is not an easy task. Such being the case, there is no other thing to do than for each country to set up plans to increase its gold and silver, and there is no faster method of doing that than commerce.[3]

The quotation not only reveals a certain lack of fit – a struggle to make lordly use of commerce seemly – but displays a thoroughly lord-centered vision of the role of trade. Commerce is a means to this end: the alleviation of the lord's financial difficulties, similar to Tosa's first attempt at sugar production in 1728. It is not

---

[1] *Yoshikawa Kōbunkan kokushi daijiten*, p. 153. Tetsuo Najita, "Political Economism in the Thought of Dazai Shundai," pp. 834–5, 838–9.

[2] As is evident with all of the Sorai school philosophers, Dazai had a strong interest in a practical approach to government and an emphasis on finances (Najita, "Political Economism"), however, his emphasis on lord-centered mercantilism is not evident in his widely read *Keizairoku* published in 1729, or in the memorials he submitted to the lord of Numata domain in 1733. All of these are included in Takimoto Seichi, *Nihon keizai taiten*, vol. 9, pp. 377–706; quotation from pp. 681–2. It seems *Keizairoku shūi* was not published until the modern period.

[3] This point is made by Kinugasa Kazuo, *Kinsei Jugaku shisō no kenkyū*, pp. 145–8.

defined as a significant public activity in itself. Shundai's ideological and intellectual role is to add scholarly legitimacy to such activity by figuring out how to make it fit with respected examples from Chinese history. Acquiring a scholarly seal of approval was important to the rulers and anyone, including merchants, professing to be literate, because it helped extend the legitimacy of their activities. However, Shundai's discussion of the relation between lordly commerce and lordly morality would have seemed an incomplete and old-fashioned view to his contemporary the Tosa iron merchant Izumiya Kaemon, or any merchant familiar with kokueki thought.

Later scholars were probably made more comfortable by Shundai's lead when they asserted their own visions of the public role of trade. Hayashi Shihei (1738–93) is an example of an eclectic scholar making use of kokueki thought in his 1763 petition to the lord of Sendai domain. The eccentric Kaiho (Kaibo) Seiryō (1755–1817) was an independent scholar who gave economic advice to a number of domains in the early nineteenth century. When Kaiho wrote his treatise *Keiko dan* sometime after 1811, he performed impressive and humorous verbal acrobatics by substituting the character "profit" (*ri*) for "principle" (*ri*) as a guide to good government. He stood the Confucian verities on their heads and turned the proper management of profit into a public activity of the highest order. The world had changed such that his festive inversion could not be taken purely as joke, and yet because the rhetoric was so subversive, he could not be taken in full seriousness by contemporaries or even some moderns.[4]

Most intellectuals were deeply engaged in the economic discourses generated by the samurai elite. Insofar as kokueki thought is concerned, however, they were followers and adapters. The rhetoric of kokueki grew out of a specific historic domainal context and spread because it filled the needs of merchants and governments heavily dependent upon exports. When it did not fill ideological needs, it was much less likely to successfully spread among the intelligentsia. This was evident with the scholars of the Osaka merchant school, the Kaitokudō. Although they encouraged the spread to the government of certain commercial values that also challenged, but from a different perspective, the economy of

---

[4] Tsukatani Akihiro and Kuranami Seiji, *Honda Toshiaki, Kaiho Seiryō*, pp. 481–500; Donald Keene, *The Japanese Discovery of Europe*, pp. 91–122; Tetsuo Najita treats Kaiho wonderfully in "Method and Analysis in the Conceptual Portrayal of Tokugawa Intellectual History," but despite the emphasis on the eclecticism of eighteenth-century thought, Najita's main interest is in the unfolding of a dialogue between intellectuals leading from Sōrai, where they appear as intelligent observers of a changing world who speak mainly to each other. I would argue that the dialogue between the intellectuals on economics was too bound by the discourse of old texts to be innovative. The crucial intellectual exchanges on the political economy were probably between these intellectuals and their contemporary merchants and officials. This point is better made by Najita in *Kaitokudō* p. 5, but in practice the main interest there is also in an intellectuals' dialog.

service of the samurai, they (as merchants of Osaka, I would argue) were not interested in kokueki thought.[5] Kokueki was a form of thought closely tied to the economy and society of domainal countries, extending its rhetorical influence into other regions only slowly. This is evidenced by looking at its historical distribution across the archipelago.

Kokueki thought quickly spread within large domains from the north to the south. Early examples of the use of kokueki thought include the 1755 petition of Tatebe Seian, a doctor of Ichinoseki domain in the far north of Japan. Another example from northern Japan is the petition the Sendai retainer Tamamushi Jūzō submitted a petition to the lord in 1784 arguing that, "Because we purchase so many products from other countries, gold and coinage leave our country, and I think this puts all of our people in poverty. Your lordship should prohibit the sale of all foreign products in the country and see that people make do with Country Products."[6] From the other end of Japan at approximately the same time comes an example from Saga domain. It is a 1767 proposal for government reform arguing that the domain should stop marketing so heavily in Osaka and sell domain goods within the domain, and that domain people should be encouraged to purchase locally made products.[7] The large domains in these examples were all experiencing the same pressures engendered by the economy of service, and yet had the territorial integrity and administrative strength to be useful to merchants.

The nineteenth century saw a great expansion in public expression and application of kokueki thought. Domain-sponsored commercial projects vastly increased, and "country products offices" (kokusan yakusho) were created in many domains to foster the local production of exportable products, sometimes by monopoly and sometimes by other means. Even the smaller domains tried to carry out policies similar to the policies of larger domains, but these programs more often ended in failure. Most small domain governments had neither sufficient political and financial strength nor the geographic control to attract the interest of domain merchants. Furthermore, most of these domain merchants were located in economically advanced areas that had already developed powerful organizations on which they could rely.[8] Without active support from

---

[5] Tetsuo Najita, *Kaitokudō*.

[6] Fujita, *Kinsei keizai*, pp. 35–9. Mountainous and northern Ichinoseki had a small *omotedaka* of 30,000 *koku* but was physically large. I have seen usage of the term *kokueki* in the office diary of the house elders of Aizu domain as early as 1743, but the usage is based on profitable rice sales and seems to mean "profit for the government" – similar to the usage of Tateda Kachū. Marui Kazuko, *Aizu-han kasei jikki*, vol. 8, p. 474.

[7] Fujita, *Kinsei keizai*, pp. 30–2.

[8] William Hauser, *Osaka and the Kinai Cotton Trade*, is an excellent study of an important industry located in such an area. He deals with merchant organization on pp. 65–80 and deals briefly with a conflict between a domainal commercial enterpise and local merchant organizations on pp. 83–4.

sections of the populace involved in industry and commerce, policies inspired by kokueki thought were failures, and the political meaning of the thought itself changed – as when the Kinai villagers used kokueki to define their sense of a common economic fate irrespective of elite jurisdiction.[9]

After the opening of the treaty ports to trade with the Western nations in 1859, almost all domains rushed to create Country Products Offices to strengthen their individual countries through trade. These belated efforts were often called "Kokueki Offices" in an attempt to capitalize on the concept. Even the faltering bakufu set up a "National Prosperity Development Office" in 1862 to sponsor and control silk and other exports through Yokohama.[10] But its attempts to monopolize international commerce away from the domains created serious conflicts and was one source of the western domains' resentment of the bakufu.[11] Domainal opposition, commoner opposition, and a faltering faith in the ability of the bakufu to unify Japan doomed the project. The bakufu failed to make clear effectively whether the "country" was intended to be the bakufu lands or encompass all of Japan. By the end, the shogun no longer embodied the idea of the public, and the Tokugawa were increasingly seen as "private" usurpers of the authority symbolized by the emperor. Authority was wrenched from the hands of the shogunate by people of the large western domains who created an imperial restoration, and ultimately the nation-state of Japan.

After Perry's arrival, people from these large domains, most notably Satsuma, Chōshū and Tosa led the response to the foreign economic and military threat posed by the West. They initially responded by intensifying their mercantilist policies in order to strengthen the political situation of their own domainal countries, and each became independently involved in the world trading system. Satsuma created the Shūseikan, an industrial and commercial office that functioned much like a large company, employing at its peak over two thousand workers.[12] It also quickly opened up secret and illegal trading relations with Western countries.[13] Satsuma's energetic participation in an international trading order is exemplified by the fact that it exhibited its products independently of the Japan exhibit at the Paris exposition in 1867.[14] Its success in marketing its image means that, to this day, the Japanese orange *mikan* is known in England as a "satsuma" – a term unknown in Japan. Chōshū domain, also illegally, and

[9] Taniyama Masamichi, *Kinsei minshū*, pp. 348–9.
[10] Yoshinaga Akira, *Kinsei no senbai seido*, pp. 202–8.
[11] Ishii Takashi, *Meiji ishin*, pp. 468–79.
[12] Haraguchi Izumi of Kagoshima University, "Shūseikan jigyō no rekishiteki igi," unpublished manuscript of paper presented 10 November 1989 in the Kyūshū History Section of the Conference of Japanese Studies held at the National University of Singapore.
[13] Ishii Takashi, *Meiji ishin*, pp. 453–502.
[14] Jansen, *Sakamoto*, p. 256.

after attack by Western forces had forced a shift in its expulsionist sentiment, welcomed foreign vessels into its port of Shimonoseki for trade.[15] Saga domain rapidly developed new industries to improve its military and increase domainal exports.[16] Tosa quickly placed export production and arms acquisition at the center of policy with the creation of the Kaiseikan. Tosa and other domains bought steamships, which they used as naval vessels and as merchant cargo carriers. Tosa not only built up its own fleet but later invested in the shipping company and navy that the renegade Tosa samurai, Sakamoto Ryōma, created independently to carry out his vision of a Japan strengthened through naval and merchant shipping power.[17] The shipping fleet Tosa created as a domain commercial enterprise formed the core of the operations of later Meiji industrialist Iwasaki Yatarō, the founder of the Mitsubishi conglomerate. Iwasaki was himself originally a peasant who became a chief domain commercial official.[18]

These domains became the central actors that toppled the bakufu and actively created the new nation-state of Japan. Within a few years, they scaled kokueki to the size of Japan and made it a very popular catch word and guide for economic policy. The more famous, but not more prevalent, call to *fukoku kyōhei*, or "enrich the country and strengthen the army," was a term adapted from Chinese texts and traditionally used by nonmercantilist scholars, but Meiji leaders invested it with the mercantilist rationale of kokueki thought.[19] Etō Shinpei returned from a council of new Meiji government leaders to his domain of Saga in 1869 and argued a very mercantilist understanding of "enrich the country and strengthen the army,"

The root of a strong army is a prosperous country. If a country is not prosperous then one cannot pay soldiers well or cover military expenses. If the country is prosperous then the military will be strong. If the military is strong there will be no foreign infractions. *The way to make a country prosperous is to see that national products thrive and to open up and expand trade* [emphasis added].[20]

Early Meiji government policies were created by such men as Etō and by numerous people who wrote in newspapers, published tracts and petitioned the government with their own commercial projects and ideas that would contrib-

[15] Ishii Takashi, *Meiji ishin*, pp. 468–79; Albert Craig, *Chōshū*, pp. 231–6.
[16] Shibahara Takuji, *Meiji ishin no kenryoku kiban*, pp. 228–38.
[17] Jansen, *Sakamoto*, pp. 241–8, 259–78. The fullest treatment of Tosa domain policy in the Meiji Restoration years is Hirao Michio, *Tosa-han ishin keizai shi*. Also see Morita, "Kaiseikan."
[18] William Wray, *Mitsubishi and the N.Y.K*, pp. 21–53, gives a brief summary of the transition from the domain enterprise to the private Mitsubishi corporation.
[19] Although I feel that they do not give enough attention to the influence of Edo period kokueki rhetoric, two great discussions of the ideology in modern Japan are Byron Marshall's *Capitalism and Nationalism in Prewar Japan*, especially pp. 13–50, and Richard Samuels, *Rich Nation, Strong Army*, especially pp. 33–42.
[20] Shibahara Takuji, *Meiji ishin*, p. 111.

ute to the kokueki, the "national prosperity."[21] Many new industries were created by nongovernment people with various forms of government support. A few, such as the railroad and arms-related industries, were created at government initiative and placed under heavy government control, paralleling earlier domainal developments. Some important industries such as silk received little effective government direction, but exports of silk and other goods on the international market were strongly supported by the government. For example, in 1874 the Meiji government invested a great sum of money, more than that of most European nations, to prepare the Japan exhibit at the Philadelphia World's Fair even though it was in severe financial straits, precisely because it valued strong support of export trade.[22]

The relationship between kokueki thought emerging out of domainal experience and the development of the modern nation state of Japan seems undeniable. The transition does pose a conceptual problem, however, because the larger domains of Japan did not ultimately develop into modern nations. The kokueki thought that was developed in the domains and used to strengthen domain political authority in the eighteenth century did not long encourage divisiveness between domainal regions in the early Meiji. This suggests that the assumptions common to kokueki thought are unlike elements of modern nationalism such as the concept of common ethnicity. An ethnic identity, once created, cannot easily be transferred to another group of people. By contrast, the ideology of the "national economy" is a general conception of the role of government, not necessarily place-specific.

This study has looked at the emergence of the "economic country" in the imagination of the people of Tosa. They were people living within the borders of the feudal realm, a realm whose economy was deeply involved in importing and exporting. The study of kokueki thought is certainly only a part of the work needed to understand the growth of the modern nation-state of Japan. Study of the expansion of publishing and of the rise of nativist studies elucidates the growing conception of a cultural "country." Study of the significance of the imperial tradition elucidates the religious country. These other countries all existed in the early modern Japanese archipelago. They became interwoven with the country of kokueki thought during the processes of the Meiji Restoration, and that is the story of the development of the modern community of Japan.

---

[21] Many such petitions can be found in Irokawa Daikichi and Gabe Masao, eds., *Meiji zenki kenpaku shūsei*. Fujita Teiichirō analyzes these in his series of articles "Meiji zenki" and analyzes one published tract in "'Kyōkyūsha engi sokō' no shōkai."

[22] Neil Harris, "All the World a Melting Pot? Japan at American Fairs 1876–1904."

Glossary of terms and manuscript document titles used in the text

Asaji no tsuyu 浅茅の露: document; the 1787 petition of Kyūtoku Daihachi

ashigaru 足軽: musketman, low level retainer

bakufu 幕府: the shogun's government

bakuhan taisei 幕藩体制: historian's term denoting the bakufu/domain structure of early modern shogunal rule in Japan

bakumatsu 幕末: declining years of the bakufu, period from 1853 to 1868

bōboku 謗木: a "petition post" used in ancient China

bu 分: unit of silver, one tenth of a momme

bugen'iri 分限入り: bushi of status sufficient to be listed in the official register of samurai retainers

bugyōshoku 奉行職: Tosa senior councillor

buichiyaku 分一役: port tax official

Bunsei sannen nigatsu yori ometsuke yaku yori dasu bun kakitsuke 文政三年二月より御目付役より出す分書付: document; a collection of memoranda from chief inspector to senior councillor

bushi 武士: warrior; includes samurai and lesser retainers

chigyōsho 知行所: fief of domain retainers and shogunal retainers

chiji 知事: governor of han and prefecture

chōnin 町人: townspeople

chūrō 中老: house junior elder; high-status retainer directly below house elder

Daigaku wakumon 大学惑問: book of commentary on the *Greater Learning* and government by Kumazawa Banzan

daimyō 大名: domain lord

demai 出米: duty levy collected from retainers throughout Edo period, and also new name for kariage after 1790

denyakufu 田役夫: village-administered irrigation repairs

Edo nikki 江戸日記: document; the Edo diary of Miyaji Umanosuke

funakata 船方: Shipping Administration

fukoku kyōhei 富国強兵: slogan meaning enrich the country and strengthen the army

gai 外 (short for togawa 外輪: the retainers who worked in positions administrating and defending the domain of Tosa (opposite of kin 近)

gedai 下代: one of the very lowest rank of retainers

gege 下々: very poor quality dry field agricultural land

gimin 義民: righteous martyr

gisō 義倉: village-administered relief warehouses

gō 郷: a group of mountain villages organized onto a district

goichimon 御一門: collateral houses of the lord

Gonjōsho 言上書: document; drafts of petitions by Tani Tannai

gōnō 豪農: wealthy entrepreneurial farmer

gōshi 郷士: rural samurai

goyō 御用: any duty requested by the lord

goyōgin 御用銀: special levy collected as a forced loan in Tosa (and other parts of western Japan)

goyōkin 御用金: same as goyōgin, but used in the gold-based currency system of eastern Japan

goyō shōnin 御用商人: purveyor to the lord

Goyō tō jiki kashiragaki 御用等自記頭書: document; collection of memoranda of senior councillor of Tosa domain

Hakuwansō 白湾藻: document; collection of Tosa-related documents compiled in 1880s.

Hakuyō nichiroku 柏葉日録: document; Tosa domain lord's diary as transcribed by Hirao Michio

han 藩: Meiji and post-Meiji term for domain, applied to Edo period domains in modern scholarship

han kokka 藩国家: domain nation-state, term created by Tōyama Shigeki

Hanshi naihen 藩誌内編: document; official domainal history compiled at end of Edo period

hanshu 藩主: domainal lord in Meiji and post-Meiji parlance, applied to daimyo in modern scholarship

harubuyaku 春譜役: spring irrigation repairs

Heso no Tanuki 臍の狸: document; satiric commentary on Tenmei reforms in fictional format

hiragami 平紙: paper free to be sold by producers at market value

Hitsuya-ke monjo 櫃屋家文書: document; transcriptions by Hirao Michio of many documents of the leading Kōchi merchant family Hitsuya

Hiuchibukuro 燧袋: document; early nineteenth-century diary of low-level retainer and scholar Kusunose Ōe

hiyō 日傭: day laborers

Hocho taii 輔儲大意: document; Yamauchi lord's copy of scholarly text and petition

hōkō 奉公: service to one's lord

hōkōnin 奉公人: contract or hereditary servant

honden 本田: field first cultivated before 1600

hongyō 本業: hereditary occupation, prescribed by status

hyakushō 百姓: status denoting hereditary landowning farmer

hyōjōsho 評定所: bakufu's high court

ichimon 一門: lord's dependent relatives

ichiryō gusoku 一両具足: self-made rural samurai of sixteenth-century Tosa

ie 家: household

ikiru kami 生きる神: living god, reference to the emperor

ikki 一揆: organized peasant protest

ikoku 異国: Edo period term for foreign country of a different culture

ipponzuri 一本釣り: single-line-and-hook fishing technique used to catch bonito

isamebako 諫箱: another name for petition box, used in Okayama domain

Ishi nenpu 医師年譜: document; book of lineages of domain-employed doctor
households

jidaka 地高: land-area assessment of production used in Tosa

Jimu ronsaku shū 時務論策集: collection by Hirao Michio of many samurai petitions

jinsei 仁政: benevolent government

jinzai 人材: men of talent

jō 上: high grade of rice fields

jōnō 上納: paying tax

kachi 徒, 歩行, 走行, 陸: foot soldiers

kachū 家中: retainers of a daimyo

kaikaku 改革: government reform

Kaizanshū 皆山集: compilation of Tosa historical documents by Matsunoo Shōko in
Meiji period – now published

kamigata 上方: region around Osaka and Kyoto

kan 貫: unit of silver, equals 1,000 monme

Kangeki zakki, Hakutō zatsudan, Kanjitsu zasshu, Hogosen 間隙雑記、白頭雑談、間
日雑集、反故撰: document; compilation of Tosa historical documents by Teraishi
Masamichi

kanjō bugyō 勘定奉行: Finance Magistrate – office created in 1787 to upgrade status
and authority of the Finance Chief

kanjō gashira 勘定頭: Finance Chief – pre-1787 head financial official

Kansei sannen okyaku chō Tosaya Kyūemon 寛政三年御客帳土佐屋九右衛門: document; record of users of Tosaya Kyūemon's inn in Bizen Fukuyama

kariage 借上: special percent-of-income levy collected from all people of Tosa, ostensibly a loan

karō 家老: house elders – highest-status households in domain

karuki mono 軽き者: general term for low-level retainer

Kashiwaba nichiroku 柏葉日録: document; Hirao Michio's transcription of selections of
domain lord's diary

katsuobushi 鰹節: bonito processed for soup base and food

ken 県: prefecture; created out of domains in 1871

Kenshōbo 憲章簿: document; compilation of Tosa domain laws sent to Hata county –
now published

kerai 家来: vassal, retainer

ki 櫃: early Chinese petition box used by empress Wu

kichimai 吉米: white rice

Kikō: Keizai zakki, jōshoan 貴稿経済雑記上書案: document; petition drafts and miscellany of economic facts by retainer-scholar Miyaji Haruki

kin 近 (short for kinshū 近習): retainers serving the needs of the lord and the Edo residence (opposite of gai 外)

kin 斤: unit of measurement for sugar and other products

kingai itchi 近外一致: single-manning of parallel posts in domain and Edo, used as a cost-cutting measure

kinshū 近習: retainers serving the needs of the lord and the Edo residence (opposite of togawa 外輪)

kirihata 切畑: slash-and-burn field

kō 公: lord, public

kōbu gattai 公武合体: union of court and military rule

Kōbun 綱文: document; Table of Contents volumes of Yamauchi-ke shiryō

Kōchi hanshi bussan rui 高知藩誌物産類: document; lists many products, production amounts, and their ports of export from Tosa domain in the mid-1860s

kogaku 古学: ancient literary studies

kōgi 公義: government authority

Kōgi narabini oie tomo mitsu shi basshō 公義並御家供密史抜抄: document; eighteenth-century extracts of compilation of various domain documents

kokka 国家: state, nation

koku 石: unit of rice measurement, equals 5.1 bushels or 180 liters of rice

koku 国: country, province, domain

kokudaka 石高: rice-value estimate of production

kokueki 国益: prosperity of the country, national prosperity

kokueki shisō 国益思想: mercantilist thought and ideology originating in the eighteenth century

kokugaku 国学: nativist studies

kokusan 国産: domainal "country export products"

kokusangata 国産方: Country Products Administration; term used interchangeably with kokusan yakusho

kokusan senbai 国産専売: domain products monopolies

kokusan yakusho 国産役所: Country Products Office

kokutai 国体: national structure and identity

komononari 小物成: "casualties," taxes on minor farm household products

Kōseshi ogakusoku 公世子御学則: document; study book of Yamauchi heir-apparent

koshō 小性: page, attendant of lord

kōtō 鈷箭: earliest Chinese form of petition box

kuchigin 口銀: initially port taxes; later sales taxes

kuni 国: domainal country, country, province

kunijū fushinpu 国中普請夫: domain-administered irrigation repairs

kuragami 蔵紙: paper purchased at low prices by domain from villagers forced to produce a certain quota kurairichi 蔵入地: demesne agricultural land

kurairi mononari 蔵入物成: taxes from demesne agricultural land

kurayashiki 蔵屋敷: domainal Osaka marketing compound

maru 丸: unit of volume for goods such as paper. Equal to 20–80 *soku* of paper according to type. Number of sheets differs according to paper type.

meikun 明君: enlightened ruler

men uri 免売: domain sale of land tax collection rights to merchant

metsuke 目付: chief inspector of domain

meyasu 目安: petition, suit

meyasubako 目安箱: petition box

mikan みかん: a small Japanese orange

minpu 民富: enrich the people

Miyazaki Hachisuke zakki 宮崎八助雑記: document; a miscellany by retainer Miyazaki Hachisuke

monme 匁: unit of silver, one thousandth of a kan

mononari 物成: agricultural tax, same as nengu

Murakami shinden 村上新田: new fields surveyed by the domain inspector, Murakami Hachibei, in the 1620s and taxed like honden fields

myōgagin 冥加銀: commercial privilege fee

nakama 仲間: merchant association

Nanroshi 南路志: document; Tosa historical document collection, compiled in 1810s by a Kōchi merchant – currently being published in full

Nanroshi yoku 南路志翼: document; Tosa historical document collection compiled in early Meiji period

nengō 年号: calendric era name

nengu 年具: annual crop taxes, same as mononari

Nikki 日記: document; diary of retainer Mori Hirosada

Obugukata kenbunroku 御武具方見聞録: document; record of visit to domain armory

ōdonya 大問屋: large wholesaler (group) that deals in many products

Ogura hyakunin isshū 小倉百人一首: document; well-known collection of medieval poetry

ōhanshi 大半紙: common size of paper

oie sōdō 御家騒動: daimyo household factional dispute

ōjōya 大庄屋: the commoner administrator of a group of mountain villages

ōkoshikake 大腰掛: waiting house outside of Kōchi castle gate, site of petition box

okuni 御国: domainal country

Okuni nendai ryakki 御国年代略記: document; a chronological table of domain history compiled in the early nineteenth century

okuragami 御蔵紙: paper bought at low price from producers as a form of tax

Okurairi omononari narabini shounjōgin tomo honbarai ōzumori 御蔵入御物成並諸運上銀共本払大積: document; domainal budget

omakanaikata 御賄方: finance office for domain

Omakanaikata tsumori mokuroku 御賄方積目録: document; domainal budget

omotedaka 表高: public record of production

on 恩: debt (and conversely) munificence

otame 御為: for the benefit of the lord, serving the lord

Osamurai chū senzosho keizu chō 御侍中先祖書系図牒: document; official lineages and history of public duty of retainers of Tosa domain

oshikari 御叱: official reprimand

oshukō 御趣向: lord's initiative or project

osso 越訴: illegal direct appeals to high officials

osukui 御救: the lord's famine relief

otameshi 御試: lord's experiment or project

Otōke nendai ryakki 御当家年代略記: document; brief annual history of domain compiled by Miyaji Nakae in 1840s

ri 利: profit

ri 理: principle governing relations, logic

rōnin 浪人、牢人: lordless samurai

ryō 領: a samurai's territory in fief, usually refers to lord's domain

ryō 両: gold monetary unit, equivalent of one koban coin

ryōbun 領分: official term for domain used by bakufu

ryōgoku 領国: domainal country

sakoku 鎖国: "closed country" term originating in late eighteenth century to describe bakufu foreign policy as isolationist

samurai 侍: upper level retainers

Sansei nichiroku 参政日録: document; 1790s office diary of Tosa junior administrator, Mori Yoshiki

sensaku 詮索: investigation

seron 世論: public opinion

Seyō nikki 世用日記: document; diary/historic chronology of Tano port by gōshi/merchant Fukushima Heitabei

shi, watakushi 私: self, private as opposed to public

Shibuya-ke monjo 渋谷家文書: document; collection of documents belonging to senior kinshū retainer household

shii 私意: selfishness

shinden 新田: field first cultivated after 1600

Shingaku 心学: townsman's moral philosphy popular from the late eighteenth century

Shinmin kigen 新民基元: document; 1830s compilation of Tosa samurai petitions of Tenmei reform era

shiokiyaku 仕置役: junior councillor

Shirin shūyō 史林集葉: document; compilation of domain documents by Hirao Michio

shogunshi 諸郡紙: paper purchased at free market price by domain

shōin 書院: Chinese Song era office accepting petitions

Shokaikyū kakushiki no kongen 諸階級格式之根元: document; a history of the status system in the Yamauchi retainer household, written by Mutō Yoshiharu in the 1830s

shōryaku 省略: government fiscal stringency plan

shōshō 少将: an imperial court rank

shoya 庄屋: village headman

shugodai 守護代: imperial governor's representative

shūmon aratame 宗門改: parish registry system

shūmon aratame chō 宗門改帳: books recording annual results of annual registry

Shūshi yoroku 修史餘録:document; compilation of domain documents by Hirao Michio

Shūwa 聚話: document; records of facts from conversations in Edo by Miyaji Nakae

Sōbōkigen 草茅危言: document; late-eighteenth-century book on political economy by Nakai Chikuzan

sojōbako 訴状箱: petition box, same as meyasubako

soku 束: bundle, a unit of volume of paper equal to 10 chō 帳(volumes); number of sheets differs according to paper type

soshō 訴訟: suit, petition

Suigyo 水魚: document; an essay on good rulership by domain heir Yamauchi Toyoteru

sutebumi 捨文: unsigned petitions left anonymously before the hyōjōsho

Tadayoshi-sama, Tadatoyo-sama, Toyomasa-sama gozai Edo oirime zōgen hikikurabe oboe 忠義様、忠豊様、豊昌様御在江戸御入目増減引比覚: document; a comparison of the Edo expenses of the second, third, and fourth daimyo of Tosa compiled by domain finance officials at the end of the seventeenth century

taimai 太米: red rice

takoku 他国: different domain or different province

takoku no hito 他国の人: person from a different domain or province

tan 反: unit of land, 0.245 acre

Tanko ibun 探古遺文: document; compilation of Tosa documents by Hirao Michio

tenka 天下: word signifying Japan in early modern usage

Tenmei shichi nen hinoto hitsuji doshi Seitokuin-sama on oboegaki, zen 天明七年丁未年靖徳院様御覚書全: document; Edo period collection of Tenmei reform declaration and petition of Yoshimoto Mushio

teppō ashigaru 鉄砲足軽: musketman

Tōbun oboegaki 当分覚書: document; biannual domain statistical brief of Tosa domain officials

tororo aoi 黄葵: variety of hibiscus used for paper making

Tosa zatsugoto yaburenunobukuro 土佐雑事破布袋: document; collection of Tosa documents by Matsunoo Shōko

tokigari 時借: regular short-term domain loans

tonya (toiya) 問屋: wholesale merchant

tozama 外様: lineage of lord who was not a vassal of the Tokugawa until 1600

uttae 訴え: suit, petition

wabun 和文: Japanese prose

wagaku 和学: Japanese studies

waka 和歌: Japanese poetry

yaku 役: duty, prescribed economic function

yamashi 山師: lumber contractors

Yamauchi-ke shiryō 山内家史料: document; early twentieth-century compilation of Tosa lord's house documents

yamaukenin 山請人: lumber contractor

yōnin 用人: low-level domain official, generally chosen from gōshi

Yonkanen narashi ginmai sōchijime utsushi 四ケ年平等銀米総縮写: document; a four-year average of domain income and expenditure

Yōsha zuihitsu 湧舎随筆: document; a miscellany of a Tosa junior elder, Yamauchi Akinari

Zakki shōhikae oboe rui 雑記諸扣覚類: document; memoranda compilation by house elder

Zennoshin kaze 善之進風: the Wind of Zennoshin, a typhoon that hit Tosa in 1757 and was popularly reputed to be the avenging spirit of a protestor named Nakahira Zennoshin

Sources for figures and tables

Figures

3.1   Population figures come from the following sources. The figure for 1665 comes
from, "Okunijū shosaku demai narabi ni hitodaka tsumori," in ms. *Nanroshi yoku*,
vol. 7, ff. 72nd–75th (original in the Tokyo University Historiographic Institute, I
used a photocopy in the Kōchi Prefecture Library). This document gives the actual
survey total for the main domain of Tosa and includes an estimate of the total for
the small branch domain of Nakamura, whose figures were not available to the
official at the time. The figures for the years 1681–1798 come from Takeichi
Saichirō, "Tosa no kuni nihyakugojū nenkan no genjū jinkō," pp. 95–105. The
original document for this article is now lost, but comparison of its numbers with
other surviving *shūmon* sources show it to be reliable. The figures in the article for
the years 1681 to 1689 do not include the population of the Nakamura branch
domain. These can be supplemented by the annual domain totals given in *TMK*,
vol. 38, ff. 82–6 (1681–2); *TMK*, vol. 41, ff. 143–6 (1682–3); *TMK*, vol. 45, ff. 102–
12 (1683–4); *TMK*, vol. 52, ff. 80–7 (1685–6); *TMK*, vol. 56, ff. 95–9 (1686–7);
TMK, vol. 72, f. 75 (1692–3); *TMK*, vol. 75, ff. 79–84 (1693–4); *TMK*, vol. 79, ff.
37–8 (1695); *TMK*, vol. 90, ff. 83–5 (1697–8); *TMK*, vol. 94, ff. 85–6 (1698–9). 1689
is from Hirao Michio, *Kōchi-han zaisei*, p. 11. The *TMK* volumes for the years 1688
and 1689 are missing. Unlike the Takeichi totals, these figures and the ones that
follow permit many breakdowns by sex, age, status, and region. The figures for
1802–3 are from a *metsuke*'s official report surviving as paper reused in a different
document (GM, no. 1354 [a large ms. tome entitled *Goyō tō jiki kashiragaki*], on
the inside of the first folio in the section entitled "Akegumi narabi ni migi hidari
orusuikumi no bu"); 1805–6, from *Nanroshi*, vol. 1, pp. 468–9; 1822, from
Kaizanshū, vol. 6, p. 477; 1823–4, from Teraishi Masaji, comp., ms. *Kangeki zakki,
Hakutō zatsudan, Kanjitsu zasshu, Hogo sen*, pp. 163–8, unclassified copy in the
Kōchi City Library; 1824–25 are from ms. *Tanko ibun*, HB, no. 119, pp. 66–7;
1844–5, from a detailed report copied in ms. *Kōchi-han keizai shiryō, zaisei hen
(2)*, HB, no. 200, pp. 116–22; 1854–5, Matsunoo, *Kaizanshū*, vol. 6, p. 477; 1861–
2, Fukao, *Onchi roku*, ff. 8–11; 1870, from ms. *Shirin shūyō (2)*, HB no. 356, pp.
63–6.

The agricultural land area (*jidaka*) figure for 1600 is the Chōsogabe survey total; 1626 adds on the findings of the domain wide Murakami resurvey (1621–6) as given in Hirao Michio, *Tosa-han nōgyō*, pp. 93–4; The 1634, 1646, 1678, and 1684 figures are from a domain memorandum, ms. "Oboe" dated 3/9/1684 in *Jōkyō monjo, Jōkyō gannen*, Kōchi Prefecture Library, and quoted in Hirao, *Kōchi-han zaisei*, pp. 3–4; 1665, from ms. "Jidaka kome ginsu honbarai daimokuroku," in Kaganoi-ke shiryō no. 16–30, in the Kōchi City Library. In *Kōchi-han zaisei* and *Tosa-han nōgyō*, Hirao gives a figure of 391,994 *koku* (*tan*) for the year 1700, and it has been quoted widely by other scholars, but this is incorrect. That figure is the *jidaka* for the year 1743. For details, see Luke Roberts, "Tosa hansei chūki" and "Genroku makki Tosa." The figure for 1698 comes from an "oboe" in a high ranking retainer's family document collection in Tokyo. I used a photographic copy held in the Kōchi Prefecture Library, ms. *Shibuya-ke monjo*, vol. 3; 1769, from "oboe" copied in Matsunoo Shōkō, comp., ms. *Tosa zatsugoto yaburenunobukuro*, vol. 1, in the Kōchi Prefecture Library (K270/16/1), pp. 141–2. The figure for 1813 subtracts the amount of slash-and-burn field from a total given in Inoue Kazuo, *Han hō, bakufu hō*, vol. 2, pp. 461–2 (slash-and-burn field total is from sect. 2 of ms. *Bunka ninen tōbun oboegaki*, GM, no. 5540). The figure for circa 1843 comes from undated ms. "Nanagun honden shinden taka chijime," in the Kōchi Prefecture Library, box of unclassified documents. Date is estimated by comparison with two other dated "oboe" recording six-county totals in the same collection. The figure for 1870 comes from Hirao, *Kōchi-han zaisei*, p. 5; 1872, from Hirao *Tosa-han nōgyō*, p. 52.

4.1   The figure for 1602 is my estimate from multiplying the *kurairi jidaka*, assessed land area paying tax to the domain (which is the *sadame okurairi* found in "Kan'ei sannen onkurairi narabi ni kyūchi chō," in ms. *Shūshi yoroku*, HB, no. 7; see also Matsuyoshi Sadao, *Tosa-han keizai*, p. 10.) by 30 percent, which is the effective tax rate given by contemporaries (*Kōchi-ken shi, kinsei hen*, pp. 50–1; *TYK*, vol. 1, pp. 596–7). The figure for 1622 is my estimate from "Ōkata kime mokuroku," in *TYK*, vol. 1, pp. 596–7; 1626, from "Kan'ei sannen..." cited above, with a 35 percent estimate of tax rate. the figure for 1665 is actual income from ms. "Jidaka kome ginsu honbarai daimokuroku," in the Kaganoi-ke document collection in the Kōchi City Library; see also Matsuyoshi, *Tosa-han keizai*, pp. 12–13. The following years are from annual tax reports ("Okurairi mononari mokuroku"): 1676–7, from "Enpō gannen oboegaki," vol. 3, f. 12 as in *NRSCS*, reel 43; 1682–3, from "Tenna sannen oboegaki," vol. 4, ff. 15–16 as in *NRSCS*, reel 44; 1684, from *TMK*, vol. 46, ff. 19–21; 1685, *TMK*, vol. 50, ff. 84–5; 1686, from *TMK*, vol. 53, ff. 23–45; 1695–6, from *TMK*, vol. 84, ff. 55–8, and "Genroku jūnenbun oboe," ff. 1–2, in *NRSCS*, reel 45; 1697–8, from orig. ms. in *Genroku monjo jūichinen*, in the Yamauchi Family Shrine Treasury and Archives; 1733, from *Nanroshi*, vol. 1, p. 459. All years from 1716 through 1755 and 1757 come from ms. *Shibuya-ke monjo*, "Kyōhō gan shin nen yori omononari oboe" (original in Tokyo private collection, photographic copy in the Kōchi Prefecture Library [Kenshi shiryō, vol. 124]). The figures for the years 1767–8 come from ms. *Miyazaki Hachisuke zakki*, ff. 45–6, in SB, no. 26; 1769, from ms. *Tosa zatsugoto yaburenunobukuro*, vol. 1, pp. 144–5, in the Kōchi Prefecture Library (K270/16/1); 1777–8, within ms. *An'ei hachinen tōbun oboegaki*, GM, no. 5500; 1781–2, *TCK*, vol. 36, ff. 136th–137th; 1783, *TCK*, vol. 40, ff. 148–50; 1799–1800, within ms. *Kyōwa gannen tōbun oboegaki*, GM, no. 5735, 1801–2, within ms. *Kyōwa sannen tōbun oboegaki*, GM, no. 5534; 1803–4, within ms. *Bunka ninen tōbun oboegaki*, GM, no. 5540; 1817, 1818, and 1819, in ms. [Mononarimai mokuroku], GM nos. 5849, 5850; 1818, 1820, 1822, 1824, 1826, and 1828, from a chart in ms. *Kōchi-han keizai shiryō, zaisei hen (2)*, HB, no. 200, pp. 11–12, which is based on the "on kurairi mononari mokuroku" quoted in *tōbun oboegaki*, no longer extant. (Hirao puts these five figures in each of the following years because he misinterpreted the tax reports in the *tōbun oboegaki* to represent the year of the titles, but in reality they represent the previous year.) The averages for 1704–6 are from ms. "Omakanaikata ōzumori," in *Hōei monjo, Hōei roku-shichinen*, in the Kōchi Prefecture Library; 1781–7, ms. "Oshūnō ginmai oboegaki utsushi," GM, no. 5833; 1787–96, from Matsuyoshi Sadao, *Tosa-han keizai*, pp. 37–8.

4.2   This chart is based on Hirao's compilation in *Kōchi-han zaisei*, pp. 100–4, but checked against available documents. Discrepancies, ambiguities and omissions exist for a number of years, so I have altered Hirao's information based on the following sources: 1729, *TNK*, vol. 16, ff. 15th–21st, and *Otōke nendai ryakki* (a domain chronology, information to be found in the relevant year's entry, below identified as *Otōke*), ms. copy in Princeton University, Gest Library; 1737 and 1738, *Otōke*; 1789, *TCK*, vol. 64., ff. 123rd–125th; 1790, *Otōke*; 1791, *Otōke*, and *TKK*, vol. 62, f. 60th; 1793, *Otōke*, and *TKK*, vol. 19, ff. 82nd–101st; 1794, *Otōke*, and *TKK*, vol. 24, ff. 17th–19th; 1797, *Otōke*, and Yamamoto Takeshi, *Kenshōbo*, vol. 1, pp. 181–7; 1802, *Otōke*, and *TKK*, vol. 58, f. 21st, and Yamamoto, *Kenshōbo*, vol. 1, p. 247; 1814, Kusunoki Ōe, *Hiuchibukuro*, vol. 3, p. 55; 1817, *Otōke*, and Kusunoki, *Hiuchibukuro*, vol. 4, p. 135; 1823, Yamamoto, *Kenshōbo*, vol. 1, p. 247; 1824, Kusunoki, *Hiuchibukuro*, vol. 9, pp. 17–18, and Yamamoto, *Kenshōbo*, vol. 1, pp. 251–2; 1825 and 1826, *Otōke*, and Kusunoki, *Hiuchibukuro*, vol. 9, pp. 36–7; 1827, Kusunoki, *Hiuchibukuro*, vol. 10, p. 77, and vol. 11, pp. 43, 46; 1831, *Otōke*, and Kusunoki, *Hiuchibukuro*, vol. 13, pp. 73–4; 1832–9, *Otōke*; 1857, *Onikki* as in ms. *Hakuyō nichiroku*, HB, no. 74, p. 77, and Inoue Seishō, *Shinkakuji nikki*, vol. 2, p. 31; 1866–67, *BMI*, vol. 6, pp. 3–14; 1868, *BMI*, vol. 10, pp. 192–9.

Actual *koku* amounts are from the following sources: 1709, ms. "Hōei rokunen okurairi omononari narabini shounjōgin tomo honbarai ōzumori," in *Hōei monjo, Hōei roku-shichinen*, in the Kōchi Prefecture Library; 1747, "Okariagemai no uchi Edo shin osakuji nyūyō mai sashihiki oboe," in *TNK*, vol. 89, ff. 32nd–46th; 1778, 1800, and 1838, from the *Tōbun oboegaki* sect. 12, GM, nos. 5500, 5735, 5668.

Tables

3.1   See sources for income cited for Figure 4.1 and various "Okurairi mononari mokuroku" in the following sources: for 1682–3, "Tenna sannen oboegaki," vol. 4, ff. 15–16 and as in *NRSCS*, reel 44; 1684, *TMK*, vol. 46, ff. 19–21; 1685, *TMK*, vol. 50, ff. 84–5; 1686, *TMK*, vol. 53, ff. 23–45; 1695–6, *TMK*, vol. 84, ff. 55–8, and "Genroku jūnenbun oboe," ff. 1–2 in *NRSCS*, reel 45; 1697–8, orig. ms. in *Genroku monjo jūichinen*, Yamauchi Shrine Treasury and Archives.

4.1   The year 1681 is based on ms. *Omakanaikata tsumori mokuroku* bound in *Tenna monjo, Tenna gannen*, in the Kōchi Prefecture Library. Its estimate of 750 *kanme* of lumber income was only for the portion of lumber income to be devoted to "regular expenses." "Irregular expenses" were covered largely by additional sales of lumber. Therefore the 750 *kanme* have been adjusted to 1,500 *kanme* because an actual lumber income document from the closest available year gives 1,573 *kanme* for 1686, and sources for 1689 and 1693 give incomes in this range as well, as in *NRSCS*, reel 44; *Oboegaki Jōkyō sannen*, vol. 4, ff. 41–4, reel 45; *Oboegaki Genroku ninen*, vol. 6, ff. 25–6; and *TMK*, vol. 74, f. 101. The figure for 1709 is found in ms. *Okurairi omononari narabi ni shounjōgin tomo honbarai ōzumori*, bound in *Hōei monjo, Hōei roku-shichinen*, in the Kōchi Prefecture Library. 1778, in ms. *An'ei hachinen tōbun oboegaki*, GM, no. 5500; 1853, in ms. *Kaei rokunen tōbun oboegaki*, HB, unclassified, and printed in Hirao, *Kōchi-han zaisei*.

4.2   The 1620 debt comes from the letter by domain Kyoto official Kurobe [Kurota?] Heita to Narumi Heidayū (probably a lord's chamberlain) dated the second month second day, no year given but clearly from 1620, f. 7th in ms. *Gonjōsho hei dai jūroku gō* in the Yamauchi Family Shrine Treasury and Archives. The 1620 income estimate comes from p. 99 of Takagi Shosaku's "Bakuhan seijishi jōsetsu – Tosa-han Genna kaikaku". This estimate is based on a domain finance document entitled "Ōgata kime mokuroku," in *TYK*, vol. 1, pp. 596–7. Takagi estimates debt at 3,000 *kan*. The figure for 1681 comes from ms. "Enpō kyūnen omakanaikata tsumori mokuroku," in *Tenna monjo gannen* in the Kōchi Prefecture Library; 1709, from ms. "Hōei rokunen okurairi omononori narabi ni shounjōgin tomo honbarai ōzumori" in *Hōei monjo, Hōei roku-shichinen* in Kōchi Prefecture Library; 1759 from "Edo Kamigata okunijū tomo shin ko okarigin ōzumori oboe," ff. 103rd–108th in *TNK*, vol. 123. The figures for 1778, 1804, and 1852 come from ms. *Tōbun oboegaki* as follows: 1778, GM, no. 5500; 1804, GM, no. 5540; 1852 from HB, box of unclassified.

5.1   In alphabetical order:

Aizu: Fukui Hisazō, *Shodaimyō no gakujutsu to bungei no kenkyū*, vol. 1, p. 2; and in Fukushima-ken, *Fukushima-ken shi 2*, p. 655.

Amagasaki: Watanabe Hisao, et al. eds., *Amagasaki-shi shi*, vol. 2, pp. 213–5, and vol. 5, pp. 386–8; and in Gifu-ken, *Gifu-ken shi, shiryō hen, kinsei 2*, p. 481.

Bakufu – all locations: Takayanagi Shinzō and Ishii Ryōsuke, eds., *Ofuregaki Kanpō shūsei*, pp. 1,204–13.

Bitchū Matsuyama: Asamori Kaname, "Bitchū Matsuyama-han no meyasubako ni tsuite," pp. 81–2.

Fukuchiyama: Fukuchiyama-shi Shi Hensan Iinkai, *Fukuchiyama-shi shi*, vol. 3, p. 118, and nenpyō p. 33.

Fukue: Kimura Motoi, et al., eds., *Hanshi daijiten*, vol. 7, p. 247.

Fukuoka: Inoue Kazuo, *Han hō, bakufu hō to ishin hō*, vol. 1, p. 450.

Fukuyama: Hiroshima-ken, *Hiroshima-ken shi, kinsei 2*, pp. 120, 147, 1,015, 1,016.

Hagi: *Yamaguchi-ken bunkashi nenpyō*, p. 136.

Hamamatsu: Ōtsuka Katsumi, *Hamamatsu no rekishi*, p. 554.

many *han* and prefectures: Meiji Bunka Kenkyūkai, ed., *Meiji jibutsu kigen*, pp. 243–7.

Hida no kuni, Bōkata village: Gifu-ken Shi Hensan Iinkai, *Gifu-ken shi, tsūshi hen, kinsei jō*, p. 1273.

Hikone: Kimura, *Hanshi daijiten*, vol. 5, p. 22.; Hikone-shi, *Hikone-shi shi*, vol. 1, pp. 545–6.

Himeji: Hashimoto Masaji, *Himeji-jō shi, chūkan*, pp. 687–8, 815; and *gekan*, pp. 20–1, 220.

Hiroshima: Hiroshima-ken, *Hiroshima-ken shi, kinsei 1*, pp. 187, 212; and *Hiroshima-ken shi, kinsei 2*, pp. 1014–20.

Imagawa Yoshimoto: Ishii Susumu, Katsumata Shizuo, and Ishimoda Shō, eds., *Chūsei seiji shakai shisō, jōkan*, pp. 206, 506–7.

Imperial court: Inoue Mitsusada, editing translator, *Nihon shoki*, pp. 349, 353–5.

Kaga: Maeda-ke henshū bu, ed., *Kaga-han shiryō*, vol. 9, p. 700.

Kaminoyama: Yamagata-ken, *Yamagata-ken shi*, vol. 3, p. 266.

Kii: Tsuji Tatsuya, *Kyōhō kaikaku no kenkyū*, pp. 119–26. It should be noted that Yūsa Norihiro has cast doubt on whether the petition box was used by Yoshimune in Kii at all, but his evidence is not conclusive ("Tokugawa Yoshimune no Kishū hansei to nisatsu no gisho," pp. 31–42).

Kokura: *Nenpyō Kokura-shi shi hōi*, p. 956.

Komono: Kimura, *Hanshi daijiten*, vol. 4, p. 419.

Kumamoto: Ōtake Hideo and Harafuji Hiroshi, eds., *Bakuhan kokka no hō to shihai*, pp. 262–3.

Kurume: *Fukuoka-ken no rekishi*, nenpyō, p. 7.

Matsumoto: Kanai Madoka, *Hansei seiritsu ki no kenkyū*, pp. 310–1.

Matsuyama: Ehime-ken Shi Hensan Iinkai, *Ehime-ken shi, kinsei jō hen*, pp. 209–10; *TNK*, vol. 121, ff. 9th–10th.

Meiji Government: Ōhira Yuichi, "Meiji shoki no meyasubako (1,2)"; Osatake Takeki, *Ishin zengo ni okeru rikken shisō*, pp. 502–15.

Minaguchi: Kimura, *Hanshi daijiten*, vol. 5, p. 51; Kōga-gun Kyōiku Iinkai, *Kōga-gun shi, jōkan*, p. 479.

Mito: *Mito-shi shi chūkan*, pp. 196–7.

Morioka: Ishii Ryōsuke, ed., *Hanpōshū*, vol. 9, pp. 279, 287.

Nagasaki Magistrate: Kodama Kōta, ed., *Nihonshi nenpyō*, p. 27.

Nagoya: Nagoya-shi, *Nagoya-shi shi, seiji hen*, vol. 1, p. 219, and vol. 2, p. 39; Nagoya-shi Kyōiku Iinkai, ed., *Nagoya sōsho*, vol. 3, pp. 96–7, 117, and vol. 5, pp. 106–107.

Nakatsu: Hiroshima-ken, *Hiroshima-ken shi, kinsei 2*, p. 227.

Nanbu: Asano Gengo, ed., *Nanbu-han shi*, p. 42.

Ōgaki: Watanabe Hisao, et al. eds., *Amagasaki-shi shi*, vol. 2, pp. 213–5, and vol. 5, pp. 386–8; and in Gifu-ken, *Gifu-ken shi, shiryō hen, kinsei 2*, p. 481.

Okayama: Fujiwara Akihisa, "Okayama hansei kakuritsu ki ni okeru 'minji' saiban kikō no keisei," in Ōtake Hideo and Harafuji Hiroshi, eds., *Bakuhan kokka no hō to shihai*, pp. 437–8.

Osaka Inspector: Osaka Shōkō Kaigisho, ed., *Osaka shogyō shi shiryō*, vol. 34, f. 163rd.

Sado magistrate: Niigata-ken, *Niigata-ken shi, tsūshi hen*, vol. 4, p. 65; Aikawa-chō Shi Hensan Iinkai, ed., *Sado Aikawa no rekishi, shiryōshū*, vol. 7, pp. 205–6 (this source has the oldest drawing of a petition box of which I am aware).

Shimoaizuki village council: Matsuoka-chō Shi Hensan Iinkai, *Matsuoka-chō shi, jō kan*, pp. 509–10.

Shirakawa: Fukushima-ken, *Fukushima-ken shi*, vol. 2, p. 655, and vol. 3, pp. 439, 450.

Takada: Kōriyama-shi, *Kōriyama-shi shi*, vol. 3, pp. 157–8; Niigata-ken, *Niigata-ken shi tsūshi 5, kinsei 3*, p. 96; Nakamura Kōichi, ed., *Takada hansei shi kenkyū, shiryō hen ichi*, pp. 57, 316–21,

Takamatsu: Takamatsu-shi Shi Henshū Shitsu, *Shinshū Takamatsu-shi shi*, vol. 1, p. 423; Inoue, *Han hō*, vol. 1, p. 450.

Takatomi: Kimura, *Hanshi daijiten*, vol. 4, p. 52; Gifu-ken, *Gifu-shi shi, shiryō hen, kinsei ni*, pp. 214–5.

Tawara: Kimura, *Hanshi daijiten*, vol. 4, p. 259.

Tosa: Kōchi-ken, *Kōchi-ken shi, kinsei hen*, pp. 503–4.

Tottori: Ishii Ryōsuke, ed., *Hanpōshū*, vol. 2, pp. 229, 234, 252–3; Tottori-ken, *Tottori-ken shi, 3 kinsei seiji*, p. 402. This source gives 1758 as date of creation but the *Hanpōshū* reveals use as early as 1734.

Tsugaru: Aomori-ken Shi Hensan Iinkai, *Aomori-ken shi* 2, p. 639; Tonozaki Satoru, "Tsugaru Nobuaki-kō no jiseki (zoku)," p. 194.

Uwajima: *Ehime-ken shi, nenpyō hen*, p. 196; Hayashi Kyūjurō, comp., Uwajima Kenkyūkai, ed., *Date-ke orekidai jiki*, vol. 1, p. 335.

Yonezawa: Inoue, *Han hō*, vol. 1, p. 450.

8.1   The amounts have been rounded off to the nearest *kan*. The figure for 1776 comes from ms. *An'ei hachinen tōbun oboegaki*, GM, no. 5500; 1781, from "Tenmei gannen kanoto ushi okuni okuchigin" in *NRSCS*, reel 46, "Tosa shiryō kakinuki dankata shūshū no bu (3) no jō," ff. 58–9. Profit is average from 1781–84, in ms. *Yonkanen narashi ginmai sōchijime utsushi*, GM, no. 5831, f. 13th; 1800, from ms. *Kyōwa sannen tōbun oboegaki*, GM, no. 5534; 1802, from ms. *Bunka ninen tōbun oboegaki*, GM, no. 5540; 1818 and 1820, from ms. "Bunsei nenkan okuragami keisan hyō," made by Hirao Michio from no longer extant *Tōbun oboegaki* in HB, no. 200, pp. 21–3; 1842, from "Tenpō jūni ushi fuyu yori dō san tora aki made okuragami chijime mokuroku," copied in HB, no. 199, pp. 47, 50–1, 99–100; 1847, from "Kokusangata sashidashi hyō" made by Hirao Michio from no longer extant documents in HB, no. 200, p. 43; 1852, from ms. *Kaei rokunen tōbun oboegaki*, in HB, unclassified and printed in Hirao Michio *Kōchi-han zaisei*, pp. 141–76; 1859, from Hirao Michio, *Tosa-han kōgyō*, pp. 117–18; 1860, from Hirao Michio, ms. *Tosa-han otesaki shōhō shi*, HB no. 230, f. 47th.

Works and documents cited

I. Abbreviations

BMI   *Yamauchi-ke shiryō: Bakumatsu ishin hen* 山内家史料：幕末維新編 See published sources

GM   Gotō-ke monjo collection 五藤家文書 See Aki City Library

HB   Hirao bunko collection 平尾文庫 See Kōchi City Library

KTK   *Yamauchi-ke shiryō: Katsutoyo-kō ki* 山内家史料：一豊公紀 See published sources

NRSCS   *Nihon rinsei shi chōsa shiryō* (microfilm) 日本林制史調査史料 See published sources under Tokugawa Rinseishi Kenkyūjo, ed.

SB   Sengoku bunko collection 仙石文庫 See Yamauchi Shrine Treasury and Archives

TCK   *Yamauchi-ke shiryō: Toyochika-kō ki* 山内家史料：豊雍公紀 See Yamauchi Shrine Treasury and Archives

TFK   *Yamauchi-ke shiryō: Toyofusa-kō ki* 山内家史料：豊房公紀 See Yamauchi Shrine Treasury and Archives

TKK   *Yamauchi-ke shiryō: Toyokazu-kō ki* 山内家史料：豊策公紀 See Yamauchi Shrine Treasury and Archives

TMK   *Yamauchi-ke shiryō: Toyomasa-kō ki* 山内家史料：豊昌公紀 See Yamauchi Shrine Treasury and Archives

TNK   *Yamauchi-ke shiryō: Toyonobu-kō ki* 山内家史料：豊敷公紀 See Yamauchi Shrine Treasury and Archives

TOK   *Yamauchi-ke shiryō: Toyooki-kō ki* 山内家史料：豊興公紀 See Yamauchi Shrine Treasury and Archives

TSK   *Yamauchi-ke shiryō: Toyosuke-kō ki* 山内家史料：豊資公紀 See Yamauchi Shrine Treasury and Archives

TTeK   *Yamauchi-ke shiryō: Toyoteru-kō ki* 山内家史料：豊熙公紀 See Yamauchi Shrine Treasury and Archives

TTK   *Yamauchi-ke shiryō: Tadatoyo-kō ki* 山内家史料：忠豊公紀 See published sources

TYK   *Yamauchi-ke shiryō: Tadayoshi-kō ki* 山内家史料：忠義公紀 See published sources

II. The archives

This book is based largely on documents in archives in Kōchi Prefecture. The characters for most of the manuscript sources are in this book's Glossary. Some of the most frequently cited major collections are referred to in the text in the abbreviated form given above in the abbreviations section. I have noted the archive for each manuscript at each citation in footnote for sources not identified by the abbreviations noted above. I have used "f." to mean folio and "ff." to mean folios. Where documents did not have folio or page numbers, I have given my own folio count using cardinal numbers, for example, "ff. 21st–23rd" means the 21st through the 23rd folios of an unpaginated document. A half-dozen documents that I use are in collections as yet uncataloged but held in one of the major archives I have described below. The process of cataloging may not reach these documents for some time, so I have photographic copies of these in my possession.

Yamauchi Shrine Treasury and Archives (Yamauchi Jinja Hōmotsu Shiryōkan) in Kōchi city houses most of the surviving documents and artifacts of the Yamauchi family, once daimyo of Tosa. Although most of the original documents were lost in the wartime bombings, tens of thousands survived and most of the surviving documents are kept here. The fullest list is in Kōchi-ken Kyōiku Iinkai, ed., *Tosa hanshu Yamauchi-ke rekishi shiryō mokuroku,* whose numbering system I have used to identify the unpublished volumes of the massive *Yamauchi-ke shiryō,* a prewar modern manuscript transcription of Tosa documents, compiled along the format of the *DaiNihon shiryō.* This and the collections below are invaluable because a large portion of the originals were reduced to ashes in World War II. Also the Sengoku bunko (SB) collection volumes and the separate Sekita bunko collection volumes housed here have thousands of transcriptions of otherwise unavailable documents. Finally, a few hundred important original documents survived miraculously in a corner of a closet in a separate shrine office building. They were discovered only recently and are still housed there. I have cited them by name and by location as Yamauchi Shrine Office documents.

Kōchi Prefecture Library (Kōchi Kenritsu Toshokan) in Kōchi city houses a large number of documents in its local history section. Because most are cataloged, they are cited by name only, except when the document name is vague, such as "Nikki" (Diary), in which case I additionally cite the call number. Many are part of various special collections and are cited accordingly. Most useful for me were the Yamauchi collection, which houses many of the Yamauchi family documents in trust; the Prefecture History documents (*Ken shi shiryō*), which are a massive collection of photographic copies of Tosa-related documents collected from around Japan; the Miyaji collection, which houses the documents of a family of official domain scholars; and the Mori collection (portions as yet uncataloged) of documents of a leading middle ranking samurai household.

Kōchi City Library (Kōchi Shimin Toshokan) in Kōchi city houses a large number of documents in its local history section. Almost all are arranged by special collections. Most important for me were the Hirao bunkō, which is described below; the Kaganoi collection, which contains many thousand documents of a senior domain official family; the Matsunoo collection, which houses the collected documents and notes of a pre-war scholar; the Aki collection, same as above; the Okunomiya collection, which houses the documents of a low-level domain official and scholar family.

Hirao bunkō (HB) is the collection of over three hundred bound volumes of documents and notes from the eminent local historian Hirao Michio. It consists of one third original documents originating in the Yamauchi collection and two thirds his research notes. Most of his research notes are extensive copies of documents made before the war. Many of the originals no longer survive, and this makes the collection extremely valuable.

Aki City Library (Aki Shimin Toshokan) in Aki city houses many collections for the Aki City Board of Education (Aki-shi Kyōiku Iinkai). I have made extensive use of the Gotō family documents described below.

Gotō-ke monjo (GM) (Gotō House Documents) are a collection of documents of the Gotō family, who were high-status *karō* (house elder) retainers for the Yamauchi and often served as chief administrators (*bugyōshoku*) for the domain. This extraordinary collection of over thirty thousand original documents relating to domain government was made public only in 1988 and has been an invaluable source of new documents.

III. Published sources

Aikawa-chō Shi Hensan Iinkai, ed. 合川町史編纂委員会編, *Sado Aikawa no rekishi, shiryō shū* 佐渡相川の歴史史料集, vol. 7, Aikawa chō (Niigata Prefecture) 合川町, 1978.

Akizawa Shigeru 秋沢繁, "Keichō jūnen Tokugawa gozenchō ni tsuite" 慶長10年徳川御前帳について, *Kainan shigaku* 海南史学, no. 30 (August 1992), pp. 28–46, and no. 31 (August 1993), pp. 25–80.

"Kinsei zenki han zaisei shi no ichi kōsatsu – Tosa-han no baai" 近世前期藩財政史の一考察——土佐藩の場合, 2 parts, *Kainan shigaku* 海南史学, vol. 1 (March 1963), pp. 1–16; vol. 2 (December 1963), pp. 25–30.

"Tosa-han shoki no suiden seisan – Tosa no jidaka chō o megutte" 土佐藩初期の水田生産——土佐の地高帳をめぐって, *Kainan shigaku* 海南史学, no. 8 (June 1970), pp. 57–66.

"Toyotomi seikenka no daimyō kokudaka ni tsuite – Chōsogabe shi kokudaka kō" 豊臣政権下の大名石高について——長曽我部氏石高考, pp. 433–48, in Akizawa Shigeru, ed., *Chōsogabe-shi no kenkyū* 長曽我部氏の研究, Sengoku daimyō ronshū series 戦国大名論集, vol. 15, Yoshikawa Kōbunkan 吉川弘文館, 1986.

Amano Masatoshi 天野雅敏, *Awa ai keizaishi kenkyū* 阿波藍経済史研究, Yoshikawa Kōbunkan 吉川弘文館, 1986.

"Kishū-han bakumatsu ki no keizai shisō" 紀州藩幕末期の経済思想, pp. 133–55, in Andō Seiichi 安藤精一, ed., *Wakayama no kenkyū* 和歌山の研究, vol. 3, 1978.

Anderson, Benedict, *Imagined Communities: Reflections on the Origins and Spread of Nationalism*, London: Verso, rev. ed., 1991.

Aoki Michio 青木美智雄, *Kindai no yochō* 近代の予兆, Taikei Nihon no rekishi series 大系日本の歴史, vol. 11, Shōgakkan 小学館, 1989.

"Murakata sōdō to minshūteki shakai ishiki" 村方騒動と民衆的社会意識, pp. 267–308, in Rekishigaku kenkyū kai 歴史学研究会, ed., *Kōza Nihon no rekishi* 講座日本の歴史, vol. 6, 1985.

Aomori-ken Shi Hensan Iinkai 青森県史編纂委員会, *Aomori kenshi* 青森県史, vol. 2, Rekishi Toshosha 歴史図書社 (reprint), 1971.

Aruga Kizaemon 有賀喜左衛門, *Aruga Kizaemon chosaku shū*, vol. 4 有賀喜左衛門著作集, Miraisha 未来社, 1974.

Appleby, Joyce, *Economic Thought and Ideology in Seventeenth Century England*, Princeton, N.J.: Princeton University Press, 1978.

Asamori Kaname 朝森要, "Bitchū Matsuyama-han no meyasubako ni tsuite" 備中松山藩の目安箱について, *Nihon rekishi* 日本歴史, no. 218 (July 1966), pp. 81–82.

Asano Gengo 浅野源吾, ed., *Nanbu-han shi* 南部藩史, Tōyōshoin 東洋書院 (reprint), 1976.

Azuma Shintarō 東晋太郎, *Kinsei Nihon keizai rinen shisō shi* 近世日本経済倫理思想史, Keio Shuppansha 慶応出版社, 1944.

Beasley, W. G., *The Modern History of Japan*, 3rd rev. ed., Tuttle Books, 1982.

Berry, Mary Elizabeth, *The Culture of Civil War in Kyoto*, Berkeley: University of California Press, 1994.

Hideyoshi, Cambridge: Harvard University Press, 1982.

"Public Peace and Private Attachment: The Goals and Conduct of Early Modern Power in Early Modern Japan," *Journal of Japanese Studies*, vol. 12, no. 2 (Summer 1986), pp. 237–71.

Birt, Michael, "Samurai in Passage: Transformation of the Sixteenth Century Kanto," *Journal of Japanese Studies*, vol. 11, no. 2 (Summer 1985), pp. 369–99.

Bix, Herbert, *Peasant Protest in Japan 1590–1884*, New Haven, Ct.: Yale University Press, 1986.

Bolitho, Harold, "The Han," pp. 183–234, in John Hall, ed., *Early Modern Japan*, in the *The Cambridge History of Japan* series, vol. 4, New York: Cambridge University Press, 1991.

Treasures Among Men: The Fudai Daimyo in Tokugawa Japan, New Haven, Ct.: Yale University Press, 1974.

Brown, Philip, *Central Authority and Local Autonomy in the Formation of Early Modern Japan: The Case of Kaga Domain*, Stanford, Calif.: Stanford University Press, 1993.

Craig, Albert, *Chōshū in the Meiji Restoration*, Cambridge: Harvard University Press, 1961.

Doi Sakuji 土居作治, *Bakuhansei kokka no tenkai – Hiroshima-han o chūshin to shite* 幕藩制国家の展開——広島藩を中心として, Hiroshima: Keisuisha 広島：溪水社, 1985.

Duara, Prasenjit, *Rescuing History from the Nation: Questioning Narratives of Modern China*, Chicago: University of Chicago Press, 1995.

Ehime-ken Shi Hensan Iinkai 愛媛県史編纂委員会, *Ehime-ken shi, nenpyō hen* and *kinsei, jō hen* 愛媛県史年表編　近世上編, Ehime-ken 愛媛県, 1986, 1988.

Fujii Shun 藤井駿, Mizuno Kyōichirō 水野恭一郎, and Taniguchi Sumio 谷口澄夫, eds., *Ikeda Mitsumasa nikki* 池田光政日記, Okayama 岡山: Sanyō Tosho Shuppan 山陽図書出版, 1967.

Fujino Tamotsu 藤野保, *Bakuhan taisei shi no kenkyū* 幕藩体制史の研究, Yoshikawa Kōbunkan 吉川弘文館, 1961.

Fujita Teiichirō 藤田貞一郎, "Bakuhansei shakai ni okeru shijō chūshin to shite no Ōsaka" 幕藩制社会における市場中心としての大坂, *Dōshisha shōgaku* 同志社商学, vol. 28, no. 3 (January 1977), pp. 88–104.

"Bakuhanseiteki shijō kōzō no hōkai – Tenpō sannen Kata ura shokoku sanbutsu kōeki kaisho ikken" 幕藩制的市場構造の崩壊――天保三年加太浦諸国産物交易会所一件, in Andō Seiichi 安藤精一, ed., *Kishū kenkyū* 紀州研究, vol. 1, Kokusho Kankōkai 国書刊行会, 1985.

"Kansei ki jōka machi shōnin no shisō – Ōkawa Uchisada cho *Tatoeba* ni tsuite 寛政期城下町商人の思想――大河内貞著『采氏弗貝』について, pp. 373–84, in Miyamato Mataji 宮本又次, ed., *Shōhin ryūtsū no shiteki kenkyū* 商品流通の史的研究, Kyoto: Mineruva Shobō ミネルヴァ書房, 1967.

Kinsei keizai shisō no kenkyū – kokueki shisō to bakuhan taisei 近世経済思想の研究――国益思想と幕藩体制, Yoshikawa Kōbunkan 吉川弘文館, 1966.

"Kinsei Nihon ni okeru 'kokueki' shisō no seiritsu to sono tenkai katei" 近世日本における「国益」思想の成立とその展開過程, *Dōshisha shōgaku* 同志社商学, vol. 34, no. 3 (October 1982), pp. 1–26.

"'Kyōkyūsha engi sōkō' no shōkai" 「協教社衍義草稿」の紹介, *Dōshisha shōgaku* 同志社商学, vol. 21 no. 5/6 (March 1970), pp. 16–25.

"Meiji ki keieisha kokueki shisō no genryū" 明治期経営者国益思想の源流, pp. 264–79, in Yasuoka Shigeaki 安岡重明 and Amano Masatoshi 天野雅敏, eds., *Kinseiteki keiei no tenkai* 近世的経営の展開, Iwanami Shoten 岩波書店, 1995.

"Meiji zenki 'kokueki' shisō tsuiseki – *Meiji kenpakusho shūsei*, o tegakari ni" 明治前期「国益」思想追跡――『明治建白書集成』を手掛りに, *Dōshisha shōgaku* 同志社商学, vol. 45, no. 2/3 (October 1993), pp. 141–169.

"Meiji zenki 'kokueki' shisō tsuiseki zokkō – *Meiji kenpakusho shūsei*, o tegakari ni" 明治前期「国益」思想追跡続行――『明治建白書集成』を手掛りに, *Dōshisha shōgaku* 同志社商学, vol. 47, no. 5 (March 1996), pp. 41–58.

"Meiji zenki no 'kokueki' shisō – *Meiji kenpakusho shūsei*, o tegakari ni" 明治前期の「国益」思想――『明治建白書集成』を手掛りに, Matsuyama daigaku ronshū 松山大学論集, vol. 4, no. 3 (August 1993), pp. 49–72.

"Tokugawa ki keizai shisō no tassei to genkai – kokueki shisō o chūshin ni" 徳川期経済思想の達成と限界――国益思想を中心に, pp. 11–32, in Sakai Takahito kyōju kanreki kinenkai 逆井孝仁教授還暦記念会, ed., *Nihon kindaika no shisō to tenkai* 日本近代化の思想と展開, Bunken Shuppan 文献出版, 1988.

Fukai Jinzō 深井甚三, "Jokamachi no jūmin kōsei to jinko" 城下町の住民構成と人口, pp. 317–52, in Toyoda Takeshi 豊田武、Harada Tomohiko 原田伴彦, Yamori

Kazuhiko 矢守一彦, et al., eds., *Kōza Nihon no hōken toshi* 講座日本の封建都市, vol. 2, Bun'ichi Sōgō Shuppan 文一総合出版, 1983.

Fukao Ryūtarō 深尾隆太郎, comp., *Onchi roku* 温知録, Osaka: privately published by compiler, 1920 (copy in Kōchi City Library).

Fukaya Katsumi 深谷克己, "Hyakushō ikki no shisō" 百姓一揆の思想, *Shisō* 思想, no. 584 (February 1973), pp. 206–27.

Fukuchiyama-shi Shi Hensan Iinkai 福知山市史編纂委員会, *Fukuchiyama-shi shi* 福知山市史, vol. 3, Fukuchiyama-shi 福知山市, 1984.

Fukui Hisazō 福井久蔵, Shodaimyō no gakujutsu to bungei no kenkyū 諸大名の学術と文芸の研究, Hara Shobō 原書房, 1976.

Fukuoka-ken no rekishi 福岡県の歴史, Fukuoka: Bungadō 文画堂, n.d.

Fukushima-ken 福島県, *Fukushima-ken shi* 福島県史, vols. 2 and 3, Fukushima-ken 福島県, 1971.

Fukushima Ōba (Nariyuki) 福島鴎波(成行), "Hōreki no ijin" 宝暦の偉人, *Tosa shidan* 土佐史談, no. 24 (September 1928), pp. 58–65; and no. 25 (November 1928), pp. 90–5.

Furushima Toshio 古島敏雄, "Shōhin ryūtsū no hatten to ryōshu keizai" 商品流通の発展と領主経済, pp. 53–101, in *Iwanami kōza Nihon rekishi* 岩波講座日本歴史, vol. 12, Iwanami Shoten 岩波書店, 1963.

Gifu-ken 岐阜県, ed., *Gifu-ken shi, shiryō hen, kinsei* 岐阜県史資料編近世, vol. 2, Gifu-ken 岐阜県, 1966.

Gifu-ken shi, tsūshi hen, kinsei jō 岐阜県史通史編近世上, Gifu ken 岐阜県, 1968.

Gotō Yasushi 後藤靖, "Bakusei kaikaku – toku ni Tenpō kaikaku ni tsuite" 幕政改革――とくに天保改革について, *Rekishigaku kenkyū* 歴史学研究, no. 176 (October 1954), pp. 38–42.

Hall, John, "The Castle Town and Japan's Modern Urbanization," pp. 169–88, in John Hall and Marius B. Jansen, eds., *Studies in the Institutional History of Early Modern Japan*, Princeton, N.J.: Princeton University Press, 1968.

"Feudalism in Japan – A Reassessment," pp. 15–51, in John Hall and Marius B. Jansen, eds., *Studies in the Institutional History of Early Modern Japan*, Princeton, N.J.: Princeton University Press, 1968.

"Foundations of the Japanese Daimyo," pp. 65–77, in John Hall and Marius B. Jansen, eds., *Studies in the Institutional History of Early Modern Japan*, Princeton, N.J.: Princeton University Press, 1968.

"Ikeda Mitsumasa and the Bizen Flood of 1654," pp. 57–83, in Albert M. Craig and Donald H. Shively, eds., *Personality in Japanese History*, Berkeley: University of California Press, 1970.

Japan from Prehistory to Modern Times, New York: Delacorte, 1970.

ed., *Early Modern Japan*, in *The Cambridge History of Japan* Series, vol. 4, New York: Cambridge University Press, 1991.

Hall, John, and Marius B. Jansen, eds., *Studies in the Institutional History of Early Modern Japan*, Princeton, N.J.: Princeton University Press, 1968.

Hanley, Susan B., and Kozo Yamamura, *Economic and Demographic Change in Preindustrial Japan, 1600–1868*, Princeton, N.J.: Princeton University Press, 1977.

Han shu 漢書, Peking: Chung-hua shu-chü 中華書局, 1962.

Harada Tomohiko 原田伴彦, ed., *Nihon toshi seikatsu shiryō shūsei* 日本都市生活史料集成, vol. 3, Gakushū Kenkyūsha 学習研究社, 1975.

Harootunian, Harry, *Things Seen and Unseen: Discourse and Ideology in Tokugawa Nativism*, Chicago: Chicago University Press, 1988.

Harris, Neil, "All the World a Melting Pot? Japan at American Fairs 1876–1904," pp. 24–54, in Akira Iriye, ed., *Mutual Images: Essays in American-Japanese Relations*, Cambridge: Harvard University Press, 1975.

Hashimoto Masaji 橋本正次, *Himeji jō shi* 姫路城史, Meicho shuppan 名著出版 (reprint), 1973.

Hatanaka Seiji 畑中誠治, "Hōreki Tenmei ki Setonaikai shohan ni okeru seisaku to sono kiban" 宝暦・天明期瀬戸内諸藩における経済政策とその基盤, *Rekishigaku kenkyū* 歴史学研究, no. 304 (September 1965), pp. 18–26.

Hayami Akira 速水融 and Miyamoto Matao 宮本又郎, "Gaisetsu – jūshichi-jūhasseiki" 概説――十七―十八世紀, pp. 4–84, in Hayami Akira and Miyamoto Matao, eds., *Keizai shakai no seiritsu 17–18 seiki* 経済社会の成立17―18世紀, *Nihon keizaishi* 日本経済史 series, vol. 1, Iwanami Shoten 岩波書店, 1989.

eds., *Keizai shakai no seiritsu 17–18 seiki* 経済社会の成立17―18世紀, *Nihon keizai shi* 日本経済史 series, vol. 1, Iwanami Shoten 岩波書店, 1989.

et al., eds., *Nihon keizai shi* 日本経済史, 5 vols., Iwanami Shoten 岩波書店, 1988–90.

Hayashi Motoi 林基, "Hōreki Tenmei ki no shakai jōsei" 宝暦天明期の社会情勢, pp. 103–54, *Iwanami kōza Nihon rekishi* 岩波講座日本歴史, vol. 12, Iwanami Shoten 岩波書店, 1963.

Hikone-shi 彦根市, *Hikone-shi shi* 彦根市史, vol. 1, Hikone-shi 彦根市, 1960.

Hirakawa Arata 平川新, "Chiiki keizai no tenkai" 地域経済の展開, pp. 111–48, in *Iwanami Kōza Nihon tsūshi* 岩波講座日本通史, vol. 15, Iwanami Shoten 岩波書店, 1995.

Hirao Michio 平尾道雄, "Hōreki kokusangata shihō to nōmin" 宝暦国産方仕法と農民, *Tosa shidan* 土佐史談, no. 73 (December 1940), pp. 25–36.

Ishin keizai shi no kenkyū 維新経済史の研究, Kōchi: Kōchi Shimin Toshokan 高知市民図書館, 1959.

Kōchi-han zaisei shi (zōho shinpan) 高知藩財政史（増補新版）, Kōchi: Kōchi Shimin Toshokan 高知市民図書館, 1965.

Tosa-han 土佐藩, Yoshikawa Kōbunkan 吉川弘文館, 1965.

Tosa-han gyogyō keizai shi 土佐藩漁業経済史, Kōchi: Kōchi Shimin Toshokan 高知市民図書館, 1955.

Tosa-han kōgyō keizai shi 土佐藩工業経済史, Kōchi: Kōchi Shimin Toshokan 高知市民図書館, 1957.

Tosa-han nōgyo keizai shi 土佐藩農業経済史, Kōchi: Kōchi Shimin Toshokan 高知市民図書館, 1958.

Tosa-han ringyō keizai shi 土佐藩林業経済史, Kōchi: Kōchi Shimin Toshokan 高知市民図書館, 1956.

Tosa-han shōgyō keizai shi 土佐藩商業経済史, Kōchi: Kōchi Shimin Toshokan 高知市民図書館, 1960.

Tosa nōmin ikki shi kō 土佐農民一揆史考, Kōchi: Kōchi Shimin Toshokan 高知市民図書館, 1953.

Yoshida Tōyō 吉田東洋, Yoshikawa Kōbunkan 吉川弘文館, 1969.

ed., "Tosa-han gōson chōsasho" 土佐藩郷村調査書(in seven parts), *Tosa shidan* 土佐史談, nos. 81–7 (October 1950–December 1955).

Hiroshima-ken 広島県, *Hiroshima-ken shi, kinsei hen* 広島県史近世編, vols. 1 and 2, Hiroshima-ken 広島県, 1981–4.

Hirotani Kijūrō 広谷喜十郎, "Genna kaikaku no ichi kōsatsu" 元和改革の一考察, *Tosa shidan* 土佐史談, vol. 100 (June 1961), pp. 96–100.

"Ōsaka ni okeru Shōtoku gonen no maki kakarime soshō mondai" 大坂における正徳五年の薪掛目訴訟問題, *Kainan shigaku* 海南史学 (in three parts), no. 1 (March 1963), pp. 17–36; no. 2 (December 1963), pp. 31–42; no. 3 (January 1965), pp. 20–32.

"Tosa hansei shoki no jōkamachi to zaigōmachi no dōkō" 土佐藩政初期の城下町及び在郷町の動向, pp. 142–64, in Yamamoto Takeshi 山本大, ed., *Tosa shi no shomondai* 土佐史の諸問題, Meicho Shuppan 名著出版, 1978.

"Tosa hansei to shoki jōkamachi" 土佐藩政と初期城下町, pp. 233–81, in Irimajiri Yoshinaga, *Tosa-han keizai shi no kenkyū* 土佐藩経済史の研究, Kōchi: Kōchi Shimin Toshokan 高知市民図書館, 1966.

"Tosa no gimin denshō" 土佐の義民伝承, *Tosa shidan* 土佐史談, no. 178 (September 1988), pp. 1–9.

"Tosa no zaigō ura machi" 土佐の在郷浦町, pp. 448–70, in Toyoda Takeshi 豊田武, et al. eds., *Kōza Nihon no hōken toshi* 講座・日本の封建都市, vol. 3, Bun'ichi Sōgō Shuppan 文一総合出版, 1981.

Honjō Eijirō 本庄栄治郎, *Nihon jinkō shi* 日本人口史, reprint in *Honjo Eijirō chōsaku shū* 本庄栄治郎著作集, vol. 5, Osaka: Seibundō 清文堂, 1972.

ed, *Kinsei jinkō mondai shiryō* 近世人口問題史料, Osaka: Keizaishi Kenkyūkai 経済史研究会, 1971.

Horie Yasuzō 堀江保蔵, *Kokusan shōrei to kokusan senbai* 国産奨励と国産専売, Hanawa Shobō 塙書房, 1963.

Wagakuni kinsei no senbai seido 我国近世の専売制度, Nihon Hyōronsha 日本評論社, 1933.

Howell, David, "Ainu Ethnicity and the Boundaries of the Early Modern Japanese State," *Past and Present*, no. 142 (February 1994), pp. 69–93.

Capitalism from Within: Economy, Society and the State in a Japanese Fishery, Berkeley: University of California Press, 1995.

Huber, Thomas, *The Revolutionary Origins of Modern Japan*, Stanford, Calif.: Stanford University Press, 1981.

Hucker, Charles O., "Confucianism and the Chinese Censorial System," pp. 182–208, in David Niven, ed., *Confucianism in Action*, Stanford, Calif.: Stanford University Press, 1959.

Ikeda Norimasa 池田敬正, "Tenpō kaikaku ron no saikentō – Tosa-han o chūshin ni shite" 天保改革論の再検討――土佐藩を中心にして, *Nihon shi kenkyū* 日本史研究, no. 31 (April 1957), pp. 23–37.

"Tosa-han ni okeru Ansei kaikaku to sono hantai ha" 土佐藩における安政改革とその反 對派, *Rekishi gaku kenkyū* 歴史学研究, no. 205 (March 1957), pp. 18–29.

Ikegami, Eiko, *The Taming of the Samurai*, New Haven, Ct.: Yale University Press, 1995.

Inagaki Takeshi 稲垣武, *Hiraga Gennai, Edo no yume* 平賀源内、江戸の夢, Shinchōsha, 1989.

Inoue Kazuo 井上和夫, *Han hō, bakufu hō to ishin hō* 藩法幕府法と維新法, 3 vols., Gannandō 巖南堂 (reprint of 1940–1 ed.), 1965.

Inoue Kiyoshi 井上清, *Saigō Takamori* 西郷隆盛, Chūkō shinsho 中公新書, no. 223, Chūō Kōronsha 中央公論社, 1970.

Inoue Mitsusada 井上光貞, ed., trans., *Nihon shoki* 日本書記, Nihon no meicho 日本の名 著 series, vol. 1, Chūō Kōronsha 中央公論社, 1971.

Inoue Seishō 井上静照, Kōchi Chihōshi Kenkyūkai 高知地方史研究会, ed., *Shinkakuji nikki* 真覚寺日記, 10 vols. (within *Tosa gunsho shūsei* 土佐群書集成 series), Kōchi: Kōchi Shimin Toshokan 高知市民図書館, 1961–74.

Irimajiri Yoshinaga 入交好脩, *Tosa-han keizai shi kenkyū* 土佐藩経済史研究, Kōchi: Kōchi Shimin Toshokan 高知市民図書館, 1966.

Irish University Press, *Area Studies Series, British Parliamentary Papers, Japan*, vol. 4, *Embassy and Consular Commerical Reports 1859–1871*, Shannon: Irish University Press, 1972.

Irokawa Daikichi 色川大吉, Gabe Masao 我部政男, et al., eds, *Meiji zenki kenpakusho shūsei* 明治建白書集成, 6 vols. at present, Chikuma Shobō 築摩書房, 1986–present.

Ishii Ryōsuke 石井良助, *Shōgun no seikatsu sono hoka* 将軍の生活その他, Jiji Nippōsha Shuppan 時事日報社出版, 1971.

ed., *Hanpōshū* 藩法集, vols. 1–12, Sōbunsha 創文社, 1959–75.

Ishii Susumu 石井進, Katsumata Shizuo 勝俣鎮夫, Ishmoda Shō 石母田正, *Chūsei seiji shakai shisō, jōkan* 中世政治社会思想上巻, vol. 21 of *Nihon shisō taikei* 日本思想体 系, Iwanami shoten 岩波書店, 1972.

Ishii Takashi 石井孝, *Meiji ishin no kokusaiteki kankyō (zōtei hen)* 明治維新の国際的環境 （増訂編）, Yoshikawa Kōbunkan 吉川弘文館, 1966.

Ishiodori Tanehiro 石躍胤央, "Nonaka Kenzan shissei makki no Tosa hansei – toku ni shinden kaihatsu to bakufu fushinyaku o megutte" 野中兼山執政末期の土佐藩政―― とくに新田開発と幕府普請役をめぐって, *Rekishi hyōron* 歴史評論, no. 293 (September 1974), pp. 37–45.

"Tosa-han 'Kanbun no kaitai' ni kansuru ichi kōsatsu" 土佐藩「寛文の改替」の一考察, pp. 1077–94, in Kobata Atsushi 小葉田淳 ed., *Kokushi ronshū* 国史論集(2) vol. 2, Dokushikai 讀史会, 1959.

"Tosa-han ni okeru Genna no kaikaku" 土佐藩における元和の改革 *Tokushima daigaku kyōyō gakubu kenkyū kiyō (jinbun shakai kagaku)* 徳島大学教養学部研究紀要（人 文・社会科学）, vol. 20 (1985), pp. 13–22.

"Tosa-han ni okeru teppōgumi ni tsuite" 土佐藩における鉄砲組について, *Tokushima daigaku kyōyō gakubu kenkyū kiyō (jinbun shakai kagaku)* 徳島大学教養学部研究紀要（人文・社会科学）, vol. 4 (March 1969), pp. 81–93.

"Tosa-han no jōmai jōgin kashitsuke seido ni tsuite" 土佐藩の城米城銀貸付制度につい て, *Tokushima daigaku kyōyō gakubu kiyō (jinbun shakai kagaku)* 徳島大学教養学部研究紀要（人文・社会科学）, no. 2 (Feb. 1967), pp. 31–46.

"Tosa-han shoki hashirimono taisaku ni tsuite" 土佐藩初期走り者対策について, pp. 127–41, in Yamamoto Takeshi, ed., *Tosa shi no shomondai* 土佐史の諸問題, Meicho Shuppan 名著出版, 1978.

Itō Tasaburō 伊東多三郎, *Kinsei shi no kenkyū* 近世史の研究, 4 vols., Yoshikawa Kōbunkan 吉川弘文館, 1981–4.

Jansen, Marius B., *China in the Tokugawa World*, Cambridge: Harvard University Press, 1992.

 Sakamoto Ryōma and the Meiji Restoration, Princeton, N.J.: Princeton University Press, 1961.

 "Tosa in the Last Century of Tokugawa Rule," pp. 331–47 in John Hall and Marius B. Jansen, eds., *Studies in the Institutional History of Early Modern Japan*, Princeton, N.J.: Princeton University Press, 1968.

 "Tosa in the Seventeenth Century: The Establishment of Yamauchi Rule," pp. 115–29, in John Hall and Marius B. Jansen, eds., *Studies in the Institutional History of Early Modern Japan*, Princeton, N.J.: Princeton University Press, 1968.

 "Tosa in the Sixteenth Century: The 100 Article Code of Chōsokabe Motochika," pp. 89–114, in John Hall and Marius B. Jansen, eds., *Studies in the Institutional History of Early Modern Japan*, Princeton, N.J.: Princeton University Press, 1968.

 ed., *The Nineteenth Century*, in *The Cambridge History of Japan* series, vol. 5, New York: Cambridge University Press, 1989.

Kaizanshu 皆山集, see Matsunoo Shōkō, comp.

Kalland, Arne, and Jon Pedersen, "Famine and Population in Fukuoka Domain During the Tokugawa Period," *Journal of Japanese Studies*, vol. 10, no. 1 (Winter 1984), pp. 31–72.

Kanai Madoka 金井圓, *Hansei* 藩政, Shibundō 至文堂, 1962.

 Hansei seiritsu ki no kenkyū 藩制成立期の研究, Yoshikawa Kōbunkan 吉川弘文館, 1975.

Kanō Kyōji 狩野亨二, *Edo jidai no ringyō shisō kenkyū* 江戸時代の林業思想研究, Nihon Ringyō Chōsakai 日本林業調査会, 1977.

Kasaya Kazuhiko 笠谷和比古, *Kinsei bukeshakai no seiji kōzō* 近世武家社会の政治構造, Yoshikawa Kōbunkan 吉川弘文館, 1993.

Katsumata Shizuo with Martin Collcutt, "The Development of Sengoku Law," pp. 101–24, in John W. Hall, Nagahara Keiji, and Kozo Yamamura, eds., *Japan Before Tokugawa: Political Consolidation and Economic Growth, 1500–1650*, Princeton, N.J.: Princeton University Press, 1981.

Kattō Isamu 甲藤勇, "'Yōsha zuihitsu' ni mieru Teshima jiken" 「勇舎随筆」に見える手島事件, *Tosa shidan* 土佐史談, no. 118 (December 1967), pp. 105–11.

Kawashima Tetsurō 川島哲郎, Sekita Hidesato 関田英里, et al., "Kirihata keiei chitai no keizai kōzō – Kōchi-ken, Takaoka-gun, Niyodo-mura, ōaza Besshi, aza Honmura o chūshin to shite" 切畑経営地帯の経済構造——高知県高岡郡仁淀村大字別枝字本村を中心として, *Kōchi daigaku gakujutsu kenkyū hōkoku* 高知大学学術研究報告, vol. 5, no. 32 (1956).

Keene, Donald, *The Japanese Discovery of Europe*, Stanford, Calif.: Stanford University Press, 1969.

Kenjō Yukio 見城幸雄, "Edo bakufu meyasubako e no ichi sojō – bakumatsu ki aru rōnō no bakuhansei hihan" 江戸幕府目安箱への一訴状——幕末期ある老農の幕政批判, *Toki no hōrei* 時の法令, no. 1031 (13 March 1979), pp. 21–32; no. 1032 (23 March 1979), pp. 22–31; no. 1040 (13 June 1979), pp. 42–8; and no. 1049 (13 September 1979), pp. 44–50.

Kenshōbo 憲章簿, see Yamamoto Takeshi, et al., eds.

Kimura Motoi 木村礎, Fujino Tamotsu 藤野保, et al., eds., *Hanshi daijiten* 藩史大事典, 8 vols., Yūzankaku 雄山閣, 1988–91.

Kinsei Sonraku Kenkyūkai 近世村落研究会, ed., *Tosa no kuni jikata shiryō* 土佐の国地方史料, Nihon Gakujutsu Shinkōkai 日本学術振興会, 1956.

Kishimoto Minoru 岸本實, "Hansei chūki ni okeru Kaifugawa ryūiki no kaitaku katei – Awa Tosa ryōkokukan no jinkō idō" 藩政中期に於ける海部川流域の開拓過程——阿波土佐兩国間の人口移動, *Chirigaku hyōron* 地理学評論, vol. 24, no. 5 (May 1951), pp. 19–24.

Kobayakawa Kingo 小早川欣吾, *Kinsei minji sosho seido no kenkyū* 近世民事訴訟制度の研究, Yūhikaku 有斐閣, 1957.

Meiji hōseishi sōkō 明治法制史叢考, Kyoto: Kyōto Inshokan 京都印書館, 1945.

Kōchi Chihōshi Kenkyūkai 高知地方史研究会, ed., *Kōchi-ken rekishi nempyō* 高知県歴史年表, Kōchi: Kōchi Shimin Toshokan 高知市民図書館, 1959.

Kōchi-han kyōiku enkaku torishirabe 高知藩教育沿革取調, Kōchi: Tosa Shidankai 土佐史談会 (reprint), 1986.

Kōchi-ken Jinmei Jiten Henshū Iinkai 高知県人名辞典編集委員会, *Kōchi-ken jinmei jiten* 高知県人名辞典, Kōchi: Kōchi Shimin Toshokan 高知市民図書館, 1971.

Kōchi-ken Kyōiku Iinkai 高知県教育委員会 ed., *Tosa hanshu Yamauchi-ke rekishi shiryō mokuroku* 土佐藩主山内家歴史資料目録, Kōchi: Kōchi-ken Kyōiku Iinkai 高知県教育委員会, 1991.

Kōchi-ken Rekishi Jiten Hensan Iinkai 高地県歴史事典編集委員会, *Kōchi-ken rekishi jiten* 高地県歴史事典, Kōchi: Kōchi Shimin Toshokan 高知市民図書館, 1980.

Kōchi-ken Shi Hensan Iinkai 高知県史編纂委員会, *Kōchi-ken shi* 高知県史, 10 vols., Kōchi-ken 高知県, 1968–78.

Kōchi-shi Shi Hensan Iinkai 高知市史編纂委員会, *Kōchi-shi shi, jōkan* 高知市史、上巻, Kōchi-shi 高知市, 1958.

Kodama Kōta 児玉幸多, and Kitajima Masamoto 北島正元 eds., *Monogatari hanshi* 物語藩史, vol. 8, Jinbutsu Ōraisha 人物往来社, 1965.

Kodama Kōta 児玉幸多, *Nihonshi nenpyō* 日本史年表, Yoshikawa Kōbunkan 吉川弘文館, 1984.

ed., *Hyōjun Nihon rekishi chizu* 標準日本歴史地図, Yoshikawa Kōbunkan 吉川弘文館, 1984.

Kōga-gun Kyōiku Iinkai Hen 甲賀郡教育委員会, *Kōga-gun shi, jōkan* 甲賀郡史上巻, Kōga-gun, 1926.

Kokushi Daijiten Henshū Iinkai 国史大辞典編集委員会 ed., *Kokushi daijiten* 国史大辞典, 14 vols. (in print), Yoshikawa Kōbunkan 吉川弘文館, 1979–present.

Kokusho sōmokuroku: chosha betsu sakuin 国書総目録著者別索引, Iwanami Shoten 岩波書店, 1976.

Kōriyama-shi 郡山市, *Kōriyama-shi shi* 郡山市史, vol. 3, Kokusho Kankōkai 国書刊行会 (reprint), 1981.

Kubokawa-chō Shi Henshū Iinkai 窪川町史編集委員会, *Kubokawa-chō shi* 窪川町史, Daiichi Hōkishuppan 第一法規出版, 1970.

Kumon Arata 公文新, "Tosa Nakamura Yamauchi-ke ni tsuite – sono naibun shihan to shite no seiritsu katei" 土佐中村山内家について――その内分支藩としての成立過程, pp. 23–50, in Yamamoto Takeshi, ed. 山本大, *Kōchi no kenkyū* 高知の研究, vol. 3, Osaka: Seibundō 清文堂, 1983.

Kurokawa Masamichi 黒川真道, ed., *Tosa monogatari* 土佐物語, vol. 2, *Kokushi sōsho* 国史叢書 series, Kokushi Kenkyūkai 国史研究会, 1914.

Kusunoki Ōe 楠大枝, auth., Kōchi Chihōshi Kenkyūkai ed. 高知地方史研究会, *Hiuchi bukuro* 燧袋, 16 vols. (within *Tosa gunsho shūsei* 土佐群書集成 series), Kōchi: Kōchi Shimin Toshokan 高知市民図書館, 1966–87.

Maeda-ke henshū bu 前田家編輯部, ed., *Kaga-han shiryō* 加賀藩史料, 16 vols., Ishiguro Bunkichi 石黒文吉, 1929–43.

Mamiya Hisako 間宮尚子, *Tosa-han no sanson kōzō – Mitani-ke monjo kōkyū* 土佐藩の山村構造――三谷家文書考究, Kōchi: Kōchi Shimin Toshokan 高知市民図書館, 1978.

Marshall, Byron, *Capitalism and Nationalism in Prewar Japan*, Stanford, Calif.: Stanford University Press, 1967.

Matsumoto Sannosuke, "The Idea of Heaven: A Tokugawa Foundation for Natural Rights Theory," pp. 181–9, in Tetsuo Najita and Irwin Scheiner, eds., *Japanese Thought in the Tokugawa Period 1600–1868 – Methods and Metaphors*, Chicago: University of Chicago Press, 1978.

Matsunoo Shōkō 松野尾章行, comp., Hirao Michio 平尾道雄 et al., eds., *Kaizanshū* 皆山集, 10 vols., Kōchi: Kōchi Kenritsu Toshokan 高知県立図書館, 1973–8.

Matsuo Masahito 松尾正人, *Haihan chiken* 廃藩置県, Chūō kōronsha 中央公論社, 1986.

Matsuoka-chō Shi Hensan Iinkai 松岡町史編纂委員会, *Matsuoka-chō shi, jō kan* 松岡町史上巻, Matsuoka-chō 松岡町 (Fukui Prefecture), 1978.

Matsuyama-shi Shiryōshū Henshū Iinkai 松山市史料集編集委員会, ed., *Matsuyama-shi shiryōshū* 松山市史料集, vols. 5 and 6, Matsuyama-shi Yakusho 松山市役所, 1985.

Matsuyoshi Sadao 松好貞夫, *Tosa-han keizai shi kenkyū* 土佐藩経済史研究, Nihon Hyōronsha 日本評論社, 1930.

Meiji Bunka Kenkyūkai 明治文化研究会, ed., *Meiji jibutsu kigen* 明治事物起源, Nihon Hyōronsha 日本評論社, 1969.

Miharu-chō 三春町, *Miharu-chō shi, Kinsei* 三春町史　近世, vol. 2, Miharu-chō 三春町 (Fukushima Prefecture), 1984.

Mikami Sanji 三上参次, *Edo jidai shi* 江戸時代史, Kōdansha 講談社 (reprint), 1977.

Minami Kazuo 南和男, *Bakumatsu Edo shakai no kenkyū* 幕末江戸社会の研究, Yoshikawa Kōbunkan 吉川弘文館, 1978.

Mitani Hiroshi 三谷博, *Meiji ishin to nashonarizumu* 明治維新とナショナリズム——幕末 の外交と政治変動, Yamakawa Shuppan 山川出版, 1997.

Mito-shi shi, chūkan 水戸市史、中巻, Mito-shi 水戸市 (Ibaraki Prefecture), 1969.

Miyamato Mataji 宮本又次, *Kabunakama no kenkyū* 株仲間の研究, (1938), vol. 1, in *Miyamoto Mataji chosakushū* 宮本又次著作集, Kōdansha 講談社, 1977.

Ōsaka 大阪, Nihon rekishi shinsho 日本歴史新書, 1957.

ed., *Shōhin ryūtsū no shiteki kenkyū* 商品流通の史的研究, Kyoto: Mineruva Shobō ミネルヴァ書房, 1967.

Miyoshi Tsunenori 三善庸礼, auth., Miyamoto Mataji 宮本又次, ed. *Kokka kanjō roku* 国 家勘定録, Osaka: Seibundō 清文堂, 1971.

Mizuki Sōtarō 水木惣太郎, *Gikai seido ron* 議会制度論, Yūshindō 有信堂, 1963.

Mori Yasuhiro 森泰博, "Shoki no Kōchi-han Ōsaka kurayashiki" 初期の高知藩大坂 蔵屋敷, *Keizaigaku ronkyū* 経済学論究, vol. 44, no. 3 (December 1990), pp. 29–47.

Moriguchi Kōji 森口幸司, "Mori Kanzaemon Hirosada no ryaku nenpu to sono shūhen – nikki, senzosho nado ni miru kakuchū bushi no seikatsu to sesō" 森勘左衛門広定の 略年譜とその周辺——日記先祖書などに見る廓中武士の生活と世相, *Tosa shidan* 土佐 史談, no. 181 (September 1989), pp. 18–26.

Morikawa Hidemasa 森川英正, *Nihongata keiei no genryū* 日本型経営の源流, Toyōkeizai Shinpōsha 東洋経済新報社, 1973.

Morita Toshihiko 森田敏彦, "Kaiseikan shihō no tenkai to sono genkai" 開成館仕法の展開 とその限界, pp. 268–321, in Ishii Takashi 石井孝, ed., *Bakumatsu ishinki no kenkyū* 幕末維新期の研究, Yoshikawa Kōbunkan 吉川弘文館, 1978.

Morris, John, *Kinsei Nihon chigyōsei no kenkyū* 近世日本知行制の研究, Osaka: Seibundō 清文堂, 1988.

Mozume Takami 物集高見, *Kōbunko* 廣文庫, 20 vols., Kōbunko Kankōkai 廣文庫刊行會, 1916–8.

Mutō Yoshikazu 武藤致和, comp. and auth.; Yorimitsu Kanji 依光貫之, Akizawa Shigeru 秋沢繁, et al., eds., *Nanroshi* 南路志, 9 vols. at present (will total 10), Kōchi: Kōchi Kenritsu Toshokan 高知県立図書館, 1990–present.

Nagano Susumu 長野暹, "Hansei kaikaku ron" 藩政改革論, pp. 201–35, in Yamada Tadao 山田忠雄 and Matsumoto Shirō 松本四郎, eds., *Hōreki Tenmei ki no seiji to shakai* 宝 暦天明期の政治と社会, Yūhikaku 有斐閣, 1988.

Nagoya-shi 名古屋市, *Nagoya-shi shi, seiji hen* 名古屋市市政治編, vols. 1 and 2, Nagoya-shi 名古屋市, 1967.

Nagoya-shi Kyōiku Iinkai 名古屋市教育委員会, ed., *Nagoya sōsho* 名古屋叢書, vols. 3 and 5, Nagoya: Nagoya-shi kyōiku iinkai 名古屋市教育委員会, 1961 and 1962.

Najita, Tetsuo, "The Conceptual Portrayal of Tokugawa Intellectual History," pp. 3–38, in Tetsuo Najita and Irwin Scheiner, eds., *Japanese Thought in the Tokugawa*

Period 1600–1868 – Methods and Metaphors, Chicago: University of Chicago Press, 1978.

"Political Economism in the Thought of Dazai Shundai," *The Journal of Asian Studies*, vol. 34 (1972), pp. 931–44.

Visions of Virtue: The Kaitokudō Merchant Academy in Tokugawa Japan, Chicago: University of Chicago Press, 1987.

Najita, Tetsuo, and Irwin Scheiner, eds., *Japanese Thought in the Tokugawa Period 1600–1868 – Methods and Metaphors*, Chicago: University of Chicago Press, 1978.

Nakai, Kate, *Shogunal Politics: Arai Hakuseki and the Premises of Tokugawa Rule*, Cambridge: Council on East Asian Studies, Harvard University Press, 1988.

Nakamura Kōichi 中村幸一, ed., *Takada hansei shi kenkyū, shiryō hen ichi* 高田藩制史研究史料編一, Fūmon shobō 風間書房, 1967.

Nakamura-shi shi hensanshitsu 中村市史編纂室, *Nakamura-shi shi* 中村市史, Nakamura-shi 中村市 (Kōchi Prefecture), 1969.

Nangoku-shi shi hensan shitsu 南国市史編纂室, *Nangoku-shi shi, gekan* 南国市史、下巻, Nangoku-shi 南国市 (Kōchi Prefecture), 1982.

Nanroshi 南路志, see Mutō Yoshikazu 武藤致和, comp. and auth.

Nemoto Makoto 根本誠, "Tōdai no tōki ni tsuite" 唐代の投匭について, *Waseda daigaku daigakuin bungaku kenkyūka kiyō* 早稲田大学大学院文学研究科紀要, no. 13 (1967), pp. 125–38.

Nenpyō Kokura-shi shi hoi 年表小倉市史補遺, Kokura-shi 小倉市, 1936.

Nihon Rekishi Daijiten Henshu Iinkai 日本歴史大事典編集委員会, *Nihon rekishi daijiten* 日本歴史大事典, 12 vols., Kawade shobō 河出書房, 1968–70.

Nihon Rekishi Gakkai 日本歴史学会 ed, *Nihon rekishi gakkai no kaikan to tenbō* 日本歴史学会の回顧と展望, vol. 8, Yamakawa Shuppansha 山川出版社, 1987.

Niigata-ken 新潟県, *Niigata-ken shi, tsūshi hen* 新潟県史、通史編, vols. 4 and 5, Niigata-ken 新潟県, 1988.

Nishikawa Shunsaku 西川俊作 and Amano Masatoshi 天野雅敏, "Shohan to sangyō to keizai seisakushi" 諸藩と産業と経済政策史, pp. 173–217, in Shinbo Hiroshi 新保博 and Saitō Osamu 斎藤修, eds., *Kindai seichō no taidō* 近代成長の胎動, Nihon keizaishi 日本経済史 series, vol. 2, Iwanami Shoten 岩波書店, 1989.

Niven, David, ed., *Confucianism in Action*, Stanford, Calif: Stanford University Press, 1959.

Nomura Kanetarō 野村兼太郎, *Tokugawa jidai no keizai shisō* 徳川時代の経済思想, Nihon Hyōronsha 日本評論社, 1939.

Nosco, Peter, *Remembering Paradise: Nativism and Nostalgia in Eighteenth-Century Japan*, Cambridge: Council on East Asian Studies, Harvard University Press, 1990.

Ōguchi Yūjirō 大口勇次郎, "Tenpō ki no seikaku" 天保期の性格, pp. 325–62, in *Iwanami kōza Nihon rekishi* 岩波講座日本歴史, vol. 12, Iwanami Shoten 岩波書店, 1976.

Ōhira Yūichi 大平祐一, "Kinsei no daimyo 'kōmu' to sono hōkai – bakumatsu no 'otetsudai,' 'jōnōkin' o tegakari ni shite" 近世の大名「公務」とその崩壊——幕末の「御手伝」「上納金」を手がかりにして, *Hōgaku* 法学, vol. 48, no. 6 (December 1985), pp. 97–156.

"Meiji shoki no meyasubako (1,2)" 明治初期の目安箱, *Ritsumeikan hōgaku* 立命館法
学, 1988, no. 5/6, pp. 753–84; 1992, no. 3/4, pp. 353–408.

Oka Takeshi 岡毅, "Senshō Oka-ke kiroku" 船匠岡家記録, *Tosa shidan* 土佐史談, no. 48
(September 1934), pp. 75–103.

"Okachū hengi" 御家中変義, *Tosa shidan* 土佐史談, no. 54 (March 1936) pp. 152–63; no.
55 (June 1936) pp. 209–32; no. 57 (December 1936) pp. 123–32; no. 59 (June 1937)
pp. 131–40; no. 62 (March 1938) pp. 140–7.

Okamoto Ryōichi, "Tenpō kaikaku" 天保改革, pp. 209–50, in *Iwanami Kōza Nihon
rekishi* 岩波講座日本歴史, vol. 13, Iwanami Shoten 岩波書店, 1963.

Ono Masao 小野正雄, "Bakuhansei seiji kaikaku ron" 幕藩制政治改革論, pp. 309–39, in
Rekishigaku kenkyūkai 歴史学研究会, ed., *Kōza Nihon rekishi* 講座日本歴史, vol. 6,
Tōkyō Daigaku Shuppankai 東京大学出版会, 1985.

Ōno Mizuo 大野瑞男, "Bakuhanseiteki shijō kōzō ron" 幕藩制的市場構造論, pp. 227–69,
in Rekishigaku kenkyūkai 歴史学研究会 ed., *Kōza Nihon rekishi* 講座日本歴史, vol. 5,
Tōkyō Daigaku Shuppankai 東京大学出版会, 1985.

Ōsaka Shōkō Kaigisho 大阪商工会議所, ed., *Ōsaka shōgyō shi shiryō* 大阪商業史資料,
vols. 2 and 34, Osaka: Ōsaka Shōkō Kaigisho 大阪商工会議所, 1963 and 1965.

Ōsaka-shi Shi Hensanjo 大阪市史編纂所, *Shokoku kyakukata hikae, shokoku kyakukata
chō* 諸国客方控・諸国客方帳, Osaka: Ōsaka-shi Shiryō Chōsakai 大阪市史料調査会,
1994.

Osatake Takeki 尾佐竹猛, *Ishin zengo ni okeru rikken shisō* 維新前後に於ける立憲思想,
Tōkyō Bunka Kenkyūkai 東京文化研究会, 1925.

Oseki Toyokichi 小関豊吉, "Tosa hansei shoki no jōsei" 土佐藩政初期の情勢, *Tosa shidan*
土佐史談, no. 32 (September 1930), pp. 76–97.

Ōtake Hideo 大竹秀男 and Harafuji Hiroshi 原藤弘司, eds., *Bakuhan kokka no hō to
shihai* 幕藩国家の法と社会, Yūhikaku 有斐閣, 1984.

Ōtsuka Katsumi 大塚克美, *Hamamatsu no rekishi* 浜松の歴史, Tōyōshoin 東洋書院, 1983.

Ravina, Mark, *Land and Lordship in Early Modern Japan*, Stanford, Calif.: Stanford
University Press, forthcoming.

  "State Building and Political Economy in Early Modern Japan," *The Journal of Asian
Studies*, vol. 54, no. 4 (November 1995), pp. 997–1022.

Renan, Ernest, *Oeuvres Completes de Ernest Renan*, tome 1, Paris: Calmann-Levy,
1947.

Rikkyō Daigaku Nihon Shi Kenkyūshitsu 立教大学日本史研究室, ed., *Tani Jinzan, Tani
Kanjō ke monjo mokuroku* 谷秦山、谷千城家文書目録, Rikkyō daigaku shozō monjo
mokuroku 立教大学図所蔵文書目録, no. 2, Rikkyō Daigaku Toshokan 立教大学図書
館, 1975.

Roberts, Luke S., "Genroku makki Tosa no jidaka ni tsuite – honden shinden jibarai
chō kankei no shinshiryō shōkai" 元禄末期土佐の地高について――「本田新田地払
帳」関係の新史料紹介, *Tosa shidan* 土佐史談, no. 182 (December 1989), pp. 156–
7.

  "The Petition Box in Eighteenth-Century Tosa," *Journal of Japanese Studies*, vol. 20,
no. 2 (Summer 1994), pp. 423–58.

"A Petition for a Popularly Chosen Council of Government in Tosa in 1787," *Harvard Journal of Asiatic Studies*, vol. 57, no. 2, (Dec. 1997), pp. 575–96.

"Tenmei shichinen no chōsan ikki to jōkamachi sōdō no shin shiryō – Nomi Reinan no 'Ōminato nikki' yori" 天明七年の逃散一揆と城下町騒動の新史料——野見嶺南の「大湊日記」より, *Tosa shidan* 土佐史談, no. 183 (December 1989), pp. 22–6.

"Tosa-han sojō (meyasu) bako no seido to kinō 土佐藩訴状（目安）箱の制度と機能," *Kainan shigaku* 海南史学, vol. 28 (August 1990), pp. 45–62.

"Tosa hansei chūki ni okeru 'jidaka' ni tsuite – 'Genroku gōchō,' 'Honden shinden jibarai chō,' 'Okuni nanagun gōsonchō' o chūshin ni shite" 土佐藩制中期における"地高" について——「元禄郷村帳」・「本田新田地払帳」・「御国七郡郷村牒」を中心にして, *Tosa shidan* 土佐史談, no. 181 (September 1989), pp. 9–17.

"Tosa to ishin – 'kokka' no sōshitsu to 'chihō' no tanjō" 土佐と維新——「国家」の喪失と「地方」の誕生, forthcoming in Kindai Nihon Kenkyūkai 近代日本研究会 ed., *Nenpō kindai Nihon kenkyū* 年報近代日本研究, no. 19, Yamakawa Shuppan 山川出版, 1997.

Rozman, Gilbert, "Edo's Importance in the Changing Tokugawa Society," *Journal of Japanese Studies*, vol. 1 (Autumn 1974), pp. 91–112.

Urban Networks in Ch'ing China and Tokugawa Japan, Princeton, N.J.: Princeton University Press, 1974.

Saito Osamu 斎藤修, "Daikaikon, jinkō, shōnō keizai" 大開墾、人口、小農経済, pp. 172–215, in Hayami Akira 速水融 and Miyamoto Matao 宮本又郎 eds., *Keizai shakai no seiritsu* 経済社会の成立, Nihon keizaishi series 日本経済史, vol. 1, Iwanami Shoten 岩波書店, 1989.

Sasaki Junnosuke 佐々木潤之介, *(Zōho kaitei ban) Bakuhan kenryoku no kiso kōzō* （増補改訂版）幕藩権力の基礎構造, Ochanomizu Shobō 御茶ノ水書房, 1985.

Sasaki Junnosuke 佐々木潤之介 with Ronald Toby, "The Changing Rationale of Daimyo Control in the Emergence of the Bakuhan State," pp. 271–94 in John W. Hall, Nagahara Keiji, and Kozo Yamamura, eds., *Japan Before Tokugawa: Political Consolidation and Economic Growth, 1500–1650*, Princeton, N.J.: Princeton University Press, 1981.

Sasaki Junnosuke 佐々木潤之介 and Yamaguchi Keiji 山口啓二, *Bakuhan taisei* 幕藩体制, Nihon Hyōronsha 日本評論社, 1972.

Scalapino, Robert, "Elections and Political Modernization in Prewar Japan," pp. 249–91, in Robert Ward, ed., *Political Development in Modern Japan*, Princeton, N.J.: Princeton University Press, 1969.

Scheiner, Irwin, "Benevolent Lords and Honorable Peasants," pp. 39–62, in Tetsuo Najita and Irwin Scheiner, eds., *Japanese Thought in the Tokugawa Period 1600–1868 – Methods and Metaphors*, Chicago: University of Chicago Press, 1978.

Sekai rekishi jiten 世界歴史事典, 21 vols., Heibonsha 平凡社, 1951–5.

Sekita Hidesato 関田英里, "'Hiragami' no hatten to 'shogunshi' no seiritsu" 「平紙」の発展と「諸郡紙」の成立, *Tosa shidan* 土佐史談, no. 100 (June 1961), pp. 79–83.

"Tosa no 'kokudaka' ni tsuite" 土佐の「石高」について, *Tosa shidan* 土佐史談, no. 91 (August 1957), pp. 34–43.

Sekiyama Naotarō 関山直太郎, *Kinsei Nihon no jinkō kōzō—Tokugawa jidai no jinkō chōsa to jinkō jōtai ni kansuru kenkyū* 近世日本の人口構造 — 徳川時代の人口調査と人口状態に関する研究, 2 vols., Yoshikawa Kōbunkan 吉川弘文館, 1958.

Shibahara Takuji 芝原拓自, *Meiji ishin no kenryoku kiban* 明治維新の権力基盤, Ochanomizu Shobō お茶の水書房, 1965.

Shigakkai 史学会, *Nihon rekishi gakkai no kaiko to tenbō* 日本歴史学会の回顧と展望, vol. 8, Yamakawa Shuppan 山川出版, 1987.

Shih-chi 史記, Peking: Chung-hua Shu-chü 中華書局, 1959.

Shikoku Minka Hakubutsukan Kenkyūsho 四国民家博物館研究所, *Sanuki oyobi shūhen chiiki no satō seizō dōgu to satō shimegoya, kamaya (chōsa hōkokusho)* 讃岐および周辺地域の砂糖製造道具と砂糖しめ小屋、窯屋調査報告書, Takamatsu: Shikoku Minka Hakubutsukan 四国民家博物館, 1987.

Shinbo Hiroshi 新保博 and Saitō Osamu 斎藤修, eds., *Kindai seichō no taidō* 近代成長の胎動, Nihon keizaishi 日本経済史 series, vol. 2, Iwanami Shoten 岩波書店, 1989.

Smith, Henry D., II, "The History of the Book in Edo and Paris," pp. 332–52, in James L. McClain, John M. Merriman, and Ugawa Kaoru, eds., *Edo and Paris: Urban Life and the State in the Early Modern Era*, Cornell, N.Y.: Cornell University Press, 1994.

Smith, Thomas, "The Land Tax in the Tokugawa Period," pp. 283–300, in John Hall and Marius B. Jansen, eds., *Studies in the Institutional History of Early Modern Japan*, Princeton, N.J.: Princeton University Press, 1968.

Nakahara, Stanford, Calif.: Stanford University Press, 1977.

"Okura Nagatsune and the Technologists," in Albert Craig and Donald Shively, eds., *Personality in Japanese History*, Berkeley: University of California Press, 1970.

Political Change and Industrial Development in Japan: Government Enterprise, 1868–1880, Stanford, Calif., Stanford University Press, 1955.

"Premodern Economic Growth: Japan and the West," *Past and Present*, no. 60 (Aug. 1973), pp. 127–60.

Smith, Thomas, and Robert Y. Eng, "Peasant Families and Population Control in Eighteenth Century Japan," *Journal of Interdisciplinary History*, vol. 6, no. 3 (Winter 1976), pp. 417–45.

Sone Hiromi 曽根ひろみ, "Kyōhō ki no soshō saibanken to uttae – Kyōhō ki no seiji to shakai"享保期の訴訟裁判権と訴え — 享保の政治と社会, pp. 263–300 in Matsumoto Shirō 松本四郎 and Yamada Tadao 山田忠雄 eds., *Genroku Kyōhō ki no seiji to shakai* 元禄享保期の政治と社会, Yūhikaku 有斐閣, 1980.

Sugawara Michizane 菅原道真, *Ruijū kokushi* 類聚國史 (zenpen), vols. 5 and 6 in *Kokushi taikei* 国史大系 series (shintei zōho hen 新訂増補編), Yoshikawa Kōbunkan 吉川弘文館, 1965.

Sugi Hitoshi 杉仁, "Kasei ki nōson ni okeru minpuron no keisei" 化政期農村における民富論の形成, pp. 61–108, in Kano Masanao 鹿野政直 and Takagi Shunsuke 高木俊輔, eds., *Ishin henkaku ni okeru zaisonteki shochōryū* 維新変革における在村的諸潮流, San'ichi Shobō 三一書房, 1972.

Takagi Shōsaku 高木昭作, "Bakuhan seijishi josetsu – Tosa-han Gcnna kaikaku" 幕藩政治

史序説 —— 土佐藩元和改革, *Rekishi hyōron* 歴史評論, no. 253 (October 1971), pp. 98–115.

Takahashi Shirō 高橋四朗, "Kitagawa-gō sōdō to Sukumō ryōmin ikki" 北川郷騒動と宿毛領民一揆, *Seifū* 青風 (published by Kōchi Kenritsu Toshokan 高知県立図書館), no. 2 (August 1978).

"Tosa-han 'shōya dōmei' kenkyū no ichi zentei" 土佐藩「庄屋同盟」研究の一前提, *Kainan shigaku* 海南史学, no. 3 (January 1965), pp. 1–19.

Takahashi Tsutomu 高橋務, "Chūki Akita-han no shakuchi seisaku ni tsuite" 中期秋田藩の借知政策について, *Shūdai Shigaku* 秋大史学, no. 34 (March, 1988), pp. 21–36.

Takamatsu-shi Shi Henshū Shitsu 高松市史編集室, *Shinshū Takamatsu-shi shi* 新修高松市史, vol. 1, Takamatsu-shi 高松市, 1964.

Takayanagi Shinzō 高柳真三 and Ishii Ryōsuke 石井良助, eds., *Ofuregaki Kanpō shūsei* 御触書寛保集成, Iwanami Shoten 岩波書店, 1958.

Takeichi Saichirō 武市佐市郎, "Tosa no kuni nihyakugojū nenkan no genjū jinkō" 土佐の国二百五十年間の現住人口, *Tosa shidan* 土佐史談, no. 33 (December 1930), pp. 95–105.

Takeuchi Makoto 竹内誠, "Kansei kaikaku" 寛政改革, pp. 1–44, in *Iwanami kōza Nihon no rekishi* 岩波講座日本歴史, vol. 12, Iwanami Shoten 岩波書店, 1976.

Takimoto Seiichi 滝本誠一, *Nihon keizai taiten* 日本経済大典, vol. 9, Meiji Bunken 明治文献, 1967.

Tamura Sadao 田村貞雄, *Nihon shi o minaosu* 日本史をみなおす, Aoki Shoten 青木書店, 1986.

Tanaka Seiji 田中誠二, "Hansei kikō to kashindan" 藩制機構と家臣団, in Fujii Jōji 藤井讓治, ed., *Shihai no shikumi* 支配のしくみ, *Nihon no kinsei* 日本の近世 series, vol. 3, Chūō Kōronsha 中央公論社, 1991.

T'ang hui yao 唐会要, in *Kuo-hsüeh chi-pen ts'ung-shu* 国学基本叢書 series, Taipei: T'aiwan Shang-wu Yin-shu-kuan 台湾商務印書館, 1968.

Taniyama Masamichi 谷山正道, *Kinsei minshū undō no tenkai* 近世民衆運動の展開, Takashina Shoten 高科書店, 1994.

Tano-chō Shi Hensan Iinkai 田野町史編纂委員会, *Tano-chō shi* 田野町史, Tano-chō 田野町 (Kōchi-ken 高知県), 1990.

Teraishi Masaji (Masamichi), 寺石正路, *Nangakushi* 南学史, Fuzanbō 冨山房, 1934.

Tilly, Charles, ed., *The Foundation of National States in Western Europe*, Princeton, N.J.: Princeton University Press, 1975.

Toba Masao 鳥羽正雄, "Edo jidai no rinsei" 江戸時代の林政, *Iwanami kōza Nihon rekishi* 岩波講座日本歴史 (First series, issue number 9) Iwanami shoten 岩波書店, 1934.

Toby, Ronald P., "The Carnival of the Aliens: Korean Embassies in Edo Period Art and Popular Culture," *Monumenta Nipponica*, vol. 41 no. 4 (Winter 1986), pp. 415–55.

State and Diplomacy in Early Modern Japan: Asia in the Development of the Tokugawa Bakufu, Princeton, N.J.: Princeton University Press, 1984.

Tokugawa Rinseishi Kenkyūjo 徳川林制史研究所, ed., *Nihon rinsei shi chōsa shiryō, Kōchi-han* 日本林制調査史料、高知藩, (microfilm, 51 reels) Tokugawa Rinseishi Kenkyūjo 徳川林制史研究所 publishers, marketed by Yūshōdō 雄松堂, 1970.

Tōkyō Toritsu Daigaku Fuzoku Toshokan 東京都立大学付属図書館, ed., *Mizuno-ke monjo mokuroku* 水野家文書目録, Tōkyō Toritsu Daigaku Fuzoku Toshokan 東京都立大学付属図書館, 1974.

Tonozaki Satoru 外崎覚, "Tsugaru Nobuaki-kō no jiseki (zoku)" 津軽信明公の事蹟(続), *Shidankai sokkiroku* 史談会速記録, Hara Shobō 原書房 (reprint), 1975.

Tosa Shimizu-shi Shi Hensan Iinkai 土佐清水市史編纂委員会, *Tosa Shimizu-shi shi, jōkan* 土佐清水市史上巻, Tosa Shimizu-shi 土佐清水市, 1980.

Totman, Conrad, *Early Modern Japan*, Berkeley: University of California Press, 1993.

    The Green Archipelago: Forestry in Pre-Industrial Japan, Berkeley: University of California Press, 1989.

    Politics in the Tokugawa Bakufu 1600–1843, Cambridge: Harvard University Press, 1967.

    "Preindustrial River Conservancy: Causes and Consequences," *Monumenta Nipponica*, vol. 47, no. 1 (Spring 1992), pp. 59–76.

Tottori-ken 鳥取県, *Tottori-ken shi, 3, kinsei seiji* 鳥取県史 3 近世政治, Tottori-ken 鳥取県, 1979.

Tōyama Shigeki 遠山茂樹, *Meiji ishin* 明治維新, Iwanami shoten 岩波書店, 1951; rev. 2nd ed., 1972.

Toyoda Takeshi, et al., eds., *Kōza Nihon no hōken toshi* 講座日本の封建都市, 3 vols., Bun'ichi Sōgō Shuppan 文一総合出版, 1981–3.

Tsuda Hideo 津田秀夫, *Hōken shakai kaitai katei kenkyū jōsetsu* 封建社会解体過程研究序説, Hanawa Shobō 塙書房, 1970.

    Kinsei minshū undō no kenkyū 近世民衆運動の研究, Sanseidō 三省堂, 1979.

Tsuda Shigemaro 津田茂麿, *Kinnō hishi Sasaki rōkō sekijitsu dan* 勤王秘史、佐々木老候昔日談, vol. 1, *Nihon shiseki kyōkai sōsho, daiyonki* 日本史籍協会叢書、第四期 vols. 4 and 5, Tōkyō Daigaku Shuppankai 東京大学出版会, 1980.

Tsuji Tatsuya 辻達也, *Kyōhō kaikaku no kenkyū* 享保改革の研究, Osaka: Sōbundō 創文堂, 1963.

Tsukahira, Toshio, *Feudal Control in Tokugawa Japan: The Sankin Kōtai System*, Cambridge: Harvard East Asian Monographs, 1966.

Tsukamoto Manabu 塚本学, *Kinsei saikō – chihō no shiten kara* 近世再考 —— 地方の視点から, Nihon Editaa Sukūru shuppanbu 日本エディタースクール出版部, 1986.

Vaporis, Constantine, *Breaking Barriers: Travel and the State in Early Modern Japan*, Cambridge: Council on East Asian Studies, Harvard University Press, 1994.

    "Post Station and Assisting Villages," *Monumenta Nipponica*, vol. 41, no. 4 (Winter 1986), pp. 377–414.

    "To Edo and Back: Alternate Attendance and Japanese Culture in the Early Modern Period," *Journal of Japanese Studies*, vol. 23, no. 1 (Winter 1997), pp. 25–67.

Vlastos, Steven, *Peasant Protest and Uprisings in Tokugawa Japan*, Berkeley: University of California Press, 1986.

Wakabayashi, Bob, *Japanese Loyalism Reconstrued: Yamagata Daini's 'Ryūshi shinron' of 1759*, Honolulu: University of Hawaii Press, 1995.

Wakita Osamu 脇田修, "Kinsei toshi no kensetsu to gōshō" 近世都市の建設と豪商, pp. 155–94, in *Iwanami kōza Nihon rekishi* 岩波講座日本歴史, vol. 9, Iwanami Shoten 岩波書店, 1975.

"The *Kokudaka* System: A Device for Unification," *Journal of Japanese Studies*, vol. 1, no. 2 (Summer 1975), pp. 297–320.

Walthall, Anne, "Japanese *Gimin*: Peasant Martyrs in Popular Memory," *American Historical Review*, vol. 91, no. 5 (December 1986), pp. 1076–102.

Social Protest and Popular Culture in Eighteenth Century Japan, Tucson: University of Arizona Press, 1986.

Ward, Robert, ed., *Political Development in Modern Japan*, Princeton, N.J.: Princeton University Press, 1969.

Watanabe Hisao 渡辺久雄, et al., eds., *Amagasaki-shi shi* 尼崎市史, vols. 2 and 4, Amagasaki-shi 尼崎市, 1966 and 1974.

Watanabe Mitsushige 渡辺光重, "Tosa-han tōgyō shikō" 土佐藩糖業史考, *Tosa shidan* 土佐史談, no. 61 (February 1937) pp. 36–72.

White, James, *The Demography of Sociopolitical Conflict in Japan, 1721–1846*, Berkeley: Institute of East Asian Studies, 1992.

Wigen, Kären, "The Geographic Imagination in Early Modern Japanese History: Retrospect and Prospect," *Journal of Asian Studies*, vol. 51, no. 1 (February 1992), pp. 3–29.

The Making of a Japanese Periphery, 1750–1920. Berkeley: University of California Press, 1995.

Wray, William, *Mitsubishi and the N.Y.K,* Cambridge: Council on East Asian Studies, Harvard University Press, 1984.

Yamagata-ken 山形県, *Yamagata-ken shi* 山形県史, vol. 3, Yamagata-ken 山形県, 1987.

Yamaguchi Keiji 山口啓二 and Sasaki Junnosuke 佐々木潤之介, *Bakuhan taisei* 幕藩体制, vol. 4 in *Taikei Nihon rekishi* 体系日本歴史 series, Nihon Hyōronsha 日本評論社, 1971.

Yamaguchi-ken bunkashi nenpyō 山口県文化史年表, Yamaguchi-ken 山口県, 1956.

Yamaguchi Tetsu 山口徹, "Bakuhansei shijō no saihen to shōhin seisan" 幕藩制市場の再編と商品生産, pp. 229–65, in Rekishigaku kenkyūkai 歴史学研究会, ed., *Kōza Nihon rekishi* 講座日本歴史, vol. 6, Tōkyō Daigaku Shuppankai 東京大学出版会, 1985.

Yamamoto Hirofumi 山本博文, *Edojō no kyūtei seiji* 江戸城の宮廷政治, Yomiuri Shinbunsha 読売新聞社, 1993.

Yamamoto Takeshi 山本大, *Chōsokabe Motochika* 長曽我部元親, Yoshikawa Kōbunkan 吉川弘文館, 1960.

"Chōsogabe seiken no henshitsu to ichiryō gusoku" 長曽我部政権の変質と一領具足, Nihon rekishi 日本歴史, no. 117, (March 1958), pp. 69–77.

Kōchi-ken no rekishi 高知県の歴史, Yamakawa Shuppansha 山川出版, 1969.

ed., *Kōchi no kenkyū* 高知の研究, vol. 3, Osaka: Seibundō 清文堂, 1983.

ed., *Tosa shi no shomondai* 土佐史の諸問題, Meicho Shuppan 名著出版, 1978.

et al., eds., *Kenshōbo* 憲章簿 (Kanematsu 兼松 [personal name unknown] comp.), 7 vols., Kōchi: Kōchi Kenritsu Toshokan 高知県立図書館, 1982–6.

Yamauchi-ke shiryō – Bakumatsu ishin hen 山内家史料 — 幕末維新編, vols. 4–15, Kōchi: Yamauchi Jinja Hōmotsu Shiryōkan 高知：山内神社宝物資料館, 1983–present.

Yamauchi-ke shiryō – Katsutoyo-kō ki 山内家史料 — 豊公紀, Kōchi: Yamauchi Jinja Hōmotsu Shiryōkan 高知：山内神社宝物資料館, 1980.

Yamauchi-ke shiryō – Tadatoyo-kō ki 山内家史料 — 忠豊公紀, 3 vols., Kōchi: Yamauchi Jinja Hōmotsu Shiryōkan 高知：山内神社宝物資料館, 1980–1.

Yamauchi-ke shiryō – Tadayoshi-kō ki 山内家史料 — 忠義公紀, 4 vols., Kōchi: Yamauchi Jinja Hōmotsu Shiryōkan 高知：山内神社宝物資料館, 1982.

Yamazaki Ryūzō 山崎隆三, *Kinsei bukkashi kenkyū* 近世物価史研究, Hanawa Shobō 塙書房, 1983.

Yano Takanori 矢野隆教, ed., *Edo jidai rakusho ruijū* 江戸時代落書類聚, Tōkyōdō 東京堂, 1984.

Yasuoka Shigeaki 安岡重明, "Bakuhansei no shijō kōzō" 幕藩制の市場構造, pp. 245–98, in *Iwanami kōza Nihon rekishi* 岩波講座日本歴史, vol. 10, Iwanami Shoten 岩波書店, 1975.

"Kansei Bunka ki ni okeru hanseki shori ni kansuru Kusama Naokata no iken" 寛政・文化期における藩債処理にかんする草間直方の意見, *Dōshisha Shōgaku* 同志社商学, vol. 14, no. 2, pp. 52–71.

Nihon hōken keizai seisaku shi ron 日本封建経済政策史論, Yūhikaku 有斐閣, 1959.

Yates, Charles, *Saigo Takamori: The Man Behind the Myth*, London: Kegan Paul International, 1995.

Yokogawa Suekichi 横川末吉, "Bunsei ki Tosa-han kokusan shihō no kenkyū – *Kenshōbo* o chūshin ni" 文政期土佐藩国産仕法の研究 — 「憲章簿」を中心に, pp. 285–316, in Irimajiri Yoshinaga 入交好脩, *Tosa-han keizai shi kenkyū* 土佐藩経済史研究, Kōchi: Kōchi Shimin Toshokan 高知市民図書館, 1966.

Chōsogabe chikenchō no kenkyū 長曽我部地検帳の研究, Kōchi: Kōchi Shimin Toshokan 高知市民図書館, 1961.

"Tosa no kokudaka" 土佐の国高, *Tosa shidan* 土佐史談, no. 106 (January 1964), pp. 10–17.

Yokoyama Toshio 横山十四男, *Gimin denshō no kenkyū* 義民伝承の研究, San'ichi Shobo 三一書房, 1983.

Gimin: hyakushō ikki no shidōsha tachi 義民：百姓一揆の指導者達, Sanseidō 三省堂, 1973.

Yokoyama Toshio 横山俊夫, "'Han' kokka e no michi – shokoku fūkyō fure to tabinin" 「藩」国家への道 — 諸国風教触と旅人 pp. 81–130, in Hayashiya Tatsusaburō 林屋辰三郎, *Kasei bunka no kenkyū* 化政文化の研究, Iwanami Shoten 岩波書店, 1976.

Yoshinaga Akira 吉永昭, *Kinsei no senbai seido* 近世の専売制度, Yoshikawa Kōbunkan 吉川弘文館, 1973.

Yusa Norihiro 遊佐教寛, "Tokugawa Yoshimune no Kishū hansei to nisatsu no gisho" 徳

川吉宗の紀州藩政と二冊の偽書, *Wakayama kenshi no kenkyū* 和歌山県史の研究, no. 13 (1986), pp. 31–42.

Yunoki Manabu 柚木学, ed, *Shokoku okyakusen chō* 諸国御客船帳 : 近世海運史料, 2 vols., Seibundō shiryō sōsho 清文堂史料叢書 series, vols. 12 and 13, Osaka: Seibundō 清文堂, 1977.

Index

abandoned land, 66, 81
Adachi Mohei, 131
agricultural land development, 66–7, 74–5,
  91–2
agricultural land surveys, 15, 36–7
  in Tosa, 37–8, 57, 65–7, 80–4, 91–2
agricultural tax, 13–14
  rates in Tosa, 50, 79–84
  sale of collection rights in Tosa, 126, 156
  totals in Tosa, 88, 89–92
Ainu, 37
Aizu domain, 108
Akaoka port town, 159
Aki City Library, 222
Aki Gonshichi, 158–9
Aki port, 45, 49, 54
Akizawa Shigeru, 170n58
alternate attendance system, 12, 13, 36, 53
  costs of, 17–18, 29, 157, 161–2, 168
  and economy, 17–18, 76–8, 101
  and population surveys, 60
Amagasaki domain, 108
Amagasakiya Matabei, 190
Amano Masatoshi, 135
Anderson, Benedict, 9
Andō Genzō, 158
Andō Yazenta, 148
Andō Yoshiuji, 33
Ansei reforms, 195
Aoki Michio, 25
Appleby, Joyce, 140n12
Arai Hakuseki, 7
Araki Sahei, 189–90
Aruga Kizaemon, 10n25
Asakura village, 42–3
ashigaru (footsoldier), 33n2, 76, 87, 121, 124,
  151
Awa, *see* Tokushima domain

Baba Yagoroku, 139–40
bakufu, 22–3
  petition box, 108, 109–10

population surveys, 57–9
  see also shogunate
"*bakuhan taisei*," 22–3
Berry, Mary, 10n25, 15
Bitchū Matsuyama domain, 108
Bizen, *see* Okayama domain
Bizen Fukuyama, 46–7
Bokata village council, 108
Bolitho, Harold, 168
bonito, 47–8
Brown, Philip, 15, 36n11
buichiyaku (port tax official), 46
bullionism, see *kokueki* thought, and
  bullionism

camphor, 194
carpenters' guild, 127
castle towns, 14; *see also* Kōchi; Urado
castles in Tosa, 50–1; *see also* Kōchi; Urado
casualties, *see* incidental produce taxes
census, *see* population
chief inspector, 104–5, 114, 124n58, 163–4
Chiya Hiromori, 75
China and petition boxes, 106–7, 110, 116
Chōshū (Hagi) domain, 108, 187, 202; *see also*
  Mōūri clan
Chōsogabe clan, 33, 34–5, 37, 39
  era policies, 49, 50, 54
Chōsogabe Morichika, 33, 34, 35n8
clothing and status, 129–30
commercial monopolies, 23–4, 25–6, 199
  abolition of, 129, 154, 159, 138, 178, 182
  license fees, 178
  opposition to, 142, 144, 152, 181, 182
  paper, 111–13, 128, 178, 181–3
  soy, 143–4, 150, 157, 159–60
  sugar 190–3
commercial taxes, 88, 89; *see also* port taxes;
  sales taxes
commoners' right to political discourse, 27,
  110, 112–13, 126, 162–3; *see also* petition
  box

243

Printed in the United States
36750LVS00005B/20